AMERICA'S ARMY

AMERICA'S ARMY

MAKING THE ALL-VOLUNTEER FORCE

BETH BAILEY

THE BELKNAP PRESS of
HARVARD UNIVERSITY PRESS

Cambridge, Massachusetts
London, England
2009

Printed in the United States of America

Library of Congress Cataloging-in-Publication Data
Bailey, Beth L., 1957–
America's Army : making the all-volunteer force/Beth Bailey.
p. cm.
Includes bibliographical references and index.
ISBN 978-0-674-03536-2 (alk. paper)
1. United States. Army—Recruiting, enlistment, etc.
2. Military service, Voluntary—United States. I. Title.
UB323.B35 2009
355.2'230973—dc22 2009023007

In memory of
Tim Moy

CONTENTS

PREFACE

IN MID-MARCH 2003, as American military forces moved toward Baghdad, the U.S. Army replaced "An Army of One" recruiting ads with commercials evoking a tradition of heroism and sacrifice. Sepia-toned closeups of soldiers' faces filled the screen in "Victors." In "Creed," army unit crests proclaimed "Not for Ourselves Alone" and "Ducit Amor Patriae" as elegiac music strikingly akin to the soundtrack from *A Band of Brothers* claimed an historical connection with World War II. These commercials were light-years from the upbeat message of the recently retired recruiting jingle "Be All You Can Be" or the grittier but slightly perplexing "Army of One" campaign that had replaced it in 2001. The language of service and sacrifice, duty and honor, had been largely absent from army advertising since the beginning of America's all-volunteer force. For the previous three decades, the primarily peacetime army had recruited soldiers with promises of individual opportunity: marketable skills, money for college, achievement, adventure, and personal transformation. In the first moments of a controversial war, those promises sounded inappropriate, if not absurd.

The army would soon return to its usual recruiting campaign and, as Operation Iraqi Freedom became an extended conflict, struggle to meet its recruiting goals. And the American public and its congressional representatives would debate the implications of fighting an extended war with an all-volunteer force instead of one based, at least in theory, on the belief that military service is an obligation of all the nation's (male) citizens. Those debates were given weight and heat by powerful divisions over the legitimacy of the war itself as well as by the steadily mounting number of American and Iraqi dead. In ways well-reasoned and naive, Americans discussed the practical limitations and foreign policy implications of relying on a military that could not supply troops on demand by simply increasing draft calls. And they worried about the social impact of a volunteer force that left one segment of American citizens and their families to carry the burden of war while asking nothing of those who chose not to volunteer.

The questions Americans raised in those difficult years were important, but the debates were in most ways moot. Short of international conflagration, the United States was not likely to reinstate the draft. When the nation began its war in Iraq, the all-volunteer force had already been in existence longer than the post–World War II draft, which had lasted—with one brief interruption—until 1973. Although the quandaries presented were evident, so were the significant successes of the all-volunteer force, the enormous political difficulties of reinstating the draft, and the almost-certain problems with the military it would produce. In 2003, as America moved toward war, the all-volunteer force was a fact of life. But its history, and the complex struggles that had given it shape, were little understood.

America's Army is the story of the making of the all-volunteer force (AVF). It traces the history of the AVF from the draft protests and policy proposals of the 1960s through the American wars in Iraq and Afghanistan. As the title makes clear, this book focuses on the army. That is in part because the army is the largest and least-specialized service and the one that requires by far the greatest number of volunteers. The army was the service most affected by the move to an all-volunteer force, and also the one that thought most inventively about how to manage that transition. The implications of that move were played out in the most fundamental ways over the decades that followed. Others have written detailed policy studies and institutional histories of the all-volunteer force. This book offers a broader framework, situating the all-volunteer army in the broader American society and analyzing how the army and its civilian overseers dealt with the changes that followed from the end of the draft and tried to imagine and create a force that was capable of responding effectively to rapidly changing and complex international situations.

Thus *America's Army* is also a history of America after Vietnam. The military played a critical role in the United States during those years, and not only as an instrument of national defense or in times of war. It was in the army, this book argues, that America directly confronted the legacies of the social change movements of the 1960s: African American claims and the problems of social inequality; women's expanding roles and their fervent opposition; gay rights. The army, competing with employers in the national labor market, dealt most directly with the rising importance of the marketplace and of consumer culture in American society. Army recruiting learned how to sell military service alongside soap and soft drinks in the consumer marketplace. And it was around the issue of army service that Americans struggled over some of the most important questions of the age: over who "belongs" in America and on what terms, over the meaning of citizenship and the rights and obligations it carries, over whether equality or liberty is the more central of American values, and over what role the military should play in the United States, not only in times of war, but in times of peace.

AMERICA'S ARMY

1 ★ INDIVIDUAL FREEDOM AND THE OBLIGATIONS OF CITIZENSHIP

THE YEAR 1968 BEGAN BADLY. The winter Tet Offensive only added to the growing certainty that something was very wrong with government claims about the Vietnam War. April brought the horror of Martin Luther King Jr.'s assassination; in June a second Kennedy brother fell to assassin's bullets. It was a year of cities burning, of racial strife, of confrontation and revolt, of anger and fear and violent passions. By August, there were tanks in the streets of Chicago.

In November, with the U.S. death toll in Vietnam approaching 35,000, a divided nation went to the polls. Though Democratic presidential candidate Hubert Humphrey had entreated Americans to "put aside recrimination and disunion. Turn away from violence and hatred," his was an impossible charge. The Republican candidate's words echoed more powerfully. "As we look at America," Richard Nixon told the nation, "we see cities enveloped in smoke and flame. We hear sirens in the night. We see Americans dying on distant battlefields abroad. We see Americans hating each other, fighting each other, killing each other at home. And as we see and hear these things, millions of Americans cry out in anguish: did we come all this way for this?" Appealing to the "nonshouters, the nondemonstrators," the "forgotten Americans," Nixon insisted that the answer was "No." Humphrey's campaign slogan was "There Is No Alternative." Nixon's was "Vote Like Your Whole World Depended On It."[1]

Two and a half weeks before the presidential election, Richard Nixon went live on CBS's national radio network and, at the height of America's involvement in the Vietnam War, called for an end to the draft. It was a politically opportunistic and Nixon-esque move, timed for the critical days before the election and meant to indicate his willingness to take bold action, his ability to resolve the national crisis. The Republican presidential candidate ended his carefully crafted speech with an appeal to conscience, framed in the language of freedom and liberty: "Today all across our country we face a crisis of confidence. Nowhere is it more acute than among our young people. They recognize the draft as an infringement on their liberty—which it is. To them, it represents a government insensitive to their rights—a government callous to their status as free men. They ask for justice—and they deserve it. So I say, it's time we looked to our consciences. Let's show our commitment to freedom by preparing to assure our young people theirs."[2]

Campaign promises are more easily made than kept, and this was a doozy. At the height of the Vietnam War, with well over half a million American troops in Southeast Asia and a total military force of about three and a half million, the Republican candidate stated his intention to end the draft and transform the nation's military to an all-volunteer force (AVF). Nixon was clear: the shift could not happen until the end of America's involvement in the Vietnam War. But he proposed to commit the nation to that goal immediately.

The problem was, Nixon didn't have any of the necessary sign-ons from those who mattered. His plan did not stem from the quietly voiced desires of American military leaders. He'd had no confidential conversations with Pentagon officials or national security advisors or even the man who would become his secretary of defense. In fact, nearly everyone with power in or over the military opposed his proposal. The last issue that the military establishment wanted to deal with, as it struggled through the final years of the U.S. war in Vietnam, was the end of the draft. Instead, the force behind the AVF proposal—and the author of Nixon's speech—was a thirty-year-old associate professor of economics who was excited by the antidraft discussions that were energizing free-market and libertarian economists in the mid- to late 1960s.

As a radical and unvetted campaign promise, the AVF should have been doomed to a rapid and embarrassing public failure or, at the very least, a politically managed and quieter death by committee. In the midst of the Vietnam War the notion that the U.S. military could ever fill its ranks with volunteers seemed improbable, if not ludicrous, and the chair of the House Armed Services Committee was widely quoted as he quipped, repeatedly, that the only way America could get a volunteer force was to draft one. But despite all the apparent obstacles, the United States drafted its last man—Dwight Elliot Stone—in December 1972. He began his "obligated term" on June 30, 1973, and the all-volunteer force became a reality the following day.[3]

Paradoxically, it was the Vietnam War that made the transformation to an all-volunteer force possible. The war created a political perfect storm. It divided the nation, but it also gave legitimacy to vastly different arguments justifying the move to an all-volunteer force. Opposition to the draft was critical to the antiwar movement from its small and unpopular beginnings in 1965 through growing public opposition as Johnson escalated and Nixon expanded the war. Young men, of course, had a great deal at stake, no matter their beliefs about the legitimacy of the war. Great Society liberals saw their concerns about social inequality manifest in a selective service system that created a "working class war." Black Americans overwhelmingly believed that the toll of the war fell heaviest on their sons; Nixon's "forgotten Americans" wondered why their sons should be "forced to sacrifice two of the most important years of [their lives], so that a neighbor's son can go right along pursuing his interests in freedom and safety?"[4] Those who hoped to curtail the power of the president to commit the nation to war without congressional mandate hoped the move to an all-volunteer force might help prevent armed conflict and constrain American adventurism abroad by forcing the president to commit troops only when he had strong public support. Conservatives on the right, in revolt against the Great Society, portrayed conscription as one more loss of individual liberty to government power.

Finally, while military leaders from the Pentagon on down worried about how they would attract large numbers of volunteers to a "broken" and enormously unpopular military, the experience of Vietnam lent the plans some legitimacy. "Reluctant" draftees did not make the best soldiers, much of the American media (and some in the army) concluded, as the battered institution increasingly struggled with poor morale, soaring AWOL and desertion rates, drug addiction, and even fragging. Although most military planners resisted such lessons, the nature of combat in Vietnam suggested the need for changes in doctrine—the way war is fought—that made a volunteer force seem more plausible, if not quite desirable.

Such widespread dissatisfaction with the draft made Nixon's proposal politically viable. But there were clear winners and losers in this competing constellation of interests. Nixon may have taken advantage of liberal and left suspicions of the draft and used the political turbulence of the time to build support, but it was not the discontent of "forgotten" Americans and the poor, nor the claims of youthful protesters in the street that mattered most. Instead, the initial and determining structure for the all-volunteer force was shaped by a group of free-market economists and libertarian thinkers who gained influence in the Nixon administration. It was they who portrayed the decision as part of America's ongoing debate about the relative importance of liberty versus equality as the nation's defining value. Instead of framing the debate about the AVF around notions of citizenship and obligation, or around concerns about the shared burden of service and social equality, they offered plans based on conservative or libertarian doctrines of market economies.

Whereas both the administration's political will to act and the public support for such a dramatic change stemmed from the power of broader turbulent forces in American life, these men placed their faith, instead, in rationality. The draft, they insisted, could be replaced by the free market; whatever inequities and inequalities that stemmed from either random chance or government-sponsored engineering (in the form of selective service exemptions) could be avoided by creating a free-market arena in which individuals made decisions based on rational understandings of their own economic best interest. They meant to replace the logic of citizenship with the logic of the market.

★

By 1968, when Richard Nixon offered his proposal, the draft (or more accurately, a system of selective service) had been in effect for almost twenty-eight years. America instituted its first peacetime draft in 1940, in the days of "dark uncertainty" (Nixon's term) before the nation committed its forces to the growing conflagration in Europe. With only a brief exception, the nation had relied on the draft through peace and war alike: as it asserted its military power in World War II, claimed superpower status in the Cold War, and fought in Korea and then in Vietnam. By the late 1960s, two generations of American men had been subject to the draft. Fathers and then their sons had been called to military duty or had, facing the possibility of conscription, volunteered. The draft had come to seem both normal and necessary. It had become a simple fact of American life.

Those who opposed the draft—especially those who opposed it on the grounds of individual liberty—frequently reminded their fellow citizens that the draft was an historical aberration. Technically, they were right. The nation had relied on a volunteer military for the great majority of its history. The draft, when it did exist, had been a wartime exception rather than a peacetime rule. And it was more often controversial than not. On the other hand, though calls to American tradition carried weight, it was hard not to acknowledge that the United States's place in the world had changed quite a bit since Congress had struggled over whether to pass the Militia Act of 1792.

Nonetheless, the history of America's experience with the draft matters to us—as it mattered to citizens in the late 1960s—because the system about which so many found so much to criticize grew out of ongoing historical struggles over the nature and role of military service in a democratic society. America's selective service system was shaped by a set of shifting ideological, practical, and structural forces that often pulled in different directions as the nation grew from a young republic into a global power.

From the beginning, most American citizens considered military service an obligation of citizenship. The original colonists had adopted the British militia system, in which all able-bodied citizens of a colony were part of a common militia, responsible for joining with their neighbors to fight a threatening foe. This system persisted in the new nation, which remained dependent on state militias despite President Washington's call for a standing army subject to federal authority. But there were critical limits to this notion of "universal" obligation. It applied only to those who were free, white, and male. And from the early days of the republic many Americans saw conscription as a threat to the higher good of individual liberty. It might be justified in extraordinary circumstances, they believed, but that bar should remain high. During the 1960s, libertarian critics of the draft sought authority in this history. The economist Richard Gillam, writing for the *Yale Review* in 1968, called upon Daniel Webster's defense of individual liberty to make his case against the draft. Even as the British set fire to Washington, DC during the War of 1812, Gillam recounted, Webster had condemned the notion of peacetime military conscription as "incompatible with any notion of personal liberty . . . a solecism, at once the most ridiculous and abominable that ever entered into the head of man."[5]

Yet even these seemingly contradictory beliefs—that military service was a universal obligation of citizenship, and that conscription represented an unconscionable and dangerous violation of citizens' individual liberty—could be allied. Those who saw conscription as an extreme measure, justified only in moments of acute danger, also presumed that in times of such danger citizens would rise to the nation's defense. As Gillam explained, "The theory [was] that the free citizen would voluntarily, by nature, spring to defense of the nation during any hour of need."[6] Thus, although the military obligations of citizenship might seem to conflict with a citizen's personal liberty, that was not the case. Armed defense of the nation and its people was—in moments of great peril—an integral, natural, and, by nature, voluntary aspect of citizenship.

Practical problems, of course, were more significant than this ideological sleight of hand suggested. Universal military service was never an actuality. Not surprisingly, there was a large gap between the ideal of universal sacrifice as an obligation of citizenship and the reality of unequal burdens. Even though each American colony claimed a "common militia" composed of free, white, able-bodied men, exemptions were specified by more than two hundred laws. Not surprisingly, most of the exemptions benefited the economically successful and the socially well-positioned. The active militia was to be filled with volunteers, but when those numbers were too low, men were conscripted from the larger "common militia." As that happened more and more frequently in the colonies and the new nation, with the burden most heavy on the poor and poorly established, potential conscripts rioted and conscripts deserted.[7]

The definition of extreme danger also posed a problem. Militias were raised by the states. Under what circumstances did the federal government have the right to call and command them? During the War of 1812, as British troops reached Plattsburgh, New York, the governor of Vermont tried to remove his state's militia from the battle, arguing that use of Vermont's militia was not justified because the British army's invasion of New York did not threaten Vermont.[8] It was not until the Civil War that federal authority—including the authority to conscript men independent of state power—was solidified. The Civil War was fought with mass armies; to raise these vast numbers—more than 750,000 in the South; 2.2 million in the North—the central governments of both turned to conscription. But in the North, men could purchase substitutes to serve in their place; in the South, slaveholders were exempted. Notions of universal sacrifice ran up against the hard realities of infantry charges and brutal slaughter. The first federal draft inductees were announced in New York just days after more than 5,500 men died in the battle of Gettysburg. Almost four times that number were badly injured, and stories circulated about men left lying in blood and filth, of battlefield amputations and gangrenous wounds. Working-class whites attacked draft offices, beginning four days of rioting that cost more than a hundred lives. During the Civil War, thirty-eight officers in charge of conscription were assassinated, with sixty more wounded in similar attempts.[9] The national draft was not easily imposed.

As the debate about the draft escalated in the late 1960s, both opponents and supporters of the draft attempted to make their cases by reaching back into America's early history. In fact, Lt. General Lewis Hershey, director of selective service since July 1941, offered a report titled "Outline of Historical Background of Selective Service (From Biblical Days to June 30, 1965)."[10] The turn to history wasn't a ridiculous strategy: Americans have frequently—and strategically—called upon the wisdom of the Founding Fathers and the philosophical claims central to the new nation, as well as on "the Word of God," when confronting difficult situations. And the calls on history were not purely symbolic: During the 1960s Americans were still arguing over the rights and duties of citizenship; the system of conscription was still mired in tensions over local control and federal authority; the questions of unequal sacrifice were scarcely laid to rest. But what most animated the struggles over the draft in the midst of the Vietnam War were the realities of the modern selective service system, which had emerged in basic form during World War I.

In both World War I and World War II the draft was legitimized by a language of universal sacrifice based in widely shared understandings that military service was an obligation of citizenship. At the same time, the selective service system—as its name makes clear—was not about universality. This system was designed by men inspired by a progressive faith in the value of scientific expertise and efficiency. They sought the most practical basis for managing manpower, both within the military and without.[11]

Simply put, there is no possibility of universal military service. Some individuals are not able; others excluded; still others protected. Economies must continue to run; domestic functions must be preserved; military personnel must be physically and mentally capable of carrying out their assigned functions. "Who serves?" is always a complicated question. Tensions between an efficient manpower policy and ideals of universal service are inescapable. Those tensions are exacerbated by changing but strongly held social values and cultural assumptions. And political concerns are always hovering over any decision about selective service policy. To complicate matters further, draft decisions were commonly made by local draft boards—"little groups of neighbors," as the selective service office liked to call them—rather than by a centralized federal agency. Draft boards were staffed by unpaid volunteers, most of them middle-class white men, often elderly veterans of previous wars.[12] These men considered individual cases, not broad social categories. They relied on national criteria, but interpreted them in light of specific local conditions—from local shortages in key occupations to local assumptions about race. Thus two potential draftees with the same characteristics—age, occupation, education, family status, health, race or ethnicity—could be treated quite differently by their respective local draft boards.

Determining the criteria for selective service selection is no easy task. Military considerations, of course, are critical. Age matters, as does physical fitness and mental capability. But where to draw those lines? How young is too young? How old is too old? Is an IQ of 85 too low? What about 70? Is one disqualified for flat feet? Nearsightedness? Asthma, diabetes, or obesity? Some of those lines have shifted through time, depending in part on changing doctrine. Increasingly sophisticated weaponry and means of warfare demand greater intellectual capacity—and often demand less physical strength. Acceptance standards tend to go up when volunteers or draftees are plentiful and down when numbers become a problem.

But selective service policy, and thus military manpower policy, has often sacrificed efficiency when it conflicted with powerful social values. Women have never been subject to the draft in the United States. This practice is based on the arguably cultural belief that women should not serve in combat; relying on this assumption, the Supreme Court ruled in 1981 that young women are not subject to the draft registration requirement that affects their male peers—even though the great majority of military specialties are not in the combat arms. Similarly, in the years following World War I, when there was no draft, many saw blacks as unfit for military service and a quota system limited their numbers in the army. During World War II, black men made up about 10 percent of the military, but were consigned to segregated units, generally restricted to support functions and heavy labor.[13] Civil rights leaders insisted that African Americans had "the right to fight," clearly understanding the association between military service and the full rights of citizenship.

During World War II, for the first time, the selective service system rejected large numbers of men for psychological reasons. The American psychiatric profession, in an attempt to establish its expertise, pushed for the psychological screening of military recruits. Such screening, they promised, could weed out the men who were likely to succumb to psychoneurotic disorders in the coming war, thus saving future taxpayers "the enormous cost of taking care" of them. WWI victims of "shell shock," they pointed out, had cost the nation more than a billion dollars in just the past two decades. Psychiatrists, advocates argued, could also identify those who would not "integrate smoothly into military service" or who might undermine the morale of the combat unit. One psychiatrist admitted that it did not seem fair to excuse "reckless, wayward, spineless, unadjusted male adults" from military service, but with war on the horizon, he argued, it was more important to build a strong and dependable army than to "discipline" the poorly adjusted. These psychiatrists were not above the common prejudices of their age: one described those prone to psychoneurotic breakdown as "dependent personalities" who would try to "get 'on the government' for life" by "breaking down in the armed forces." As the war ground on, the psychiatrists learned the limits of their expertise; hardly anyone, they discovered, could withstand combat stress for more than about forty-five days. In any case, there were far too few trained psychiatrists or psychologists to fully implement the screening program. Local general practitioners often stood in for experts, diagnosing what was then defined as the "psychiatric illness" of homosexuality by asking young men such questions as "How often do you date girls?"[14]

As draft and manpower policy excluded some Americans, it also worked to protect institutions Americans deemed culturally important. Sometimes such protection worked directly against efficient manpower policy, as when World War II draft legislation declared that "the maintenance of the family as a unit is of importance to the national well-being," and put married men with dependents (wives were considered dependents) into a "hands off" classification of 3-A. Despite the War Department's insistence in early 1943 that the army was having to turn to illiterates and other undesirables to fill its ranks because draft policies protected fathers, a subsequent Gallup poll found that 68 percent of the American public believed that single men doing essential war work should be drafted before fathers were called.[15]

There were other deferments or exemptions that were arguably related to national security. Farm workers received special deferments during World War II, as the draft removed and highly paid war work lured too many young men from the farms and food production. But the farm lobby ensured that even tobacco was listed as an essential crop and that deferments continued even as food surpluses began to pile up in the nation's warehouses. Universities, as well, made a strong case for deferments. The War Department concurred when it came to students in specific defense-related fields. But how broadly should those fields be defined? Would America's more intellectually talented youth best serve the nation by completing their academic training, or did student deferments simply offer those whose families could afford to pay for college a means to buy their way out of military service?

During World War II, the nation achieved neither the most efficient use of manpower nor universal sacrifice from all the nation's citizens. But the selective service system did register 49 million men, of whom 19 million were judged eligible to serve. Of the 16 million men who wore U.S. military uniforms during World War II, 10 million were draftees, though in part that was because the military, as part of a larger attempt to better manage civilian and military manpower, largely stopped accepting volunteers. Though current ideas about the fully shared sacrifice of the "greatest generation" are naively romantic, the military—in part because it contained such a large proportion of the nation's younger men—was fairly inclusive and relatively egalitarian, with race—though not ethnicity—as a critical exception. And so the public saw it. Ninety-three percent of Americans believed the draft operated fairly in 1942; by May 1945, it still had the confidence of 79 percent.[16]

Nonetheless, many Americans expected the draft would end when the war did. With the single exception of the fourteen months before the United States entered World War II, the nation had never tolerated peacetime conscription. But World War II had changed America's position in the world. Faced with American commitments to furnish occupation forces in Japan and Germany and the nation's growing concerns about the intentions of the Soviet Union, Congress twice extended the Selective Training and Service Act of 1940. But in March 1947, President Truman urged Congress to allow the draft to expire. The Joint Chiefs of Staff wanted a professional standing force; given the dangerous levels of instability extending from the Middle East through much of Europe and into Asia, they believed such a force would allow for more rapid mobilization than one that relied upon the draft.[17]

The army faced a difficult challenge. Its goal was to maintain a force of 1 million men, fed by volunteer enlistments of up to 40,000 per month.[18] Army recruiting advertisements noted the benefits of enlistment: "opportunities for education and travel in a well-paid career," but made their case in the language of liberty, national danger, and citizen's obligation. In support of the unwieldy but expansive slogan, "Your Army and Air Force Serve the Nation and Mankind in War and Peace," an ad designed for the popular magazines *Look* and *Collier's* read:

> Uncle Sam has always found young men ready to answer his call when the security of the nation was in peril.
>
> This is not a time of war. Yet never before except in wartime has America been threatened with graver danger than today. The democratic peoples of the world look to us as the only power strong enough to hold the balance of peace. If we fail them, the day must surely come when we find ourselves alone and friendless, fighting to defend the last slim footholds of freedom . . .
>
> You, who have enjoyed the liberty of a free country since your birth, are now face to face with the duty of protecting liberty. Your conscience—your honor—your patriotism will tell you whether you can shirk that obligation.[19]

The timing of this attempt to return to a volunteer force was terrible. With the civilian economy booming, only about 12,000 men were volunteering for the army each month—well below the thirty to forty thousand volunteers it required. Military leaders hesitated to recruit large numbers of African Americans, even as they sought places in the service. But tensions in the world continued to grow, and following the February 1948 coup in Czechoslovakia Truman reversed his previous position and called for reinstatement of the draft.[20]

Congress reimposed the draft in mid-1948. The threat of conscription, however, meant that few men were actually drafted. The number of draft-induced volunteers soared as young men sought greater control over the terms of their service, and the quality of enlistees improved. In 1949 the secretary of defense began reducing the size of American military forces. Not a single man was drafted that year. Faced with Truman's call for another extension of the draft, which was due to expire in June 1950, Congress balked. But then North Korean troops crossed the 38th parallel, the official boundary separating Korea's communist north and U.S.-allied south. Truman pledged American support in what he framed as a worldwide struggle against communism, and debates about the extension of the draft quickly disappeared.[21]

Throughout the 1950s, the idea that military service was an obligation of citizenship remained strong. Dwight D. Eisenhower, former commander-in-chief of WWII allied expeditionary forces in Europe, argued that military service was "an obligation that every citizen owes the nation" during his run for the presidency in 1952.[22] That case was made to millions of American high school students in a multipart film series, *Are You Ready for Service?* distributed by Coronet Films, which was perhaps better known in high school classrooms for such instructional films as *Are You Popular?* (1947), *Going Steady?* (1951), and *What To Do on a Date* (1951). "Service and Citizenship" was the third installment in the *Are You Ready for Service?* series. Produced and distributed in 1951, it managed to avoid all mention of the Korean War, picturing instead a "citizen army" made up of "thousands of . . . guys" who were "being trained to fight, if necessary . . . to defend our way of life."

"Service and Citizenship" was in most ways a stock instructional film, even though it listed the Department of Defense (DoD) as a consultant. A voice of authority—here, the "older and considerably more mature brother" Bill, who pronounces "mature" as "matoor" and adds a touch of sarcasm to his reading of that line—gives advice to younger brother Howie, who has gotten carried away by "snappy" military uniforms and wants to drop out of high school and enlist. In a letter from basic training, Bill urges Howie to finish school first. School, insists Bill, offers essential training in citizenship: teamwork, responsibility, and obedience to rules.

Despite the heavy stay-in-school message, the film is about the obligations of citizenship. Citizenship, students learn, is "the earning of rights by fulfilling responsibilities." As Bill and Howie's father, who served three years in the navy during World War II, explains: "You can't take things out of life without putting something in. We've got a good life here, boys.

The way we live. The privileges we enjoy. But these things aren't all free. We pay for them one way or another." "Service in the armed forces," he tells them in fatherly tones, "is the heaviest responsibility of citizenship." Though, he concedes, Mom's PTA work counts, too.[23]

The film's insistence on the importance of schooling was in keeping with emerging selective service policy. In 1958, the director of selective service told Congress that "inducting men is now only a collateral, almost, a byproduct of its operation." Despite some continuing public discussion of the obligations of citizenship and the importance of universal sacrifice, those who made policy increasingly linked national security to scientific development. In the years following the Soviet Union's successful launch of Sputnik, the nation poured funds into scientific education and training. The director of the Scientific Manpower Commission rather coldheartedly argued, on the subject of the draft, that a GI was quickly trained and easily replaced, whereas a physicist was not.[24] In keeping with such understandings, the selective service system offered an extensive set of college deferments in an attempt to channel men into "engineering, into physics, and many other pursuits which have to do with this atomic age."[25] In fact, such deferments expanded to cover most college students who were passing their courses.

Despite the tension between the idea of universal obligation and the reality of extensive deferments, deferments were not especially controversial because very few men were drafted. By the end of the 1950s, the army had fallen from 1.5 million to 860,00 active-duty troops. Only the army relied on draftees during this period, and the percentage of men who were conscripted into the army fell from 58 in 1954 to 22 in 1961. Only about 10 percent of those entering the U.S. military system each year in the early 1960s were draftees.[26]

Those who made military policy, like most Americans, were well aware of the pig-in-the-python effect of the baby boom. The population bulge that caused elementary schools to sprout on the American landscape at the beginning of the 1950s was about to translate into a flood of young men eligible for military service in the early 1960s, and the birth rate remained high.[27] Deferment categories expanded; entry qualifications were raised. But there were still too many young men available for the shrinking armed forces, and no way to conceive of enough legitimate deferments to manage the glut of available manpower.

By 1958 (which was, though no one yet knew it, the year following the height of the baby boom), the Pentagon was seriously discussing ending the peacetime draft and moving to an all-volunteer force. The issue got some attention in the 1960 election: Democrats vying for the nomination criticized the selective service system in its current form, and it was in this context that John F. Kennedy proposed the Peace Corps. Republican candidate Richard Nixon insisted that the draft was critical to the nation's defense.[28] But the public had little interest in the draft. It was an accepted backdrop, most effective as a spur to voluntary enlistment in both the active forces and the Army Reserve. Though Congress had to renew the president's induction authority every four years, the renewals were routine in 1955, 1959, and 1963.[29] The draft was once again a minor campaign issue in 1964 when Republican candidate Barry Goldwater, true to his libertarian beliefs, announced plans to do away with it. President Lyndon Johnson, who was facing his first election after assuming the presidency following John F. Kennedy's assassination, ordered the Department of Defense to study the issue.[30]

That report, however, was irrelevant almost before it was completed. In the election year of 1964, as Goldwater and Johnson struggled to convince Americans to support their very different visions of the nation's future, there were fewer than 24,000 American military men—"advisors"—in Vietnam. But in March 1965, the newly elected president sent 3,500 marines to Danang, where, in one of the odd moments of that war, the marines stormed the beach in full battle gear, complete with naval air support, only to find the mayor of Danang waiting to welcome them. That summer, at the request of General William Westmoreland, the president authorized a large-scale build-up of American ground troops in the Republic of Vietnam.[31] Johnson had spent almost two months agonizing over this decision, debating it with advisors, worrying over its implications, fretting over its impact on his Great Society programs, well aware that success was unlikely. But he buried this announcement—one that would lead to more than 58,000 American military deaths—in the midst of a July 28th press conference announcing his nomination of Abe Fortas to the Supreme Court. To reporters' questions, he insisted that this action "did not imply any change in policy whatever." At this moment Johnson announced one more critical decision. He would not call up the reserves.[32]

Johnson—always with an ear to the ground—was making a political gamble. He wanted to downplay the Americanization of the war. In his inimitable words: "If you have a mother-in-law with only one eye and she has it in the center of her forehead, you don't keep her in the living room." Thus he sought the option that would draw the least public attention. Johnson had promised to provide General Westmoreland with an additional forty-four battalions, or about 125,000 troops. He had three means of doing so: a dramatic redistribution of the current active military; calling up the reserves and potentially the national guard; or increasing current monthly draft calls.[33]

The active military totaled more than 2.6 million in 1965, but the Cold War had many fronts and America had military commitments throughout the globe. Shifting large numbers of troops to Vietnam was essentially impossible without undermining an interlocking set of complex foreign policies and international relationships. There simply weren't enough men to do it all. The obvious answer, most thought, was to mobilize the reserves, which numbered slightly more than the active military. But mobilizing the reserves, in Johnson's estimation, was a greater political threat than increasing monthly draft calls. Calling up the reserves would involve congressional approval, and Johnson, who later explained that "I knew the Congress as well as I know Lady Bird," also knew quite certainly that Congress would explode into angry debate about his war plans.[34] Mobilizing the reserves also seemed a more disruptive option than extending the draft. Men in the reserves were, on average, older and more established than those in the draftee pool. They were more likely to have jobs and families. Deploying reserve units to Vietnam would strip small communities of their firefighters and police officers, take fathers away from young families. There would be an immediate and tangible effect. People would pay attention. So Johnson disregarded the advice of former president Eisenhower, who warned him in 1965 that "sending conscripted troops to Vietnam would cause a major public-relations problem," as well as the strong recommendation of the Joint Chiefs of Staff that he rely on the reserves, supplemented by the National Guard. He more than doubled monthly draft calls in the last days of July 1965.[35]

Lt. General Lewis B. Hershey, head of the selective service system, took it all in stride. When questioned about securing 35,000 men a month, he told a reporter for *Life* magazine, "Hell, that's nothing. In 1943 we were drafting 450,000 a month—that's 2,000 an hour, 10 hours a day, six days a week." The "we" was literal: Hershey had been head of the draft since 1941. He was a larger-than-life figure, the son of an Indiana farmer who had pursued Pancho Villa through Mexico in 1916 and fought with the artillery in France during World War I. In 1965, at the age of 71, he was six feet tall, 200 pounds, and blind in one eye. "My grandfather was a stonemason," he liked to explain, "and was blinded when a piece of rock broke off as he was hammering it and hit him. I lost my eye when I got hit by a mallet playing polo at Fort Sill in 1926—which tells you something about the degeneration of the species." He wasn't completely joking about the degeneration of the species. Hershey had little patience for the increasing number of young men who complained about the draft. His opinion of those who opposed the draft was clear: "A society that hasn't got the guts to make people do what they ought to do," he insisted, "doesn't deserve to survive."[36]

Given that there were close to 17 million young men of prime draft age, the jump from 16,000 to between 35,000 and 40,000 calls per month still affected a relatively small percentage of them. But that was the crux of the problem. Over the preceding decade, the selective service system had developed an extensive system of deferments, meant to manage the overabundance of potential draftees. Of almost 17 million young men in the potential draft pool, more than two-thirds were either deferred or ineligible. The deferments had generated little concern while draft calls were low and the nation was at peace. But as draft calls increased, and as more and more American servicemen died on foreign soil, these deferments mattered.

When Johnson began Operation Rolling Thunder, the sustained bombing of North Vietnam, in February 1965 and committed the first official combat troops to Vietnam that March, most Americans supported his actions. Johnson, who had little foreign policy experience, had worked hard in the 1964 election to portray himself as a thoughtful but decisive leader, firm in the nation's defense but clear in his conviction that "we are not about to start another war." Some of those who had supported Johnson's vision of responsibility and restraint in opposition to Republican candidate Barry Goldwater's doomsday proclamations and talk of using small nuclear weapons to "defoliate" trees that gave cover to guerilla forces in South Vietnam were outraged by Johnson's actions.[37]

Opposition to the war emerged quickly on college campuses. At the University of Michigan faculty members organized a Vietnam War "teach-in" in late March 1965 that drew 3,000 students, dozens of journalists, and a Michigan State Supreme Court justice who told those who opposed the teach-in that "these professors are doing a vital service to their country." More than thirty-five other universities followed suit. When the University of California–Berkeley staged its teach-in in late May—by this point, a much more directly antiwar event—30,000 people joined in.[38] The Berkeley teach-in got a lot of news coverage, in part because the arrest of 800 student protesters in the Free Speech Movement Sit-in was only about six months in the past, and Berkeley was already synonymous with student revolt. Nonetheless, throughout the nation, college students were more likely than most other Americans to support Johnson's war policies.

At half past five in the afternoon of July 30, 1965, a couple of days after Johnson announced the expansion of the war and the escalation of draft calls, about 400 people gathered at New York's city hall and marched down Broadway to the army recruiting and induction center at 39 Whitehall Street. The group marched mainly in silence, some carrying signs: "L.B.J.—We Are Not a Nation of Killers—Negotiate." At the induction center—after one young man, in civilian clothes, shouted down from an upstairs window, "You're too late!"—at least five young men burned their draft cards. The *Times* reporter checked with New York City's director of Selective Service, Col. Paul W. Akst, who told him they'd done nothing illegal. "It's just a nuisance," he said. "They'll just come in to their local boards in a few days and get a duplicate card."[39]

Mendel Rivers, chair of the House Armed Services Committee, was outraged. The 62-year-old representative from South Carolina rarely hesitated to take a stand about things that mattered to him. In the early 1960s, with twenty-eight years of House service behind him, Lucius Mendel Rivers wore his hair in the flowing style of South Carolina "hero" John C. Calhoun and was proud to say that he had stood up to President Truman when Truman had pushed Congress to pass an antilynching bill in 1948. Such a bill, Rivers had insisted, would instead "lynch the Constitution." The congressman from South Carolina had a pretty serious drinking problem, back in the days when reporters knew but didn't tell, and a military authorizations bill had recently languished in the Armed Services committee while he "rested" in Bethesda Naval Hospital. But Rivers saw himself as the last line of defense for the ordinary soldier.[40] He couldn't let young men get away with such an insult to the military and a challenge to the government. On August 9th, Mendel Rivers submitted a bill making it illegal to "knowingly destroy" or "knowingly mutilate" a draft card. The penalty: a $10,000 fine or imprisonment for no more than five years.

"The House Committee on Armed Services," the accompanying statement noted, "is fully aware of, and shares in, the deep concern expressed throughout the Nation over the increasing incidences in which individuals and large groups of individuals openly defy and encourage others to defy the authority of their Government by destroying or mutilating their draft cards." In the current "critical situation of the country," it continued, these acts "pose such a grave threat to the security of the Nation that no question whatsoever should be left as to the intention of the Congress that such wanton and irresponsible acts should be punished." The bill moved quickly through the House, where Representative William Bray of Indiana described the imagined protesters as "generally filthy beatniks," passing 393–1 on a roll call vote, and in the Senate was taken forward by South Carolina senator Strom Thurmond. Thurmond also knew how to hold a line; he'd staged the longest filibuster in Senate history when he spoke for a straight twenty-four hours and eighteen minutes in opposition to the 1957 civil rights bill. The Senate version of the bill was shorter than the House version, but a bit more ostentatious. It described the "defiant destruction" of draft cards by "dissident persons" as "contumacious conduct" which, "if allowed to continue unchecked . . . represents a potential threat to the exercise of the power to raise and support armies."[41]

It's not clear what large groups of individuals were destroying or mutilating their draft cards. The only precipitating event that shows up in major newspapers or magazines is the protest on Whitehall Street; it merited brief coverage in the *New York Times* but seemingly nowhere else. (*Life* magazine belatedly published a photo of that card burning on August 20th, when it reported the new law criminalizing such acts.) On August 5th the *Washington Post* noted, in an article buried deep in its interior pages, that an antiwar group was planning a march in Washington that might include the burning of draft cards. The only other public draft-card burning on record since 1947 had taken place in (where else?) Berkeley back in early May, and had won demonstrators only about three column inches on an interior page of the *New York Times*. Protesting "the invasion of the Dominican Republic," several hundred students had marched on the Berkeley draft board headquarters and presented its coordinator with a black coffin. About forty students burned their draft cards. One student, not so well schooled in protest tactics, confided to a reporter that the act was "purely . . . symbolic": "We have been told we can get new cards if we apply for them."[42]

Though politically clueless, the young man was correct. Draft cards were easily replaced because individuals' draft information was on record. The physical existence of a draft card made little difference one way or another. If a man was registered with the selective service system, his information was on file. It didn't matter if his draft card lay in ashes. If called up, he would receive a notice. At that point he would comply . . . or not. As members of Congress well knew, there was no way that a few—or even a few hundred—draft-card burnings would impede the ability of the Congress "to raise and support armies." But because Rivers could not resist engaging the protesters in the realm of symbolic politics, the outcome was virtually predetermined. What member of Congress was going to vote in support of draft-card burners? Thus what could have remained a "nuisance" gained political significance.

Selective Service System officials—who had nothing to do with this law—were slightly baffled by Congress's action. They didn't know how many draft cards had been destroyed, they told reporters, but didn't believe it was many. Nonetheless, one said, perhaps the law would discourage protesters from destroying them in public, "thus depriving the practice of much of its point."[43] They couldn't have been more wrong. Antiwar activists saw the opportunity immediately. The young man pictured in the August 20 issue of *Life* magazine burning his draft card at Whitehall Induction Center in New York on July 30, though identified as a student, was actually a member of the pacifist Catholic Peace Fellowship (CPF) and associate editor of the *Catholic Worker*, the publication of the pacifist-anarchist Catholic Worker Movement. As Congress reacted, CPF's publications director rejoiced: "Now the government is angry . . . Of course this means we must have a public draft card burning soon." And an alliance of antiwar groups resolved, at a national meeting near Bloomington, Indiana, on September 6th, to work to build a national antidraft movement "whose purpose would not necessarily be to abolish the draft, but to build an antiwar movement around the draft issue."[44]

The first person to defy the law was a sophomore engineering major at the University of Iowa. Stephen Smith had been part of the 1964 Freedom Summer in Mississippi; he was a man of conscience who had learned, from the civil rights movement, that while there is no substitute for hard, day-to-day struggle when one hopes to change the world, sometimes a brief moment of public attention can make all the difference. "I do not feel that five years of my life are too much to give to say that this law is wrong," he said, preparing to burn his draft card. "Picketing is so common that it is not really effective any more. A dramatic means of expression is needed to keep the public alert to, and discussing, moral and social issues." Smith was arrested and then freed on $500 bail. But his act passed largely unnoticed, used by George Starbuck—a lecturer at the University of Iowa that year—in his powerful poem "Of Late," but missed by *Life, Time,* and the national news.[45] It was Iowa, after all.

Organized protest was more savvy—or at least better located. When 22-year-old CPF member David Miller climbed atop a sound truck in New York during the October 15–16 International Days of Protest, the television cameras were ready. Holding his draft card (1-A), and neatly dressed in a conservative gray suit, he told the crowd: "I believe the napalming of villages in Viet Nam is an immoral act. I hope this will be a significant political act, so here goes." He struck a match, but it blew out. Someone passed up a cigarette lighter from the crowd, and he set the card on fire. People cheered; a few shouted "treason," and "beatnik." But nothing more happened. The following day the state commander of New York's Veterans of Foreign Wars announced that unless the authorities took action within twenty-four hours, he intended to make a citizen's arrest himself. FBI agents arrested Miller two days later at a service station in New Hampshire, where he'd stopped to change a flat tire. The recent graduate of Jesuit-run LeMoyne University had been traveling as part of a "peace crusade" through New England colleges.[46]

October's International Days of Protest included demonstrations in eighty U.S. cities and several European ones, and although Miller seems to have been the only person to publicly defy the law that day, the antiwar movement had used antidraft sentiment as an organizing force. The draft drove the war home to many young people; it made the war something that could not be ignored. Concerns about the draft, about the potentially immediate impact of the war on their lives, drew many young Americans into the antiwar movement. And draft-card burning was a useful tool: it was controversial, photogenic, and symbolically powerful. It captured public attention. But it was a complicated choice, not fully appreciated in advance. Members of the draft resistance movement who burned or destroyed or returned their draft cards over subsequent years were quite serious in their opposition to the war and willing to accept the consequences of their acts. At the same time, use of the draft as a major organizing issue blurred the larger point: many Americans were powerfully opposed to the Vietnam war. Lyndon Johnson, commenting on the International Days of

Protest demonstrations from his bed in Bethesda Naval Hospital, where he was recovering from surgery, said he was "dismayed" by this "antidraft movement" and wanted it investigated for communist influences. Covering his comments, the *New York Times* framed the protests as antidraft, not antiwar: "Johnson Decries Draft Protests," the front-page article proclaimed.[47]

The antiwar and antidraft movements were overlapping and intertwined throughout the Vietnam War, but supporters of the nation's war policy were sometimes too quick to dismiss antiwar protest as driven primarily by fear of the draft. In fact, despite the sometimes agonizing and always highly publicized "generation gap," young people continued to support the war in large numbers. Some did worry about the draft, but those worries were never sufficient to explain the broadly based and growing antiwar movement. Nonetheless, as late as May 1970, when hundreds of thousands of Americans exploded in outrage over President Nixon's secret invasion of Cambodia and recoiled from the image of four young people shot dead by National Guard troops at Kent State University, *U.S. News and World Report* chronicled the "revolts on campuses across the land" and asked: "What induces such uprisings?" The answer: "Primarily, the youth of America for the last decade have been worried about the prospect of being drafted to fight in the war in Vietnam. Restlessness has resulted. Careers could not be planned."[48] The draft was a too-convenient answer to the "problem" of mounting antiwar protest, but it provided an opening for action. Perhaps war protest would quiet if the draft were not such an issue.

Richard Nixon understood that opportunity, and he understood the power of symbolic politics. So during the presidential election of 1968, as he offered a "secret plan" to end the war, Nixon also promised to end the draft. He wasn't breaking new ground as he spoke on the radio that October about "a matter important to us all, but especially young Americans and their parents." The call for a volunteer military wasn't unprecedented, even in national politics. The Wednesday Group, a set of liberal to moderate congressional Republicans that included Donald Rumsfeld, future secretary of defense, had called for an end to the draft in 1967. Various bipartisan bills had been introduced in Congress but foundered on strong opposition from the Armed Services committee. Nonetheless, executive commitment was quite different from congressional interest, and that was what Nixon was promising.

Nixon, however, did not talk about complicated political struggles in Washington or about antiwar dissent when he made his case to the American people. Instead, he offered a careful argument in language that seemed to transcend politics. Fundamentally, he claimed, America's national defense needs were changing. In a nuclear age, Nixon instructed his listeners, "huge ground armies operating in massive formations would be terribly vulnerable." The nation now needed a smaller number of "motivated men, trained in the techniques of counterinsurgency," and with the "higher level of technical and professional skill" necessary to operate the "complex weapons of modern war." That smaller but more highly trained force, Nixon told his audience, could be created through voluntary enlistments. How? The military, he explained, had been protected by the draft. The armed forces were the "only employers today who don't have to compete in the job market . . . They've been able to ignore the laws of supply and demand." Higher pay and increased benefits, he claimed, would make military life "more competitive with the attractions of the civilian world" and make an all-volunteer force a true possibility.[49]

Most listeners took away the political message: Nixon pledges to end the draft. But in policy terms, Nixon's explanation of how this process would work, along with his larger rationale for its necessity, is critical. Nixon's economic argument—that competitive pay and benefits would solve the problem of recruitment—is a free market–driven claim that fits neatly with his larger rationale. Nixon offered Americans a case against the draft built on the conservative/libertarian claim that liberty is the most central of American values. The draft, he explained, raised "the question of permanent conscription in a free society." He quoted the conservative senator Robert Taft, who had opposed instituting a draft even as the United States moved toward involvement in World War II because he believed conscription interfered with the "principles of individual liberty." Allowing that conscription was the easiest and cheapest way to raise an army, Nixon claimed that the tradeoff was too great. No longer must Americans endure a "Hobson's choice" that required the nation to "constrict the freedom of some, or endanger the freedom of all." The solution to the dilemma was a market-driven all-volunteer force.[50]

A great many Americans—especially young men—cared little about the ideological basis for Nixon's claims, but those who followed policy recognized that he was affiliating himself with an already well-articulated position in an ongoing public discussion. It was easy to find opposition to the draft; difficult to find support. Policy-oriented liberals, "tormented by Vietnam," hoped that a volunteer force would be more difficult for a president to commit abroad. Other liberals, appalled at the inequality of sacrifice in the still-expanding war, thought a universal program of national service would offer greater equality.[51] Policy-oriented conservatives were much less likely to tie their support for a volunteer force to Vietnam. Instead, they presented the draft as a "gross infringement on personal liberty." It was an ideologically conservative argument, but one that easily completed a political circle to the left: calls to limit state power resonated with those suspicious of the government; the language of personal freedom was not incompatible with exhortations to "Do your own thing," no matter how appalled conservative ideologues might be by some of their new bedfellows.

Nixon's call to end "permanent conscription in a free society," his description of the draft as an "infringement on . . . liberty," puts him squarely in the conservative camp. Yet, despite his calls upon free choice and liberty, on market forces and "hidden taxes," Nixon was, as usual, more the pragmatist than the ideologue. He wanted to gain whatever political advantage possible, to defuse the issue of the draft, to "quell the restless students."[52]

Why, then, did notions of individual liberty and the free market shape his proposals? Chance and contingency mattered more than design. In 1967, Martin Anderson, then a young associate professor of economics at Columbia University, got into a political "discussion" with another young man during a dinner party. At some point the other man, who worked for the law firm Mudge, Stern, Baldwin & Todd, where Richard Nixon had been a senior partner since 1963, got exasperated and told him, "You should work for this guy Nixon. You think like he does." Not long afterward Anderson joined Nixon's pre-campaign task force.[53]

Anderson, who had joined the Reserve Officers' Training Corps (ROTC) at Dartmouth and then served as a second lieutenant in the Army Security Agency in 1958–59, was drawn—as an economist—to discussions about the draft that engaged prominent free-market economists at the time. In late 1966, at a University of Chicago conference on the topic, both Milton Friedman and Walter Oi had urged an end to the draft; the following spring, both had written antidraft articles for a special issue of the *New Individualist Review,* a libertarian journal published by University of Chicago students. That summer Anderson drafted an article titled "An Analysis of the Factors Involved in Moving to an All-Volunteer Armed Force." Anderson's political insight—that coming out against the draft could make a real difference in voter support—captured Nixon's attention. But Anderson was the one who briefed Nixon on the issue, and he was the one who wrote the speech calling for an end to the draft. Thus Nixon made his proposal in the free market, libertarian language used by the Chicago school of economics.[54]

With Nixon's victory, Anderson left Columbia for a staff position in the White House, where he continued to shepherd his plan.[55] On January 29, 1969—just nine days into his presidency—Nixon wrote a memorandum to his new secretary of defense, Melvin Laird. It began: "It is my firm conviction that we must establish an all-volunteer armed force after the expenditures for Vietnam are substantially reduced," and requested that Laird "immediately" begin to plan a commission that could develop "a detailed plan of action for ending the draft." Laird, who in January 1969 did have other things on his mind, and who philosophically was committed to notions of shared responsibility rather than defense through free-market principles, tried to slow down Nixon. The Department of Defense —having seen the writing on the wall—had already begun studying the feasibility of an all-volunteer force. Nevertheless, Pentagon officials made clear to Laird that while the DoD preferred volunteers and had no objection to change, it was "alarmed" by Nixon's reliance on economists who were "fanatic opponents of the draft" and might not offer a "careful, objective study of the problem."[56] Despite Laird's cautions, Nixon held firm. On March 27th he announced the creation of the President's Commission on an All-Volunteer Armed Force, for which Anderson served as White House liaison. Nixon's charter was clear: the mission was not to evaluate the possibility of ending the draft, but to "develop a comprehensive plan for ending conscription and moving toward an all-volunteer force."[57]

The commission was chaired, at Laird's suggestion, by Thomas Gates, the former secretary of defense. Gates, reportedly, told Nixon at the outset that he was "opposed to the whole idea of a volunteer force." Nixon replied (according to Anderson's later account): "That's exactly why I want you as the Chairman . . . If you change your mind and think we should end the draft, then I'll know it is a good idea."[58] The White House meant to have the endorsement of the committee, but it didn't ignore the obvious credibility issue. No one wanted the committee to look like a stacked deck, even if most hoped it would function like one. Thus the fifteen members were appropriately distinguished and carefully chosen. Retired generals Alfred Gruenther and Lauris Norstad, both of whom had served as Supreme Allied Commander, Europe, represented the military. There were major figures from secondary and higher education, from industry, and from the civil rights community. Several members filled multiple roles. Jeanne Nobel, the only woman on the committee, was a professor at New York University, the Vice President of the National Council of Negro Women, and a former member of the Defense Department Advisory Committee on Women in the Services (DACOWITS). Stephen Herbits, a 26-year-old law student at Georgetown, was meant to represent "youth." But his congressional connections were substantial: he had been the key staff person for the Republican "Wednesday Group" study supporting an all-volunteer force. The commission also boasted three prominent economists: Milton Friedman, Alan Greenspan, and W. Allen Wallis.[59]

Nixon had charged the commission to develop a plan of action for ending the draft. But—by design—the commission was not uniformly in favor of an all-volunteer military. Five members, including all the economists, were strong and public supporters of an AVF. Five members had strong, but not public, reservations. And five had, seemingly, given the matter little thought. It became quickly evident at the first commission meeting that there were some very serious discussions ahead, and not simply about means and methods.

The commission members and staff came together for the first time on May 15, 1969, in the Roosevelt Room of the White House. Chairman Gates conferred Nixon's charge, making clear that the president had "the desire and a commitment" to do something about the draft "problem." Almost immediately the touchy question came up: were they "obligated to recommend" the AVF plan? Gates said no. The commission, he believed, could decide to offer a plan and at the same time present its critique of that plan. Although much of the meeting dealt with procedural issues—how to handle public relations; how to handle relations with Congress (Mr. Gates weighed in on the side of using "good manners"); how to handle hearings and testimony; confirmation of the proposed staff—commissioners also began staking out their positions.[60]

Throughout the commission's life, the most energetic exchanges took place between Crawford Greenewalt and Milton Friedman. Greenewalt had been president of the DuPont Corporation from 1948 through 1962 and in 1969 continued as chair of DuPont's finance committee. But

Greenewalt was also a gifted engineer. Assigned to the Manhattan Project during World War II, he'd served as liaison between University of Chicago physicists and DuPont engineering and construction crews and had impressed all by his rapid grasp of the physics involved. Typical for the DuPont family (he had married Irinee DuPont's daughter), Greenewalt was a man of broad interests. In other circles, he was best known for his knowledge of hummingbirds. His published photographs, made possible by new high-speed photography techniques he'd developed, had been compared favorably to the work of photographer Eliot Porter. Greenewalt had made the cover of *Time* magazine back in 1951. "DuPont's Greenewalt," read the cover caption. "Cellophane, nylon, a wrinkleproof suit—and the H-bomb."[61]

Milton Friedman, just seven months away from his own *Time* magazine cover (which would bear the banner headline, "Will There Be a Recession?"), was probably the best-known economist in the United States. A member of the University of Chicago's department of economics since 1948, Friedman had shaped and enhanced that department's reputation as a scholarly center for proponents of a free-market economy. Since 1966, he'd written a regular column for *Newsweek* magazine, frequently offering economic analysis on policy issues that was at odds with *Newsweek*'s more (twentieth-century) liberal vision. Though the Chicago school was an outlier among economics departments in the 1960s, Friedman was in good company in the Gates Commission. His fellow economists, University of Rochester president W. Allen Wallis and economic consultant Alan Greenspan, both embraced free-market ideology. Greenspan, in fact (like Martin Anderson), was a friend and follower of Ayn Rand and shared her commitment to "rational egoism" and laissez-faire capitalism.

The key division emerged quickly, and it was not so simple as pro- and anti-AVF. At the initial meeting, as economists suggested that the AVF was really a labor market issue to be solved by competitive pay and Stephen Herbits, the law student, urged the staff to "consider labor/capital 'tradeoffs' after calculating true manpower costs," Crawford Greenewalt made clear that he had "serious philosophical reservations about paying people to die for their country." Milton Friedman then "observed" that "it was far worse to use the draft to force young men to sell their lives cheaply and that it would be infinitely preferable to pay those risking their lives a decent wage." When Greenewalt ventured, over lunch at a subsequent meeting, that "there was something immoral in seducing people to die for their country," and that "risking one's life for his country was not just another job," Friedman replied that "he could not see how morale and effectiveness were enhanced by paying people substandard wages," for the "logic of such an approach would dictate paying them nothing."[62] Greenewalt's objections were sustained and powerful, but never so fully developed as the manpower calculations and system-to-system comparisons offered by the economists. Greenewalt, with no evidence one way or another, doubted whether increased pay would draw a sufficient number of volunteers, especially in times of war. But he was also uncomfortable with the way the discussion turned so heavily on notions of supply, demand, and fixed elasticity. He was convinced that there was a moral issue involved, and that it couldn't be reduced to economic terms.

The White House, represented by Martin Anderson, did not stand idly by. The administration wanted a report as soon as possible, in part because Anderson worried that pending draft reform would undermine the case for a volunteer force, but it also wanted maximum credibility. To that end, the White House suggested the commission create a youth advisory committee. Politically savvy members of the Gates Commission thought a youth committee would be "trouble in the long run." Instead, the commission decided to hold a series of hearings throughout the nation as a way to generate public support. However, Nixon's key advisor and Anderson's immediate superior Arthur Burns cautioned that public hearings would likely become forums for Vietnam War dissent. At the same time, a public relations expert Gates consulted made clear that certain groups—such as the Veterans of Foreign Wars (VFW) and the American Legion—would "feel slighted" if not "allowed to appear personally before some members and staff." In the end, the commission decided to invite representatives of key groups, including organizations of young Americans that Stephen Herbits insisted were critical if the commission hoped to claim legitimacy, to testify at an informal meeting in Washington, D.C. They also sent a stock letter to groups ranging from the United Auto Workers to Students for a Democratic Society, from the Air Force Association to the American Friends Service Committee. It's not clear how the American Farm Bureau Association or the American Association of Dental Schools was meant to respond to the stock question, "What flow of enlistees will be required to maintain the desired active duty and reserve effectiveness at several alternative force levels?" On the other hand, there is no evidence that responses to these letters were ever compiled or circulated to commission members.[63]

Only four commission members attended the informal hearings on

September 6th: Norstad, Gruenther, Gates, and Herbits. More than anything else, those invited to testify made clear how little support remained for the draft. Selective Service director Lewis B. Hershey did argue that the urge to end the draft was an "overreaction" to Vietnam.[64] James R. Wilson, director of the National Security Commission of the American Legion, made the case that "service to ones [*sic*] country is a privilege and an obligation of citizenship," and that changing the "concept of military service from a citizen responsibility to a 'paid job'" would not serve the "best interests of the nation."

But opposition was strong, and it came from avowed opponents: The leftist National Student Association (NSA) initially stated simply that "conscription is immoral," while the conservative Young Americans for Freedom (YAF) called the draft "involuntary servitude." Randall Teague, executive director of Young Americans for Freedom (draft status "1-Y on physical infirmities," with no military service, as he informed those present) took advantage of the opportunity to explain to two former Supreme Allied Commanders, Europe and a former secretary of defense that the United States was "fighting the wrong kind of war" in Vietnam and that he "definitely felt that the current 3.4 million force was too large."

Gates, however, found the YAF representative more compelling than the NSA's Jim Sutton, who'd tried to disarm the commission by beginning his testimony: "Good morning, gentleman. My name is Jim Sutton, and I have the unlikely middle name of Hercules." Sutton took the opportunity to lecture the group on broad inequities in American society, prompting a staff member to "recommend" that he "focus on the military's sole [*sic*] and operation and not the ills of society." Sutton then opined that only 1–2 percent of young men were "basically martial" and would be interested in volunteering. When Mr. Gates "suggested that recruits would be patriotic youths and not necessarily ones with a 'martial orientation,'" Sutton replied that he "rejected an interpretation of patriotism as blind obedience to the nation's leaders." General Gruenther asked if Sutton still "thought the draft was an immoral system," to which Mr. Sutton replied in the affirmative, noting that he would nonetheless favor its use in times of emergency. It may have been 26-year-old Herbits who found the testimony hardest to sit through. If these two set the standard, it was not going to be easy to gain—or even to seek—credibility with the nation's youth.[65]

Though the testimonies raised critical issues, including the way the

Vietnam War affected public opinion of conscription, the relationship between citizenship and military service, and questions of social equality, they made little difference in the commission's trajectory. The frame of the debate had already been set, well before these men testified, well before the commission even met. It was the staff—not the commissioners—that proposed the agendas, that directed the research, that drafted the report. And while the commissioners represented an even division of opinion, the commission staff most certainly did not. Four of the five senior staff members were anticonscription free-market economists with significant reputations of their own: William Meckling (the executive director), Walter Oi, Harry Gilman, and Stuart Altman.[66] All of them were public supporters of an all-volunteer force.

Of course, the commission members were not railroaded by the staff's enthusiasm for an all-volunteer force. It's difficult to imagine two retired four-star generals and a former secretary of defense being cowed by the opinions of their staff. What mattered most was not the staff's opinions but their methods—more precisely, the way that this staff understood the nature of evidence. They had no use for general arguments or philosophical debates. These economists sought clear data and quantifiable proof.

To make their case, the commission staff first dealt with common objections to the all-volunteer force. They generated a list of thirty-five objections, which they sorted into five major categories of concern: (1) an all-volunteer force would be alienated from civilian society, thus undermining civilian control of the military and increasing the likelihood of a coup d'état; (2) an AVF would have a negative effect on civilian society because military service offers education and training and makes men better citizens; (3) an AVF would lead to unnecessary military involvements overseas; (4) an AVF would lower military morale and be less effective; and (5) an AVF would be less flexible and less able to meet emergencies. Commission members pointed out that this list omitted the frequently voiced concern that an AVF would be "all-black"; the staff found this scenario unlikely, "given present military standards" for admission.[67]

Aware that the commission would have to deal with these objections, staff members tried to either locate or generate research that supported or negated these major concerns. For example, the Gates Commission staff attempted to assess the claim that military service benefited civilian society by giving men valuable educational or work experiences and so making them better citizens. If the nation moved to an all-volunteer force, fewer men, drawn from a narrower range of American society, would have military experience; thus, if such benefits existed, their impact on civilian society would decrease. The staff attempted to "investigate [that] category of arguments" by "answering two questions: (1) how much skill transference takes place, and (2) how much more do veterans earn than non-veterans." As to the first question, "several studies indicated that a veteran's post-service job was primarily a function of his pre-service education rather than the training he had received in the military." And to the second: "a preliminary answer . . . seemed to be that military service improved one's post-service income only in the case of veterans in lower mental groups."[68]

On the citizenship question, a staff member told commission members, there was little "empirical evidence" to be had. Lacking any compelling data, the staff had decided to generate its own by analyzing responses to nine questions previously posed in Gallup, Roper, and other surveys. They found "little evidence of any correlation between one's having served in the military and his subsequent attitudes." One can't help but wonder what questions they chose, and what attitudes would have indicated good citizenship. Commission members, in fact, suggested that the staff's analysis of answers to nine questions from public opinion surveys "did not reach the fundamental question of whether veterans were better citizens."[69] But the staff meant to furnish reliable data, not to raise fundamental questions. Postservice income was quantifiable; better citizenship was not. Everyone involved in the commission understood, in the late 1960s, that Americans were struggling—both in the courts and in the streets—over the meaning of citizenship. And so the more complex question receded from view as the staff furnished objective data about the economic effects of military service.

The staff relied heavily on the concept of a "hidden tax" to make its case for the AVF. This shorthand term summed up the argument that conscription imposed a virtual "tax" on draftees. Unlike those who escaped the government's hand, draftees sacrificed not only the difference in income between poorly paid military service and civilian jobs, but also years that could otherwise be spent in education, professional training, or job advancement—and thus the accumulated benefits from those lost years. This quantifiable, economic argument satisfied some, but it also exposed divisions among those who supported the AVF. Herbits was second only to Friedman in his desire to end the draft. But he—like Greenewalt—felt that something was missing in all the economic analysis. As he wrote Gates, the commission's chair, on August 1st: "I am not prepared to accept the economic cost factor or the implicit tax factor as the only viable arguments. In fact, to many, those arguments pale in comparison to a simple statement that in a Free society we must allow people to choose their own destiny when we can do so without endangering the national security."[70]

In the end, members resisted the staff's desire to begin the final report by describing the draft as "involuntary servitude," at least in part because raising questions about the constitutionality of the draft seemed ill-advised when most commission members wanted to maintain a "stand-by" draft in case of major "conflagration."[71] They also moderated the staff's plans to hinge the commission report on the notion of an implicit tax. As Gates argued, such an argument was "difficult to understand" and "involved fairly esoteric reasoning," likely requiring four or five pages of explanation. Economist Allen Wallis agreed with Gates. Discussions of an implicit tax, he said, "would sound like doubletalk to the average layman."[72] Agreement on the final draft was almost derailed by a long and heated debate about the meaning of the word "can," as members argued about whether or not the phrase "an all volunteer force *can* be implemented" underplayed reservations and implied "a categorical belief that an all-volunteer force could under no circumstances fail to succeed." Greenewalt, Norris, and Norstad, at the final meeting, still flirted with the idea of filing caveats. But when the committee forwarded its report to President Nixon on February 21, 1970, the letter of transmittal noted that "it is somewhat remarkable that, starting from different backgrounds and opinions," the commissioners had found "total agreement."

In the end, the commission's report unanimously endorsed the move to an all-volunteer force and recommended the nation end the draft on July 1, 1971. Although the report relied heavily on quantitative economic studies, it made its philosophical case around issues of individual freedom and liberty. It paid little attention to the question of fairness, simply suggesting that free-market forces would be fairer than government engineering. The most recent study of the draft versus a volunteer force, distributed to commissioners early in the process, had been titled "In Pursuit of Equity: Who Serves When Not All Serve?" In contrast, the "inch-thick" report on the AVF being prepared for President Nixon was, according to *Business Week*, tentatively titled "Protecting the Free Society."[73] That tentative title was downgraded to a chapter subheading by the time the report appeared, but the opening chapter of the Gates Commission report, which ran in the *New York Times* on February 22, 1970, justified the volunteer force as "the system for maintaining forces that minimizes Government interference with the freedom of the individual to determine his own life in accord with his values." The first and most important step in the transition, it noted, was to "remove the present inequity in . . . pay" between civilian and service scales. The "traditional belief that each citizen has a moral responsibility to serve his country" was dispensed with in a brief paragraph on page 14. Conscription, the report claimed, "undermines respect for government by forcing an individual to serve when and in the manner the government decides, regardless of his own values and talents." Thus, "a voluntary decision to serve is the best answer, morally and practically, to the question of who should serve."[74]

On April 23, 1970, President Nixon sent a message to Congress endorsing the basic findings of the Gates Commission. It is not surprising, given that he was in the process of secretly expanding the Vietnam War into Cambodia, that Nixon did not accept its proposal to end the draft when conscription authority expired at the end of June 1971. But he laid the groundwork for the end of the draft, primarily by accepting the concrete recommendations of the Gates Commission. In his message to Congress, Nixon proposed a series of increases in military pay and benefits. And he moved, in conclusion, to a broader philosophical justification that drew equally on "timeless" truths and Cold War visions:

> With an end to the draft, we will demonstrate to the world the responsiveness of republican government—and our continuing commitment to the maximum freedom for the individual, enshrined in our earliest traditions and founding documents. By upholding the cause of freedom without conscription we will have demonstrated in one more area the superiority of a society based upon belief in the dignity of man over a society based on the supremacy of the State.[75]

Nixon had kept his promise.

The all-volunteer army was born of chaos and division. As people struggled not only over the war but over their radically different visions of American society, presidential candidate Nixon had seen a political opportunity. Although most of the protest Nixon hoped to quell came from the political left, it was conservatives and free-market economists who seized the momentum and shaped the path toward an all-volunteer military. These men set aside the notion that military service is an obligation of citizenship; they walked around issues of fairness and shared sacrifice. Instead, they worked from two major assumptions: individual liberty is the most essential American value, and the free market is the best means to preserve it. Economists had not yet begun to factor irrational forces into their calculations, so these men relied on fairly basic labor market models of supply, demand, and competitive wages. Offer young men a decent wage, they claimed, and a sufficient number would enlist. Individuals would make decisions based on rational understandings of their own economic self-interest.

During the twelve months in which the Gates Commission met, from March 1969 through February 1970, 6,106 American servicemen died in combat in Vietnam.

2 ★ REPAIRING THE ARMY

TRANSFORMING THE ARMY would be a huge task, especially as the Vietnam War continued with no clear end in sight. By chance, not design, that job fell to General William C. Westmoreland, commander of the war in Vietnam until Lyndon Johnson brought him home in mid-1968 and made him chief of staff of the army. The 54-year-old four-star general had wanted that job since he was a plebe in West Point's class of 1936, so much so that his roommate took to calling him "Chief." But with the war in Vietnam going badly and with his own reputation compromised—in large part by his willingness to make the Johnson administration's case for war in an address to Congress in the spring of 1967—Westmoreland knew that hardly anyone saw this coveted appointment as a promotion.[1]

Nonetheless, Westmoreland had, for decades, been portrayed as the model American military officer. At West Point he'd risen to first captain, the highest possible rank. His uniform bore the insignia of three wars: medals and campaign ribbons from North Africa and Sicily, France and Germany, Korea, Vietnam. Few reporters could avoid the term "ramrod" in reference to his posture; when *Time* magazine named him "Man of the Year" for 1965, the authors described the commander of U.S. forces in Vietnam as "the sinewy personification of the American fighting man." Even as public support for the war waned, Westmoreland still appeared in print as the "jut-jawed epitome of a 'straight arrow' soldier," "the paradigm of the professional military man . . . as straightforward as he is straight-backed."[2]

Westmoreland found straightforwardness a handicap in the political tides and eddies of late 1960s Washington. The new administration had little use for him: Nixon saw the general as a political liability, and his national security advisor Henry Kissinger held Westmoreland responsible for the failures of the Vietnam War. Believing that Westmoreland was too invested in the war in Vietnam to offer strong leadership as chief of staff of the army, the secretary of the army and the chairman of the Joint Chiefs pressured him on staff appointments. The new army chief certainly lacked the autonomy and clear lines of power he'd had in Vietnam. Just months into his appointment, a frustrated Westmoreland decided he would best serve the army outside Washington, DC. In early 1969 he began traveling around the nation, speaking to audiences at universities and civic centers and town halls in an attempt to salvage the image of his beloved army, which had declined along with support for the war.

Westmoreland's stock speech was on the role of the military in a democracy. And even though he was routinely greeted with organized protests by demonstrators who waved signs labeling him a war criminal and interrupted his careful words, even though he privately believed, with great bitterness, that his commander-in-chief had given away a U.S. victory in Vietnam by not following his advice to expand the war, Westmoreland made a clear, firm point. The U.S. military was subject to civilian control and the armed forces were the "staunchest supporters" of that policy. "The Army is profoundly aware," he told an audience at Kansas State University in 1969, "that it exists for the American people and operates under the command and control of dedicated civilians who owe their position and authority to constitutional processes."[3]

But no matter how completely Westmoreland believed in the constitutionally mandated fact of civilian control, it cannot have been easy for him—or for his fellow senior officers—to read the words of the President's Commission on an All-Volunteer Armed Force in the spring of 1970. Men who loved their army, men who had committed their lives to its values, men who were losing hundreds of their soldiers a month in a war that would not be won, who saw respect for their proud institution draining away—such men found it difficult to confront the power of a civilian commission that treated soldiering as just another job, that seemed to presume that the nation's defense could be managed through the supply-and-demand forces of the labor market and that a competitive wage would be sufficient to motivate men into combat. No one had anything against better pay for enlisted men. But military leaders all knew that better wages would not be enough—and that is exactly what they had told the civilian commission the president had appointed. The army, especially, was never so sanguine about the ease of creating an AVF as were the distinguished members of the Gates Commission.

It was not that the army was surprised by the Gates Commission's findings. Politics are not confined to politicians, and the army had its fair share of people with political savvy. Rumblings in Congress over the draft had prompted Westmoreland, more than a month before Nixon made his campaign promise, to order a study of the feasibility of an all-volunteer army. Faced with the possibility of such a major transformation, army officials worked hard, behind the scenes, to shape the debate and control the process. The army's senior officers, however, knew that this was one of the worst possible moments to end the draft. The Gates Commission had pretty much ignored the Vietnam War, but the army couldn't. The war, of course, demanded the full force of the army's attention. But the war also created the climate from which the army would have to recruit.

Volunteer rates had remained relatively strong throughout the Vietnam War, but that was mainly due to the draft. Those who volunteered had more control over the terms of their service than those who were drafted. Even though volunteers served longer terms, they were less likely to be sent to Vietnam than were draftees. According to the army, 49.7 percent of volunteers in 1969 were "draft-motivated." By 1970, draft-motivated volunteers outnumbered "true volunteers," and of those true volunteers, only 2.5 percent joined the infantry.[4] Everyone knew that without the pressure of the draft, volunteer rates would plummet. Most believed that even once the war ended it would have a lasting effect. Fewer and fewer men saw military service as desirable, war or no war. Finally, the army knew that it wasn't just a question of numbers, not just a steady supply of men moving through basic training. The army needed *combat* troops—something the Gates Commission, for all its debate about whether or not it was moral to pay men to risk their lives, didn't ever quite confront, even when army representatives suggested combat arms might require a different measure of "flexible elasticity."

By the late 1960s, the army faced an even bigger challenge. It had gone to war in Vietnam with what most saw as the strongest, best-trained force in the nation's history. By the end of the decade, the army was in crisis.[5] The flood of news articles about drug addiction and combat refusal, fragging and racial conflict, undermined the army's public image. But even worse, those in charge knew those stories contained a core of truth. Four years into a difficult war, it was impossible not to see the trouble. Thus, the army faced two enormous challenges. It had to move to a volunteer force in the wake of an unpopular and divisive war. And it had to repair a failing institution. Of necessity, the army confronted those two problems together—it worked to strengthen and rebuild itself, and at the same time to create an army that young people might want to join.

None of this happened in a vacuum. The Vietnam War was the overwhelming context; the war made it possible to end the draft, just as it made ending the draft so difficult. But the war was not the only force roiling American society in those difficult years. Vast numbers of Americans had lost faith in their government and in the nation's public institutions. As violence and mounting anger threatened to tear the nation apart, the new president blamed "permissiveness." The generation gap, many on both sides concluded, was unbridgeable. This was the larger world in which the army had to remake itself. And in this world, attempts at reform ran into the fundamental and perpetually difficult questions that lay at the base of military practice: How does one forge a disciplined fighting unit? What is leadership, and how does it best function? What is the proper relation between the military and the values and practices of the larger society? Like much else in the 1960s, these questions were not resolved. But it is impossible to understand the all-volunteer army without understanding the internal struggles that gave it birth.

Though the draft had been in effect—with only a brief respite—since 1940, army policy was to fill its ranks with volunteers, so far as possible, and then use the draft to make up the difference. In 1968, despite the relatively large number of draft-motivated volunteers, the army had to make up an awful lot of difference. No one with any real authority thought that ending the draft in the middle of the war was feasible, much less a good idea. But many, including Westmoreland, understood what a politically difficult position the army was in during the summer of 1968.

The military had no control over the draft process, but a great many

Americans didn't understand that fact. The distinction was confusing, for the selective service system—a civilian institution—was run by Lt. General Lewis Hershey, who held his rank in the U.S. Army. After almost three decades in charge, Hershey had an almost proprietary attitude when it came to the draft. He said what he thought with a bluntness that rivaled LBJ's, and he increasingly put his disdain for those who opposed the war or resisted the draft into action. When Hershey decided that college students who were arrested or detained in war protests should lose their student deferments—and so notified those down the line—he opened up a huge political can of worms. And his public statements on the topic were hardly conciliatory.[6] Hershey, whose draft notification letters—beginning with "Greetings"—had changed the lives of American young men for decades, had by 1968 become the nightmare of many American 18-year-olds. Much of their anger and frustration redounded onto the army, which was where most draftees were bound. As public discussion of reforming—or even ending—the draft became louder and more insistent during the summer of 1968, army officials knew they must be prepared to take an official position just in case all those words spilled into print actually mattered. They also knew they had to think hard about how to present that position in a way that didn't create more public resentment.

In September 1968, General Westmoreland ordered army staff to investigate the feasibility of an all-volunteer force. The resulting study, conducted by Lt. Col. Jack R. Butler on a "close-hold" (extremely limited access) basis, was not encouraging. An all-volunteer force was feasible, the report concluded, depending of course on the size of the regular army and reserves in the years following the Vietnam War. But it would be expensive, with many fewer "high quality" soldiers. And the social implications were not good. Like most military leaders at the time, the authors of this report believed that military service was an obligation of citizenship and that ending the draft would sever that connection. Nonetheless, despite powerfully worded reservations, Butler encouraged Westmoreland to "take a positive approach." Direct opposition would be politically costly; expressions of willingness to work toward a zero-draft army would be much more politically acceptable. According to army historian Robert Griffith, the Butler report's verdict on the prospects of an all-volunteer army was "gloomy . . . but not hopeless."[7]

Westmoreland scarcely had time to digest the Butler study when a "bootleg" copy of Nixon's January 1969 letter to his secretary of defense,

Melvin Laird—the one that laid the basis for the President's Commission on an All-Volunteer Armed Force—landed on his desk. Westmoreland wasted no time; within days he had initiated a major study of the army's own, which functioned under the unusually pronounceable but slightly tortured acronym PROVIDE (PROject Volunteer In DEfense of the nation). The PROVIDE group completed its report in June, just a month after the Gates Commission held its first meeting. PROVIDE was a broad-ranging and thoughtful effort to determine how the army might "stand a reasonable chance of achieving the objective" of an all-volunteer army. Unlike the Gates Commission, which would conclude that the fundamental answer lay in "economic incentives," the PROVIDE group offered a comprehensive and specific set of recommendations for simultaneous action. Better pay was critical, but so was reducing the number of "irritants" (such as reveille) that plagued the life of the enlisted man. Better dental plans, more relevant recreational options, and improved housing might make a difference. PROVIDE recommended that the army improve the quality and training of recruiters, expand (and publicize) the role of women in the army, and use commercial advertising to counteract the poor image of the army that pervaded the society from which it would have to recruit. On the broader issue—whether to support the proposed move to an all-volunteer force—the group recommended that Westmoreland should "seize the initiative" and appoint a task group to plan for that transformation.[8]

Westmoreland was not quite ready to go that far. PROVIDE, in Westmoreland's mind, belonged to a sort of broad category that included bomb shelters and war games: much better to be prepared for what one hopes will never come. Certainly, Westmoreland did not want army studies to encourage Nixon's agenda. Thus army testimony to the Gates Commission that June fell somewhere between cautionary and negative. Officials offered full responses to questions commissioners posed but neglected to mention the existence of PROVIDE or any of its many recommendations. Such purposeful omission probably made little difference. The Gates Commission staff focused on manpower and economic issues, and even when the army provided detailed comments on a draft of the report in January 1970—and included many of their noneconomic recommendations—the Commission paid little attention.[9]

The move to an all-volunteer force seemed a done deal. But many of those who mattered, from the chairs of the congressional Armed Services committees to the secretary of the army, didn't see it that way. They believed that Nixon had gained what he needed, politically, and that the notion of an all-volunteer force would gradually slip from his—and the nation's—attention. After all, the President's Commission on an All-Volunteer Armed Force was the *fifth* such commission since 1964. Nothing was being budgeted for the transition, either in the immediate fiscal year budget for 1971 or in the five-year plan for the budget of the DoD. But pressure from the White House continued. It was becoming increasingly clear that the commander in chief was serious about ending the draft. So in October 1970 General Westmoreland publicly pledged the army's full commitment to achieving an all-volunteer force and summoned all concerned to face the challenge with "imagination and full energy."[10]

Nonetheless, the prospect of an all-volunteer force was rarely the most important issue confronting the chief of staff of the army. It would have been irresponsible for him to ignore Nixon's pledges and Gates's report and even the ongoing pressure of antidraft sentiment among the nation's youth. But the Vietnam War was always his central concern, the army in Vietnam more immediately important than some imagined volunteer army of the future.

To put things into perspective, when Westmoreland ordered the initial study of the feasibility of an all-volunteer force in the fall of 1968, he was much less concerned about congressional plans to end the draft than he was about his inability, as chief of staff of the army, to influence then-president Johnson's decisions about the war he'd been ordered to leave. During his first year and a half as army chief, Westmoreland was profoundly annoyed—some said obsessed—by what he saw as fawning press coverage of his successor in Vietnam, Creighton Abrams. *Time*'s article on the shift in command had described Abrams as a "onetime tank commander who could inspire aggressiveness in a begonia"; by fall of 1969 a long *New York Times* magazine feature implicitly contrasted Abrams with Westmoreland, noting that Abrams had clear military brilliance, but "at the stage at which he inherited command" in Vietnam "the problems were so thick and tangled that even brilliance could only dent them."[11]

In early 1969, about the time that Westmoreland came into possession of the bootleg copy of Nixon's letter to Laird and authorized the PROVIDE study, he began a national speaking tour that left him painfully aware of widespread antiwar sentiment and the declining public reputation of the army. In late March of that year, Nixon created his commission on the all-volunteer force. Two days later army Vietnam veteran Ron Ridenhour sent an anguished letter to members of the U.S. Congress. "Exactly what did, in fact, occur in the village of 'Pinkville' in March, 1968 I do not know for certain," Ridenhour wrote, "but I am convinced that it was something very black indeed. I remain irrevocably persuaded that if you and I do truly believe in the principles, of justice and the equality of every man, however humble, before the law, that form the very backbone that this country is founded on, then we must press forward a widespread and public investigation of this matter with all our combined efforts."[12] This letter, also, came to Westmoreland's desk. While the PROVIDE group, on Westmoreland's orders, was analyzing the potential impact of improved pay and better dental plans on volunteer rates, Westmoreland's office was concerned with the details of the massacre of men, women, and children in My Lai. The investigation was quiet but taken very seriously. And everyone knew that the story would eventually break.

The decline of the U.S. Army hadn't yet become a stock story in the American press in the spring of 1969, though stories about racial tension and drug abuse and "disillusioned" G.I.s were increasingly frequent. In August, correspondent Peter Arnett chronicled the "combat refusal" of the 196th Light Infantry Brigade's Alpha Company and then, on the *Huntley-Brinkley Report,* NBC's Kenley Jones speculated that the "brief revolt of Alpha company" might signal that as U.S. strategy shifts toward "disengagement," some soldiers are deciding that "the stakes are too high."[13]

As the PROVIDE group briefed Westmoreland in October 1969, millions of Americans were joining local War Moratorium protests. November began with *Harper's* publication of letters from men who had survived the eleven consecutive assaults on Hill 937—"Hamburger Hill"—in the A Shau Valley the previous May. Neil Sheehan, a former war correspondent, wrote by way of introduction: "Perhaps there is no difference, but it ought to be one thing to perish on the beaches of Normandy or Iwo Jima in a great cause and another to fall in a rejected and unsung war." The letters published in *Harper's* ranged from "passionate and eloquent protest[s] against the battle and the war itself" (Sheehan's language) to the words of "simple soldiers who . . . no longer believe" and in whose letters, "innocent of grammar but wise in the ways of war," now "flows a bitterness, uncomplicated, apolitical, and abiding." Sheehan's eloquence seems badly overblown when set beside the words he chose to end this collection:

"[A]ll I can say," wrote an unnamed sergeant, "is that quite a few people are suffering because of how fucked this war (of senior officers) has become."[14] On November 15th the largest antiwar protest in the nation's history was staged in Washington, DC. The My Lai story—complete with photographs—broke toward the end of the month. This was the November during which Westmoreland established the PROVIDE task force. He also launched a commission under the leadership of Lt. General William Peers to examine "the nature and the scope" of the original U.S. Army investigation of the events at My Lai.[15] Clearly the feasibility of an all-volunteer army was not the main focus of Westmoreland's attention.

In February 1970 the President's Commission on an All-Volunteer Armed Force issued its report, calling for an end to the draft in sixteen months. In March, the Peers Commission submitted its enormous and exhaustive report on the army's preliminary investigations into the My Lai incident. But General Peers also handed Westmoreland a secret memo. Moving beyond the measured language of the commission report, Peers told Westmoreland that he believed something had gone badly wrong with the army's officer corps. Westmoreland, moved to action not only by the report's findings but by Peers's clear outrage, ordered the commandant of the U.S. Army War College to conduct an "Analysis of Moral and Professional Climate in the Army." "By no means," wrote Westmoreland, "do I believe that the Army as an institution is in a moral crisis." But at the same time, he noted, "several unfavorable events occurring within the Army during the past few years" have been of "grave concern," and suggest a need to evaluate the "state of discipline, integrity, morality, ethics, and professionalism" in the army.[16] Westmoreland's letter arrived at Carlisle Barracks at almost exactly the same time that Nixon publicly endorsed the move to a volunteer force. Then, just over a week later, on April 30th, the United States invaded Cambodia.

Events in the United States quickly spiraled out of control. On May 4th, national guardsmen sent to contain student antiwar demonstrations at Kent State University, where the campus ROTC building previously had been torched in protest over Nixon's move into Cambodia, opened fire on university students. National Guard troops shot thirteen people. Four of them died. As anger reached a boiling point on campuses throughout the nation—over the invasion of Cambodia, over the deaths at Kent State—chancellors and trustees at more than five hundred colleges and universities decided it would be best to close down their campuses. The National

Guard troops at Kent State had not been federalized—they were under the command of the governor of the state of Ohio. But to many that made little difference. These were men in military uniform, carrying loaded weapons, who had killed four of "America's children." Even early newspaper editorials that offered a parallel rejection of "student violence" and government action charged the National Guard officers with a "gross lack of control of the men under their command" and condemned the shooting as "an unconscionable act of military panic."[17]

Army leaders in the summer of 1970 faced a growing crisis. The war in Vietnam was going badly. Antiwar sentiment was increasing at home. Newspapers offered a constant barrage of reports on problems within the army—reports largely confirmed from the field. Racial friction, drug use, small acts of indiscipline, failure of morale. And then there were the serious failures, the ones that were, in Ridenhour's words, "very dark indeed." Respect for the military—at an all-time low—would sink even further. The American public ranked the army lowest among the services—below the air force, navy, and marines. Worse—and this was according to an army-sponsored survey—army veterans did, too. The quantified fact that 70 percent of army veterans would advise others to join the navy or the air force instead of the army was unsettling, at best.[18]

Many career army men who had come of age during World War II or Korea were infuriated by the raw anger of civilian antimilitarism in the late 1960s. But many were truly anguished by the problems they saw within the army itself. As chief of staff of the army in that awful summer, caught in that moment of torment and that lifetime of duty, Westmoreland faced two challenges. As the War College study on army ethics and morality made clear, even beyond the evidence of his own eyes, he had to try to repair his army. And, as it was becoming increasingly obvious that Nixon was serious about ending the draft, he had to figure out how to move the draft-dependent army to an all-volunteer force.

The army would address these tasks in tandem, and its approach to both depended on the answers to a set of interrelated questions: Were the problems plaguing the army due to the war in Vietnam? Were they reflections of the broader society, as military culture was overwhelmed by the culture of contemporary youth, by "permissiveness," by young people who rejected both authority and discipline? Or were the problems internal, army problems created by army practices?

The answers to those questions would shape the army's move to an all-volunteer status, and they came primarily from the War College study of army ethics, which was delivered to Westmoreland's office on June 30, 1970. The report, which buried the terms "discipline, integrity, morality and ethics" under the title *Study on Military Professionalism,* was a powerful indictment of army practices. The authors' bureaucratic language obscures their sense of urgency, but they were clearly struggling with their findings. General G. S. Eckhardt, the commandant of the War College, prefaced the report "on the heart and soul of the Officer Corps" with a clear acknowledgment of the study's "emotional overtones" and an assurance that it was designed "to minimize the intrusion of emotionalism or group bias"; later, the authors pointed out that they had relied upon the behavioral sciences "and their preoccupation with being as unemotional and non-subjective as possible."[19]

The report argued that there was, indeed, a crisis in the army's officer corps, a "significant difference between the ideal values and the actual or operative values of the Officer Corps." The army's problems, according to War College analysis, were not due to external factors ("no direct evidence that external fiscal, political, sociological, or managerial influences are the primary causative factors of this less than optimum climate"), nor were they short-term effects of the war in Vietnam ("Neither does the public reaction to the Vietnam war, the rapid expansion of the army, or the current anti-military syndrome stand out as a significant reason for deviations from the level of professional behavior the Army acknowledges as its attainable ideal"). And they were not due to the corrosive effects of youth culture: young officers, those most steeped in the culture of youth, those most affected by "societal change such as the anti-war, anti-establishment movements," the report claimed, were the solution to the problem, not its cause. Young officers, the study argued, were more idealistic than their elders and, in keeping with the "stereotype of the better informed and somewhat skeptical youth of today," quicker than their elders to criticize "substandard performance" and failures of integrity.[20]

The *Study on Military Professionalism* concluded that the problem with the army was the army's own fault, the combination of a flawed "system" with what they described as the basic facts of human nature. Being human, officers were self-interested. They were motivated by the desire for reward—in this case, promotion. But the army system of evaluation—translated into the Officer Efficiency Report (OER)—created an "unrealistic demand for perfection." There was no room for failure; evaluations demanded "perfection or the pose of perfection at every turn." Those who took risks and made honest mistakes risked their careers; those who falsified reports to meet the unreasonable standards or who pressured junior officers to do so ascended the ladder. The system, moreover, rewarded "trivial, measurable, quota-filling accomplishments," creating officers who, in the words of another critic less burdened by the language of bureaucracy, were so festooned with medals and badges that they "resemble[d] walking Christmas trees." The system emphasized "ticket-punching" at the expense of expertise. The system was the problem.[21]

It seems counterintuitive, but this was welcome news. "It is in fact an optimistic finding," the War College study concluded, "that seemingly correctable flaws in various self-designed army systems might be prime causes of variances from ideal standards."[22] There was little the army could do about rapid societal change and the contemporary culture of youth. It wouldn't be easy to fix the internal structural problems—after all, the army's senior officers were products of this system; they were the ones who had best manipulated it, who were most invested in its continuation. But at least that problem was somewhat under army control.

The *Study on Military Professionalism* focused solely on the army's officer corps. It was the problem of filling the enlisted ranks, however, that worried those charged with moving to an all-volunteer force. There should have been little overlap between the War College study and the challenge of creating an AVF. But the subordinate claim of this study—that youth culture was not the problem, that youth, in fact, might be part of the solution—carried over into efforts to create and portray an army that young men might want to join.

No matter what else demanded the attention of the army chief, the all-volunteer army was not going to go away. Martin Anderson, in the White House, was determined to keep it on the front burner. When Westmoreland told the president during one of Nixon's regular meetings with the Joint Chiefs of Staff that the army could not then or in the near future meet its need for infantry soldiers without the draft and that, furthermore, he was worried that Congress and the American public were getting a different impression, Anderson was furious. Though Westmoreland denied that White House pressure had any impact on his actions ("The decision was made by the President and transmitted to me by the Secretary of Defense; I complied," he said), it also seemed clear that if the army didn't "get out in front publicly," it might lose control of the process. Westmoreland decided it was time to act. All the internal studies in the world might be for naught if he didn't make a public and powerful statement of the army's commitment to achieve an all-volunteer status.[23]

During the fall of 1970, as plans for the transition began to take shape, it was ever more obvious that it needed a project manager. Army bureaucracy was complex and often rigid. The fundamental changes planners envisioned rarely fell within a single line of authority. The only way the army would pull off this change, both the chief of staff and the secretary of the army came to believe, was if someone with sufficient rank and experience took control of what would almost certainly be a logistical nightmare and without doubt a difficult and politically charged process.

It took Secretary of the Army Stanley Resor and Chief of Staff Westmoreland less than twenty-four hours to decide who would be Westmoreland's new "special assistant." George Forsythe was, at that time, commanding general of the army's Combat Developments Command at Fort Belvoir, Virginia; he'd recently commanded the 1st Cavalry Division in Vietnam. Those who had watched Forsythe's career described him as "energetic, bright, can-do," someone who "talked very well." One who worked closely with Forsythe remembered him as self-assured and open-minded, a "renegade brigadier who could do a hundred things at the same time with complete indifference to politeness and customary military propriety." The phrase "hard-charging" came up sometimes, and not always fondly; Forsythe was more likely to call himself "hard-headed." Westmoreland had seen Forsythe handle some particularly complicated political and practical issues in Vietnam, not in his command of the 1st Cavalry Division but in the Civil Operations and Revolutionary Development Support (CORDS) program. Lyndon Johnson had appointed a civilian—Robert Komer, who had been running Johnson's "other war" (the one to win the hearts and minds of the people of the Republic of Vietnam) from Washington, DC since 1965—to direct a program charged with coordinating all civil and military pacification efforts in Vietnam. The complications of the job are obvious, but they were magnified by the introduction of civilian authority within military command. CORDS was located within the Military Assistance Command, Vietnam (MACV), the unified command structure for all military forces in Vietnam. Komer, with the personal rank of ambassador, claimed status equivalent to General Abrams, who was then deputy to Westmoreland. Some large part of Forsythe's job was managing tensions in this unorthodox arrangement; he'd shown an aptitude for communicating the CORDS agenda to both military and civilian actors.[24]

As "special assistant" for the all-volunteer army, Forsythe offered Westmoreland something beyond his demonstrated facility at unorthodox command and civil-military relations. As both assistant commandant and commandant at the Army Infantry School at Fort Benning, Georgia, Forsythe had given a fair amount of thought to the relationship between young men and the army. On Westmoreland's instructions, he had recently been spending time at summer ROTC camps, trying to engage in "free-flowing" conversations that might help him figure out "what was bugging the young ROTC guy who was about to enter the Army." Forsythe, in the continuum of concern over the apparent conflict between the nation's youth and its army, came down pretty strongly on the side of youth. He had a 21-year-old son in the fall of 1970, which may help explain his sympathies.

Forsythe understood that it was a big deal to voluntarily put on an army uniform and walk around a college campus in 1970. The young men who were doing so wanted answers; they wanted to understand the role of the army, the significance of its history and the justification for its current actions. They wanted to be able to go back to their campuses equipped to defend the choice they'd made. The sergeants who were training them in the summer ROTC camps, in Forsythe's telling, had no patience with them. Not with college students, in general. And not with college students' "screwy questions" that were really "none of their damn business." Forsythe's analysis is clearly—if not self-consciously—based on his understanding of social class: he saw a natural tension between these sergeants and the better-educated youth they were training. The young men, Forsythe believed, saw much in the army that didn't seem "realistic or relevant," that "didn't make sense." He thought that, on the whole, they had a point. Forsythe believed it was the army that needed to change, not its youthful critics.[25]

Just as the War College study focused on the officer corps, not on the tens of thousands of enlisted men the army would need to recruit every month by mid-1973, Forsythe was concerned with those he hoped would become army officers, not with the enlisted men completing combat training at Fort Benning. But he didn't draw an absolute line between the two—nor did more influential public analyses. In 1968 the nonprofit Battelle Institute conducted a major study for the Office of the Deputy Chief of Staff for Personnel on how to meet army personnel needs over the next decade. The *Army 75 Personnel Concept Study* (most commonly known as the *Army 75* study) simply assumed that the draft would continue, suggesting that the promised move to an AVF was not taken as gospel by even the best connected in 1968.

The study's authors, nonetheless, spent a fair amount of space on the challenge posed by the nation's youth. Both for officers and "enlisted input," they wrote, "we must dip into an activist cauldron of riots in the slums and unrest in the colleges, LSD, sex and hippies." The army would have to deal with young people who had been raised "permissively, unaccustomed to being told no," a group "that has been catered to, and whose every whim has been satisfied . . . with nary a moral judgment of whether the whim should be gratified or forbidden." At the same time, they insisted, "the issues raised by the young hold promise and excitement for dignity, human values, and a sense of identity in a depersonalized world." As American youth had become better educated, they'd also become more sophisticated, more questioning, more challenging. The results were not all good, certainly, but they were also not all bad. The nature of American youth had to be taken into account, the study insisted, as the army thought about manpower and personnel policy in the difficult days ahead.[26]

Historians and participants still debate how committed the army was to what it would call the MVA—the Modern Volunteer Army. Certainly some careers foundered in the effort, and some who were there claim that no matter how no-nonsense Westmoreland's public statements were, he had serious reservations about both goal and means. At the same time, the choice of Forsythe as SAMVA (Special Assistant, Modern Volunteer Army) is significant. Before Westmoreland asked Forsythe to take on the MVA, he invited him to lunch and had a serious conversation about the army. Forsythe told Westmoreland about his discussions with young men and the problems they saw in army life and army practices. Westmoreland told Forsythe about the War College study and its findings. Westmoreland explained the imperative to create an all-volunteer army, and, Forsythe remembered, he told Westmoreland that, volunteer army or not, they had to make some major changes. They had to trust their young soldiers more. They had to give them challenging and relevant work. They had to "open up a dialogue" with them. Westmoreland didn't offer him the job—didn't even raise the notion—until the end of this conversation. If it hadn't been clear before, it was clear then: Forsythe was in the fix-the-army camp, not the permissive-society-is-the-problem one; he was interested in and sympathetic to American youth; and he was willing to throw himself into the process of reform and transformation. Clearly, Westmoreland knew what he was getting when he put George Forsythe in charge of the future of the army.[27]

On October 13, 1970, Westmoreland stood before the gathered members of the Association of the United States Army in Washington, DC, and committed the army to an "all-out effort" to move with "imagination and full energy" to a "zero-draft" status. This was the dramatic public commitment the White House was looking for. But something else was going on that night. Westmoreland had chosen his words carefully. For while "zero-draft" and "all-volunteer" would, in practice, have the same outcome—a volunteer army—they had very different meanings. Zero-draft, simply put, was the ultimate success of the army's current practice: to rely first on volunteers and then use the draft, as necessary, to fill the ranks. The phrase "all-volunteer," at that moment in history, was firmly attached to free-market principles that exalted individual freedom and called upon liberty as the highest good. Many in that camp denied the legitimacy of the draft and the notions of citizens' rights and obligations upon which the draft was based. Of course plenty of people used the phrase without accepting those assumptions, including most of the army men who'd been studying the issue. But Westmoreland was making a point. The army would do its utmost to carry out the president's orders, but it wasn't signing on to the Gates Commission's vision of the army as just another competitor in the national job market. The White House got what it wanted, but not quite as it might have desired. Westmoreland wasn't the only one who tempered his support. The Pentagon had announced its commitment to achieving an all-volunteer force a few days before Westmoreland's speech. "Asked if the timing were political," *Time* magazine reported of the Pentagon announcement, Secretary of Defense Melvin Laird "could not suppress a smile." "'I don't know how you came to that conclusion,'" he told the reporter.[28]

In the relative privacy of the army Westmoreland spoke much more directly about his true concerns. He wove his keynote address to the Army Commanders' Conference that November around his twinned and intertwined agendas: the mandated move to an all-volunteer force and his powerful desire to rebuild the army. His announced topic was "achieving a Modern Volunteer Army," but the War College study shadowed every word he spoke. He showed no enthusiasm for the MVA—"an objective that has been assigned to us," he called it—but insisted that they could "take advantage of the situation" to improve the army. Westmoreland had no carefully crafted argument. He told the assembled commanders that he planned to speak "very bluntly and informally," and the sole record of this speech is an edited transcript. As Westmoreland circled around the coming of the MVA in a talk anchored around words such as "disappointed" and "concerned" and "unhappily," full of references to "dark days" and "serious errors" and "scandals," he returned repeatedly (though without attribution) to the substance and implications of the War College study and to Forsythe's arguments about contemporary youth. Westmoreland made it clear that the army could not hold itself fully apart from the society in which the young men who became soldiers had grown up and to which most would soon return. "Personal freedom," he said, had become more important to young people; they were more skeptical and less willing to submit blindly to authority. "We simply have to recognize," Westmoreland told his audience, "the fact that these changes have occurred and will continue. We cannot alter these trends ourselves, and we should forget about trying."[29]

Westmoreland wasn't willing to go as far as Forsythe or even as far as the authors of the War College study. He didn't see youth as the hope of the army or as a reservoir of idealism and honor. But he did see the possibility of their salvation. "I believe," he told the assembled commanders, "that the young men of our country are looking for responsibility. They are looking for respectability. They are looking for challenge. They are looking for adventure." The army, he believed, could offer them these things. How? It all came back to leadership. Leadership was the issue on which the army would rise or fall. Like the War College study, Westmoreland focused first on the failures of the officer corps: "Gentlemen," he said, "the Army cannot afford the type of leader who gets the job done in the narrow sense of meeting immediate requirements, when in so doing he creates devastating side effects by exploiting his people for his own personal betterment. This is quite obviously prevalent." But at the same time, he turned to army commanders—those who rose through that system—for the solution to the army's dual problems. The challenge of command today, he said, is to bring out the best in every leader. In the Modern Volunteer Army, authoritarianism must give way to real leadership. In today's world, that meant finding ways to "engage the imagination and enthusiasm of the men," to create a "continuous dialogue" that is "sensitive to their needs and aspirations," to "enhance their self-respect," and to accept them "as partners in a mutual endeavor."[30]

If they wanted the Modern Volunteer Army to succeed—and Westmoreland insisted they had no choice—they were going to have to figure out how to make the army more attractive to potential recruits. The "keynote" of the MVA, he announced, would be a series of changes designed to make army service "more enjoyable, more professionally rewarding, and less burdensome in its impact on our people and their families." He stipulated the end of what the army henceforth referred to as "needless irritants" (things known more colloquially as "Mickey Mouse" or "chickenshit"). There would be no more morning reveille formations. "Unreasonable ['spit and polish' to the extreme] inspection standards" were now a thing of the past. The army would liberalize pass policies, let soldiers drink beer on post, and, as a rule, give them Saturdays and Sundays off. Westmoreland knew that a majority of the men in that room had serious reservations about an all-volunteer force. He shared many of them. But as chief of staff of the army, he believed he must carry out the orders of his commander in chief to the best of his ability. And that day, he declared an end to debate. "The decision has been made," he said. "I expect your full support."[31]

Westmoreland's no-nonsense address to army commanders set the tone and began the slower process of altering the practice—the specifics of which he'd assigned to Lt. General George Forsythe. General Forsythe knew all too well that he faced an enormous challenge. His job was to create a comprehensive plan that would allow the army to move to an all-volunteer status by the middle of 1973. That gave him thirty-two months in which to design and implement a plan that would directly affect close to a million people and that relied on the decisions of institutions and entities over which the army had no control—Congress, the American public, and, perhaps most difficult of all, the average American eighteen-year-old. Forsythe had no office and no staff. He knew that the army recruiters were not up to the challenge, that the army's reputation was at its lowest point ever. He knew that support within the army for this transformation was thin and that people all up and down the line disagreed not only about ends but about means. He knew that the Armed Services committee was opposed to the AVF. He was aware that there was no money in the existing budget to implement any of his ideas, and that for the immediate future what limited funding there was had to come from reprogramming existing funds. He knew that the move to a volunteer force would hit the army much harder than any of the other services, but that the navy, air force, and marines would fight tooth and nail to preserve the current balance of funding. He knew there was no time to create a careful long-term plan that could be gradually instituted. But the bottom line was that beginning in mid-1973 the army was going to need to find more than 200,000 "true" volunteers a year. The promise of $183 a month would not fill the ranks. It was going to take bold, unconventional thinking and some major changes in the day-to-day practices of the army to even have a prayer that this would work.

Forsythe assembled a staff of creative and committed younger officers—a group that included Major Pete Dawkins, U.S. Military Academy "star man," Heisman Trophy winner, and Rhodes scholar—and told them to think about how to draw young men to the ranks of a volunteer army. The SAMVA Warriors, as they styled themselves, discussed psychologist Abraham Maslow's hierarchy of needs; they studied Ford and GM, and then Volvo, trying to understand what did—or did not—make work gratifying; they considered the results of Elton Mayo's Hawthorne experiments on worker productivity and asked how the army might better "pay attention" to its soldiers. They started with notions of human need, with what they saw as the inborn desire for fulfillment and for meaningful work, but it was with a clear historical understanding of how institutions have turned those human needs to their own advantage. As well-educated men of their time, they called upon empirical research and they understood the value of marketing. Social science research, they explained, could tell the army what young men wanted; advertising could sell young men their own desires in the army's form.[32]

Market research and high-profile advertising played a key role in the move to the volunteer army, as did a thorough overhaul of the recruiting process and a significant increase in pay for the lower ranks. But Forsythe, like Westmoreland, saw the transformation as an opportunity to reform and strengthen the army. In January 1971, he launched a series of experiments under another oddly pronounceable acronym: VOLAR, for "VOLunteer ARmy." VOLAR was an unusual move to local autonomy and grassroots experimentation on the part of a massively bureaucratized and centralized institution: commanders at four major U.S. posts (Fort Benning, Fort Bragg, Fort Carson, and Fort Ord) were given limited funding and full authority to try out locally generated ideas to improve army life.[33]

With VOLAR, as in so many other cases, the army's current problems shaped its approach to the future. A great many of the experiments tried in the VOLAR program were not speculative changes aimed at imagined future recruits. They were, instead, built on attempts to manage growing disciplinary problems in the army of the moment. The SAMVA office did rely heavily on the PROVIDE reports. But the true model for VOLAR was Fort Carson. Fort Carson, at that point, was one of the most controversial places in the army. Like most posts in 1970, it was plagued by a host of problems: racial conflict and violence; excessive drug use; a spike in crime; a decline in morale; failures of discipline; and simply too many disaffected draftees and Vietnam returnees who had no love for the army. The army had always experienced problems of "indiscipline," but in 1970 none of the tried and true methods seemed to work. Not the clear exercise of authority, not isolating the troublemakers, not punishment, not vigorous training or peer pressure or any of the various attempts to create pride or build unit cohesion.

Faced with this mess, post commander Major General Bernard Rogers shifted his tactics from military to managerial. Instead of authority, he tried cooptation. Rogers established a Junior Enlisted Man's Council and met regularly with its nineteen representatives. They, in turn, proposed a long list of ways to improve life for the men in the lowest ranks—and Rogers listened. He let men divide their barracks into semi-private spaces and decorate them as they pleased: black lights, psychedelic posters, Playboy centerfolds. Attempting to foster free communication, he set up regular rap groups (a term that had a different meaning in the early 1970s than today) and improved recreational options, with both a fine arts program "designed for those soldiers, low in rank and pay, whose tastes were along more sophisticated cultural lines" and topless go-go girls in the enlisted men's club.[34]

Such changes were not universally popular. Bill Mauldin's 1971 *Life* magazine cover, which depicted WWII cartoon G.I.s Willie and Joe watching in amazement as an infantryman buckled on a motorcycle helmet adorned with a peace symbol and painted in psychedelic patterns, created a big stir among the army brass. An article on Fort Carson in the army *Recruiting and Career Counseling Journal* then attempted to smooth the waters, addressing complaints about changes that undercut the chain of command. Revealingly titled "What Hasn't Changed," it explained that the Junior Enlisted Man's Council was formed "because of the realization that the traditional chain of command, although capable and thorough, did not provide a sufficient line of communications between the lower enlisted . . . grades and the top command." But according to army reports, the switch from "authoritarian to participatory" procedures seemed to work: statistics showed that significant disciplinary problems declined by one quarter and reenlistment rates jumped. The man Forsythe had chosen as his deputy, Col. Robert Montague, came directly to the SAMVA office from Fort Carson. Forsythe had confidence in him because they'd previously worked together (and it probably didn't hurt that Westmoreland had been Montague's scout master when he was a boy). Montague was a huge believer in the Fort Carson experiment. He thought it should be the model for the MVA.[35]

In its most optimistic version, VOLAR built on four basic—and historically specific—understandings of human nature. First and most fundamental were notions of dignity and respect. All people, a whole variety of army reports and memos asserted, wanted to be treated with dignity. Attempting to put that insight into practice, Fort Benning developed a new seven-hour course on "enlightened leadership" for its noncommissioned and commissioned officers. "Our style of leadership," the course manual explained, "must respect the individual dignity of every man. There is no room in today's Army for the shouting, screaming, harassing style of leadership." Treat men like men, a second claim asserted in the language of the day, and they'll act like men. Bed checks and pass forms and sign-ins and sign-outs, as an article in the *American Legion* magazine put it, were "notorious affronts to the notion that the army makes men." Lots of VOLAR initiatives were based on (in Westmoreland's words) "the principle that if we treat a young soldier like a responsible man he will act like one." Besides, asked the author of the *American Legion* article, "who ever heard of your civilian boss coming around to see if you're in bed at midnight?"[36]

Assumptions about the specific nature of modern youth were central. No matter how often the army claimed that it could solve problems of discipline and motivation by changing the way it forged soldiers, few were able to completely reject the notion that, as a *Washington Post* headline asserted baldly, "The Army: Its Problems Are America's." The army had little success drawing a firm line between civilian and military life. It had to contend with young men who had been raised in civilian society and who embodied all its contemporary problems. There was little the army could do about racial tensions or the growing drug culture in American society. But VOLAR spokesmen found strengths in what others called weakness. American young men were not resistant and antiauthoritarian, but instead curious and independent. They were not mired in racial prejudice and anger, but frustrated by the lack of opportunity for honest communication. Youth, by their very nature, had much to offer. "The young man we have to deal with today is a fine young man," explained General Westmoreland, "but he is a man who asks 'Why?'" Today's young soldier, the training manual for the Fort Benning leadership course reported, "rejects and resents imposed solutions and dogmatic answers." America's youth, it stated as truth, "have re-emphasized many of the values the older people have been preaching about the value of the person, the dignity of the individual, honesty, integrity, compassion. These are excellent values on which to build a nation and a modern Army."[37]

Finally, those who crafted VOLAR believed wholeheartedly that most people seek fulfillment through meaningful work. "There is a theory of motivation," Pete Dawkins explained to representatives at an Armed Services subcommittee hearing, "which I hold as being very powerful and persuasive." Quite obviously, he acknowledged, there are problems in the army—"things such as pay, things such as living conditions"—that demand reform. But those reforms will not make a better army. Material improvements will not motivate men. Better pay will not make them better soldiers. The congressmen needed to understand, Dawkins told them, that in the new MVA, soldiers would "build real commitment," "want to serve, and to perform well and with competence." Thus the army would have to "address a whole different set of factors . . . such as the ability to grow in one's work, the ability to achieve recognition for achievement, the opportunity to really have work which challenges . . . These are the facts that fuse commitment and motivation."[38]

All these fine terms—commitment and motivation, dignity and respect, individuality, compassion, challenge and fulfillment—translated into a host of practical changes, some of them obviously significant, some of them almost embarrassingly mundane. Within a month, Fort Benning had instituted eighty-two "significant" innovations, with twelve more pending. Forsythe, in fact, said he'd compiled a list of "670 Jim-Dandy ideas" from the army's previous studies. Many of the most significant changes were to the training process. Drill sergeants were advised to exhibit "concerned leadership" and "sensitivity," to tell men "why" rather than simply claim authority. Fort Benning's Command Sergeant Major described the shift as "cutting out the harassment and treating our soldiers like gentlemen." At Fort Ord, where troops went through basic training, the commanding general set up a civilian-military task force to redesign the training program in its entirety. Experts in psychology, training, and testing came up with a plan that re-centered training from the group to the individual, letting each man master skills at his own pace and offering performance-based advancement and other rewards to those who moved most quickly. Recruits who learned rapidly, in this plan, could finish the sixteen-week training program with three infantry military occupational specialties (MOSs) rather than one and a grade of E-4.[39]

All the VOLAR posts, following Westmoreland's directive, tried to end "needless irritants" and make-work. They hired civilians for KP (kitchen patrol) and the most menial groundskeeping tasks, thus allowing soldiers to concentrate on training. This was an expensive experiment: half of VOLAR's $5 million budget at Fort Benning went to pay those civilian workers. But as the slickly produced booklet on the MVA explained: "In the new Army, the primary job of soldiers will be soldiering . . . A proud, competent soldier can only be so when he knows that his primary job is so important that no one wants him to be anything else." Following Westmoreland's directive, VOLAR posts dispensed with reveille formations. "If reveille causes a solider dissatisfaction and aggravation by causing him to stand out in the rain for no reason, we can do away with that," Dawkins testified to the congressmen.[40]

Many of the experiments were meant to convey to the young soldier that he was, in Forsythe's words, "our nation's most valuable asset." The term for the enlisted man, "EM," which had replaced "G.I." after the Korean war, was largely dropped; it turned out that enlisted men much preferred to be called "soldiers." Nonetheless, "Enlisted Man's Councils" appeared at all the VOLAR posts, often along with some version of a "Racial Harmony Council." These elected representatives had a real voice—direct and unmediated contact with the post commander and responsibility for suggesting changes in policy and practice that had a good chance of being implemented. But officers, all the way up to the top, were also encouraged to drop by and "rap" with whatever men happened to be around—in order to make clear, in practice, that the army truly cared what its privates thought.

Finally, there were a whole host of "lifestyle" experiments, ranging from the truly wacky to the ones that, as an officer at Fort Benning said, were "just legislating common sense." All sorts of restrictions were eased and dispensed with, including those that required close-cropped hair. (*Time* magazine traced the hair initiative to the navy, where the commander of the Miramar Naval Air Station in San Diego boasted that he'd sent the base barber to hairstyling school. "You might think we're going a little gay around here," Navy Captain "Hap" Chandler told the reporter, with evident pride.)[41] Fast food showed up as an alternative to standard fare, and vending machines with 3.2 beer went into the barracks. Some barracks were partitioned into smaller shared rooms that allotted basic trainees seventy-two square feet per man. These rooms were furnished with lamps, tables, chairs, and rugs—and presumably beds, though they were not mentioned in the official description. In most places, soldiers could decorate to their—and their roommates'—individual tastes. Such lifestyle changes were instituted in patchwork fashion, coming and going with little warning, and they often relied heavily on subjective criteria. Commanders were sometimes "appalled" to discover "splashy wall displays of hard-core pornography" created under the vague guidelines of "good taste," while varying notions of what constituted "neatness" when it came to hair length was a constant point of contention. In the midst of all this experimentation, a sergeant at Fort Benning told reporters, "We're going to have to standardize standards to make [VOLAR] work."[42]

Many of these VOLAR initiatives were adopted quickly, without a coherent pattern, without adequate funding, and often without adequate thought, training, or preparation. Forsythe and his staff had an unbelievably short time in which to come up with a plan to transform the army. VOLAR, to these men, was a set of experiments. Some of them would work. Some of them wouldn't. Forsythe's staff intended to evaluate the results, using the objective criteria of the social sciences, to create specific, useful knowledge for the enormous task of creating a Modern Volunteer Army.[43] None of them had ever intended the various experimental mixtures of 670 Jim-Dandy ideas to be confused with the MVA itself.

That confusion was common—though most pervasive in the civilian press. An article in the *Christian Science Monitor* in March 1973—nine months after the VOLAR program ended—began: "'Volar,' as the new

Army is called, has a confident, healthy look. All those eager officers and non-abusive sergeants doing exercises with bright-eyed 17-to-21-year-olds . . ." And a *Commonweal* article asked, in 1974: "Can the Army Survive VOLAR?" The *New York Times*, in 1971, ran several articles describing VOLAR programs as the "new" army—the MVA. But even within the army, the six-month review of VOLAR found, soldiers tended to use the two terms interchangeably.[44]

VOLAR did get a lot of national press. The army was responsible for some of it: hoping to portray the army's "new and better" nature as it looked ahead to all-volunteer status, public information officers drew attention to many of the "lifestyle" reforms. But the more sensational lifestyle reforms were also much easier to write about—and to draw readers with—than changes in banking practices on army posts or the move toward individual-centered training. Too often, the national press boiled down VOLAR, MVA, and the all-volunteer army to "beer in the barracks."

Stories about the new army were not written—or read—in a vacuum. These were days of anger and division, and it was in that context that people made sense of the changes in the army. The "army in crisis" narrative appeared most frequently. In September 1971, for example, the *New York Times* ran a front-page photograph of a trainee during drill, balancing his M-16 one-handed while he bit a fingernail on his other hand. Army leaders, the article noted, "often seem as bewildered as the rawest recruits, compromising, innovating, ordering strategic retreats from tradition, tossing out the training manual—all with uncharacteristic pliability." It continued: "The desertion rate soars, so they do away with bed checks and permit psychedelic posters on barracks walls. The troops are bored, so they take them skiing and put beer machines in the day room. The troops refuse to advance, so they talk it over with them and try to find another way."[45]

The army-in-crisis narrative evolved quickly into another major theme—permissiveness. The description was by no means restricted to the army; "permissiveness" was one of the most important terms in the moral discourse of the age. It emerged as one of Nixon's brilliant political strokes, though it was widely used before he adopted it, a word that tied together all the anger and frustration of hard-working white folks who opposed Great Society giveaways to people they saw as freeloaders, who couldn't believe that black people might be angry enough to burn down their own neighborhoods, who were afraid of the rising crime rate, who were appalled by young people who'd been given nothing but the best, spared the hard times of depression and world war, who threw it all away for sex and drugs and undisciplined pleasure, who grew their hair long and used foul language, who rejected both respectability and the respect owed authority. Nixon had appealed directly to such divisions in 1969, calling out to the "silent majority." By 1970 he had moved from his 1968 promises of "law and order" to this even more complexly coded condemnation. "Permissiveness," Nixon told Republican strategists during the 1970 congressional campaign, "is the key theme." In a similar vein, conservative columnist James Kilpatrick argued that members of the National Guard were not to blame for the four young people lying dead on the campus of Kent State University. The fault lay instead with the "sickness of permissiveness" that pervaded American society.[46]

Forsythe was well aware of the power of such condemnations. Constant discussion of the new, permissive army made all sorts of actions more complicated. It undermined support for VOLAR and the MVA within the army. The label made it difficult for members of Congress to support—and thus to fund—SAMVA proposals. Endorsing permissiveness created political problems, even for liberal Democrats, and a fair number of congressmen and senators looked back on their own military experience, though not always with fondness, with a powerful and abiding sense of how things had been—and ought to be—done. Chair of the House Armed Services Committee F. Edward Hébert had no military service himself; he was forty years old and already serving in Congress when the Japanese bombed Pearl Harbor. But Hébert had no more enthusiasm for VOLAR than he had for the all-volunteer military, and he was equally outspoken on the topic. "When you turn the military into a country club," he told a writer from *Life* magazine, "discipline goes out the window."[47]

Forsythe, however, was politically savvy; that's one of the main reasons he'd been given this job. He was committed to the process he'd begun, though he knew they had made mistakes. But he also knew that he had to re-cast the "new Army," to change the framework of understanding. So when the first set of assessments from commanders at VOLAR posts arrived that July, he paid close attention. Perhaps they'd been talking amongst themselves, but more than one of the commanders suggested that the SAMVA office was making the obvious difficulties worse. By emphasizing lifestyle changes that might attract new recruits to the future all-volunteer army, SAMVA had strengthened internal resistance and fed right into the cultural conflicts of the age. Wasn't the larger objective, suggested one commander, to create "a highly professional Army"? Professionalism, Robert Griffith notes, is "the Army's equivalent of motherhood," a notion that was virtually impossible to oppose.[48] The framework of professionalism fit perfectly with both Forsythe and Westmoreland's belief that their major goal was to improve the army.

By summer 1971, the SAMVA office was working hard to reframe the debate. Selling the Modern Volunteer Army to young men was critical, but first they had to sell their reforms to the army itself—and to Congress. More than anything else, they understood this as a sales job. Forsythe didn't change his programs or funding priorities; he and his men instead put "a new label on an old bottle." They tried to replace "permissive" with "professional," both within the army and without, and they thought hard about new metaphors that might better explain change.[49]

In late September 1971, General Forsythe was called to testify before the House Armed Services' subcommittee on the recruiting and retention of military personnel. The army needed to convince the Armed Services committee that its transformation plans made sense—in large part because the move to an all-volunteer army was going to be costly. Increased salaries were a significant line in the budget proposal, but it would also cost real money to remodel barracks and to hire cooks and groundskeepers and the other civilian employees who would let "soldiers soldier." The subcommittee before which Forsythe appeared was chaired by Virginia congressman "Dan" Daniel, a conservative Democrat who had first been elected to Congress in November 1968. Daniel, unlike Hébert, did have military experience. He'd served in the navy during World War II; just over a decade after the war ended he was elected national commander of the American Legion. In an attempt to win over the committee, Forsythe brought along Pete Dawkins. It wasn't too far into his testimony before Forsythe drew Dawkins's accomplishments to the committee's attention: "I would like to ask Pete, sir, a Heisman Trophy winner, . . . to explain to your committee . . ."[50]

From the outset, Forsythe was on the defensive. It was a privilege to testify, he told the committee, for "probably due to our fault in many cases, there hasn't been a proper level of understanding as to what is really happening in the Army." "General," replied Mr. Daniel, in the language of politics, "I am sure we are all working toward the same goal."

After Forsythe's introductory statement, the conversation moved quickly to beer in the barracks. Forsythe himself raised the issue. It was going to come up; beer in the barracks was one of the most controversial and widely reported of army "reforms." Forsythe tried recontextualization: General Westmoreland believed in treating young soldiers like mature adults, and that's all the 3.2 beer represented. Daniels, completely missing the point, agreed: "It is like taking the top off the cookie jar. If you keep the top on, kids will go and look in. If you keep the top off, they will seldom look." General Forsythe didn't give an inch: "It is treating men like men," he replied. Missouri congressman Dick Ichord, who was also chair of the House Un-American Activities Committee (recently renamed the Internal Security Committee), joined in. He had served in the navy, and he'd been the "sort of kid" who had snuck beer into the barracks. He didn't agree with the cookie-jar analogy: "if you have beer in the barracks, I think I would have drunk a lot more beer than I did when I was compelled to sneak it in. If a man drinks too much beer, he might not be a good fighting man." Forsythe politely noted that they weren't selling that much beer. "For most of my 32 years of service," he said, "I thought soldiers were beer drinkers. Today's soldier is not a beer drinker, he is a Coke drinker, a Teem drinker, and a milk drinker."[51]

With that issue satisfied, Ichord raised his major concern: what sort of men would an all-volunteer force draw? "The Spartans had one way of doing it and the Athenians another way," Ichord noted. "The Spartans developed a tough, motivated, dedicated individual. You don't think we can do that in today's society?" As Forsythe suggested that Sparta might not be a good model for contemporary America, Ichord broke in with an anecdote about the difficulties of taking a man from an affluent home and turning him into a "hard, tough, football player" (water skiing, for some reason, figured prominently in the tale). "If you soften the Army," Ichord asked, "are we going to be dealing with the same thing? Are we going to have a hard, tough, fighting man?" Forsythe was clearly pleased to trade the Spartans for professional football. Professional football was the SAMVA office's analogy for army reform, and Vince Lombardi was Forsythe's answer to all the charges of permissiveness. "If Vince Lombardi sent his offensive backfield off to cut the grass on the football stadium one day," Forsythe told the representatives, "and the next day the tackles and two ends were out selling tickets (these jobs are 'mission related') he wouldn't have much of a football team."[52]

The football metaphor was not a one-time effort, nor was it restricted to events with Dawkins present. Forsythe's point, repeated and refined over time, was that sending men off to work details every morning during training destroys the teams: "the fire teams, the squads, and the platoons . . . the teams that on the battlefield win the skirmishes and the battles." He insisted that the army was not only getting rid of "needless irritants" (the army's original language), but giving the men back to their sergeant for real training and so enhancing professionalism.[53] When the *New York Times* ran an article on the "softening" of recruits' training, Colonel Montague used the same language. "We want professionalism, job satisfaction as the civilians say," he began, and turned quickly to football. "Football is cited," ran the *Times* subhead, as Montague explained why, in *NYT* paraphrase, "tank drivers should drive tanks, not wash dishes or pick up trash." "We can hire other people to do those things," Montague said. "KP doesn't have anything to do with discipline. A football team achieves discipline and spirit and competence without the coach having to worry all the time about where every tackle and halfback hangs his shoulder pads."[54]

The article continued: "Many regulars, particularly drill sergeants, would say to Colonel Montague that a halfback is not the same as a tank driver or a rifleman, but not even the new Army encourages such free discussion." In fact, some fairly free and often heated discussion of VOLAR and the MVA took place in the pages of the *Army Times*—which had previously drawn Westmoreland's fury by publishing the provisions of his close-hold report from the PROVIDE task force almost as soon as it hit his desk. And feelings often ran high. An anonymous "Sergeant Major" posed the rhetorical question: "Are we, after years and years of 'old' Army standards and disciplines, expected to accept these complete reversals with a smile? It's comparable to being raised into a God-fearing son by a God-fearing mother and then suddenly find that she has decided to become a prostitute!" Sergeant First Class Theodore Evans had little use for such analogies. "As a professional soldier," he wrote in June 1971, "I am sickened and shocked by the bickering and non-professionalism displayed by too many of my contemporaries regarding the Army's efforts to make life a little better for low-ranking enlisted men." Dismissing complaints about lost discipline with a blunt "Poppycock," he argued that such claims are "being parroted now by the same non-professionals who said that black boots and socks wouldn't last because the dye would ruin people's feet, that the green uniform wouldn't last because it wouldn't look good on fat soldiers (like what does?), that the M1 rifle couldn't be replaced. Etc."[55]

Many letters adopted the language of the generation gap. "Captain MVA"'s "Letter to Sarge" began dismissively ("Dear Old Soldier") before asking (again, rhetorically): "Have you ever noticed how bald and fat you are getting? . . . I would rather have a slim soldier who could brush the hair from his eyes to fight alongside of me than a fat soldier who can't even brush the bushes aside because of his fat belly." To which M.Sgt. James C. Guyton of Fort Washington responded: "[Noncommissioned officers] by far can out-walk, out-shoot, and out-soldier any group of officers, in the same age bracket, any day of the week. If this seems rather partisan, it is, and I am."[56] Another writer let haircut policies sum up his problems with VOLAR. The army, he suggested with heavy-handed irony, should replace current headgear with the "Napoleon hat." Not only would it fit more easily on the "'Army Afro' or the now standard near duckbill cut," he argued, but it might also provide a "symbol our youth might identify to, as an era of haberdashery excellence and imminent revolution . . . if properly adorned with the customary plume it would provide a basis for continued association between our newly acquired soldiers and their recently separated 'hippy' friends." "Remember," he concluded, "it is essential that the Army continue and strengthen its ties to the civilian society from which it springs."[57]

Much of this months-long debate sounds petty: the arguments over hair length and army policy on sideburns, the sniping back and forth between generations and among ranks. But once again, the letters must be read in context. And the overwhelming context was not the coming volunteer army, but the war. Both internal army documents and less carefully controlled statements to the press tended to focus on noncommissioned officers (NCOs) as the barriers to progress. Lt. Col. Willard Latham told a writer for the *Recruiting and Career Counseling Journal,* "It's an absolute truism that any NCO opposed to VOLAR is on his way out," while "Sergeant Major" claimed in his letter to the *Army Times* that "Senior NCOs are under increasing fire from all directions for being the 'big problem' in everything from civil rights to VOLAR."[58] NCOs on VOLAR posts were more likely than anyone else to oppose the reforms, though their reasons varied. Perhaps the most significant reason was a sense of responsibility. Though Nixon's policy on Vietnam meant that far fewer American troops were being sent there (by the end of 1971 the number of American service personnel in the Republic of Vietnam had dropped from a high of over half a million to 156,800), 2,357 deaths of American servicemen were recorded that year. Most posts were chosen for the VOLAR experiments because men were trained there. The men who were responsible for training soldiers knew that what they had to teach mattered, that doing their jobs well might make the difference between life and death. The debate about hair length and access to beer and reduced irritants was not only about the transition from a draftee to a volunteer army. It tied into the debate about whether soldiering was just another job, whether the army was simply another competitor in the national labor marketplace. And it was a debate about the proper relationship of the military to civilian society. While few took up Congressman Ichord's notion that Sparta could be the model for the U.S. military in the early 1970s, not a few military men suggested that it would be difficult to forge soldiers out of men who still had at least one foot in civilian society and who only belonged to the army from nine to five, Monday through Friday.

The officers who promoted VOLAR experiments were caught between worlds: between the army they had and the volunteer army of the future; between their own experiences and the social science research on human motivation and on what might make military service attractive to contemporary youth. In fact, General Forsythe's words on leadership were not revolutionary. The "style and character" of leadership may change, he said, but "the principles of leadership do not." He insisted to members of Congress that it was a "long developmental process" of training that came together on "that fine day when [a soldier] is on the field of battle." (In another sign of the times, Forsythe's term "fine" is edited out of the official congressional record).[59] Nonetheless, NCOs and junior officers in the leadership course at Fort Benning were taught the findings of social science: that, for young men coming into the army, "hard work is no longer necessarily a virtue"; that today's young soldier is motivated by the desire "for self-gratification, the ego needs, for self-realization." The civilian-military committee that altered the training process at Fort Ord looked to social science research demonstrating that men would be best motivated by individual reward, and instituted "merit points" to be traded in for weekend passes and other such incentives.[60] In general, the army promoted these changes as a recognition of the dignity of the individual and an incentive to enlistment. Undoubtedly the new policies led to less harassment. But many of those in charge of training cared less about a trainee's individual dignity than about his eventual survival. Once again, the war was a more immediate and important fact than the future army of volunteers.

The army's move toward a volunteer force was profoundly shaped by its particular moment in time, a moment of national division, of internal anguish, of perceived crisis. The army, as an institution, did not resist the commander in chief's order to move to an all-volunteer status. No matter what reservations remained, the army was both proactive and imaginative in its efforts. But the reforms it instituted—and the resistance to them—were always primarily about the challenges facing the army in 1971. General Forsythe had brought a clear mission of reform to his work as SAMVA. In the words of the *Recruiter Journal,* his goal was "a better army better advertised."[61] But the two did not fit together so neatly. Army advertising would look toward the all-volunteer army of the future while most everyone else had to contend with the army they had.

3 ★ THE ARMY IN THE MARKETPLACE

ON FEBRUARY 23, 1970—the day after the *New York Times* printed the substance of the Gates Commission report—forty-two agencies got letters soliciting bids for the army's recruiting advertising account. The timing is the stuff of Hollywood film and television sitcom, the fortuitous coincidence on which the course of history turns, though ever so slightly. The army would need tens of thousands of volunteers every month. Those volunteers would have to be young people. Young people in 1970, however, were generally opposed to military service. Most certainly didn't want to enlist. So how would the army convince young men to volunteer? Through the genius of advertising; by employing the most sophisticated tools of America's consumer marketplace. All-volunteer force = massive marketing campaign. It was a virtual certainty that turning from the draft to an all-volunteer force would create a major windfall for U.S. advertising and marketing firms. But that outcome, which seems inevitable in retrospect, was not so clear in 1970. Not a single one of these forty-two firms, nor any of America's 615 leading advertising agencies, realized how potentially lucrative the army's account might become. Competition for the army account plodded forward, drawing little attention and only four bids.[1]

The army certainly did nothing to signal new possibilities. Though the PROVIDE task force made clear that the all-volunteer force could not succeed without a major advertising campaign, that close-hold document wasn't circulated to those who managed the army's ongoing advertising contract. The purchasing and contracting officer at Fort Monroe was not following up on the PROVIDE proposal when he sent those forty-two letters. He was simply complying with federal regulations: such contracts were to be opened for bidding every three years. As required, the army advertised the contract competition. But the ad didn't run in *Advertising Age*, the key publication for the advertising industry. Instead, it appeared as a 1.75 inch notice in *Commerce Business Daily.* The contracting agency, according to the notice that ran under the heading for "Photographic, Mapping, Printing, and Publication Services," would be responsible for "preparation of the advertising headlines; preparing the rough forms of all illustrations; selecting the lettering to be used," and other such basic technical tasks. Neither the letters nor the *Commerce Business Daily* ad contained the phrase "all-volunteer." And neither gave any indication that the regular $3-million-a-year army account was about to increase by 600 percent.[2]

Once the advertising world realized what it had missed and started its carefully phrased, behind-the-scenes complaining, investigators found that many of the army's solicitation letters had gone to businesses such as Space Age Engineering, Lane Art Services, or Dynatech Systems, rather than to America's major advertising agencies. Thirty-five of the forty-two firms the army originally contacted, according to an outraged article on the process, were not advertising firms at all. Most of the questions army officials asked the agencies were generic procurement questions, focused on logistics, not on creative content. One senior advertising executive told a reporter, "I didn't believe the Army bought advertising as though it were shopping for machine guns. But that's the impression I got from the questions we were asked—'Do you object to periodic audits?' and things like that." The decision on the advertising contract, according to an *Army and Navy Journal* exposé, was made by the assistant secretary of the army for installations and logistics.[3]

Perhaps, in some universe, this made sense. After all, according to the Gates Commission and the commander-in-chief, the success of an all-volunteer force was most fundamentally a problem of supply and demand. The draft had protected the military from the laws of the market. Now, the laws of the market would make an all-volunteer force possible. If military pay rivaled that of civilian jobs, the army would have no difficulty filling boots. According to this logic, advertising was no more important to a volunteer force than to one based on conscription.

As American troops fought in the jungles and deltas of Vietnam and as blood flowed in American streets, economists in seminar rooms at the University of Chicago, meeting rooms in the Pentagon, and presidential briefings in the Oval Office made their case for a market-based military. They declared their faith in the laws of supply and demand and in the rational economic choices of individuals. These economists were right about one thing: the shift to an all-volunteer force *was* a move toward the primacy of the market in American society. But it was not a move toward the rational. These were not days of measured rationality in American society. And the market, in 1970s America, was not simply a realm of rational individual economic choice. It was a site of consumer desire; it was a volatile space of inchoate needs, hopes, and fears.

The military officers who managed the transition to the all-volunteer force, paradoxically, understood the complexity of this "market" much better than the Chicago-school economists. Perhaps it was because they had dealt more directly with the problem of human motivation, or because they were more accustomed to a language of intangibles ("Duty, Honor, Country"), or because they were painfully aware of how badly the military fared in current public estimation. Of necessity, they accepted the marketplace model, but not as it was envisioned by the free-market theorists. They understood that they had to compete for young Americans. But they were certain that a sufficient number of eighteen-year-olds wouldn't join the military, most particularly in the wake of the Vietnam War, because it was an arguably rational economic decision. They moved from models of free-market rationality to models of consumer capitalism, and with mixed feelings, they adopted consumer capitalism's most powerful tools.[4]

Despite its origins in ideologies of rational choice and free-market competition, the MVA was shaped from its beginnings by the best available social science–based market research and caught uneasily in the logic of mass-market advertising, as even some army officers began to reframe potential recruits as "customers" and the army itself as a "product." When the nation adopted a marketplace model for military service in the early 1970s, it joined the power of the state with the less direct but still critical power of major advertising and marketing firms who worked to shape the unruly desires of consumers.

The army had to recruit far more young men than did the navy, air force, or marines. And it came in dead last of the four in public regard. So no matter how strongly some proponents of the all-volunteer force insisted that it was all a matter of labor force competition, army leaders knew better. They saw fundamental problems with the labor market model. Young Americans were not simply rational economic actors. The army was not just another potential employer, and these were not normal times. Pay increases were welcome, and they would make a difference. But in the words of the PROVIDE task force: "unless the Army is viewed favorably, our ability to attract voluntary personnel will be greatly limited."[5]

When the authors of the PROVIDE report argued, in 1969, that the army must develop a sophisticated, big-budget, commercial advertising campaign, they were asking the army to do something unprecedented. Military advertising, of course, was nothing new. Because the post–World War II military relied first on volunteers, drafting men only to make up any shortfall, all four services had established recruiting systems and contracts with advertising agencies. J. Walter Thompson served the marines; Grey Advertising the navy. N.W. Ayer, which held the army account during the 1940s, had taken it on again in 1967. But these were relatively minor accounts. When it came to the powerful forces of television and radio, the military relied on public service announcements. No one was sure whether any federal agency or institution had used commercial broadcast advertising before. It was not clear that such a move was legitimate.[6]

Nonetheless, the army made commercial advertising a key part of its transition plans. Perhaps that decision was easier because the secretary of the army, Stanley Resor, was the son of two of the most important figures in the history of American advertising. His mother, Helen Lansdowne Resor, was one of the greatest copywriters of her generation. His father, Stanley B. Resor, headed J. Walter Thompson for forty-four years; he brought his faith in scientific research to the agency, hiring behavioral psychologist John B. Watson and attempting to rationalize the business of advertising. Resor's family history may be irrelevant, but when the army lobbied the Department of Defense for resources, commercial advertising was at the top of the list. "Let advertising do for the Army," proposed Assistant Secretary of the Army William K. Brehm, "what it has done successfully for business." Here, he joined army reform and army advertising in the language of the consumer marketplace: proposed improvements in army life, from civilianizing KP and grounds maintenance to improving housing, were now "product improvements."[7]

N.W. Ayer, the agency responsible for army recruiting ads, did not anticipate how important it would become to the future of the army. Ayer had taken over the army account in mid-1967, when the army was becoming more and more difficult to sell. Antiwar protest was growing; draft cards were being burned; induction offices were targeted. But in many ways, little was at stake. The U.S. Army was a minor account in 1970, worth only $3 million to an agency that represented such corporate giants as AT&T and DuPont. Army recruiting advertisements were intended to convince draft-induced volunteers to join the army instead of one of the other services. The role of advertising was peripheral, at best.

In this climate, Ayer created a national print campaign and prototypes for local newspaper ads. Most army advertising, however, ran on radio and television. Military recruiting ads counted as public service announcements, which broadcast media were required to air as a condition of licensing. So although print advertising was costly, broadcast advertising was free. Of course, these ads usually showed up right before the networks played the national anthem and signed off for the night—or perhaps just before the 5:30 A.M. farm report the following morning.[8] They had little visibility and little real impact.

A major advertising firm was not going to put its major resources into a minor account, especially one that constrained their creativity. In October 1968, when the deputy chief of staff for personnel offered direction for the 1970 army advertising campaign, he requested ads that presented "the Army truthfully as a serious instrument of national security dedicated to our country's interests" and portrayed "the United States Army as it is, an honorable institution dedicated to the service of our country in peace and war." His vision was an attractive one, focused on "an Army which is mission oriented, dedicated, dignified, and disciplined," that emphasized dignity and fair treatment regardless of race, color, or creed, and offered young men a world in which "competence and ability," not the "politics of social background," brought success. But he clearly knew little about advertising or about his potential market, for he assured his readers that such images would "counteract elements that are doing all possible to ridicule the Army and undermine its foundations" and at the same time "draw intelligent young Americans to our service." "Therefore," he concluded, only two months after antiwar protesters faced tanks in the streets of Chicago during the Democratic National Convention, "the recruiting message can afford to be subtle."[9]

With such guidance and with little other incentive, Ayer had developed the subtle and, as later characterized by an Ayer executive, "uninspiring and low visibility" slogan: "Your future, your decision . . . choose ARMY." The SAMVA office was not impressed. "We need the very best advice and execution from N.W. Ayers [sic]," insisted a talking paper prepared for the first of their weekly planning meetings. "We may even want other agencies to review our campaign to insure it is appealing and imaginative." The SAMVA office immediately requested that N.W. Ayer and the Recruiting Command present a "full-scale review" of army advertising; at that meeting, Ayer was given two weeks to "review the entire advertising campaign, give it imaginative treatment, expand it to match the 18.1 million budget level, and present its ideas."[10]

"It was a brutal assignment," N.W. Ayer's director of creative services said later, "because the Army's prospects were so low." Not that anyone at Ayer said that out loud, at least to anyone in the army. Given an ultimatum—produce a "head turner" that will generate "a *dramatic* increase in enlistments" (and, as one SAMVA warrior noted, "If N.W. Ayer can't do it, we'll find someone who can")—Ayer presented the assignment to the army as "A Copywriter's Dream," the "most important assignment in the Advertising Business," a task "Of critical importance to the country."[11] It's worth noting the words Ayer capitalizes—and the ones it doesn't. But despite such visible confidence, everyone involved understood what a challenge Ayer faced.

The Vietnam War was an enormous obstacle. Though American troops were no longer fighting in Vietnam when the military moved to an all-volunteer force in mid-1973, no one knew how long America's involvement in Southeast Asia would last. And no one knew how long the experience of Vietnam would shape American youths' attitudes toward the military, even after the U.S. combat role ended. Pointing to growing antimilitary sentiment among the general public, the authors of the PROVIDE report broke from their usual stilted style to quote William S. White's *Washington Post* editorial: "the hang-up against the very term 'military' has reached a point little short of hysteria."[12] The powerful and growing youth culture presented another problem: so much that distinguished youth from age at that moment in history was antithetical to military life. From the oft-quoted demand to "question authority," to modes of dress and behavior that many adults saw as absolute rejections of discipline and order, to highly visible participation in the antiwar movement, all signs were that this generation would not flock to recruiting centers, no matter how "competitive" the pay. To complicate matters further, growing racial tensions promised difficulty on all fronts. And no one was sure what the women's liberation movement would mean for whatever plan they implemented.

This was the situation confronting N.W. Ayer in the early winter of 1971, when it took on the task of completely recasting army advertising. Ayer was inspired by the fact that the army advertising budget was rising rapidly; it seemed certain that the work would not be wasted on a $3 million account. Army advertising was budgeted at $18.5 million in fiscal year 1971, $10 million of that intended for a "test" of army advertising on commercial broadcast television and radio, and the figure of $60 million for the future campaign was floating around.[13] Prospects for a lucrative relationship were good. Nonetheless, Ayer had to come up with a campaign for an unpopular "product" that seemed to be in the midst of a controversial internal transformation. The "market" for this product, research discovered repeatedly, was generally hostile to it. Even if the Vietnam War were over—and that was a big "if"—young American men feared that if they joined the army, they would lose their personal freedom, submerged in an institution that showed no respect for individuality.

Ayer, in what probably should have given the army pause, described the problem they faced as "like trying to sell a double-breasted suit to a Phi Beta Kappa." But the agency people had good instincts. They made clear that the first step was to hear from the army—and not "some junior official who is handling advertising." They asked for meetings with the secretary of the army and the army chief of staff. They got them. The Ayer executives and their creative people came down to the Pentagon to meet with General Westmoreland and various members of the SAMVA office. Westmoreland and his people waited for the briefing to begin. The Ayer people, skilled in presentation, simply sat there. Finally, one of the Ayer execs said, "Sir, we're here to listen to you."[14]

Westmoreland made the pitch he was perfecting by that point—that the army is a young man's business, that the army likes young people and understands them, that the army can help young Americans develop a value system and, in exchange, young people can give the army energy and enthusiasm. The volunteer army, he said, should be a partnership between an old institution and a new generation of Americans, and so he emphasized the changes the army was making to accommodate youth. The Ayer people went back to Philadelphia for a couple of weeks of very intense work.[15]

The Ayer group was briefly inspired to try a hip campaign, and flirted with the idea of using a picture of a chicken wearing dog tags over the title "Bye, Bye Birdie." They figured everyone would understand it: an army without "needless irritants" (the "chicken" or "chickenshit" of infantry-speak). No one seems to have commented on the awkwardness of using a photo of a chicken to advertise the U.S. Army. And the "Army generals," reportedly, "loved it."[16] But the idea fell by the wayside. The Ayer group was certain that it must convey, in a single "surprising" expression, two concepts: "join" and "'improved' product." Copywriting toward the idea yielded some slogans that made "Your future, your decision . . . choose ARMY" look inspired:

Join the New Army
Enlist in the New Army
Join a Better Army
Join an Improved Army
Join a Changing Army
Join Today's Army
Today's Army Wants You[17]

When the Ayer group met with Generals Westmoreland and Forsythe again, in the Pentagon, they pitched a single idea. They showed the army officials a photograph of a young man—a civilian—with the caption: "Today's Army Wants to Join You." As General Forsythe described the army's reaction in an interview conducted three years later: "We all looked at it and thought, 'They can't be serious. A big outfit like this and they can't come up with something better than this?'" Ayer executive Tom Regan remembered that General Westmoreland asked, "Do you have to say it that way?"[18]

The Ayer staff had two answers. Most fundamentally, they argued, the ad campaign wasn't meant to appeal to army generals. It was meant to grab the attention of young men who might possibly be prompted to contact a recruiter or ask for information about joining the army. It was clear, they said, even from the limited amount of research done thus far, that traditional appeals would not work. In order to get the attention of a new generation the campaign had to show a clear break with the past. Their term was "interruptive."[19]

They believed that "Today's Army Wants to Join You" turned the traditional call to service on its head. Instead of summoning young men to service with a stern-featured Uncle Sam and a declarative command, this slogan would leave young people thinking that "The Army is interested in *me,* in *my* needs as well as its own." Replacing "I WANT YOU . . . as in 1917" with "*we* need each other as in 1972" would recreate the relationship between the army and the recruit. As the army suggested, "Let's get together for *mutual* gain," young people would think: "There is something in it for me."[20]

This slogan, Ayer creatives insisted, would help transcend the bitterness, the hostility, the antimilitarism of American society. "The Army wants to 'join the people,'" they explained, was a "public assertion of the Army's concern over the many forms of 'divisiveness' confronting our society—including some *Anti-Militarism* sentiment." "Today's Army Wants to Join You," Ayer implied, could help "pull this country together." The army representatives still hated it—though perhaps not so much as most of the rest of the active army would once the ads started appearing—but Westmoreland took a deep breath and set the campaign in motion.[21] Signing on for "Today's Army Wants to Join You" was a key moment in the shift to the logic of the market. Despite their discomfort with almost everything about the Ayer proposal, Westmoreland, Secretary of the Army Robert Froehlke, and Forsythe decided to defer to the expertise of advertisers and marketers. The perceived "needs" of American youth would drive the campaign.

All involved understood that the new army recruiting ads had to compete in the larger world of consumer advertising and meet new standards of production quality and creative innovation. They would have to break through a cluttered medium, making the army visible in the consumer marketplace. In this new world, the army would have to sell itself as a specific "product" (in competition with other "products"—the other military services), but within a larger category that left most potential "consumers" cold. Few consumer goods had to overcome a general hostility to the product category itself: Ford didn't have to convince people that cars were desirable, just that they'd rather drive a Mustang ("Sitting still . . . it looks invincible") than a Corolla ("You can fit a lot of important things in Toyota's $1876 Wagon"). For the army, the advertiser's task was not capturing consumer desire, but creating it—or at the very least, undermining the consumer resistance that was amply demonstrated in ongoing market research.

That said, few of those involved lost sight of the fact that joining the army was a more significant "consumer decision" than buying a Coke or even a car. Although members of the SAMVA office and later of the Recruiting Command often claimed that an all-volunteer force could not be created or maintained without large-scale commercial advertising, most didn't see the advertising as selling the "high-cost" act of enlisting so much as the low-cost act of writing for information or contacting a recruiter. Nonetheless, those involved in this move to the consumer market understood the larger challenge. Even if they imagined their task as motivating the low-cost phone call rather than the high-cost enlistment, they believed that everything hinged upon healing the army's public image, especially among youth.

Research indicated that the army's most likely prospects were poorer, younger, less-educated males from rural or small-town America. These young men, according to findings, were more likely to watch primetime television than to read magazines. In the early 1970s, however, primetime television meant broadly-targeted shows on the three major networks, any of which might be watched by up to 70 percent of the viewing public. The army ran its initial ads on *Gunsmoke, The Man from Shiloh, Hee Haw,* and *Love American Style,* thus capturing audiences for westerns, country music, and "hip" comedy that ranged from toddlers to the geriatric. Neither Ayer nor the army complained that they could not target more effectively, for they meant the ads to play two roles: they hoped to improve the army's image with the general public and to attract the attention of potential volunteers.[22] Moreover, though research made clear that the most efficient use of advertising dollars was material aimed at 18-year-old rural youth, army officials endorsed advertising that pictured and was meant to appeal to young men from a broadly defined middle class. Concerned about the declining quality of volunteers as opposed to inductees, they meant to reach young men on the road to success, not those who joined only because they saw no other option.

In working with the army, the Ayer team claimed expertise based on past creative success. But even more than creativity, they stressed their state-of-the-art marketing research. Ayer, like most American advertising agencies that tried to sell to young people, had already turned to the sort of youth-oriented research that Eugene Gilbert had pioneered in the 1940s when he, at age nineteen, founded the Gilbert Youth Research Organization to offer American businesses insight into the growing teenage consumer market. Ayer offered to let the army piggyback on consumer research it had already commissioned for large clients. And as funding became available, the SAMVA office and Ayer jointly commissioned research on American teens and young adults, trying to understand their worldviews, their goals, their needs and desires. The Department of Defense was fully on board; by the early 1970s the DoD sponsored Gilbert surveys on youth and the military and made them available to appropriate army officials. In 1971 the DoD also began the long-lived Youth Attitude Tracking Study, or YATS, a semiannual survey of young men aged 16–21. (Young women were not included until 1980.)[23]

The army, relying on market logic in its attempts to create and maintain a volunteer force, defined the market as a site of consumer desire, a sphere in which the emotional weight of individuals' hopes and dreams and fears was more powerful than that of rational decisions based on practical information. The advertising that became crucial to recruiting campaigns was consumer driven, even as the consumer was constructed through research profoundly shaped by historically specific assumptions about everything from models of psychological development to assumptions about family structure, peer culture, and the meaning of masculinity and femininity. The focus on the "important psychological needs" and desires of potential volunteers was given added weight by the market surveys and social science research that offered quantitative evidence about what young men and women wanted.[24]

It is probably not surprising that studies conducted in the early 1970s would emphasize psychological needs, or that the psychological needs they discovered in young men concerned their desire to be treated as individuals and to have "freedom." These initial findings were supported by other surveys commissioned by SAMVA and Ayer. In 1971 the Opinion Research Corporation (Princeton, NJ) reported that, in addition to military pay increases, young men wanted more freedom in their use of personal time and a guarantee that every individual could "retain his individuality." And in 1972 the Cinecom Corporation (Cambridge, MA) argued that the all-volunteer force could draw enough volunteers if the army had a "clear recognition of the several needs, attitudes, and expectations" of young men. Cinecom research had found that many volunteers, especially those most likely to choose combat arms, saw themselves in situations of "failure" and believed the army offered a low-risk escape and an opportunity to start over. The army could attract more such young men, Cinecom advised, by making clear that it would meet the "youth's perceived need for a *structured situation in which he may gain maturity*" while also reassuring him that he would be "treated with dignity—as a *volunteer* in a volunteer system which . . . *has respect for his individuality.*" These research firms listed such psychological "needs" as potential answers in multiple-choice survey research. But respondents chose them in great numbers, and both N.W. Ayer and the army focused on those responses.[25]

There was a fundamental disconnect, however, between the felt "needs" of potential recruits in the early 1970s and the reality of army life. It was hard to use the desire for individuality and freedom as reasons to join the army. Nonetheless, in a vote of confidence for the power of irrational desire, that's exactly what N.W. Ayer did. The signature advertisement for the "Today's Army Wants to Join You" campaign, created in April 1971, appeared the following fall in *Senior Scholastic* magazine. The ad was a two-page spread. On the left were nine class pictures of young men, three rows with three portraits on each, the men's pictures separated from each other only by thin black lines. The young men were clearly chosen to illustrate diversity of race, ethnicity, and youth culture. In 1971 they likely looked a bit—though not profoundly—conservative; their hair was far from short by today's standards, but every single haircut left ears visible. The right page led with the army's new slogan in heavy boldface text, followed by a carefully produced list of acknowledgments and inducements:

> We know you have pride in yourself and in what your Country can be.
>
> We know you have a brain and your own ideas.
>
> We know you'd like to share these ideas with hundreds of young men and women from all parts of this Country.

> We know you'd like to build your mind and body.
>
> We know you'd like to further your education, become expert at a skill, have opportunity for advancement, travel, and 30 days vacation a year.
>
> We also know you put a price on these things. The price is your individuality. And you question the Army's willingness to pay this price.
>
> Today's Army is willing to pay this price.
>
> We're committed to eliminating unnecessary formations, skin-head haircuts, signing out, signing in, bed checks, and "make work" projects. You'll find more mature policies at every level.
>
> If you'd like to serve yourself as you serve your Country, Today's Army wants to join you.[26]

The following month an almost identical version of this ad targeted young women. The same nine slots were filled with photographs, but the text offered some additional reassurances: "In today's Army a girl can be a girl. Live her own life on her own time. Date. Marry if she wants to."[27] Women, though included in the new advertising campaign, were not a priority. The army needed combat troops in 1971, and women were then, as now, not allowed to serve in the combat arms.

As the army and Ayer planned the new campaign, portrayals of race had gotten much more attention than those of gender. The potential role of African Americans in an all-volunteer force had been controversial since the earliest debates about ending conscription. Many opponents—coming from all points on the political spectrum—feared that an AVF would be dominated by poor blacks. Some were worried about the exploitation of black Americans, in part because the belief that African Americans had been treated as cannon-fodder in the Vietnam War remained powerful, and in part because many recognized that "volunteers" drawn heavily from the nation's most disadvantaged group would not be true volunteers. Others feared an army composed of poor—and thus presumably angry, or degenerate, or unskilled—black men. Some arguments were clearly racist, others more complexly situated in the often violent racial tensions of the time, and others purportedly based only on the need for "quality" in a new, smaller, more technologically sophisticated force.[28] These emotional debates left Ayer walking a fine line: black men and women had to appear prominently but, at the same time, could not seem over-represented.

Army advertisements in "general interest" publications were carefully racially inclusive, and advertisements featuring black men and women only ran in publications such as *Essence* or *Ebony.* Young black men, researchers found, were more concerned about salary than were young white men, and they wanted assurance they would be joining an institution that treated people fairly irrespective of race. But army advertising rarely offered racially targeted appeals during this era, even in ads intended for black publications. One advertisement, a photograph with the heading "When was the last time you got promoted?" had four versions: white man, black man, white woman, black woman. Each man was shot on a loading dock; each woman in an office, standing beside a mail cart. Sex changed the surroundings dramatically; race changed nothing. The settings were identical; white and black people completely interchangeable.[29]

While some ads in this initial campaign emphasized job experience or skill training, many elaborated on the original themes of individuality and personal freedom. A widely used ad promised: "We care more about how you think, than how you cut your hair." Another turned to the language of youth: "We'll make you an expert at whatever turns you on." A series of ads for enlistment in the combat arms—the army's greatest challenge in recruiting an all-volunteer force—even offered: "Take the Army's 16-month tour of Europe." The slogan was a witty turn on the multiple meanings of "tour," at least for those who did not dwell too long on the difference between the grand tour of Europe and the military tour of duty. Accompanying illustrations varied, from a small shot of a smiling flight attendant (because most people still thought troops traveled on troop ships and air travel was considered a luxury), to a montage of the tourist sights of Germany, to a photo using the classic advertising techniques of the age. The young man in this image—in civilian clothes and a haircut that could pass for civilian—sat with a pretty blonde woman in an outdoor café. The background was suggestively foreign, shot in soft focus. A column rose behind the man; a large salt shaker and a small wine carafe stood on the table between them. Just in case someone missed all that heavy-handed imagery, the woman was shown raising an open lipstick tube toward her mouth. "Sex sells," after all, was an advertising truism. And for those young men not convinced by the blonde, the army offered an alternate version: "Mike, Leroy, Rocky, Vince and Bunts are taking the Army's 16-month tour of Europe. Together."[30]

There was some element of cynicism in these ads. Their point was to attract recruits, not to offer an honest representation of life in the army. If putting on an army uniform in 1971 did not guarantee the attentions of beautiful blonde fräuleins, neither did Listerine transform the bridesmaid into a bride (1923), nor drinking Coca-cola bring world peace (1971). The army's ad campaign was, at its most basic, built on the wisdom of the market: advertising does not sell the product; it sells the dreams of the consumer (whether of blondes or of buddies). There are, however, less cynical justifications for the army's direct or implicit promises of individuality, exotic travel, and sex. One draws on wisdom that might be described as parental: maybe the kid will eat spinach if you play airplane with the spoon. That analogy, of course, depends on believing that joining the army would be good for someone. Although Ayer was right about powerful antimilitary sentiments in 1971, many in the army continued to believe that military service offered young men the discipline and the leadership skills that would transform their lives. As General Westmoreland argued with full confidence, in exchange for the energy and enthusiasm of the young, the army would teach them values.

A final justification for this advertising strategy depended on the relative nature of truth: compared to the old "Brown Shoe" army, the MVA did offer a great deal more freedom (the end of bed check and reveille, liberalized pass and alcohol policies) and more tolerance for individuality. The narrator for an episode of the television program *The Army Reports,* "Today's Army: Is It Your Bag?" promised viewers that the army was responding to young people's need for "free choice." "What is Today's Army?" he asked, and offered this answer: It is "made up of individuals who reflect the complexities, contradictions, and strengths of America today . . . Today's Army is changing to meet the needs of its soldiers, so that they will be able to fulfill themselves while contributing to the defense of the country."[31]

Notions of service and contribution had not completely disappeared from these advertisements and programs, even though they were subordinated to a promise of self-fulfillment. Army officials were not quick to relinquish the language of service, even as they sought to attract volunteers and recreate the army's image. And in 1971, the draft was still in effect. The war in Vietnam continued, with no clear timetable for an American exit. Advertising "Today's Army" without mentioning Vietnam was a stretch; mention of service or defense, even in a supporting role, made the ads seem more credible.

For the SAMVA office, much hinged upon a ten-week "test" of commercial television advertising scheduled for spring 1971. There was a lot at stake, for the army's planned shift to commercial broadcasting had found more opposition than support. The army had a strong case to make. Public service announcements were nowhere close to sufficient. The army averaged three to four public service announcements a week in most television markets, with less than 4 percent of them in prime time. And if every commercial station in the United States agreed to run a public service army recruiting ad between 7 and 8 every weekday morning—something that was not at all likely—they would still reach only about a third of the number of 18- to 24-year-old men as would a single ad in *Good Housekeeping* ("hardly a publication we would use to reach this audience," army researchers noted). Other branches of the military, however, were well aware that the army's move was likely to destabilize the entire system. If the army paid for its advertising slots, why would the media offer the other services time for free? Each service was trying to protect its territory and its budget during the uncertainties of transition. Although the army had the most to worry about—the most volunteers to recruit, the worst image to overcome—the navy, air force, and marines saw many of the army's more innovative proposals as challenges. The "Army move" would weaken the "unity" of the services, complained the air force. The navy sniped that army ineptness was creating "deep resentment" at radio and television stations throughout the nation.[32]

Tensions among the services were obvious. Columnist Art Buchwald, satirically predicting a coming advertising war, proposed a new air force slogan: "GET HIGH IN THE AIR FORCE." But it was the marines who greeted the Army's new advertising campaign with the greatest condescension and hostility. As the army offered blondes and the buddy option, a sixteen-month European tour, thirty days paid vacation and transportation by transatlantic jet, the marines' recruiting ads replied: "If you just want to be one of the boys, stick with the boys. The Marines are looking for a few good men." *Advertising Age* characterized the marines' new campaign as a response to the army's "surprise recruiting attack," and its description is accurate. The marines intended to exploit army weaknesses, even floating a prototype ad with the line: "But don't kid yourself; nobody's joining you, you are joining *us*." Someone leaked that ad to the army, prompting a flurry of protests and denials and intervention by the office of the secretary of defense. The army won that skirmish, but the marines' "counterattack" was effective. "The Marines Are Looking for a Few Good Men," framed in response to army claims, long outlasted "Today's Army Wants to Join You." In the bigger picture, however, the other services were right about the impact of army initiatives. In early 1971 J. Walter Thompson, which had handled the marine advertising campaign for the past twenty-four years, had only five people assigned to the account. That would quickly change. And by the end of the decade, public service announcements would be the exception, not the rule. The new world of consumer advertising would be significantly more intense, and significantly more expensive.[33]

In April 1971, the army launched its controversial thirteen-week test of radio and television advertising. The majority of the ads pitched combat arms, but with humor: a sergeant, in car-salesman mode, pointed out the features of a heavily armored tank to a young man who, impressed, signed the papers and drove the tank away; a pretty airline stewardess gradually disappeared under a pile of soldiers' coats as they boarded a jetliner bound for Europe. For thirteen weeks, the army was one of the most heavily promoted goods or services on the nation's airwaves.[34] The SAMVA office hoped the test would prove the worth of commercial advertising and so justify large increases in the army's recruiting budget. The test was followed by a study, which the SAMVA warriors believed would demonstrate advertising's importance in clear and unambiguous numbers. Unfortunately, the quantitative evidence was grim. Rome Arnold & Company found that the percentage of men in test areas who would definitely "like to enter the Army" dropped from 4 percent in pre-test sampling to 3 percent in the post-test version, whereas the percentage who "probably" or "definitely" would not like to enter the army rose from 86 percent to 88 percent. These are marginally significant changes at best, but they hardly made a strong case for large-scale funding of commercial advertising.[35]

What the survey discovered, however, was that young men registered the transformation of the army's appeal. Young men who liked the army commercials described an army that was "becoming more 'relevant.'" The commercials, they suggested, "made Army service seem to be 'fun' or 'more of a pleasure.'" Those who viewed the army positively, Rome Arnold reported, saw the army as something "other than a military duty." To them, the army seemed "'more like an opportunity and not an obligation.'" On the other hand, young men who were not persuaded by the commercials described them as "misleading," "unreal," "dishonest," "slick garbage," and "bullshit."[36]

As army officials attempted to explain the limited or seemingly negative effect of television advertising, they noted that the "television advertising elicited a great response and projected a very positive view of the army at, as fate would have it, the height of the Calley trial." (That spring, Lieutenant Calley faced court-martial for his role in the My Lai massacre.) In fact, many who called the number listed in the army ads simply wanted to register their opinion, one way or the other, about Calley's actions and the eventual guilty verdict. My Lai was not the army's only public problem that spring; American newspapers, magazines, and television news were full of stories about the collapse of morale in the army, rampant drug use, corruption, desertion, racial conflict, and fragging. It was not a good time to experiment with selling the army, though of course this was the same climate from which the army was expected to recruit tens of thousands of volunteers.[37]

Despite the bad news, both N.W. Ayer and the SAMVA people were encouraged that the new slogan had captured the public's attention: by December 1971 "Today's Army Wants to Join You" easily beat "Ford has a better idea" and 7-Up's "The Uncola" in public recognition. And they emphasized the good news: television advertising had generated steadily increasing numbers of live leads and of subsequent enlistments, which dropped when the test ended and advertising appeared only as public service announcements.[38]

In the end, the disappointing quantitative data wasn't nearly as big a problem as congressional opposition. F. Edward Hébert, the chair of the House Armed Services Committee, cared little how well the army spun the numbers or argued for the critical importance of commercial advertising. "Not one cent of appropriated money," Hébert insisted, "would be used to buy something that the Government already owned." He had no problem with paid print advertising or with advertising in general. But on the topic of paid broadcast advertising, he moved quickly from warning to threat. He would do everything in his power, he said, to prevent such a step. If the army defied him, he would use "all power within his command" to make things difficult for them.[39] Hébert's intransigence had deep roots. Like President Nixon and many other major government officials, Hébert believed that American network news was undermining the U.S. military mission in Vietnam. As a strong supporter of the armed forces—according to his understanding of their needs—he regarded the media with suspicion. But he had been pushed past reason by *The Selling of the Pentagon*, a major CBS documentary that aired in February 1971.

The Selling of the Pentagon stepped into America's increasingly angry debate about the war in Vietnam with all the credibility the network news then possessed and all the most persuasive techniques of documentary filmmaking. The Department of Defense, narrator Roger Mudd told his audience, admitted to spending $30 million a year on public relations efforts intended "not merely to inform but to convince and persuade the public on vital issues of war and peace," but the actual figure was closer to $190 million.[40] *The Selling of the Pentagon* revealed that army colonels had been dispatched, at taxpayer expense, to deliver speeches defending American policy in Vietnam—a practice in direct violation of army regulations. Cameras followed paunchy and graying "influential civilians" who played at war on a Pentagon-sponsored guided tour complete with "four-star chaperons." Mudd even pointed out the failings of its own Walter Cronkite, duped or complicit in Pentagon propaganda. Much of the documentary's power, however, lay in its visual, not its verbal, argument. Under Roger Mudd's measured narration ran close-ups of children's faces, footage of children seduced by weapons of war, cheering as they watched violent demonstrations by army Green Berets. Mudd told viewers that "nothing is more essential to a democracy than the free flow of information." Hébert, chairman of the House Armed Services Committee, proclaimed that "the most vicious instrument in America today is network television." No matter how many people agreed with him, Hébert did not come off well in *The Selling of the Pentagon*.[41]

Almost everyone involved in the ensuing struggle between the army and the House Armed Services Committee over commercial television advertising understood that Hébert's complete intractability stemmed from his outrage over the CBS documentary. Proclaiming it "the greatest disservice to the military I've ever seen on television, and I've seen some pretty bad stuff," Hébert said that "CBS taking money from the Army after denouncing it on tv is like Mary Magdalene pleading she is a virgin." So long as Hébert chaired the House Armed Services Committee, he made clear, there was no way that CBS would profit from army advertising.[42] *The Selling of the Pentagon* provoked a congressional investigation over alleged bias against the DoD, and the ensuing controversy over freedom of the press and government interference roiled the American media for months. This larger struggle was the context within which the army tried to make its case for commercial recruiting advertising.

On April 8, 1971, the House Commerce Committee served CBS a subpoena demanding all materials related to the production of *The Selling of the Pentagon.* On April 21 and 22, 1971, a subcommittee of the House Commerce Committee held a hearing on House Concurrent Resolution 215, a "sense of Congress" resolution that "the Federal Government . . . and departments and agencies thereof should not expend public funds to purchase time for the carriage of advertisements by radio or television broadcast stations." The resolution specifically identified the army advertising test, and warned that broadcast stations' opportunity to profit from government funds "raises the specter of Government influence over this sensitive media." In fact, the hearing focused solely on the army's use of commercial advertising.[43]

Underlying definitions of "market" structured some of the debate, as representatives adopted the rational-choice labor market model and suggested that the military pay raise—perhaps in conjunction with a "liberalized . . . life-style"—should be sufficient to draw the required number of volunteers. The Department of Defense was not solidly supportive, as the other military branches remained opposed to the army move. The larger philosophical issues of government power and freedom of the press were also invoked, especially given that the U.S. newspapers were full of such debates in the growing controversy between CBS and the House Commerce Committee over the subpoena for *The Selling of the Pentagon* materials. How much power would dispensation of large advertising budgets give the government in its relations with the broadcast media? Might the move to paid broadcast advertising do harm to the freedom of the press? One representative observed, borrowing his language from a recent editorial in *Advertising Age,* the "official organ for the advertising industry": "We're troubled by the spector [sic] of the Federal Government pouring millions of dollars into ad budgets aimed at molding public opinion in favor of one Government program or another . . . There is great temptation to use Government advertising for partisan purposes, and as far as we can see there aren't any built-in safeguards against this sort of misuse."[44]

The House of Representatives, in the end, supported CBS's stand on freedom of the press and ended the Commerce Committee's efforts to subpoena journalistic materials. It also supported the "sense of Congress" ban on federal departments and agencies using commercial broadcast advertising. The army, stymied at this critical moment, did manage to increase its advertising budget according to its requests, and turned heavily to print advertising. The ban on paid broadcast advertising would last five years, until Representative Hébert ended his term as chair of the House Armed Services Committee.[45]

In some ways, both congressional acts are victories for freedom of speech and freedom of the press. In the late stages of the Vietnam War, they show limited support for public dissent and concern about proper limits on government power. As one representative told the assembled committee at the hearing on the legitimacy of paid recruiting advertising, commercial advertising seemed "an unfortunate weapon to deal with the problem [of attracting volunteers]."[46]

The complication, of course, was that there were few real choices of weapon. Moved—largely against its will—into the marketplace, an old and proud institution was struggling to figure out how to prevail in unfamiliar territory. As Ayer executive William Kelley explained it, "It hurt the Army's ego. After all the years of service to the country the Army saw itself as having to stoop down to the 18 year old's level."[47] But the army actually showed enormous flexibility and initiative in adopting the best weapons possible. It embraced the use of state-of-the-art market research and sophisticated advertising techniques. It adopted an advertising campaign geared toward the problematic youth market of the early 1970s, even though the notion that the army "wants to join you" appalled some large number of those in the active army. And perhaps most impressively, the army faced its own problems and attempted real reform, using the moment of transformation to try to create a stronger, more people-oriented, and more professional force.

High-cost, high-quality commercial advertising and major ongoing market research allowed the army to compete in a marketplace that transcended both the labor market and the market of rational economic choice. As tools—or weapons—these lacked great precision. But they were nonetheless powerful, and they had significant consequences for both the army and the larger American society.

In the 1970s, many of those charged with training and supervising the new volunteers were concerned by what they encountered. The army had to recruit large numbers of young men from a racially, culturally, and politically divided society in the wake of a very bad war. The military entrance qualification test was misnormed for a while during the late 1970s, and falsely high test scores led the army to admit a great number of volunteers it would otherwise have rejected. But many of those in charge also insisted publicly, and in writing, that young men drawn by promises of "individuality" and "freedom" (and blondes and buddies and the tourist sites of Germany) made difficult soldiers. Recruits often felt the same way. A late 1970s study by a congressional representative from Tennessee charged that recruits felt "misled" by army advertising. In response, the army and N.W. Ayer introduced the "This is the Army" campaign, in which ads bore headlines such as "In Europe You're on Duty 24 Hours a Day, but the Rest of the Time is Your Own."[48]

Nonetheless, the young men who commented on the army's initial advertising campaign in the early 1970s understood its sales point very well: The army was not about obligation, but opportunity. Those who had worked to redefine the meaning of military service in the early 1970s, replacing notions of citizen's duty with marketplace options, had found unwitting support in army actions. The cold and rational logic of the labor market was not alone sufficient to draw volunteers for military service; the emotional logic of consumer desire was essential, as well. The army's increasingly sophisticated efforts to discover the desires and psychological needs of American youth and to offer the army as their fulfillment was a critical part of the shift from duty to market, from obligation to opportunity. This new emphasis on opportunity would play a powerful role in the struggles of a nation trying to come to terms with the social change movements of the 1960s and 1970s.

4 RACE, "QUALITY," AND THE HOLLOW ARMY

Scarcely had the last draftee completed basic training before reporters and pundits began chronicling the faults of the all-volunteer army. By April 1974 the *New York Times* seemed ready to call an end to the whole misbegotten experiment with its "conspicuous . . . hazards and shortcomings," and *U.S. News and World Report* headlined "Volunteer Army in Trouble: Back to the Draft, or What?" only three and a half months after the draft's demise.[1] Of course, the decline-of-the-army genre was already well established: Vietnam had yielded a story of sinking morale and combat refusal and atrocity; VOLAR a tale of permissiveness and lost discipline. Accounts of the failure of the all-volunteer army fit neatly into that larger narrative of decline. But the key criticism of the all-volunteer force was something different, a concern fully appropriate to an era of limits and a climate of national malaise. The army, many argued, was facing a crisis of quality.

"Quality," today, is one of the most important measures of the health of the volunteer force, and it has a very specific meaning. "Quality" recruits are those who have earned a high school diploma (not a GED) and who score in the top 50th percentile in the test given to all potential recruits. That's an immensely precise measure of an imprecise concept. But that definition of quality, with all its quantifiable precision, coalesced during the first decade of the all-volunteer force. As the nation applied the lessons of the marketplace to the problem of national defense, a very astute national defense specialist pointed out in a 1981 report to Congress, it had turned to "the dominance of economic criteria, market-place analogies, and quantitative analysis" as bottom-line measures of success.[2]

Whereas definitions of quality were shaped by the military's dramatic shift to the marketplace model, and concerns about quality were voiced in the language of limits and loss that pervaded a decade of economic failures, debates about quality and the AVF were also driven by the fallout of the social change movements of the 1960s. During the 1970s, the problem of race was inescapable. These were days of anger and mistrust and violence, of continued white racism and of black separatist desires. During this decade Americans were forced, time and again, to confront the legacy of centuries of oppression and discrimination. This was as true within the military as in American society as a whole. In the 1970s, every discussion of "quality" and the army was shadowed by assumptions about race.

Concern about "quality" and how to measure it was nothing new. As America's military faced the challenge of inducting and then allocating and training millions of young men during World War I and World War II, Korea and Vietnam, it had developed measures and standards based on the best scientific knowledge—however flawed—of each era. During the twentieth century, the draft (even with the widespread exemptions that existed during the Vietnam War) swept up men with all levels of ability and preparation. The military increasingly relied on standardized tests to screen out those it deemed untrainable and to sort inductees into a hierarchy of "mental categories" that were then used to assign individuals to different military occupational specialties, or MOSs. Who would dig the ditches and who would file reports was determined less often by demonstrated ability than by test scores.

As the draft was replaced by the marketplace, whether conceived as labor market or as consumer market, the nature of the army's control over who entered its ranks changed. It could reject those deemed undesirable, and it could woo those it wanted. But it no longer had the power to compel their presence. As the numbers of those from the top mental categories dropped sharply with the end of the draft, heated debates began. What level of "quality" was necessary for a "modern" volunteer force—the smaller, leaner, more technologically sophisticated one that was to take the place of the unwieldy military of days past? Did it matter that the army, with the declining mental quality of its enlisted ranks, looked less and less like the U.S. population as a whole? Should the military play a social welfare role, serving as employer of last resort or offering remedial training to America's disadvantaged youth? Finally, what could the military do to shape its force, given that it had no authority to guarantee the profile of its new recruits? The answers offered to these questions in the 1970s were closely tied to the nation's evolving understandings of the role of the military and the meaning of military service in American life.

The army first adopted what was then called "mental testing" during World War I. The move to standardized testing would likely have come sooner or later, in any case, as a push for rationalization and efficiency reached ever more broadly through American society during the first years of the twentieth century. But the war created an immense and immediate pressure. In April 1917, when the United States entered the Great War, the nation's armed forces counted only 210,000 men, a full third of them in the National Guard. Only slightly more than 100,000 men served in the U.S. Army. In the nineteen months to follow, the nation would register 24 million men for military service. Close to 5 million men would serve, by far the largest share of them in the army. The logistical challenges were enormous, even for an institution that had fully embraced the principles of modern organization. The American military was not such an institution. As the draft lottery began supplying hundreds of thousands of men, there was no mechanism for classifying recruits or sorting them by talent, skills, or aptitude. Even officers were promoted solely on the basis of seniority. As one of those who helped develop the testing and classification system wrote later, at the beginning of World War I the process most resembled "the British colonel in the Boer War who stood at the gangplank of a troop ship in Capetown and tapped each descending recruit with his riding crop, diagnosing by some process of occult divination: 'Infantry! Cavalry! Artillery! Er—Medical Corps!'"[3]

Some Americans saw a major opportunity in the challenge of mobilization. To these influential citizens, World War I was not only the war to end all wars, the great battle to make the world safe for democracy. It was also a chance to demonstrate the efficacy of the new tools of modern society, to bring the lessons of science to bear on major social problems. The American Psychological Association, some members of which had been experimenting with mental testing and had adopted the concept of an "intelligence quotient" not long before the United States entered the war, offered its expertise. Not only could psychologists help screen out suspected "mental defectives," the president of the association promised, they could create a test that would allow the military to classify men by ability and so more efficiently assign them to different military occupations. Psychologists and concerned members of the public debated whether these new "IQ" tests measured innate ability or achievement, nature or nurture, but the army cared little. It simply needed to allocate millions of inductees in the most successful and efficient way possible.[4]

Despite the psychological association's promises, it had yet to develop an appropriate test. This was a daunting task, and Robert Yerkes, president of the association, approached it with missionary zeal. By June 1917 he and six colleagues had produced a test they felt fairly confident about. In fact, they had produced two tests: one for those who were literate in English, and one for those who were illiterate and/or did not understand the English language. The first of these, "examination alpha," took only fifty minutes and could be given to groups of up to five hundred men at a time. Its substance would be more-or-less familiar to most Americans who have taken the Scholastic Aptitude Test. There were analogies and logical reasoning questions, sentence completions and number sequences. The other, "beta" examination, was much more challenging to create, to administer, and to complete. Instructions were given in pantomime—a standardized sequence of movement performed by trained examiners. Because Yerkes's committee was committed to scientific reliability, these pantomimed instructions could not vary from examiner to examiner, place to place. Thus examiners, many of them graduate students in psychology, attended a newly created "school of military psychology" at Fort Oglethorpe, Georgia, where they practiced administering the tests until the instructions were like a second language. They, also, felt a missionary zeal. But imagine playing charades with men from a dozen different nations—as well as unschooled men from the most rural and isolated parts of the United States—with only one approved way to act out a word. Bowing to the difficulties of administration, regulations restricted the size of beta test groups to 300.[5]

By May 1918, the army was testing 200,000 men a month, ranking them on an alphabetic scale of A to D. Men who scored between 135 and 212 points (the highest possible) were labeled "A," while scores between 0 to 14 points earned a "D." Some army officers found the scientific data useful, but many remained unconvinced. Looking back, one general called the psychologists "mental meddlers," and even as they did their work the commander at Fort Dix made clear that psychologists were just as useful as "a board of art critics to advise me which of my men were the most handsome, or a board of prelates to designate the true Christians." The army quickly ended the mass testing program at the end of the war. Although mental testing made sense in a period of rapid mobilization, many concluded, intelligence was not the only quality that mattered. The work of "civilian scientists whose knowledge of military affairs is usually meager" was, in any case, no substitute for the personal evaluations of experienced officers. Pointing to a D-rated draftee who was "a model of loyalty, reliability, cheerfulness, and the spirit of serene and general helpfulness," one commander asked: "What do we care about his 'intelligence?'"[6]

The results of the mental tests were more compelling to America's civilian society, which was attempting to absorb enormous numbers of immigrants, than they were to the army. The now-quantified supposedly substandard intelligence of Italians and Jews, as well as of blacks, lent weight to calls for immigration restriction and evidence in support of the eugenics movement. The reported results of the tests—that even the native-born men tested had an average "mental age" of thirteen—fed fears about the problem of democracy in a complicated age. As the opening sentence of a 1919 *New York Times Magazine* article, "Secret Mind Tests of the Army," asserted: "Misfits encumber the world."[7]

By the time the military mobilized for World War II, psychologists had developed a much-improved classification test. The Army General Classification Test (AGCT) was, according to the *New York Times,* "as reliable a measure of native intelligence, quick thinking and learning aptitude as anything that advanced psychologists have devised." "[I]n an Army seeking out brain power," the article continued, the AGCT "is the most effective single means of determining how much a soldier's mind can be expected to absorb," even if "there will always be a mother of some intellectual broadcasting her horror that another potential colonel has been made a latrine orderly." Based on AGCT scores, the army sorted potential soldiers into categories I through V. The categories were based on a bell curve, not equal quintiles, so Category III included men who scored between 31 and 64 on the 100-point test, while only those who scored between 93 and 99 were designated Category I.[8]

As historian Paula Fass points out, "where subnormal mentality was the bombshell of the First World War draft, illiteracy and unequal educational opportunity became the equivalent shocker of the Second." The problem was largely one of race. Until 1943, the military had a race-based quota for those who could not read or write: up to 10 percent of all whites and 10 percent of all blacks inducted on a given day could be illiterate. But that quota was enforced locally, not nationally. Because so many young black men in the South had been denied education, southern whites were drafted at extraordinarily high rates while southern blacks were equally highly deferred. In June 1943, under pressure from all directions, the selective service system ended its literacy requirements. The army, which had to figure out how to use these men, created remedial educational units to "salvage" illiterates, the more capable of the Category V recruits, and those who spoke no English. The Special Instruction Units were not restricted to Negroes, though they were segregated. Nonetheless, they are evidence that the army, as an institution, understood the social origins of black inequality. Even though its motivation was efficiency rather than justice, the army did teach many black men to read and write, and so made a significant difference in their lives.[9]

Throughout the war, the army relied heavily on AGCT scores. As a twenty-five-cent booklet with a cover that promised readers, "*Get the Job You Want in the Army! Pass High on the Inductee's Mental Test,*" explained to its audience, the army worked "carefully, using sound scientific principles" to construct the tests, for it "doesn't propose to make any gross errors in classifying its men. The stakes are large for which this war is being fought and mistakes can be costly beyond calculation." The AGCT was described as a "democratic" tool that allowed the army to classify men by ability rather than by class, education, or position. Scores, however, revealed enormous disparities between black and white men, as well as between men from different regions of the country. The army insisted that the gaps were a result of "environmental factors which have modified for better or for worse the *native* intelligence with which [an individual] was originally endowed." A pamphlet created for commanding officers of Negro units emphasized that while the AGCT is "a roughly accurate measure of what the new soldier knows, what skills he commands, and of his aptitude in solving problems[, *i*]*t is not a test of inborn intelligence.*"[10]

The military's experience with classification tests as it mobilized millions during World War II convinced decision makers of their usefulness, and such mental tests grew steadily in importance. Beginning in 1950, the military adopted a service-wide Armed Forces Qualification Test (AFQT), each successive version of which was normed against the distribution of AGCT scores of men on active duty as of December 1944. A series of other service-specific exams tested for vocational aptitudes. The Department of Defense introduced a unified exam, the Armed Services Vocational Aptitude Test (ASVAB), in 1968; it was offered to high schools as part of a student testing program. In 1976, ASVAB (which incorporated a version of the AFQT) replaced all individual service exams as the basic qualification and classification test for entrance into military service.[11]

One lesson from the army's experience in World War II was that classification and qualification exams were useful. Another was that racial inequalities were closely related to social and educational inequalities, and that the military could, through remedial instruction and disciplined attention, make a positive difference in individual lives. That, in the best possible reading, was the thinking behind Project 100,000, Secretary of Defense Robert McNamara's plan to use the military as a part of the Johnson administration's antipoverty drive, "salvaging" tens of thousands of young men from "poverty-encrusted" backgrounds first for "productive military careers and later for productive roles in society." Men culled from the ranks of draft rejectees, McNamara explained, "will be given the opportunity to return to civilian life with skills and aptitudes which for them and their families will reverse the downward spiral of human decay." McNamara's August 1966 announcement of Project 100,000—which caught the Pentagon by surprise—came as the United States was rapidly increasing the number of combat troops in Vietnam.[12]

Although, as one study, *Low-Aptitude Men in the Military,* notes, McNamara "probably didn't deserve the Nobel Prize for a solely selfless interest in helping the country's young people" through Project 100,000, the program was not simply to produce cannon fodder for the Vietnam War. As in the case of so much that happened during the 1960s, one historical trajectory was overtaken by another, and original intentions were lost or betrayed in a very different world. In 1962, Americans were alarmed to learn that a full third of the 18-year-olds summoned for draft examinations had been rejected, half of them for reasons of mental aptitude. President Kennedy, not long before his term was cut short by an assassin's bullet, created a task force to investigate the problem. "A young man who does not have what it takes to perform military service," he argued, "is not likely to have what it takes to make a living. Today's military rejects include tomorrow's hard-core unemployed." Kennedy's claim meshed neatly with other contemporary fears, as Daniel Patrick Moynihan began to voice his growing concern about a black "culture of poverty"—its complex racial politics further complicated by assumptions about gender—arguing that young black men from single-parent families must be rescued from a woman-dominated world and given proper male discipline. One proposed solution, born of President Johnson's War on Poverty and the legacy of racial remediation in World War II, was the 1964 Special Training Enlistment Program (STEP), which would enroll about 11,000 men into a remedial army program. Critics were quick to dub STEP the "moron corps," and Congress was equally quick to deny funding. The army, it explained, was not the proper place for socioeconomic experiments.[13]

In 1964, opportunities for training in a peacetime army seemed attractive, even if the rationale was paternalistic. But in 1966, reclassification of those formerly rejected by the draft seemed much less an "opportunity." Project 100,000 put 350,000 "New Standards" men into the military. Seventy percent of them were draftees, not volunteers. Sixty-six percent of them went into the army, with the remaining 34 percent shared more or less equally among the air force, navy, and marines. More than a third were assigned to combat arms—a not unreasonable use of unskilled men in the course of a war, but certainly not a source of training, education, and racial uplift. Of these New Standards men, 38 percent were black. And for these men, the median AFQT score was 13 out of 100.[14]

This was the world in which the army began planning for a move to an all-volunteer force. It had come to rely heavily on quantitative measures of aptitude and capacity despite occasional reminders of the critical importance of individual observation and informed opinion. It was well aware of the problems presented by those of low aptitude. It was frustrated by attempts to use the military as an engine of social welfare, and it was highly aware of the problem of race.

In discussions of quality, as with so much else in the transition to an all-volunteer force, the army often focused less on what was coming than on the specific problems of that moment late in the Vietnam War. Virtually everyone understood that the "quality" distribution of new enlistees would change as the army adopted the principles of supply and demand. The working assumption was that the all-volunteer force, and the army in particular, would draw many fewer of those in the top quality rankings—the best educated, those scoring in the top two mental categories—than had been supplied by the draft. Nonetheless, many who needed to plan for the future AVF focused on what was frustrating them in the present. They obsessed about the "problem" of bright youth, those better educated than their NCOs, prone to ask questions and to expect answers. They wanted to figure out how to draw those men in, to make them a source of informal leadership instead of a source of trouble. Thus in 1972 when General Westmoreland argued that the generation gap was a major problem for the army, his description of youth was ambivalent. "They want to know all the answers," he told reporters, with some frustration. "They want to know why, and they want to talk philosophy of war and philosophy in general, and the non-coms haven't been able to communicate with them at that intellectual level." Fourteen percent of draftees were college graduates in 1971, he pointed out, and "many" had advanced degrees. New inductees often had more education than noncommissioned officers and were at least as well educated as their officers. "It was," he noted, "sometimes very difficult for the sergeant, who perhaps had a high school education or less, to communicate with this highly educated private."[15]

Congress, too, took up this problem. When the House Armed Services Committee held hearings on recruiting and retention in 1972, it sought testimony from one of those well-educated soldiers, the chair of the Junior Enlisted Council at Fort Dix, SP5 Stephen Fanteau. Fanteau's surname may have been Fateaux or Fauteux, as the hearing transcript referred to him by all three, and he, when the chair of the subcommittee rather argumentatively insisted that he couldn't pronounce the witness's name, said just to call him Foxtrot and that would be fine. Fanteau argued that the enlisted council helped overcome the barriers of the generation gap. The Junior Enlisted Council, he told the gathered congressmen, could give insight into "the feelings of . . . junior enlisted men" and "provide the command with a source of totally undiscolored information." Specialist Foxtrot noted that he had been distressed at being drafted upon graduation from Yale, as his summons to military service required him to decline a Carnegie Fellowship to teach at his alma mater. His testimony—"it seems there is a strong passivist [sic] tradition, especially in the young people, which exerts itself against the uniform as a symbolic target"—was articulate and insightful. But selecting Fanteau as the spokesman for the army's junior enlisted ranks, both at Fort Dix and in the halls of Congress, perpetuated the notion that one of the biggest problems the army faced was poorly educated NCOs faltering in discussions of philosophy with graduates of Yale.[16]

That's not to say that no one was worrying about the quantity-quality balance. But the army's attempts to deal with the issue were complicated by congressional decisions and shifting military manpower policy. When Congress voted in September 1971 to extend the draft for two more years, it also ordered the army to cut its strength by 50,000 men in the following nine months. That was a battle the army had lost, and thus a bureaucratic mess it could not avoid. It had to accomplish a rapid reduction in force (RIF) in the midst of a continuing war while trying to figure out what the army would look like without a draft. The result was what the army calls "personnel turbulence": because overseas units had to be maintained at 95 percent strength, when soldiers in Europe or Korea took advantage of early release programs, others had to be transferred in to fill those vacancies. This downsizing and the resulting shifts in assignments put enormous stress on personnel managers. But personnel managers weren't immune to the turbulence, either, and many with the knowledge and experience necessary to manage the process were transferred or released themselves.[17]

The rapid RIF created havoc in individual lives and in army units. It also created two problems for the coming volunteer force. Temporary manpower shortages meant heavier workloads for many enlisted men, thus betraying the Modern Volunteer Army promise of regular hours and dependable schedules. Those who hoped to reenlist in the army were often turned away—or pushed out—even as the army was using "Madison Avenue approaches" (in the words of a critical report from the House Armed Services Committee) to lure new recruits. That's not because the right hand didn't know what the left hand was doing; it wasn't even "the Army way" (as in "there are three ways of doing something: the right way, the wrong way, and the Army way"). No matter how it looked to the public, army logic was clear. The military relied on new enlistees to keep balance in age and in rank. Privates are essential to the functioning of an army; it was not possible to reduce the size of the force by shutting down the recruiting offices and weeding out the bottom ranks. But the consequences of this reduction in force undermined the army's credibility with its own enlisted men, with potential recruits, and (even though the RIF was mandated by Congress) with influential members of the House Armed Services Committee.[18]

In that same session, Congress also prohibited the Secretary of Defense from setting quotas based on mental categories. The congressmen behind this move believed that some in the DoD would do anything to prove the AVF a success—including lowering quality standards to whatever level the market most easily supplied.[19] This legislation ended McNamara's Project 100,000. It also created greater flexibility—and uncertainty—as the military moved into the marketplace. How would marketplace forces drive the balance between quantity and quality? What level of quality was necessary? There was no unanimity on those questions.

Two arguments about quality developed within the Department of Defense. One group insisted that clear and unchanging quality requirements should be set for each military occupational specialty. The other fully embraced marketplace principles: they believed that quality standards must be flexible, rising and falling depending on how many high-quality men were willing to join the military. The army manpower office understood the stakes very well: relying solely on an unregulated marketplace was bad for the army. As research revealed with depressing regularity, the army fell last of the services in public esteem. "High-quality" recruits were much more likely to join the air force or even the navy. And the marines only needed "a few good men" compared to the twenty to thirty thousand a month the army had to recruit. So although those in the Department of Defense were intent on making numbers—the quantity part of the equation—the army insisted that it could not ignore quality.

This debate was not about those scoring in Category I and II—or even in Category III. The manpower specialists were arguing over men in Category IV. It had become clear that the army would be able to meet its recruiting goals if it relied heavily on those who scored 30 or lower on the AFQT. But those men—in aggregate—were harder to train. They had difficulty mastering technical skills. Many couldn't read and write. They caused more disciplinary problems. The army even offered quantitative evidence: research showed that about two-thirds of those who scored in the top portion of Category IV (with 21–30 scores on the AFQT, which the army had defined as roughly equivalent to IQ scores of 82 to 91 on the Stanford-Binet test), could—with enough repetition in training—learn some of the more technical skills required to meet current army shortages. But only a third of those in the bottom of the category, with test scores of 10–15 (71 to 81 IQ), could do so. But these last were the men the marketplace most easily supplied. So despite DoD disapproval—"How many Viet Cong riflemen had Ph.D.s?" was the exact and slightly contemptuous phrasing—the army began giving recruiters specific "sub-objectives" for skilled MOSs and denying them credit for recruits who scored in the bottom half of Category IV.[20]

To many of the most fervent supporters of the AVF in the Nixon administration, this action seemed a clear sign of resistance. Many of them had never believed the army was really on board with the move to a volunteer force. Westmoreland, despite his firm public commitment to the AVF when he was chief of staff of the army, had expressed serious concerns in a private letter to Nixon as he left the position, and General Creighton W. Abrams, his successor, was a traditionalist who had little use for the term "Modern Volunteer Army" and pretty much despised the phrase "Today's Army Wants to Join You." But not even the most suspicious had been able to point to direct evidence of "sabotage"—until now. Even army analysts admitted that it would be harder to meet recruiting objectives if standards were higher. Did army officials think, some began to ask, that a quick and decisive failure would deliver the larger victory?[21]

In May 1973, as induction authority moved into its last weeks, Nixon appointed a new secretary of the army. Howard H. Callaway, known to everyone as "Bo," was an interesting choice. Graduated from West Point in 1949, he "knew how to salute" even though he'd not chosen a military career. He was a Republican from Georgia back when they were fewer and farther between, a man who'd joined the Goldwater bandwagon in 1964 and won election as Georgia's first Republican congressional representative since Reconstruction. In 1966, the self-proclaimed conservative had run against Democrat Lester Maddox for the governorship of Georgia. Lester Maddox was an unreconstructed racist who had never graduated high school. He was best known for brandishing an axe handle in defense of his right to choose who to serve—and not to serve—in the Pickrick Cafeteria, his Atlanta restaurant. Callaway, in contrast, came from a wealthy family that Georgians knew best as the owners of Callaway Gardens, a vacation resort not far from FDR's Warm Springs. Though Callaway won the plurality of the popular vote, he did not claim a majority, and the almost completely Democratic state legislature voted Maddox in. Many of Georgia's better-educated citizens, appalled at the vulgarity of the new governor, proposed amending the state constitution to require that the state's governor be a high school graduate. The Nixon administration, however, was more interested in Callaway's term in the U.S. Congress and the invaluable access to current members it gave him. Given that the House Armed Services Committee—and its chair, F. Edward Hébert—had turned out to be the most powerful opponent of the AVF, Callaway's connections couldn't hurt.[22]

Callaway understood the politics of the all-volunteer force and the challenge it posed to the army. Personally, he had a lingering fondness for the World War II–era draft, the full mobilization version that drew men from all segments of the population. But like many others on both sides of the liberal/conservative divide, he saw the highly limited draft as unfair—though in his case it was not because of exemptions that favored those with more social advantages, for he found the randomness of the lottery system equally troublesome. If not all were expected to serve, he claimed, briefly adopting the language of the free-market economists, the draft was involuntary servitude. "It is slavery by definition," he later penciled into the transcript of an army oral history. Callaway knew that, despite the sentiments of Hébert and other members of the Armed Services committee, there was no way that Congress was going to reinstate the draft. So he positioned himself as the all-volunteer army's chief cheerleader, determined that if the army was going to be all volunteer, it would be as good an all-volunteer army as he could make it.[23]

In October 1973, less than four months after draft authority had expired, Bo Callaway stood before the assembled members of the Association of the United States Army (AUSA)—the same audience before which Westmoreland had pledged the army's commitment, and one that had not fully embraced the move to a volunteer force—and offered them a choice that was no choice: "a successful volunteer Army or failure for the Army." And then he proclaimed, as directly and succinctly as possible, that "the volunteer Army is working!" The pre-circulated version of the speech was complete with an exclamation point, and the press release prepared by the army skipped over Callaway's admonishments to the AUSA and catalogued all the ways in which the volunteer force was "excelling."[24] It's not clear that any news source outside the army picked up this pre-packaged account of Callaway's speech. The Arab-Israeli Yom Kippur War saturated the papers that week, and that grim story was scarcely leavened by reports that Henry Kissinger, then deep in Middle East negotiations, had been awarded a Nobel Peace Prize for his diplomatic efforts in the Vietnam

War. But if anyone did print "Army Secretary Confident that Volunteer Army is Working," it was the best press the army would get that decade.

Callaway understood very clearly that the interests of the Department of Defense were not identical to the interests of the army, and that the army's success or failure had much to do with how it negotiated its role in relation to the other branches of the armed forces. The army had relied the most heavily on the draft. "The navy, air force, and marines had all kinds of sex appeal," Callaway said later, and "we were talking about trenches." The new secretary of the army was certain, and not without reason, that the other services were quite willing to "skim off the high quality," leaving the army to take "the dregs."[25] And that was where he drew the line.

Avoiding the usual football metaphors, Callaway reached back to the radio programs of his Depression-era youth to make his case. The army certainly needs "people who can carry the ammo," he said, men who "don't want to be company commander by the second day; who don't have the mentality." But, he insisted, it also needs at least some "Jack Armstrongs" (as in "Jack Armstrong, the All-American Boy"), young men who are "bright and . . . able," "entrepreneurial and . . . energetic."[26] Callaway lacked the reforming zeal of General Forsythe and his SAMVA warriors, who had meant to transform the army. But he had a very practical bent, and understood that if he meant to recruit quality soldiers, he needed to turn away from the philosophical claims, whether about professionalism or individuality, to the critically important process of recruiting.

Recruiting, during the roughly three decades of the draft, had been a fairly low priority for the army. At the end of 1970 there were about 700 recruiting stations in the United States, most of them in the basements of post offices or other federal buildings, furnished with hand-me-down equipment and staffed by men who, in army terms, were "order takers," processing volunteers who were heavily motivated by the draft. Well aware that a volunteer force would ultimately rely on the success of recruiters, the army had already begun to increase their numbers—from 3,000 in early 1971 to 6,000 by early 1974—and to rethink the training process. Here, once again, was the language of the market. "You are going out to be salesmen," the speaker at the closing ceremony told graduates of the Army Recruiter and Career Counselor training course in October 1971.[27]

Callaway, however, sought more fundamental change. Recruiting assignments, he directed, would no longer be the last stop for noncommissioned officers nearing the end of a career, a way of easing men into retirement. Instead, army recruiters would be "top caliber" NCOs with promising careers ahead of them, men with distinguished combat records, hand-picked by special teams sent out to canvass army installations for candidates. Many of the high-caliber NCOs identified by these special teams feared the recruiting assignment was a sign their careers had gone badly off track, no matter what promises were made, and such beliefs were not restricted to sergeants. When Callaway appointed General Eugene Forrester to USAREC, the army recruiting command, Forrester seriously considered resigning rather than accepting the appointment. But for NCOs, the end-of-the-line image faded quickly. By late 1974, competition was stiff: recruiting, like the army itself, was by that point solely on a volunteer basis, and volunteers had less than a one-in-three chance of being accepted for a recruiting assignment. By early 1975, chances were less than one in four.[28]

Potential recruiters—at this point mostly men in their twenties, and usually combat veterans of the Vietnam War—completed a five-week course of instruction at Fort Benjamin Harrison, Indiana. It was a world of young men and high spirits, and perhaps not unexpectedly—though certainly not officially—many decided the best place to practice the salesmanship skills they were learning was on the women of neighboring Indianapolis. (Throughout the 1970s recruiters, reportedly, had a very high divorce rate, and although the long hours and stress of recruiting strained marriages, well-honed sales skills played a role all too often.) Recruiters were preparing for an atypical army assignment, sent to live in a civilian world—and the best recruiting was usually not from the most desirable cities and towns in the nation—to pay civilian prices for food and housing, to forego the social support of an army post, to operate with an enormous amount of autonomy. Recruiters cultivated high school principals, counselors, coaches, and teachers; they chaperoned dances and coached kids' baseball teams; they wore their uniforms to church, befriended Rotarians, addressed parent-teacher organizations, and made their sales pitches to the guys pumping gas and the girls waiting tables. "Oh, come on Earl," said Sgt. Dan Bailey to the teenager pumping his gas in Goldstone, NC, in footage from a long *MacNeil/Lehrer Report* segment on recruiting the new volunteer army. "What are you staying around here for, Earl? She'll be waiting for you when you come back . . . you ain't doing nothing here in Goldstone . . . just kinda hanging around the service station here." Lehrer, a former Marine, made his disapproval clear: "'You're not doing anything anyway, so why not join the army?' . . . Perhaps the scars of Vietnam make it difficult to sing the army's praises . . . but . . . what kind of man would that pitch appeal to?"[29]

The Washington Post had offered a more sympathetic portrayal in its 1972 profile of Sergeant First Class Louis E. Manley, a 30-year-old former Army Ranger working from a recruiting station in Northeast DC. Manley ticked off his triumphs: he had enlisted several undercover narcotics agents who "blew their cover" and had to get out of town fast, a high school football player who planned to go into the undertaking business and joined the army to learn auto mechanics ("Someone," he explained, "has to keep the hearses working"), and a black power activist who accused Manley, who was also black, of recruiting other black men as cannon fodder for white men's wars and ended up, in the words of the *Post,* turning in "his dashiki for a guaranteed course of training in electronics." The reporter clearly found Manley's enthusiasm appealing, and made much of his engaging confidence. Manley, the reporter noted in the article's second paragraph, "amplif[ied] his eagerness to 'join' any 'qualified candidate'" by restating his answer to an officer who asked him if he thought he could recruit rural southern whites: "I told him . . . that if the man had a body temperature of 98.6 degrees, and a 50 per cent desire to join the Army, I'd get him in."[30]

Callaway's insistence on quality recruiters was a major step. But he expected the recruiters to provide quality volunteers, as well. By August 1973, he'd instituted a new system for allocating credit to recruiters for enlistees, one borrowed from the air force and retuned to army purposes, and one that very definitely didn't take "a body is a body" as the bottom line. *The Recruiting and Career Counseling Journal* (the official publication for those charged with recruiting and reenlisting soldiers) attempted to explain the new graduated point system in the October 1973 issue with an "example designed to illustrate the computations involved in the point system, and the manner in which it encourages achieving overall objectives, while additionally obtaining accessions beyond objectives." The following year, with a slightly revised system, they tried again . . . a bit more clearly: "Each enlistment is worth a fixed number of credits based upon the civilian education and the mental category of the enlistee. In short, Albert Einstein would be worth ten credits, while any one of the Three

Stooges would be worth one." That wasn't, in fact, true. Under the Qualitative Incentive Procurement program (or QIPS, which was, the article noted, pronounced "Kips"), enlistees from mental category IV brought no additional credit, and those from categories I, II, or III were worth exactly the same: one additional point.[31] Nonetheless, the metaphor was effective. Quality mattered.

The *Recruiting and Career Counseling Journal* continually reinforced that message. The journal's December 1974 issue pictured Santa Claus busily turning out "Quality Volunteer Soldiers" for packages addressed "To: Hon. Bo Callaway." The commanding general of USAREC lectured recruiters on the importance of quality in the September 1974 issue. The quality soldier, General William B. Fulton wrote in a "message" that was emphatic if a bit incoherent, "must be of sound moral character—tell right from wrong. We don't need a bunch of bums who are one step ahead of the sheriff." A soldier's intelligence, also, is critical, for "a deep sense of duty and responsibility are more quickly understood and accepted by the more intelligent and better educated soldier." Those from the "lower mental categories," he continued, "many of them are losers to start with," more likely to be disciplinary problems, less likely to make it in the army. "The Army has lost a lot of money and time with these guys," Fulton pointed out, "and you have to start over and enlist their replacements. Quality pays off, not only for the Army, but for *you,* too." He ended with his usual admonition: "get crackin!"[32]

Fulton's point about "losers" was driven home by QIPS. Not only did recruiters earn more points for volunteers who scored in the higher mental categories and who had high school diplomas, they could lose points for non–prior service recruits who did poorly and were discharged or chose to leave the army under the new 179-day Training Discharge program. This, also, was Callaway's initiative, and it was a controversial one. In a conscription-based army, the possibility of a quick and nonprejudicial "separation" would have given reluctant draftees a great incentive to fail in basic training; in the volunteer army, quick discharges seemed the best way to avoid troubles later on. Drill sergeants who were once judged by how many men they got through basic training now were encouraged to weed out the difficult and the incapable. For many, it went against the grain. But by mid-1974 almost 12 percent of army volunteers were discharged or released during that first 179 days.[33]

QIPS was not only a way to calibrate recruiting objectives and sub-objectives more finely. It was also a point-driven system of rewards for successful recruiters. Awards began with gold stars for the silver recruiter badge (and the first recruiter in each of the five recruiting battalions to earn a gold star was flown to the New Orleans commanders' conference in late 1974 and personally awarded that star by Callaway); then a gold recruiter's badge to replace the silver one, and then a series of stars with small sapphires for the gold badge, and finally a "Super Bowl" recruiter's ring with a green stone. General Forrester, who commanded USAREC from 1975 to 1978, mused that he didn't understand the point of providing such symbolic awards—"gaudy," he called them—but nonetheless they seemed to work. It seems an odd statement from a man who'd spent almost four decades in an institution that awarded its highest honors in the symbolic form of ribbons and medals.[34]

For all the cheerleading about quality, it was clear that some recruiters were not happy with the complicated point system or the world view it mirrored. A body was a body, some believed. If a high school diploma was required, one could be provided. All it took was an original diploma, a little scotch tape, and a photocopier. "Clean" police records were more complicated, but not impossible. If the police did a record search on just a part of someone's name—and lots of middle names might as well be surnames—likely they'd find no record. It was easy enough to add the surname to the form after it came back clean. Qualifying tests were the most difficult to finesse. Sergeant Manley in Washington, DC, gave all his potential volunteers six or more practice tests to prepare them for the real thing, and coached them on vocabulary and mathematical word problems. Pep talks and coaching, he insisted, could boost scores by as much as 20 points. A bit south, in Hickory, North Carolina, recruiters convinced the exam administrators at the Catawaba Valley Technological Institute to let them proctor and score the tests.[35] Results were uniformly good.

Chair of the House Armed Services Committee F. Edward Hébert—the man who had blocked the army's attempt to use paid broadcast advertising, the man who had worn the wit out of his claim that the only way to get an all-volunteer army was to draft one—saw the emerging stories of recruiter malfeasance as another way to demonstrate the impossibility of a well-run all-volunteer force. He launched an official investigation of recruiting among all the services. Focusing on the months from January 1972 through October 1973, investigators followed up 1,600 complaints about army recruiters (total cases investigated in the other services were navy, 69; marines, 71; air force, 73). They discovered 298 cases of proven malpractice by army recruiters (navy, 3; marines, 19; air force, 9), for which 250 army recruiters were disciplined. The national media was quick to portray recruiter malpractice as just one more failure of army credibility. At a July 1973 news conference, reporters seamlessly linked the investigations of recruiter malpractice to charges that the army was trying to sabotage the AVF to army misrepresentations to Congress about bombing in Cambodia. Deputy Secretary of Defense William Clements sputtered, in response to reporters' questions: "I don't think anybody can run, as an example a Seven-Eleven stores [sic], they've got about 1,800 or something like that, and I'm sure that they're going to have a certain number of managers and some kind of default."[36] Bad press, indeed.

The recruiting scandal, however, offered fuel to supporters of the all-volunteer force as well as to its critics. In October 1973 Stephen Herbits, the former "student" representative on the Gates commission who was now in the Department of Defense, framed his attempt to scuttle the army's stricter quality standards as concern for the plight of "hard pressed" recruiters. Herbits believed, fully and wholeheartedly, that the army was using the issue of quality to sabotage the AVF, and he urged the secretary of defense to prevent the army from refusing volunteers who scored in the bottom half of Category IV. Callaway, under pressure, lowered the army's high school graduate to nongraduate goal from 70:30 to 50:50.[37]

The argument against higher quality standards, however, also got a clear and forceful public airing. Conservative columnist George Will, writing in the *Washington Post,* wasted no concern on army recruiters as he set forth his charges of sabotage. "Some people in our 'action Army,'" he began, "—the one that 'wants to join you'—have swung into action to discredit the idea of a volunteer force." The army's concerns about quality were nonsense, he claimed, and its new quality standards were "arbitrary," designed primarily to "impede" recruiting and thus prove the AVF impossible and unsustainable. Halfway through the article, however, Will made what seems an immense leap from notions of quality to questions of race. "But one more thing must be said," he wrote. "The Constitution will not permit the racial 'mix' of recruits to be treated as a 'problem.' The percentage of black recruits in August (29.7), as in other months, was higher than the percentage of blacks in the population. But so what?" "Current Army talk about recruits being 'too few' or 'inferior' or 'too black' is devious and corrupt nonsense," Will continued, "designed either to get conscription reinstated or to justify a massive budget shift among the services, in favor of the Army."[38]

Will, in linking discussions of quality and race, was squarely within the established parameters of the debate. Although the common and unthinking equation of black with "low quality" had roots in white racism, many of those who paid attention to the numbers—whether white or black, and of all political stripes—saw two key facts clearly. Black men were enlisting in the army at rates much, much higher than their proportion of the American population. And blacks, in aggregate, scored lower on the "mental tests" than did whites. Though most who struggled with the implications of those facts would have accepted one reporter's explanation for those lower scores—"the education situation of the blacks in urban areas, rural areas too"—it remained true that the army had a disproportionate share of black men and that a disproportionately large percentage of black men in the army were Category IV.[39]

The army had significant experience with lower-level Category IV draftees, as Project 100,000 had brought more than 230,000 such men into the army during the Vietnam War. The officers and NCOs who had trained and commanded these men had strong reservations about their use. There were some success stories, but in almost all cases Category IV soldiers took longer to train and needed more frequent reinforcement. The army was fairly confident that it could train most such men, if they had the motivation to learn. But there were more fundamental concerns. Bottom line, the New Standards men were more frequently killed or wounded than other combat soldiers. They were less likely to survive combat and more likely to endanger other members of a platoon. Military analyst Eliot Cohen made the point bluntly in 1982: "Those who assure us that stupid soldiers can make good infantrymen should ask themselves whether, if *they* had to go on a patrol behind enemy lines, knowing that a lapse in alertness, willing cooperation, or initiative could lead to death in a sudden ambush, they would prefer stupid to bright comrades. The dull-witted soldier does not simply get himself killed—he causes the death of others as well."[40]

There was, however, a big difference between the draftee army in Vietnam and the new peacetime all-volunteer army. Those attempting to sell the army had been working hard to reposition it, to portray it as an opportunity, not an obligation. By mid-1973 General Abrams had succeeded in getting rid of the hated "Today's Army Wants to Join You" slogan. N.W. Ayer would have a new campaign in place, complete with supporting social science research, by mid-1974. But for a while, the army would simply proclaim itself "Today's Army." This wasn't much of a recruiting slogan, but it worked well with a variety of subordinate themes, almost all of them about opportunity in its most practical form.

The promises of individuality and self-fulfillment that structured Ayer's initial campaign had spoken to a real concern of contemporary youth, even as the ads fed the charges of permissiveness and indiscipline that plagued the transition to the volunteer force. But as the war ended and the volunteer force became a reality, advertising increasingly emphasized the practical opportunities the army offered. Thirty thousand young men between the ages of 18 and 21 had mailed inquiry cards in response to a *Reader's Digest* ad with the caption: "We Have Over 300 Good, Steady Jobs" in 1972, the same year the army ran an ad in *Ebony* that began, "It's tough to get ahead when you start so far behind. No skills. No experience. No jobs to look forward to, except the ones anyone can do." Quality volunteers, research showed, were drawn by the promise of learning a skill, by the possibilities of education, training, and travel. As the largest group of baby boomers yet neared the end of their high school years, and as the unemployment rate jumped from 4.9 percent in 1973 to 8.5 percent in 1975, the army promised: "The job you learn is yours to keep"; "Good jobs that take you places"; "A two-year education." Callaway counted the creation of a "skill catalog" that related training for army MOSs to comparable civilian jobs as one of the army's major accomplishments of 1973.[41]

Many Americans believed that drafting poorly educated young men from the lowest acceptable mental categories and sending them to fight in Vietnam was exploitation, no matter how much Secretary of Defense McNamara described Project 100,000 as a form of social welfare. But what if there were no draft? What if there were no war? What if the army really was about opportunity? In that case, was all the concern about "quality" simply a way to limit the number of blacks in the military, to deny them opportunity?

From the beginnings of the debate about the all-volunteer force, race had played a critical role. A member of the Gates Commission had argued that "emotional language," such as "all-black army," undercut public acceptance of the idea of a volunteer force, and many of the strongest arguments against the AVF hinged on notions of race. Representative Charles

Rangel, a Democrat from New York, argued strongly that a volunteer force would depend most heavily on America's poor, black citizens, that those who had fewest opportunities in the civilian sector would find themselves conscripted, in essence if not in fact, by economic factors. But by 1973, a strong black claim for equal access to the military had emerged. Its most powerful voice was Ron Dellums, a black congressman from northern California who'd been elected on an antiwar platform in 1970. Dellums was a former marine with a master's degree in social work from Berkeley and strong ties to the progressive community in both Berkeley and Oakland. One of just thirteen black members, Dellums was, by the standards of the 92nd Congress, clearly a troublemaker. He set up a "war crimes" display in the annex to his congressional office, large posters of American atrocities in Vietnam splashed with sprays of red paint to emphasize his point. In April 1971 he began a series of hearings on American war crimes, which remained unofficial because the House of Representatives refused to endorse them. He joined with the other black members of Congress, including Shirley Chisholm and Rangel, to form the activist Congressional Black Caucus. Dellums quickly won a spot on President Nixon's enemies list.[42]

Dellums's actions had not been calculated to win the hearts of the Vietnam-era military, but he did take military issues seriously. The Black Congressional Caucus, in one of its first actions, investigated charges of racism in the military. Dellums boldly asked the questions about quality and race. As a member of both the Black Caucus and the Armed Services committee, he was someone who could not be ignored.

Questions began with the marines. On October 11, 1973, Congressman Dellums wrote the deputy assistant secretary of defense for equal opportunity to ask about stories that the Marine Corps was using racial quotas in recruiting. The stories were, in fact, true. The Marine Corps, trying to limit the number of black Category IV recruits, had instructed recruiters that minorities could account for no more than 15 percent of Category IV accessions each year. The 15 percent figure was roughly equivalent to the percentage of minorities in the national population, though not necessarily to the proportion of minority males in the prime recruiting age group. But most who paid attention to issues of race and representation still assumed, in 1973, that "minority" was just another word for black.[43]

The Department of Defense overturned Marine Corps policy immediately. Race-based limits were not going to fly. So the marines tried something different. This time they set limits on both white and minority recruits: no more than 10 percent of minority accessions and no more than 10 percent of white accessions could be drawn from mental category IV. The General Counsel, condemning racial quotas even when applied similarly to whites and minorities, deemed that plan "unconstitutional" even though the fundamental Supreme Court decision outlawing racial quotas was still a few years in the future.[44] Meanwhile, it was early February of 1974 and no one had answered Dellums's letter.

The (civilian) office of the secretary of defense (OSD) and the Marine Corp officials charged with managing this issue defined it very differently, and their conflict went to the heart of the struggle over race, quality, and access. Dellums, in writing to the office of equal opportunity, implicitly defined military service as an opportunity, as a source of employment and training, as an American institution whose advantages blacks were quite possibly being denied. And the DoD's equal-opportunity officers worked from the same set of assumptions, adopting a language of opportunity and the logic of the job market. Their "proposed reply" to Dellums explained in fairly impenetrable bureaucratese that the Marine Corps had grown concerned that blacks made up such a large percentage of Category IV recruits (43 percent in the 1973 fiscal year). This "maldistribution" was creating a low-skilled "occupational ghetto" for black marines. The Marine Corps—with methods all now understood were problematic—had believed it might help equalize black representation in more attractive "hard skill" and technical positions by limiting the percentage of minority Category IV recruits. The quotas had been well-intentioned, the letter made clear, motivated by desire to improve the opportunities the Marine Corps offered black Americans. That goal had not changed, though methods had: the marines were now trying a "computer based mathematical methodology" to optimize "fair-share proportionate distribution" without use of racial quotas.[45]

The Marine Corps did not take well to this reply's muddled language, to its apologetic tone, or to the notion that the Marine Corps was a job-and-training program. The Marine Corps fought wars, and it took heavy casualties. The author of the marines' "cannot concur" response to the OSD noted somewhat caustically that the Corps was not acting out of concern about the quality of blacks' job training. The Corps was concerned that Marine rifle companies were so heavily black. This "occupational ghetto," he pointed out in borrowed OSD language, made it absolutely certain "that if combat occurred, a highly disproportionate ratio of blacks would be killed."[46]

In early 1974, many Americans would have heard the echoes of "cannon fodder" and "genocide" in that line. More than a few would have remembered black nationalist Stokely Carmichael's charges that by waging war in Vietnam "the [white] man is moving to get rid of black people in the ghettos."[47] In their struggle over the proper answer to Congressman Dellums, the marines and the assistant secretary of defense were arguing over whether the military should be seen as a source of jobs for American youth or treated as the fundamental instrument of national defense. That debate would play a critical and expanding role in the future of the AVF. But at that precise moment in American history, the issue of race was more raw and more powerful.

Black Americans felt its immediacy. In early 1974 the Civil Rights Act, born of blood and sacrifice, was less than a decade old. The assassination of Martin Luther King Jr. was a recent memory. Few blacks in America had been spared the consequences of white racism, the threats of violence, the stifled opportunities, the force of rage that had spilled on the streets of America's cities. Young black men, in the early 1970s, had not come of age in the struggle for integration, with its emphasis on respectability, nonviolence, and Christian forbearance. Their political consciousness had been forged in the rising tide of black separatism and cultural nationalism, shaped by an ideological insistence on symbolic forms of black identity and self-respect that did not sit easily with white institutional authority.

Many white Americans, even those who understood its sources, feared black anger. Even more, as the Black Panthers understood clearly, they feared the thought of black men with guns. In the aftermath of riots in Watts and Detroit and just days before James Earl Ray murdered Martin Luther King and despair turned to rage in the streets of cities all across the nation, the establishmentarian liberal *New York Times* had run a long magazine piece by New Left author Sol Stern, of *Ramparts* magazine, on the "potential threat" posed by the black veterans of the Vietnam War. Returning from Vietnam to a world that ignored their sacrifices and offered them few opportunities, to a world in which the racial divide had grown even broader and undeniably uglier, Stern wrote in March 1968, black veterans might well grow bitter. "Militant black ghetto organizers" already saw, in these men, a powerful resource. "They have been trained to kill," explained organizer Carlos Russell. "If rebellions break out and they see their black brothers and sisters slaughtered by racist cops they will come to the defense of their own. They offer a good resource of skills and technical know-how to those in the movement who feel the only solution is armed struggle."[48]

Whitney Young, executive director of the Urban League, feared that same possibility. "Disillusioned and hostile" black veterans, Young wrote, are "full of fresh memories of an environment where life was cheap and where the order of the day was kill or be killed. It would . . . be realistic to expect such experts of mines and booby traps and other forms of destruction to . . . use these skills and risk their lives against the enemy of personal injustice as they did against the enemy of Communist aggression." Negro veterans, he said, "could make Rap Brown look like Little Lord Fauntleroy."[49]

Policy makers, inside the military and out, believed in this threat. As Stern argued, the current administration, already "jittery" over the racial tinderbox they saw in America's cities, could hardly ignore the possibility that black men might put their military training to use much closer to home. But Stern went further. Black veterans, he was certain, are likely to "move with the tide of militancy and nationalism now rising in the ghetto." But it was black men *in* the military, he claimed, who posed the greatest threat. If America falls into race war, he asked, and the military must keep peace, is it not reasonable to think that the black G.I. will see himself as "black first and soldier second, and turn his gun around"?[50]

Today Stern's rhetoric sounds extreme, at best. But in the late 1960s and early 1970s, within the military, racial violence was very real. The strain showed in Vietnam, though not so much in front-line units. "When you drink out of the same canteen and eat off the same spoon, you get real tight together," one black paratrooper told a reporter. But graffiti in the latrine at Danang Navy headquarters read, "I wouldn't compare a gook to a nigger." And on the day of national mourning for Martin Luther King, someone raised a Confederate flag in front of that same building. In August 1968 a race riot broke out in the Long Binh army detention center outside Saigon. A gang of black prisoners, high on smuggled amphetamines, overpowered their guards and, shouting "kill the chucks," beat a white prisoner to death. Sixty more whites, including the stockade commander, were injured. Black prisoners, according to reports, donned "war paint," turbans, and African-style robes and "beat out jungle sounds on oil drums." The army line, "there's only one color here, and that's olive drab," was increasingly unconvincing.[51]

Race was a problem not only in Vietnam. Racial tensions grew on army installations all over the world. A study ordered by General Westmoreland in 1969 concluded that racial discord was "the greatest morale problem" faced by the army. The *Chicago Daily Defender,* reporting on the study, found it no surprise that "Negroes are losing faith in an army system that allows junior and non-commissioned officers to call them 'stupid black niggers.'" It dismissed the army's claim that "the army . . . has a race problem because our country has a race problem" as disingenuous at best. The army, the *Defender* reminded the generals, "is supposed to be a disciplined body with wide jurisdiction over the lives and behavior of those who serve under its authority." The military had the necessary tools to end racist behavior, if only its leadership would use them.[52]

Ebony magazine examined the army's struggles over race in a long article in early 1974, exactly the same time that the marines and the OSD were attempting to frame their reply to Congressman Dellums about Category IV black accessions. "Bloody clashes" between black and white troops in West Germany in 1971 had "sent shock waves through the remotest corners of the Pentagon," *Ebony* reported. The Department of Defense had investigated, as had the NAACP and all thirteen members of the new Black Congressional Caucus. *Ebony*'s story of the "Battle the Army Can't Afford to Lose" chronicled subsequent army efforts "to defuse the most explosive internal crisis to confront the U.S. Army in its entire history," to prevent "a black mass-mutiny and a second 'Battle of the Rhine,' only this time between black and white Americans," and to repair the "racial polarization that had threatened the services' virtual disintegration as a combat-ready fighting force." In its own investigation, *Ebony* found much to praise—most particularly the efforts of Major General Frederic E. Davidson, the first black man to command an army division, who had begun a major equal-opportunity initiative. And *Ebony* generally approved of the army's Race Relations School (RRS), which had been established in September 1972 to train volunteers who returned to their units and helped provide the eighteen hours of race relations education now mandated for all members of the U.S. military. Musing on the "strange bedfellows" created by the RRS course, the author described "a white discussion leader lectur[ing] enthusiastically, though with an unmistakably

Deep South twang, to a mixed class of blacks, whites, Puerto Ricans and Orientals on the evils of slavery and the heroic deeds of black historical figures such as Frederick Douglass and slave revolt leader Nat Turner."[53]

But *Ebony* also found trouble in the new army. The officer charged with enforcing equal opportunity in the U.S. Army, Europe (USAREUR), in words that must have haunted him for the rest of his life, explained to the article's author that one of the main reasons for racial tension in Germany was that "he (the black soldier) can't just blend into downtown Heidelberg as *our* (meaning white) soldiers can because of his skin color. He has more difficulty making the acquaintance of reputable German girls than *American* (brief pause) than the white soldier does." Not all the trouble, this bourgeois black publication concluded gingerly, was with the deeply rooted racism of white Americans—or with what it described as the growing racism of Germans. Profiling Pfc. Donald Washington, a 20-year-old black man from Mississippi, the *Ebony* author offers Washington's response to his question about the army: a "contemptuously slurred 'sh . . . . t.'" Washington had joined the army because he couldn't find a job and was "tired of hanging out on the block." This "thoroughly alienated high school drop-out" had no interest in any of the army's "numerous educational activities" or "vast education programs." He'd caused his share of trouble, including one encounter with the military justice system for getting into a fight with a "jive Oreo . . . sergeant" (which *Ebony* felt necessary to define as "black on the outside, white on the inside") who had ordered him not to give the black power salute while in ranks. Men like Washington, *Ebony* made clear, did the cause of black soldiers no good.[54]

But other black Americans, including Congressman Augustus F. Hawkins, a Democrat from California and a member of the Black Congressional Caucus, saw acts such as Washington's as "legitimate protest against adverse military activities." White officers were all too quick, Hawkins argued, to treat Afro hair styles, black power handshakes, black power arm bands, and the like as evidence of conspiracy against the military rather than as legitimate expressions of black identity.[55] Certainly many black soldiers saw it that way, especially after all the army advertisements claiming that the army would not ask them to sacrifice their individuality. Army officials, in the early 1970s, struggled mightily not only with the outward manifestations of white racism, but also with questions such as how large the circumference of an Afro might legitimately grow, and whether black power salutes necessarily interfered with military discipline.

This was the world Secretary of the Army Bo Callaway had to manage. And when it came to race, Callaway was a man with some baggage. As Benjamin Mays pointed out in a *Chicago Defender* column following Callaway's Senate confirmation, as a Georgia congressman Callaway had voted against federal civil rights legislation. During the Georgia governor's race, while he had privately made commitments to Georgia's Negro leaders, he had not had the courage to publicly seek black support. Now, however, Callaway had publicly admitted the existence of racial discrimination in the army. And he had declared, flatly, that "it has absolutely got to quit." As a southerner, Mays noted, Callaway would be under special scrutiny when it came to race, but it was clear in this column that he was giving Callaway a cautious endorsement. Throughout his time as secretary of the army, the mainstream black press gave Callaway a fair amount of support, especially given the manifest suspicion of the age. "Blacks Get 'Square Deal' in Army, Callaway Avows," read an *Atlanta Daily World* front-page headline in 1974, following Callaway's visit to the *World* newsroom to meet with the paper's top managers and reporters. This voice of Atlanta's black middle-class and elite community found Callaway's message persuasive. "No good person," it quoted Callaway, "is going to be kept out of the army because of his race." Though Callaway insisted there would be no racial quotas that would keep qualified blacks from learning one of the more than 300 "trades" the army offered, he also told the *World* that the army needed "better recruitment of your whites to become military people."[56]

It was called, in retrospect, the "Callaway shift": moving recruiters from the relatively easy territory of urban ghettos, where employment opportunities were few, to the more difficult terrain of middle-class white suburbs and small towns. Callaway was trying to keep the race numbers somewhat in line with the population—to achieve a "representative Army," as he described it. He worked hard to keep black leaders on board—not simply through his pilgrimages to the black press, but through regular meetings with the Congressional Black Caucus. In his meetings, he stressed army equal-opportunity programs; race-blind notions of quality, opportunity, and training; and efforts to increase the percentage of black officers.[57] For a while, it seemed to work.

But in 1974, 30 percent of the new recruits who joined the army were black. The number set off alarms. Military planners and manpower analysts were convinced that the army was approaching a tipping point—a moment when, no matter what economic inducements or advertising campaigns the army tried, white men would no longer be willing to join what they saw as the low-status "all-black Army." In the first months of 1975, however, the number of black accessions dropped sharply. As jobs became scarcer in the worsening economy, charges surfaced in the black press that the army was using its admissions tests to "weed out" blacks who sought what increasingly seemed employment of last resort. "A disproportionate number of Blacks, according to Black political leaders," reported the *Amsterdam News,* "test in the lowest category" of military admissions tests. Many of these young men, the *News* claimed, might well succeed in the army if given the opportunity. But Category IV recruits were limited to 18 percent overall, and in the first months of 1975 the army had cut back even further, to 6 percent of new accessions. It was not difficult to see a purposeful relationship.[58]

Congressman Dellums pursued the matter with the secretary of the army, submitting what Callaway described as a list of detailed and penetrating questions. And Callaway gave him detail back: enlistment rates that refuted the charges that had appeared in the press; precise figures on the dramatic underrepresentation of blacks in the officer ranks and the parallel over-representation among enlisted men; the percentage of minorities in ROTC programs (24.5 percent) and enrolled at the U.S. Military Academy (9.3 percent); the current minority recruiting advertising budget (rising, from $191,000 to $223,941 that year); and the exact distribution of blacks in different "career management fields" as of the end of fiscal year 1974. Callaway's data demonstrated the impact of equal opportunity and affirmative action efforts within the officer ranks, with "black advantage" over whites in selection averaging around 150 percent, and pledged the army's "continuous good faith" in assuring minority opportunity.[59] (As was typical of the time, Callaway used the terms "black" and "minority" interchangeably, and it is not clear whether the statistics on minority representation actually include all nonwhites or only African Americans.)

The secretary of the army was markedly direct and uncompromising on two key points. "I am sure you are aware," Callaway wrote Dellums, "of the considerable concern by black organizations of the minority casualty problem" in the Vietnam War. If combat units have a high percentage of black soldiers, black soldiers will sustain a high level of casualties. "This is wrong," he wrote with some force, and it is the army's responsibility to prevent any single group of Americans from suffering "the brunt of wartime casualties."[60] The man who volunteers for a peacetime army has no guarantee that peace will remain; the army, thus, can never assume that the question of representation is irrelevant.

Callaway was also adamant about quality. The army did not use "quality" to limit black enlistment. "Nothing could be further from the truth," he wrote. Here, though, marketplace principles appear: "competition for available opportunities in the Army has become keener," Callaway informed Dellums, though in one place he attributed that keenness to the army's new emphasis on quality and in another to the current scarcity of civilian jobs. Then, without comment, Callaway offered a table showing the enormous disparity between "Caucasian" and "minority group" recruits. The bald numbers translated into alarming comparisons. One thousand white volunteers yielded twenty-seven Category I soldiers, whereas 1,000 minority volunteers produced only two soldiers in Category I. The more significant differences, however, were in categories II and IV. White recruits were close to three times as likely to score in Category II than black recruits, whereas black recruits were more than twice as likely as whites to score in Category IV. The army had not kept records—oddly, given how much racial data it had compiled—of volunteer acceptance rates by race. But in fiscal year 1974, 352,933 applicants had taken the army classification test. Failure rates were even more revealing than the mental category distributions—even without percentages to give them context: 24,261 blacks and 17,992 whites had failed.[61]

Callaway had mastered both languages: the Army's traditional language of combat and shared sacrifice, and the marketplace language of the all-volunteer force. In both cases, the weight of his data seemed incontrovertible—unless, like Jimmy Carter's secretary of the army, one rejected such quantitative measures of quality altogether. Clifford Alexander, sworn into this position on Valentine's Day, 1977, was—like Callaway—an activist secretary. His activism, however, had different roots. Alexander was the first black secretary of the army, a man who, at the age of 43, had already forged a distinguished career in public service. Born in Harlem in 1933, he'd been the only black student in most of his classes at the Ethical Culture School and then at the Fieldston School, both of which had awarded him scholarships. He'd gone on to earn degrees from Harvard

(B.A., with honors, '55) and Yale (Law, '58), and had served his six-month stint as a private in the National Guard in 1959. He'd completed brief terms as assistant district attorney for New York County and as executive director of the Harlem Youth Opportunities organization before the Kennedy White House appointed him to the National Security Council. Through the 1960s, Alexander had played important roles in Democratic administrations, moving from his foreign affairs post to serve as a close advisor to President Johnson, who in 1967 appointed him chair of the EEOC—the Equal Employment Opportunities Commission established by Congress in 1964 to enforce the new civil rights legislation. Alexander's vigorous efforts drew the ire of influential Republicans and the new Nixon administration forced his resignation in 1969.[62]

Throughout the years of Republican ascendancy, Alexander maintained his political edge. He joined a prominent Washington law firm; came close to winning the Democratic primary race for mayor of the District of Columbia; taught at Howard University and Georgetown University Law Schools; hosted a weekly television program called "Black and White." The new Democratic administration of Jimmy Carter clearly understood what it was getting when it offered Alexander the position of secretary of the army in 1977. He would be a strong advocate for equal opportunity and his appointment would serve as a clear sign that this administration, headed by a man many still called "the peanut farmer from Georgia," meant to address the problem of race head on. And Alexander clearly had the temperament to do so. Friends and colleagues described him to reporters as "sensitive, mild-mannered, and easygoing," though almost all were quick to confide that he was also "aggressive, highly competitive, and always looks to win."[63]

Alexander, like Callaway, was a cheerleader for the all-volunteer army. But unlike Callaway, who was greatly concerned about questions of quality and the (racial) "representativeness" of combat units, Alexander believed that "quality" was a cover word for racism and that the percentage of black troops in the army was "immaterial." You should be asking, Alexander chastised an interviewer, "why there is almost 40 per cent unemployment among black teen-agers before you ask why they enlist." Alexander saw virtually all opposition to the volunteer army as racist, whether it came in the form of internal questions about the deficiencies of new recruits or in the rising tide of editorial opinion and journalistic analysis that declared a crisis of quality in the army but not in the other branches of the armed forces, all of which had a much smaller proportion of African Americans.[64]

Alexander was irrevocably certain that the army's measurements of quality—an earned high school diploma and an AFQT score in Category III or above—were unnecessary and prejudicial. Dismissing army statistics demonstrating that there was an enormous disparity between high school graduates and dropouts (with high school dropouts, 1,400 volunteers yielded about 940 soldiers at the end of the first six months, whereas 1,000 high school graduates yielded approximately the same), Alexander insisted that what mattered was the ability of an individual to perform his or her assigned task. Army manpower analysts agreed—when it came to individuals. But their repeated attempts to discuss how well these predictive factors worked in aggregate, as the army tried to calculate how many trained soldiers its recruiting efforts would yield, given existing rates of voluntary separations and less-than-honorable discharges, did not interest the secretary of the army.[65]

Alexander had even less use for military testing. He believed that the Armed Services Vocational Aptitude Battery (ASVAB), which was offered to high schools as a free "aptitude test" for graduating seniors, was useful in assigning soldiers to MOSs. But he saw the "mental category" scores, which were based on verbal and mathematical subtests that paralleled the old AFQT and ignored the results of the vocational sections, as irrelevant and prejudicial. Category IV, he informed members of the House Armed Services Committee, was "not a mental category because it is not based on an intelligence test." When one congressman asked him what category he thought a "retarded person" would end up in, Alexander insisted that there was no way to know. Fully confident that such quantitative measurements were pernicious, Alexander had AFQT scores removed from the files of 400,000 soldiers in order to prevent their "abuse."[66]

Manpower experts were well aware of the problems with "mental tests." There was little question that an exam that relied heavily on analogies, general information, and the vocabulary of the educated classes would be subject to cultural bias and reflect the results of educational disparities. Military analysts were, like Alexander, aware that exam results opened doors and, just as decisively, closed them. Offering practical advice, *The Recruiter Journal* warned recruiters not to let prospects go drinking and carousing the night before the exam, for a hangover was particularly deadly in combination with a three-and-a-half-hour test and a bad morning after a long night could easily turn a Category III recruit into a Category IV. Although the army was confident its exam results correlated closely with "trainability" *in aggregate,* on the individual level there would always be those who had bad mornings, and not necessarily through any fault of their own. The results of a single pencil-and-paper test, given the army's new faith in quantitative assessments, could rule out a potentially good soldier or blight a future career. Not everyone was happy with the growing tendency to rely so heavily on quantitative measures rather than "subjective" but "informed" judgments of experienced officers and NCOs.[67]

Through the first decade of the volunteer force, the official line was that the all-volunteer army was a success. But from the beginning, there were rumblings from the field. Congressional fact-finding missions tended to see what they were looking for: complaints for the critics; reassurance for the supporters. The army was good at what Eliot Cohen described as "the art of bureaucratic self-preservation." But the unease was there, and it leaked into the press. NBC's portrayal of "A New Kind of Army" in late 1973 so disturbed the U.S. Military Academy's social science faculty that they launched—with command blessing—their own investigation of the "much-maligned" Category IV volunteers. In 1978, ABC aired its own television special: "The American Army: A Shocking Case of Incompetence." Alarming statistics wove through stories on the all-volunteer army throughout that first decade; "too dumb, too black, too costly" was one of the more compelling pull-out lines. But nothing matched a good anecdote to make the point. *Time* magazine, in a June 1980 cover story, quoted a member of the military police from Fort Benning, Georgia: "'I've had people come up to me and say, 'How do I get back to my unit?' I ask, 'What's your unit?' And then they answer that they don't know. So I ask them what their orders say. They reply, 'I can't read my orders. All I know is that my unit is in a big, white building.'" Falling capability among recruits, *Time* noted, fit poorly with the rising complexity of weaponry. "The modern Black Hawk helicopter," it offered as example, "has 257 knobs and switches, 135 circuit breakers, 62 displays and 11.7 sq. feet of instruments and controls."[68]

Despite the official pronouncements, the army was well aware of the problems it faced. Volunteers were not necessarily more committed or more pro-military than the draftees they replaced. GI "disaffection," by army measures, was rising. According to the *Army Times,* 40 percent of recruits did not complete their enlistments. A 1976 study at Fort Benning found that 53 percent of enlisted men read at *or below* the fifth grade level. In 1979, 41 percent of the army's enlisted ranks were high school dropouts. Category IV recruits remained a problem. An army study conducted during 1977–78 found that it took 50 percent longer to train a Category IV recruit than one from Category III, and the same ratio held true for the amount of training reinforcement required. The army rewrote training manuals, shifting both language and explanation from eleventh to seventh and eighth grade reading levels. Others reappeared in comic book format.[69]

James Fallows, writing in the *Atlantic Monthly* in April 1981, summoned the image of an army in which "such soldiers as do enlist stand befuddled before the space-age machinery they must operate." The mismatch between the skills brought by a high school dropout and the technical abilities required to run and maintain a computerized tank was, Fallows noted, a significant problem. But his concerns were not so much about what the army ever less frequently called "mental categories" and more about class. In 1974, the commander of a basic training company at Fort Ord had described the problem: "A lot of these guys are young kids who never finished anything they started . . . this is just one more place they've drifted to." Of the men he would likely discharge before the end of basic training, he said, "every one of them was just knocking around, living off the land, and a couple of them were literally hungry the day they enlisted. They wanted a meal, a roof, a shirt on their backs . . . I'd say there's a whole generation out there right now, the new drifters, almost like the bums during the Depression, except they're younger, they've got long hair. But they're just as uneducated, just as broke, just as hungry." Two years later the commander at Fort Dix explained: "We've always had recruits from all walks of life, but since the draft ended, the percentages have changed dramatically. The majority today haven't enjoyed the leadership at home that more privileged youths receive."[70]

In 1981, Fallows offered a more positive portrait. "Taken one by one," he wrote, "most of the soldiers in the volunteer force command an outsider's respect." The issue is not the failings of the individual soldier, but a failure of balance. "While the soldiers individually may be tough, humorous, appealing, as a group they clearly come from outside the mainstream of American life." Quoting a Marine Corps major on the military in general, Fallows made his point: "you can . . . feel the change in social class. There used to be a general expectation that people would conform to middle-class values in the military . . . the balance has shifted to those who come from areas without discipline, and there's not the implied standard for them to conform to." Here Fallows turned to the work of military sociologist Charles Moskos, whose analysis of the army's shift from "institution" to "occupation" clearly informed Fallows's discussion of the "civilianization of the Army" and the conversion of its "operating principles to those of the workaday world." The mixture of middle-class men in the draft army, Moskos explained, had had "a modulating effect." They made it easier to socialize recruits in the beginning; they made it easier "to sustain discipline." And while many discussions—both in the army and in the press—of the cultural conflict between volunteers' origins and the discipline of basic training were very much centered on race and notions of black cultural identity, Moskos made clear that it was white recruits who presented the greatest challenge. Black recruits were significantly more likely to have high school diplomas than were whites, more likely to come from at least the lower ranks of the middle class. White volunteers, in the late 1970s, came overwhelmingly from the least educated portion of the white population.[71]

Some critics assigned much of the fault to the army itself—though, in part, this was a criticism of the turn to the market. "First of all, you have to look at the advertisements that have been put out for the military," fumed Representative Robin Beard, whose office had produced a highly critical report on the all-volunteer force. "'See Europe through the Army's eyes; get a college education; 30 days paid vacation; free medical care; learn a trade.' It looks like a General Motors ad." Recruiters, he continued, are under enormous pressure to make their quotas, and it's not surprising that while they're selling the "free medical and free college and this type thing, they may forget to mention, 'By the way, you might be out in the middle of the field some night in 20° weather with ice and snow all around.'" No wonder, Beard said, that up to 40 percent of recruits aren't finishing their first term. The concerns of the information officer at Fort Ord were more specific. "How do you teach a guy to fight, to be a goddamn soldier, when the whole emphasis now is on learning a specialized trade? . . . The Army advertisements claim, 'We can teach you this, we can teach you that.' But what we've really got to teach these guys is how to kill somebody."[72]

The army fairly quickly registered the anger that resulted from betrayed expectations. It revised its system to allow recruiters to really guarantee school assignments for qualified candidates. And recruiters were officially advised to "tell it like it is." The army, explained the recruiting *Journal,* using one of its odder similes, is "like a great green pickle: a fine item but not without a wart or two." If you paint too "rosy" a picture, it warned, you're likely to make an enemy, and one who won't be shy about telling all his friends and neighbors that army recruiters are not to be trusted. Army advertising, its message shifting wildly through the 1970s, followed a moving market and changing targets. By 1978, struggling to compete with the navy and air force, army advertisements ("Join the People Who've Joined the Army") emphasized army benefits, travel, education. The Beard Study's charges that potential recruits were badly misled both by recruiters and by advertising prompted a quick shift in direction. Demonstrating just how distant World War II's "This is the Army, Mr. Jones" now seemed, Ayer offered a new theme in 1979. "This is the Army" gave potential recruits the inside story on basic training. Thirty days paid vacation in Europe disappeared, replaced by "In Europe You're on Duty 24 Hours a Day, but the Rest of the Time is Your Own." Making recruiters' job even more challenging, Congress had recently cut funding for advertising by 36 percent servicewide and reduced the number of army recruiters by 400. Sometimes, for the army recruiting command, Congress seemed as much a moving target as the average American 18-year-old.[73]

No matter the explanation given or the efforts at change, the army was having trouble with its recruits—disaffection, attrition, lack of motivation, and difficulty in training. AWOL and desertion rates were climbing. Drug use was common; alcohol abuse more so. Sixteen thousand soldiers were in alcohol abuse rehabilitation programs in 1979, 24,000 in 1980. Crime was rampant: the number of soldiers in army prisons jumped 47 percent between 1978 and 1980. At the same time, quantitative data showed steadily rising AFQT scores. The percentage of Category IV recruits was down—dramatically. Back in 1969, under the draft, 24 percent of the army had been Category IV. Rates in 1977, the *New York Times* reported (possibly conflating army with militarywide statistics), were 6 to 8 percent.[74] According to all previous research, there should have been a close correlation between high percentages of "quality" recruits and success. Here the opposite seemed true, and no one could figure out why.

Senator Sam Nunn of Georgia, who had emerged as the most thoughtful congressional critic of the AVF during the late 1970s, offered the answer to the army's dilemma—with much fanfare—in a hearing before the Senate's Subcommittee on Manpower and Personnel. In recent years, Nunn claimed, there had been a steady stream of complaints from NCOs and officers about the quality of new recruits. But just as consistently the Department of Defense had insisted that the quality of volunteers was steadily rising. Even President Carter had weighed in, noting, in 1978, that "assessments of performance that are done on a scientific and objective and accurate basis show that we do have a very high level of quality in our armed services." How to make sense of the conflict between the "scientific and objective and accurate" data and the perceptions of experienced NCOs? Nunn squared the circle with "a most serious revelation": the scientific data were wrong.[75]

The most recent version of the military entrance exam, introduced in 1976, had not been properly calibrated against scores on earlier versions of the exam. The misnorming had affected low scores most dramatically, and although statisticians were still struggling with the data, it was clear that there were a great many more Category IV recruits in the army than there should have been, men Nunn described as falling between the 10th and 30th percentile of the population in mental ability. It was quite possible, Nunn continued, that men from Category V, the "borderline intelligent" and "mentally deficient" who were supposed to be excluded from military service by law, had filled out the ranks of America's armed forces.[76]

The response of the Department of Defense was masterful. Quality, explained Mr. Robert Pirie, the assistant secretary of defense for manpower and reserve affairs, to members of Congress, is difficult both to assess and to predict. "The quality of an individual's performance is the product of individual traits—honesty, integrity, skill, loyalty, commitment, and motivation." (Note what is missing from that description.) "It will also be," he continued, "a product of situational variables—the work environment, unit esprit, training and leadership." He confided to the senators that he could not measure quality with certainty, and suggested that the Department of Defense had all along been "skeptical and concerned about the accuracy and interpretation of the results of our aptitude measure—the Armed Forces Qualification Test (AFQT)." Pirie then offered a respectfully complex explanation of all the ways that Senator Nunn had misunderstood the meaning of the test results, which were measured against the population of men under arms in the United States during

World War II, not against the general U.S. population or the current population of American youth.[77]

The battle was engaged over scientific data versus the informed evaluation of the officers and NCOs, but no one was quite ready to take science's side. When Nunn questioned representatives from the Department of Defense—prompting one to "stipulate for the record, Senator, that the capacity of Army tank gunners is not anything like yours for sustained force"—he suggested that data about quality were much more simply had. "When all else fails," Nunn said, "I suggest you have a conversation with a group of sergeants and chief petty officers." In the House of Representatives, John Murtha made the same point about scientific data, though to a different end. The commanders in the field praised their troops, Murtha informed Mr. Pirie, so "I think you would take the word of a commander over a test score, which you keep changing around all the time." All this talk about test scores served only to "degrade the services," Murtha complained, for the record. "It's the same old story. If the people who are against the strong defense don't have the ammunition, you guys give it to them. You figure out a way to come up with a score that is headlines and makes the service look bad." In fact, "Shy" Meyer, the current chief of staff of the army, had praised troop quality both in public writings and in official army speeches. But during a meeting with President Carter at Camp David in December 1979, he had warned the president that quality was declining. Untrainable and undisciplined recruits were a present problem, he cautioned, but they were also a threat to the army's future. It was privates, after all, that rose through the ranks to become non-commissioned officers.[78]

In spite of the congressional rhetoric about the superiority of command judgment to scientific evaluation, nobody was really planning to go back to nineteenth-century forms of assessment. Scores were recalculated, and they were worse than anyone had thought. In fiscal year 1980, half of all army recruits scored in Category IV. Not 6 percent. Not 8 percent. Fifty percent. Congress stepped in with statutory restrictions: the only Category IV enlistees now acceptable were those with high school diplomas. The Pentagon spent 3.5 million dollars over two years, evaluating and renorming the tests. The results? The military, according to the Pentagon, was getting "more than our fair share of the above-average people." Based on a comparison of 1980 military recruits with a national sample of Americans between the ages of 16 and 23, tested the same year, the median score for the military was 52 out of 100, compared to a civilian median of 51. These numbers, of course, included all the services, bolstered by the generally higher scores of air force recruits. The army median would have been lower than the median for the military as a whole.[79]

More complicated was the breakdown by race and ethnicity. Whites in the civilian group scored a median of 59, compared to a white military median score of 58. No significant difference there. But for blacks, the civilian median of 17 fell far short of the military median of 33. And for Hispanics (now listed separately), the score spread was similar: military median of 41; civilian median of 23. The Department of Defense wasn't at all sure what to do with that information, and consulted with the NAACP and the Mexican-American Legal Defense and Educational Fund before releasing it. In many ways, this data lent credence to what analysts had been saying all along: that the army was recruiting "the cream of the lower middle-class blacks." These young people scored significantly higher than their civilian peers and were significantly more likely than white volunteers to have earned a high school diploma. Cross-race comparisons of scores, however, suggested a less positive story. The large gap between the median scores for whites and those for blacks and Hispanics made conversations about "quality" much more difficult to have, and raised yet more questions about the usefulness of such "scientific" measures.[80]

In the summer of 1980, however, Senator Nunn was more than willing to push the issue of military quality. It had been a very bad year, internationally, and his ongoing concern about the all-volunteer force took on new weight as questions of combat readiness seemed more urgent. On November 4, 1979, Iranian protesters had overrun the U.S. Embassy in Tehran, taking its American personnel hostage. With yellow ribbons of remembrance tied around trees in front yards throughout America and the new show, *Nightline,* chronicling each day of the ongoing "crisis," a sense of anger and impotence inflamed the public. A military rescue attempt had failed, dramatically and publicly, the following April, leaving eight U.S. servicemen dead. And the Cold War was escalating again, detente seeming an ever more distant dream. The Soviet Union had invaded Afghanistan on Christmas Eve 1979, and neither United Nations pressure nor President Carter's threat to boycott the Moscow Olympics had any effect on Soviet resolve.

In the midst of international turmoil, with the clear possibility of military action, stories of a military in crisis had new significance. Ninety percent of nuclear weapons maintenance specialists, America's free press reported to an interested world, had failed their qualification tests in 1978. The same was true for 82 percent of Hawk surface-to-air missile crews and 89 percent of track vehicle mechanics. One study found that 17 percent of tank commanders in Europe "didn't know where to aim when employing battlefield gunnery techniques." The army band, one publication noted, was one of the few specialties in which scores were consistently good. In the meantime, the army lowered passing level for its skills qualification tests (SQTs) from 80 to 60 percent and the DoD's Mr. Pirie once again downplayed quantitative evidence, asking a concerned member of the House subcommittee: "What do these SQT scores really tell us?"[81]

Senator Nunn called a news conference on Capitol Hill to level a charge that army leaders were engaged in "a campaign of deception" to hide the deteriorating quality of U.S. troops. "Have these leaders forgotten why we maintain our armed forces?" Nunn asked, with some vehemence. "Our Army is not an armed WPA and we must not permit it to become a jobs corps equipped with tanks and nuclear missiles." Nunn said not a word about race—but the leap was there for others to make. "Army Secretary Alexander Under Attack By Nunn," proclaimed the black-focused *Atlanta Daily World* to readers already well aware of the racial subtext of the quality debate. Is all this concern really about "fear of the Russians," *Black Enterprise* asked, or is it instead "fear of giving blacks good opportunities in American society"?[82]

The American debate, with all its racial overtones and shadows, didn't stop at the U.S. border. Allies and enemies followed it carefully; public discussion of an army in crisis played a role in both international negotiations and national decisions. In his 1980 presidential campaign against the embattled Jimmy Carter, Ronald Reagan promised a stronger U.S. military and a broader American presence in a dangerous world. Shortly after Reagan's landslide election, Moshe Dayan, the former defense minister of Israel, demonstrated the international impact of the quality debate in words of startling racial insensitivity. More U.S. troops in the Middle East would be welcome, he said, but he had serious concerns about the quality of the American military. The U.S. Army, he informed Israeli television viewers, "is composed only of volunteers, of those who have to make a living out of the army's payment. Therefore, up to the rank of sergeants, most of the soldiers are Black who have a lower education and intelligence." Perhaps the United States should return to the draft, he suggested, for the U.S. Army "should be getting better blood and brains." European allies, it turns out, were making much the same point—though more quietly and with greater care. In 1982 a top official in the Defense Department—speaking off the record—acknowledged that NATO leaders had expressed concern about the army's combat readiness and asked the Pentagon to limit the number of black troops deployed overseas. The Pentagon, he said, had denied the request.[83]

★

As American society tried to come to terms with changes fostered by the social movements of the 1960s and early 1970s, the army struggled over the role of race in an all-volunteer force. Debates about the viability of the AVF were, from the beginning, deeply embedded in American beliefs about race. The issue of race—the legacy of racial discrimination and the continuing fact of social inequality, in particular—vastly complicated discussions about military efficiency. Racial sensitivities, angers, and prejudices made it more difficult to address the issue of quality. The fundamental tension between notions of military service as opportunity and as exploitation almost always circled back to race. But even though the issue of race muddied and complicated debates about the AVF, there was a more fundamental problem. By the end of the 1970s many doubted the AVF would survive. The transition to the market had not been easy. Volunteers were scarcer than the Gates Commission had imagined. Quality safeguards had failed. And many recruits who had seen the army as an employer of last resort carried serious behavior problems with them from civilian to military life. Those who trained and commanded the troops were all too aware of the all-volunteer army's failings, and so were many of those who watched carefully from abroad.

In the spring of 1980, with Americans held hostage in Tehran, escalating unrest in Africa, and Russians in Afghanistan, President Carter asked Congress to reinstate registration for the draft. It was a sensible move. Virtually no one, even among the strongest supporters of a volunteer force, imagined that the nation would go to war without reactivating conscription. No one expected to fight a war with a volunteer force. In a moment of multifront crisis, having a system in place was only prudent. But in 1980, the crisis was not only international. At home, the military faced problems of quality, of numbers, of racial anger, and of mistrust. Carter's move to reinstitute draft registration was meant to demonstrate American resolve to the restive Soviet empire. But many saw it as something more: an admission that the all-volunteer force had failed.

5 ★ "IF YOU LIKE MS., YOU'LL LOVE PVT."

ON JANUARY 23, 1980, a visibly exhausted president stood before the joint houses of Congress and before the nation, summoning resolve to deliver a State of the Union address that offered little in the way of consolation or reassurance to a beleaguered people. Gone was Jimmy Carter's trademark and much-caricatured smile, nowhere in evidence the self-confidence that had propelled him—to the horror of his Secret Service detail—to abandon his limousine and stroll down Pennsylvania Avenue hand-in-hand with his wife and advisor Rosalynn and their nine-year-old daughter Amy during his inaugural parade three long years before.

"This last few months," Carter began, "has not been an easy time for any of us. As we meet tonight, it has never been more clear that the state of our Union depends on the state of the world." The decade had begun in turmoil and strife, Carter told an audience that knew that all too well. "At this time in Iran, 50 Americans are still held captive, innocent victims of terrorism and anarchy. Also at this moment, massive Soviet troops are attempting to subjugate the fiercely independent and deeply religious people of Afghanistan. These two acts—one of international terrorism and one of military aggression—present a serious challenge to the United States of America and indeed to all the nations of the world."

There were few words of inspiration in this speech, despite Carter's call upon "a bright vision of the America we want," an America "strong and free," an America "at peace," an America of "tolerance and justice and compassion," an America with equal rights for women, "guaranteed in the Constitution." What he instead offered the nation as it faced a new and dangerous world was the certainty that, in words Carter attributed to Walter Lippmann, "You took the good things for granted. Now you must earn them again . . . There is nothing for nothing any longer." It was in this framework, in a call to sacrifice that was not inspirational but resigned, that Carter announced plans to reinstate registration for the draft. Television cameras cut to a triumphant Sam Nunn, who had built his Senate career on criticism of the all-volunteer force.[1]

Carter's promise to reinstitute selective service registration—even with his firmly expressed "hope" that there would be no need for a draft—set off a few protests on college campuses, prompted some talk about slippery slopes and excessive government power. But selective service registration wasn't the whole story. The president could not paint a "bright vision" of America's future that included the Equal Rights Amendment (ERA)—and that was what Carter meant by the constitutional protection of women's rights—and at the same time plan to restrict selective service registration to men. Writers for *Newsweek* pointed out the silence, reporting that Carter was expected to decide the woman question by February 9th. "One clue," *Newsweek* added. "Rosalynn Carter favors registration for women as well as men."[2]

Just over two weeks after his State of the Union address, the president boarded his helicopter for Camp David, leaving White House aides to release a written statement to the press. As a means to preserve the peace, it declared, President Carter was asking Congress for authority to register young men. He was also requesting the authority to register women—for "non-combat service." The decision to include women, the statement continued, "is a recognition of the reality that both women and men are working members of our society." Women do all sorts of work in contemporary America, and they do it well. Large numbers of women currently serve in the armed forces, and they also do it well. "There is no distinction possible," Carter concluded, "on the basis of ability or performance, that would allow me to exclude women from an obligation to register."[3]

Carter knew his proposal would run into trouble. At this moment he was more intent on sending a message to the Soviets than on defending the principle of gender equity, so he submitted two proposals to Congress: one for registration of men and women, one for registration of men only. It rapidly became clear that Carter's proposal to register women would not make it to a vote on the floor of Congress. The House Armed Services Military Personnel Subcommittee, which had the power to bury proposed legislation, called a member of the Eagle Forum of Haleyville, Alabama as its first witness. The Eagle Forum was, in essence, Phyllis Schlafly; in 1975 she had expanded her STOP ERA base into a broader grassroots political organization that offered members tactical coaching and training in conservative practical politics. Mrs. Eidson, who had no expertise in the military but who did have a teenage daughter, told the assembled congressional representatives, in scripted words: "The Liberated women do not speak for me; nor do they speak for the majority of Americans. I may once have been one of the 'silent majority,' but no more. We've had enough. This, I will not stand for, nor will the American people stand for it. You cannot draft our women." When the sole female member of the committee congratulated the witness for expressing her own views better than she could herself, Mrs. Eidson allowed that "If I didn't feel so violent about it I wouldn't have come. You couldn't drag me."[4]

One member ventured criticism; he had two daughters in the military and could not agree with Eidson's statement that women did not belong there. "Sir," replied Mrs. Eidson, "I am not saying military [sic] is not for every American woman. I am saying it is not for the majority. It would take my daughter—and I am thinking of her closer friends—2 days in basic training before I know there would be total havoc in that camp. I can see her saying, 'Oh, you have got mud on my pants. I can't fix my hair.' This is the type of girls they are." Most women, Eidson claimed, did not wish to join the military and that choice was their prerogative. A witness from the Coalition Against Drafting Women, testifying on behalf of Phyllis Schlafly, who was home sick with the flu, put it this way: "our young women have a constitutional right to be treated like American ladies." Carter's new director of Selective Service, Bernard Rostker, noted somewhat wryly, "I am sure that the men who are drafted don't necessarily want to be there" either, but it made no difference. Nor did the mountain of data offered by the National Organization for Women on womanpower and military effectiveness, or NOW's claim that such efforts to "protect" women ultimately deprive them of "the right to first-class citizenship." In the end, the committee voted 8 to 1 to table the bill. Mr. Won Pat, of Guam—proud father of two servicewomen—stood alone.[5]

The short-lived debate over women's registration was conducted in much the same language as the larger debate over women's role in the all-volunteer force. The differences between the two are obvious: voluntary service is not the same thing as military obligation. But the conflation does make some sense. During the 1970s major legal and judicial challenges, along with social changes, had begun to normalize women's roles in the AVF. Although some argued that the growing number of women undermined national defense, a much larger number argued that women played critically important roles in the modern volunteer military. Why should that be true only in times of peace? If war pushed the nation to draft its citizens, they asked, why would the nation not require the service of women as well as of men?

Whether women were the salvation or the potential downfall of the all-volunteer force—and both were claimed—their numbers grew rapidly throughout the 1970s. In 1971, women made up 1.3 percent of the armed forces' enlisted ranks; by 1979, women accounted for 7.6 percent of military troops. The shift in the army was greater yet: from 1.2 to 8.4 percent.[6] In some ways this shift simply mirrored the changes taking place in American society during those years, as women made up a larger part of the paid workforce, as fewer families survived on the single wage of a male breadwinner, as the average age at marriage rose, as expectations about what women could do—and should do—underwent seismic change. And in many ways, the expanded use of women in the military was a byproduct of the move to the market, the shift from the powerful cultural traditions of military service to the structural imperatives of labor-market competition.

The nation's reaction to this dramatic shift in women's roles and representation in the military was complicated. Sometimes it went unremarked. Women rarely appeared in the key debates over the creation and development of the AVF. As Americans engaged the difficult questions surrounding the move to an all-volunteer force, arguing over notions of citizenship and obligation, over the nature of military service, permissiveness and professionalism, over questions of quality and military ability, over race and representation, over the balance between opportunity and the need for a strong national defense, they almost always assumed they were talking about men. "Women in the military" was a discrete category of conversation and concern. Even though the increasing presence of women in the armed forces sometimes complicated these debates over the AVF and its future, public discussions were more likely to frame the role of women as one of the problems. "This Man's Army," the regular army had long proclaimed itself, and that was a powerful construct.

Women's expanding role in the military grew more—not less—controversial as the decade progressed. The Equal Rights Amendment had sailed through Congress at the beginning of the 1970s, supported by Democrats and Republicans alike. The U.S. military and the Department of Defense took the ERA seriously. Various working groups began analyzing—and modifying—existing military policy and practice in full expectation that the ERA would be ratified by the states. Virtually no one in the early 1970s anticipated the strength of the backlash that was coming, the ways that issues of gender and sexuality would unite conservatives and give them a political voice. For although the 1970s may have given America "the year of the woman," they also produced the countervailing forces of STOP ERA, the Eagle Forum, the Coalition for Decency, and the Moral Majority. And even the opportunities offered by the ERA, it turned out, would have paradoxical results. The pending constitutional amendment opened doors for women in the military during the 1970s. But as the military insisted—publicly—that women now played a vital role in the nation's armed forces, it gave opponents of women's equality their most potent weapon: an image of women—America's wives and daughters—drafted and dehumanized, sent into combat, brutalized, maimed, raped, and killed.

Debates about women's proper role in the military were shaped by debates about women's proper roles in American society. And what's most striking, in retrospect, is how ugly these debates were, how quickly sexism and misogyny came to the surface. Race provides a useful comparison. Few would argue that racism had been vanquished from America in the 1970s. But racist claims and explanations were no longer accepted in mainstream discourse; racist stereotypes were anathema. Congress, when considering bills focused on black Americans and issues of race, did not bring in average white citizens to testify that "their Negroes" were just like children, or psychiatrists to discourse on the inherent nature of black people. The military and the press *always* gave racial discrepancies in "mental test" scores their social context. No matter what people may have said in private, no one publicly argued that black Americans were simply mentally inferior.

None of this was true when it came to women (and in discussions of women race was rarely mentioned, even though African Americans made up more than a quarter of army women by 1978). In the halls of Congress and the pages of the press, the careful cases put forth by liberal feminist lawyers and equal opportunity officers were countered by "experts" on God's plan for humanity and women's inherent nature. In 1976, the year after Congress opened the nation's military academies to women, General William Westmoreland—now retired and so able to speak his mind—told the *Washington Post:* "Maybe you could find one woman in 10,000 who could lead in combat, but she would be a freak and we're not running the military academy for freaks."[7]

The army struggled mightily over women's proper place in the new all-volunteer force. Most of what appeared on paper was in tune with directives about equal opportunity and the expansion of women's roles, but there was no unanimity, especially when it came to women in nontraditional fields. And resistance did not come solely from poorly educated male privates and the stereotypical crusty old sergeants who couldn't make peace with the world as it was. The leaders of the Women's Army Corps (WAC), which was a separate branch of the army until 1978, had grave concerns about the changing roles of women soldiers. And the army, as an institution, had serious questions about women in combat. Some were based in cultural assumptions and prejudices, some centered around differences in the average physical capacities of men and women, and some looked to the unknown impact women would have on unit effectiveness and morale.

But both civilian and military leadership understood that no matter how many times the words "non-combat roles" appeared in discussions of women in the military, it often just wasn't that simple. The line between combat and noncombat was not as clear as it appeared on paper, especially in the wars the army expected to fight. And finally, there were significant logistical concerns. The army was a massive personnel management system. Decisions about the appropriate number of women in the army and the roles they could play had consequences for everything from the initial military occupation specialties (MOS) of accessions to the percentage of promotions by gender to the design of equipment and the provision of uniforms. None of these things could be changed overnight; it often took years to properly implement policy changes mandated under civilian control. And Congress, caught in the turbulent politics of the decade, was spinning like a leaf in the wind.

The move to an all-volunteer force jumpstarted a gender revolution in the military. The rapid expansion of both women and their roles within the army would not have been possible without change in the larger society, of course, for the demands of the labor market do not automatically override strongly held cultural norms. But the imposition of free-market models and the powerful social changes of the 1970s were not the only forces shaping the army's approach to women in the AVF. Women had a history in the army, albeit a brief one. And that history was—to borrow a policy term—not "gender-neutral." Women's participation in the U.S. Armed Forces, from the beginning, was built around understandings of appropriate gender roles. The distinction was simple: men fought; women didn't. Before the twentieth century, even as large-scale warfare grew more logistically complex, armies were mainly composed of combat troops. In America's wars, women "camp followers" joined civilian nurses to support and care for the troops—cooking, sewing, washing, and tending to the various needs of men under arms. But as the nature of warfare changed, waging war relied increasingly on skills that had been designated as female: not only on cooking and washing and nursing, but on the mechanisms of bureaucracy and the new technologies of communication. The military needed women to type, to operate telephone switchboards, to do what had already been defined, in the civilian economy, as women's work.

The army, while it was the only service to embrace modern "mental testing" during World War I, fell well behind the navy when it came to efficient use of women. The navy—seeking experienced clerical workers, typists, and switchboard operators—enlisted 13,000 women as "Yeoman-Fs," or "yeomanettes," for shore duty during the war. These women had full military rank and status, though that required some maneuvering. According to navy regulations, every yeoman must be assigned to a ship. Women, however, were not allowed to serve offshore. The solution: the navy assigned its yeomanettes to a tugboat that lay buried and unmovable, stuck in the mud where it had sunk in the Potomac River. It wasn't a long-term solution, but it worked under pressure of war.[8]

The army, like the navy, needed people with clerical and communications experience. And the army, like the navy, turned to women. But the army was not interested in soldierettes, or private-ettes, or whatever they would have been called. The women who supported army war efforts during World War I were civilians. The navy had a clear advantage there, for yeomanettes were subject to order and under military control; unlike the army, the navy did not have to contend with the vagaries of the labor market or the shifting circumstances and choices of civilian workers.

Women were demobilized after World War I when the American military returned to a smaller, peacetime core. But some in the army thought about lessons learned, and two proposals for according women military status were floated. One, a proposal for a "women's service corps" submitted in 1926, was rejected outright. The other, Major Everett S. Hughes's well-developed plan to integrate women fully into the army, had an even less-dignified end. As Mattie Treadwell, author of the first major internal history of the Women's Army Corps, describes it:

> A dejected-looking sheaf of handwritten scraps of paper indicated that the studies were carried back and forth from G-1 [Personnel] to the Chief of Staff to the Secretary of War to G-1, bearing notations of diminishing intensity, such as "Hold until Secretary of War decides"; "Hold until fall when women return to their homes after summer activities"; and, finally, merely "Hold." The last one in the series, dated 5 January 1931, stated: "General B. [Brigadier General Albert J. Bowley] says may as well suspend; no one seems willing to do anything about it."[9]

When Europeans went to war again in 1939 and a divided America began its long path toward intervention, a member of the U.S. Congress raised, once again, the idea of a women's corps. Edith Nourse Rogers, who had served as a Red Cross nurse during World War I, worked with army leaders on a bill she introduced in the spring of 1941, as Americans continued to struggle over the nation's proper role in the war. Rogers's bill disappeared into the depths of bureaucracy, stalled if not completely lost, until Pearl Harbor changed the stakes. The Women's Auxiliary Army Corps (WAAC) was authorized by Congress on May 14, 1942; the "auxiliary" designation was removed in 1943, though the Women's Army Corps was not fully integrated into the regular army until 1948.[10]

World War II required almost total mobilization of the American public, but decisions about who should do what were heavily influenced by national values and cultural beliefs, not least those about gender. Military needs, however, had become increasingly complex by the middle of the twentieth century. The military needed men to fight, but they were just the sharp end of the spear. The U.S. military's tooth-to-tail ratio during World War II was approximately 1:8. In other words, there were at least eight men (or women) in uniform supporting each man in combat. This ratio was due in part to decisions about manpower allocations, for Japan's tooth-to-tail ratio was very close to 1:1. But it was also due to the vast scale and scope of U.S. participation in that war and the complex logistics of supporting troops spread over much of the world. No one was suggesting breeching the fundamental divide between men and women—that men fight and women don't. But the army needed skills that had been defined as appropriately female, and it knew from experience that it was better to have those skills under military command. Nonetheless, the Women's Army Corps was a difficult sell, even on a purely voluntary basis. Congressmen thundered objections. "Take the women into the armed service," a Republican congressman from Michigan asked, ". . . who then will maintain the home fires; who will do the cooking, the washing, the mending, the humble, homey tasks to which every woman has devoted herself?"[11]

Women served with distinction in World War II. Almost 350,000 women joined one or another branch of service, with the majority of them in the Women's Army Corps. WACs created a strong military culture of their own, with standard GI gripes (many concerning the ill-fitting mud-colored underwear), marching chants, and songs from training camps that bore an uncanny resemblance—in tone, not topic—to those written and sung in women's colleges during the interwar years. Most women did what was considered gender-appropriate work in health care, administration, and communication, though the less educated, including a high proportion of black women, were assigned domestic service duties: laundry, cooking, cleaning. WAC songs even endorsed this division of labor by sex: "I don't wanna march in the Infantry/Ride in the Cavalry, shoot in Artillery/I don't wanna fly over Germany/I just wanna be a WAAC," one went.[12]

Still, some women took on new roles, serving as air traffic controllers, truck drivers, mechanics, and parachute riggers. Distinctions remained, even in such jobs. Male parachute riggers, for example, were required to jump using one of the parachutes they'd rigged; female parachute riggers were required to watch a man jump with one of their parachutes. And WASPs (Women's Airforce Service Pilots), blocked from incorporation into the Army Air Force by male pilots, carried out dangerous and highly skilled military duties as civil service employees. Nonetheless, servicewomen followed combat troops to North Africa; WACs landed in Normandy thirty-eight days after D-Day and followed closely behind the invasion forces for the ten remaining months until V-E Day; 5,200 WACs were stationed in Australia, New Guinea, and the Philippines. Most servicewomen—like the great majority of servicemen, in fact—did not come close to combat. "Free a Man to Fight" was the WAC recruiting slogan, and it did little to endear WACs to male soldiers. But for all those women volunteers who did essential clerical work on the U.S. mainland, some significant number of women braved the blood and the mud and the chilblains or the leeches and earned high praise at war's end for their unfailing support of the American war effort.[13]

The end of World War II, like the end of World War I, saw a massive demobilization. The strength of the nation's armed forces dropped from more than 12 million in 1945 to about 3 million in 1946. But something significant had changed. As Colonel Mary Agnes Hallaren, director of the Women's Army Corps, put it in a 1950 memo, "Today, we [the United States] are Number One in line of battle." The United States had ended the war as the most powerful nation in the world. And the Cold War that began even as Americans and Soviets embraced on the banks of the Elbe meant that there was no way that the nation's military could shrink once again to a small peacetime core. Some people believed women must be prepared to play a major role, should war come again. Hallaren, writing on the eve of the Korean War and with a sense of impending doom, insisted that the nation must register American women through the selective service system and make them available for the draft in the case of "a total emergency." Not unreasonably, she made the case that since half the American population is female, a "total war effort must include the mobilization of women."[14]

According to Hallaren, voluntary service would not suffice. She insisted that her case for registering women had already been made by men: the volunteer force had failed in the late 1940s because sufficient numbers of men did not volunteer. And, as Hallaren pointed out, when it came to volunteering for military service, men had far fewer "inhibitions" to overcome than women. Hallaren's strongest evidence came from World War II. She wasted no time in this memo honoring WAC contributions. Her point was that it had been next-to-impossible to get women to serve. Though conservative estimates suggested that WACs could fill 1.5 million army jobs, "it took three years, millions of dollars, battalions of personnel and tons of advertising to recruit 140,000 women." Why, she asked, are we assuming that 1.5 million women will volunteer for service "when it takes a draft to procure 800,000 men"?[15]

Hallaren was proved right during the Korean War. In 1951 Anna Rosenberg, the assistant secretary of defense for manpower, personnel and reserve, was charged with recruiting 72,000 women into the armed forces. Though this was far short of Hallaren's imagined 1.5 million, the task still proved impossible. At Rosenberg's urging, Secretary of Defense George C. Marshall summoned fifty civilian professional women—one from each state and from Alaska and Hawai'i—to Washington to discuss the recruiting crisis. From this meeting grew the Defense Advisory Committee on Women in the Services (DACOWITS), which would play a key role in all issues concerning women in the military over the coming decades. But even with the committee's advice and its members' local endorsements, the U.S. Armed Forces succeeded in recruiting only 50,000 women by the end of the war—almost 50 percent short of their original goal. The Women's Army Corps reached a peak strength of only 11,500, despite pleas for volunteers. But DACOWITS, now with a federal charter, and with its current and future members awarded a "protocol rank" of lieutenant general by Marshall, continued to advise the Department of Defense. Members initially focused on strategies to attract women volunteers to the military. The group soon began studying and offering informed advice on women's training, assignments, and quality-of-life issues.[16]

By the early 1960s, as President Kennedy established a Commission on the Status of Women and questions of gender equity began emerging in American society, DACOWITS was lobbying for equal opportunity for women in the military. They had their work cut out for them. Women, according to legislation passed in 1948, were restricted to 2 percent of the nation's active forces. The highest permanent rank a woman could hold in the army was Lieutenant Colonel, though the director of the Women's Army Corps was designated Colonel for the term of her appointment. Women could not hold command authority over men. Pregnancy brought a mandatory discharge; no woman with a child under the age of 18 could serve. Married women could not enlist, though women could marry while in the service. In 1967, women could be assigned to just over a third of army occupational specialties, almost all of them in the traditionally female fields of health care, administration, and communication, but that figure radically overstated the possibilities. Fewer than 1.5 percent of army *positions* were actually open to enlisted women.[17]

Seven years of DACOWITS lobbying paid off in 1967, when Public Law 91-30 removed restrictions on women's numbers and rank. But the army itself was also discussing possible change. Writing in the midst of the domestic warfare of 1968, the authors of the *Army 75 Personnel Concept Study* (a truly odd mix of policy proposal and philosophical musing) pondered the impact of national divisiveness, violence, and fragmentation on the future of the army. "So long as Congress has the Constitutional right to raise Armies," the authors noted, ". . . the Army is guaranteed a source of accessions—even though in most likelihood its [sic] motivation will not be love of country or the urge to right an international wrong." But in these times, they asked, how many will choose the army as a career—especially as the government continues to create new avenues for people to "gain upward social mobility"? Given the mounting anger over the draft, how might the army reduce the number of unwilling soldiers in its ranks? The future of the army, they suggested, might very well depend on women.[18]

The authors of the report struggled with the whole concept of "woman," veering wildly among nineteenth-century notions of separate spheres and essential natures, labor market statistics, and patronizing reassurances of women's potential capacity. Women, the report noted, would make up 50.9 percent of the American population by 1975, and so must constitute an "essential . . . part of our manpower resources." And as "the belief in the innate inferiority of the female sex" is undermined and concerns about the "intellectual capacities and emotional traits of women" are allayed by women's increased participation in the public world, "technological development and the demands for manpower will help to erode the barriers of sexual prejudice." "[W]hen he steps back to evaluate objectively the Americal [sic] woman of the '60's," the authors wrote, positing an unspecified male observer, he finds "an intelligent, well-educated, forceful and extremely versitile [sic] individual. She recognizes the advantages and privileges available to her and she seizes the opportunity, not to assume a passive, parasitic role, but to fulfill the attendant obligations and duties inherent in this society." The modern American woman contributes to all aspects of life, they explained, but in so doing, "retains those traits peculiar to her sex—for womanly charms and virtues are a distinct asset and complement and enhance those of her male counterparts." As "woman" has "never expressed ideas that would destroy the race, every member of which she has, at the risk of her own life, brought into being," it is possible that "womanly charms and virtues" can be "utilized in direct contribution to the primary mission of the Army." Women are capable of doing some jobs "even better than men," the authors concluded, and they also "add the 'feminine touch' to Army life, which can be very hard at times. The old saying, 'Behind every great man is a woman,' has much truth to it, as history has proven; so can this be true in the Army."[19] Despite the assumptions on which it rested, the *Army 75* study was making a progressive argument, championing women's expanded roles in the army of the future.

The *Army 75* study, predicated as it was on the continued draft, was rendered largely irrelevant by the growing certainty that the nation would soon move to an all-volunteer force. But it was published in 1969, the same year that Westmoreland set up the PROVIDE task force to evaluate the army's possible transformation, and the logic of this study's argument about women nonetheless informed army plans, whether because of direct influence or simply because of widely shared assumptions. *PROVIDE* was more grounded in labor statistics and policy considerations than *Army 75*, evaluating comparative costs of procuring and training women versus men and explaining how increased numbers of WACs would impact existing facilities. And *PROVIDE* did not propose to broaden women's roles. Its authors noted instead that "the social and biological limitations of women" are "paramount" in consideration. But like the authors of the *Army 75* study—though with far less enthusiasm for women's special contributions—the authors of *PROVIDE* emphasized the difference between men and women: "Although women have become better educated and more independent than ever before, they are nevertheless women, and accordingly tend to shy away from occupations that encroach on their femininity. For this reason, young women must be shown that their true value to the service is not that they are capable of replacing men, an unfeminine connotation, but that they are women and the feminine touch is required to do the job better."[20]

From the beginning of the transition from the draft to an all-volunteer force, the army emphasized the importance of advertising. In 1971, N.W. Ayer replaced "Your future . . . your decision . . . choose ARMY" with "Today's Army Wants to Join You," explaining that the new slogan was an updated version of the classic "Uncle Sam Wants You!" that would appeal to contemporary youth. This gallery of photos illustrated the army's claim. The text that accompanied this illustration used the new slogan as the headline. N.W. Ayer Advertising Records, Archives Center, National Museum of American History, Smithsonian Institution.

Take the Army's 16-month tour of Europe.
Right out of high school.
In today's Army you can enlist for European duty that guarantees at least 16 months with one of seven crack outfits stationed in Germany.
France, Denmark and Switzerland are just across the border. Within easy reach of any free weekend. Italy and the Riviera are just a few hours away. Just waiting for you on some of that 30 days paid vacation you earn each year in the Army.
This is your chance of a lifetime. To live and work in Europe. To get to know places like no tourist ever can. To get to know the people. Pick up the language.
If you want to live and work where tourists only visit, drop us the coupon. Or talk to your near-by Army representative about enlisting in Armor, Artillery or Infantry for European duty.
Today's Army wants to join you.
Army Opportunities
I'd like to spend 16 months in Europe.
Send me more information on European duty in today's Army.

The new recruiting advertisements emphasized the opportunities of army life—from tangible benefits provided by the army ("30 days paid vacation") to other, less official perks. The plethora of phallus-shaped objects surrounding the pretty blonde fräulein in the café in this 1971 ad clearly suggests sexual opportunity, and the "16-month tour of Europe" headline links the soldier's "tour of duty" to the backpacking tours ever more commonly taken by college youth in the 1960s and 1970s. N.W. Ayer Advertising Records, Archives Center, National Museum of American History, Smithsonian Institution.

The prospect of attracting 20,000 volunteers a month seemed dubious when American youth culture appeared so much at odds with Army expectations. This cartoon appeared in the recruiters' journal in 1970.

RECRUITING
U S
ARMY
- WALTON -
" WHAT ARE YOU INTERESTED IN — REGULAR ARMY OR THE WACS ? "

General Eugene Forsythe, as "Special Assistant, Modern Volunteer Army," managed the move to an all-volunteer army. In contrast to many fellow commissioned officers and NCOs, he expressed confidence in American youth. This sketch of him appeared in the army recruiters' professional journal in 1971.

In this cover photograph for a 1972 issue of the army recruiter journal, a recruiter discusses enlistment with two "prospects."

Following graduation from the army recruiting course, each recruiter receives a silver recruiting badge bearing three silver stars. Recruiters gradually earn gold stars to replace the silver, as shown. In the photograph above, Secretary of the Army "Bo" Callaway congratulates a recruiter from the Portland District Recruiting Command during a ceremony held in November 1974 to award the first five gold stars earned under the new QIPS (Qualitative Incentive Procurement) program.

When was the last time you got promoted?
When the only jobs you can get are the jobs anyone can do, they're not very likely to get you anywhere. Like delivering the office mail, or waiting tables at the local pizza parlor.
Jobs with a future take skill and experience. Today's Army can give you both.
We have over 300 jobs in fields that offer you a future in the Army or in civilian life. Data processing, intelligence, air operations support, medical, communications, administration, to name a few.
They're jobs we'll pay you to learn. At the same starting salary our men get. With the same opportunity for regular promotions and raises. And the salary you earn in today's Army goes a long way because we provide your meals and housing while medical and dental care are free.
You can save most of your salary, or spend it on the 30 days paid vacation you'll get every year. Or stretch it by buying the things you want at post exchanges where prices are lower than in civilian stores.
And if you would like to continue your education while in the Army, we'll help you. Then help you again after you're out with up to 36 months of financial assistance at the college of your choice.
If you're looking for a job with a future, but want some time off first, we can arrange that too. With our Delayed Entry Option you can sign up for the training you want today, and take up to six months before coming in.
For more information, talk it over with your nearest Army Representative.
Today's Army wants to join you.

This 1973 army recruiting advertisement is part of a four-ad series that reveals early 1970s army assumptions about race and gender. A second ad simply replaces the black woman with a white woman; nothing else in the photograph or the text changes. The same is true of the ads featuring men, though the setting is a loading dock. In these ads, gender makes a critical difference. Race does not. N.W. Ayer Advertising Records, Archives Center, National Museum of American History, Smithsonian Institution.

Clifford Alexander, secretary of the army during the Carter administration, had a strong background in civil rights. He believed the army offered opportunity to young Americans and pushed to guarantee access to racial minorities and women. His policies ran counter to those who meant to use social scientific assessments to ensure the "quality" of the all-volunteer force. U.S. National Archives.

Many experts credit Maxwell Thurman, commander of USAREC from 1979 to 1981, with saving the all-volunteer army. He used his faith in quantitative analysis and management techniques to transform the process of recruiting. U.S. Army.

The Army needs girls as well as generals.
Generals make the Army go. But so do girls.
Girls who can keep things moving in the office. Handle personnel. Figure the payroll. Work in fields like photography, medicine, public information.
Girls who can do these and dozens of other jobs get every chance to further their education. To advance in rank and pay. To travel and share the Army adventure.
Off duty, they meet and make dozens of new friends. It's a big Army, after all, and it's full of young people who want to go places and do things.
If you'd like to be somebody that others depend on, the Army needs you.
Just ask a general if that isn't so.
The Women's Army Corps
Use coupon or write: Army Opportunities, Dept. 450A, Hampton, Va. 23369
Army Opportunities
4 CE 12-69
Dept. 450
Hampton, Va. 23369
Please send me more information about the "new world" of the Women's Army Corps.
Name Age
Address
City County
State Zip Phone
Years schooling completed

Army recruiting ads before the end of the Women's Army Corps in the late 1970s commonly emphasized Army opportunity . . . for meeting husbands. This 1969 ad was less concerned with respectability (notice their hands) than most previous ads. N.W. Ayer Advertising Records, Archives Center, National Museum of American History, Smithsonian Institution.

SOME OF OUR BEST MEN ARE WOMEN.
If there's one place where opportunity is genuinely equal, it's in the Army. Because in the Army, people get assignments based on ability. And they get ahead the same way.
With few exceptions (mainly in Combat Specialties), women have the same skill training programs to choose from as men. And the same opportunities for promotion.
If you've always wanted to drive a truck, or be a carpenter and drive nails, no one will stand in your way.
On the other hand, if you've always wanted to learn how to cook. Or type. Or take dictation, well, you can do that, too. If you're willing to compete with men.
But whatever you decide to do in the Army, remember, everyone is judged on ability and how hard one works. Isn't that the way it should be?
For more information about the hundreds of equal opportunities in today's Army, send one of the postcards, or call toll free: 800-431-1234. In New York, call 800-942-1990.
JOIN THE PEOPLE WHO'VE JOINED THE ARMY.

As the army attempted to recruit more women for nontraditional MOSs, images of femininity and romance gave way to the language of the women's movement and promises of equal opportunity, as in this ad from the late 1970s. N.W. Ayer Advertising Records, Archives Center, National Museum of American History, Smithsonian Institution.

pride (prīd), n.
1. The quality or state of being proud. 2. Justifiable self-respect. 3. Delight in one's position, accomplishments and achievements.
JOIN THE PEOPLE WHO'VE JOINED THE ARMY.

Research demonstrated that young people were not motivated by appeals to patriotism, service, or sacrifice, but congressional committees nonetheless believed in the power of such calls. Army advertising regularly included at least one ad to satisfy their congressional overseers. This visually arresting ad from the late 1970s was isolated among more practical appeals. N.W. Ayer Advertising Records, Archives Center, National Museum of American History, Smithsonian Institution.

The army introduced "Be All You Can Be" in 1980; the catchy jingle and its advertising slogan survived for more than two decades. While the music and lyrics carried the campaign, BAYCB was introduced in print media by this ad, which included the words to the new army jingle: "Be all that you can be/Keep on reaching/Keep on moving/Be all that you can be/Find your future in the Army." N.W. Ayer Advertising Records, Archives Center, National Museum of American History, Smithsonian Institution.

By the 1990s, army recruiting advertisements presented all soldiers as members of a team, playing down discussions of difference while making "diversity" very visible. This still shot, which draws our attention to the female soldier in the ranks, comes from a video sequence used first in the 1990s "Soldier's Pledge" and then in the 2005 "Army Strong" theme commercial. U.S. Army.

The "Army Values" poster draws attention to the ethnic and racial diversity of the army as much as to its central values. U.S. Army.

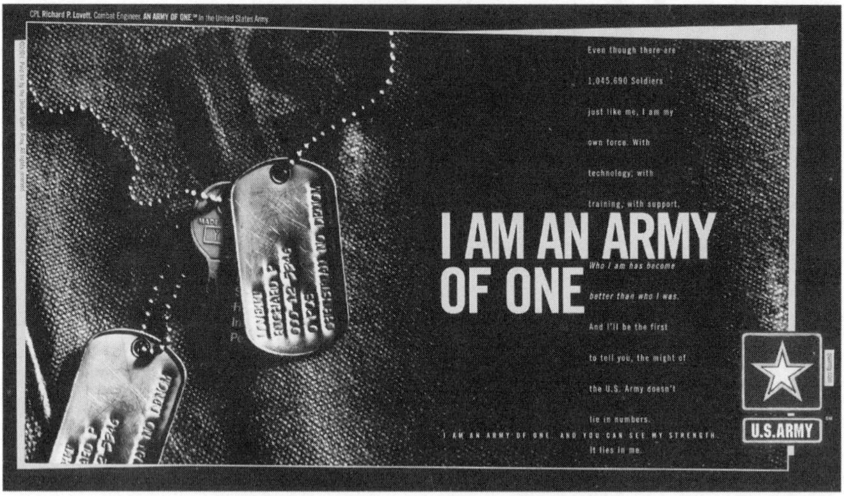

Though the "Army of One" campaign was introduced in early 2001—before the September terrorist attacks—it countered criticism of a "kinder, gentler army" with images of a "warrior" culture. U.S. Army.

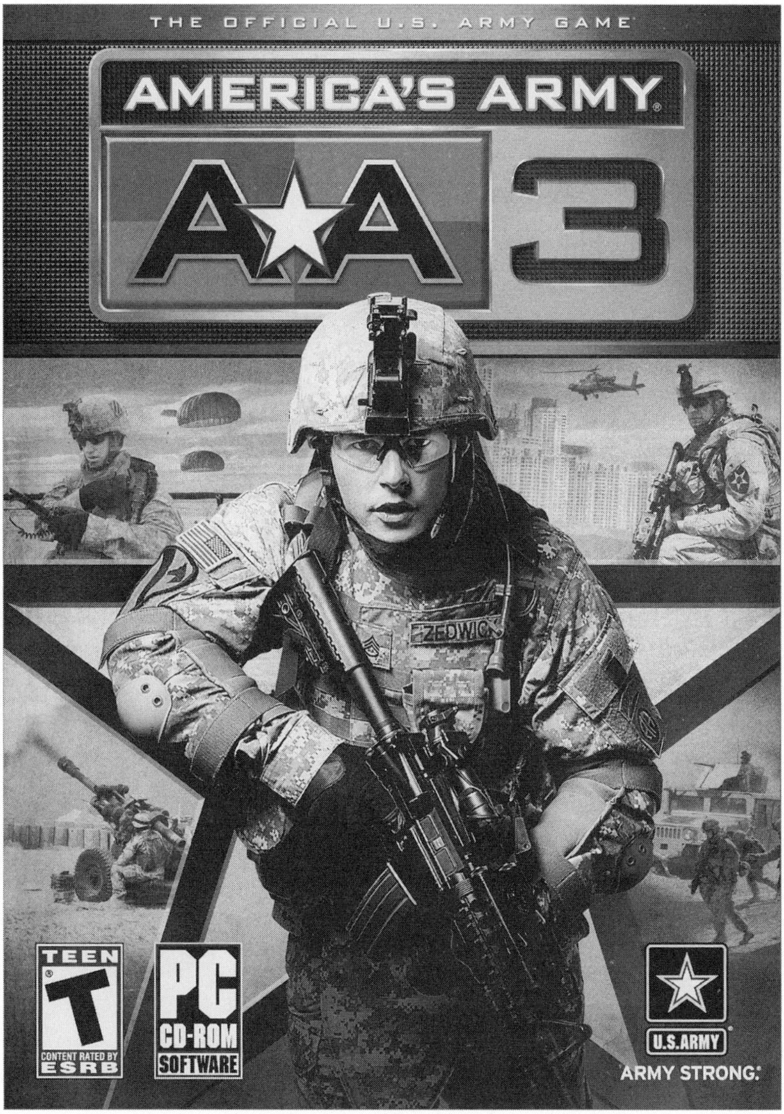

America's Army, the army's free team-based, multiplayer first-person-shooter computer game, was introduced at E3, the Electronic Entertainment Expo, in 2002. Designers focused on technical accuracy, and the army argues that the game provides insight into "soldiering," as players are bound by rules of engagement and mission success depends on "adherence to the seven Army Core Values." Rated "T" for Teen, the game had 9.7 million registered users in early 2009. U.S. Army.

SOMETIMES BEING STRONG
IS AS SIMPLE AS BEING SUPPORTIVE.
WARREN
U.S.ARMY
If your sons or daughters want to talk to you about joining the U.S. Army, take a listen. The Army offers over 150 job opportunities and money for college. It's worth hearing about. You made them strong. We'll make them Army Strong. To learn more visit goarmy.com/for_parents.
Specialist Gary Warren
©2007. Paid for by the United States Army. All rights reserved.
U.S.ARMY
ARMY STRONG.

According to army research, during the war in Iraq, parents—especially mothers—were the greatest obstacle to their children's enlistment. Advertising campaigns targeted parents with slogans such as: "You made them strong. We'll make them Army strong" and "Help him find his strength." U.S. Army.

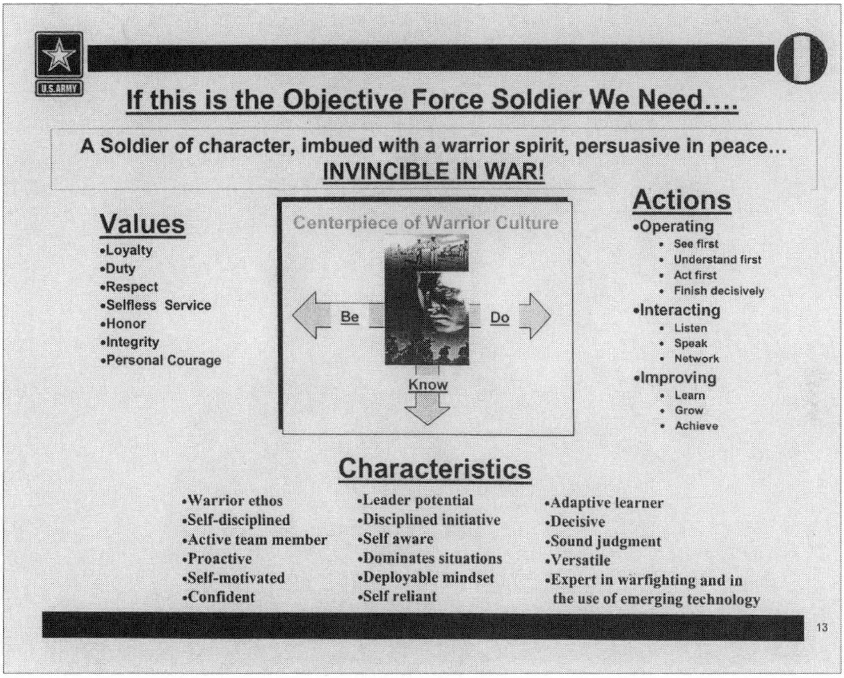

A 2003 army slide, complete with talking points, offers a portrait of the ideal soldier: "persuasive in peace, INVINCIBLE IN WAR."

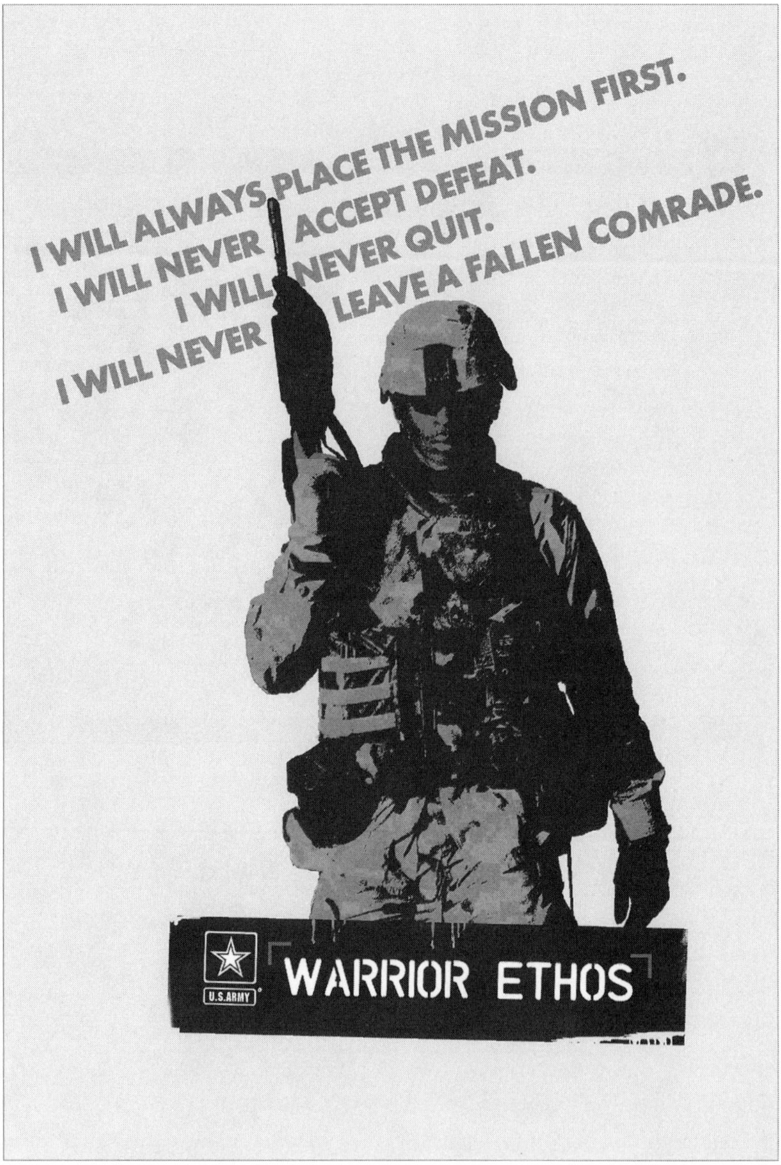
I WILL ALWAYS PLACE THE MISSION FIRST.
I WILL NEVER ACCEPT DEFEAT.
I WILL NEVER QUIT.
I WILL NEVER LEAVE A FALLEN COMRADE.
U.S.ARMY
WARRIOR ETHOS

This statement of the "warrior ethos" is part of the new "Soldier's Creed" the army adopted in 2003. These lines, engraved on all soldiers' dogtags, are meant to emphasize that all members of the army are, first and foremost, warriors. U.S. Army.

Such claims would soon be identified, by some significant portion of American women, as "male chauvinism." But it was not only male officers and consultants who defined women's femininity as a primary concern. The director of the Women's Army Corps, at that point Col. Elizabeth F. Hoisington (who had been given a low skill rating when she joined the WAAC in 1942 because she didn't know how to type) had helped produce the *Army 75* study. And her successor, BG Mildred Bailey, celebrated the thirty-second anniversary of the founding of the Women's Army Corps in 1974 with these words:

> Today, there is no doubt that a member of the Women's Army Corps is feminine and in the future this quality will be maintained by the high standards which we have set for ourselves. It required, literally, years to dispel the myths, to alter the stereotypes and to discredit the lies which portrayed the WAC volunteer as less qualified than her male counterpart and a threat to all American womanhood. But, this has been accomplished![21]

Both the *Army 75* tribute to women's life-giving properties and the frequently stated concerns about women's limitations have powerful histories, even if it is surprising to see them voiced so recently and with so little self-consciousness. But Hoisington's support for the *Army 75* study and Bailey's comments on femininity came from a clear and powerful history, as well—if a more specific one. Both Bailey and Hoisington had served in the Women's Army Corps during World War II. This service had been the shaping experience of their lives, the source of a sense of duty and commitment that led each to a career in the WAC. But just as their World War II experience shaped their commitment to the Women's Army Corps, that same experience shaped their understandings of what was necessary for its survival.

Public opposition to women in the military was ferocious during World War II. And it wasn't only grandstanding members of Congress, sputtering about the timeless roles of the sexes and asking, rhetorically, who would do the laundry ("the humble, homey tasks"). There was public outcry and public muttering, there were rumors about boatloads of pregnant WACs sent home in disgrace, about dens of lesbians, Amazons, and masculinized women, about barracks full of cheap whores, their uniforms a cover for their true mission as "morale boosters" for male officers. Such relentless condemnation weighed heavily on WACs and their families, and it vastly undermined WAC recruiting efforts. The War Department characterized such "malicious gossip" as "Nazi-inspired propaganda," and a WAC song took the same line: "Oh, pity the lot of the poor little WAC/Whom the axis decided to stab in the back./According to them she's a 'Frivolous Sal,'/A rug-cuttin', high-livin' kind of a gal/Whom Uncle Sam's paying to play with the boys."[22]

There are many ways to undermine an institution or to attack its members. These rumors, however, were some of the most insidiously effective of their time. Promiscuous, prostitute, lesbian, Amazon: each of these labels, in those days, defined a woman as unmarriageable. It mattered little whether the claim was accurate. Americans frequently said, in the mid-twentieth century, that a woman's most valuable possession was her reputation. And during that particular moment in U.S. history, reputations were quickly stained and easily lost. Association with the less reputable was enough, as was membership in a suspect group. To most young American women of that era, the prospect of marriage—a good marriage—mattered greatly. Marriage was not only an expected step in the course of life (and the average age at marriage for women dropped to 20 during the 1950s), it was also the most dependable source of economic security offered women back when jobs were still segregated into well-paid "male" and poorly-paid "female" categories. Not every American woman found full satisfaction in home, husband, and family—though many did—but it was a powerful, *normalized* expectation that they would. In addition, although one might venture that any lesbians among the WACs cared little about marriage prospects, most did care about respectability and reputation, if only for the sake of their families. Given WAC recruiting standards, the vast majority of its members came from "respectable" families of origin, not the sort that saw "prostitute" as a legitimate employment option or, to be honest, lesbianism as a legitimate lifestyle choice. The rumors were very hard on WACs' parents, even if their daughters privately believed they'd found some welcome freedom in the Women's Army Corps.

These were the challenges that shaped the WAC from the end of the war through the mid-1970s. WAC leaders believed it essential to guard against such claims and charges, important to emphasize the femininity and the "high moral standards" of all members of the Women's Army Corps. So although the WAC stressed pride in performance, professionalism, and a certain spirit of adventure, it remained virtually obsessed with the issue of femininity, with appearance, with "high standards," and with respectability. Such concerns were not restricted to the WAC; "reputation" was a concern for all women's services. Thus when DACOWITS tried to promote the armed services to young women during the 1950s, the group emphasized femininity and the respectability of the middle class. The cover of a tri-fold promotional pamphlet bore a drawing of a fresh-faced young white woman, her dark hair in loose curls, a flowered skirt of fashionable fullness emphasizing her narrow waist. She, in turn, holds a brochure picturing the uniforms of all four services. "The Fashionable Choice," reads the actual pamphlet's title. Those drawn to open the front flap found another drawing, this time of four uniformed women shopping for souvenirs in someone's idea of a traditional Asian market, their beautifully fitted uniforms and four-inch heels suggesting little of the obligations of military life. The inner pages are more informative, with assurances that women receive the same pay and privileges as men and a promise that living arrangements are "similar to those in a college dormitory." Photos of women operating impressive sorts of technological equipment are paired with the useful information that "many women in the services marry." But the recruiting appeal's basic message was: "It is truly a fashionable choice when young women elect to serve their country and wear the smart, feminine uniforms of the WAC, Women Marines, WAVES, and WAF."[23]

Col. Mary Agnes Hallaren, director of the Women's Army Corps from 1947 through early 1953, saw protecting the reputation of the Women's Army Corps as one of her most important jobs. Hallaren, who pushed for selective service registration for women, managed the full integration of the WAC into the regular army in 1948, and led army women through the process of racial integration and the challenges of the Korean War, was no stay-at-home traditionalist. Born in Lowell, Massachusetts in 1907, she earned a two-year teaching degree in 1927 and spent the next fifteen years teaching and traveling around the world before joining the WAAC—at the age of 35—as soon as recruiting opened in May 1942. Graduating in the first WAAC Officer Candidate School (OCS) class, she commanded the first WAAC unit in Europe and by the end of 1945 had served in England, France, and Germany. Hallaren never mastered—or perhaps never accepted—the neutral bureaucratic tones of the army memo. As American fighting men pushed north from Seoul in the tenth month of the Korean War, Hallaren sent a blistering message to all WAC officers. Although "more than 90%" of service women were "measuring up" to the high standards of the WAC, she wrote, there are "a few women who are a disgrace to the uniform they wear and to the country they are failing to serve." These women, she made clear, were putting the entire Women's Army Corps in "jeopardy."[24]

Her complaints were three. The "first and most common failing," she wrote, is liquor. There is nothing "objectionable in a woman taking a drink," she allowed, but there is also "no more pitiful sight than a human being who has become the inferior of a jelly fish." Drunkenness is "deplorable" in a civilian woman, intolerable in a servicewoman whose behavior "reflects upon every woman in uniform." The second deadly sin, according to Hallaren, was gossip. "The super-bazooka is a child's toy compared with a malicious tongue," she wrote. "Bazookas may penetrate Stalin tanks, but malicious tongues can pierce entire commands." And while old tanks "may be replaced with new ones," the "wrecked reputations can never be mended."[25]

Hallaren's final concern was with "abnormal actions." "There is no room in the Service," she insisted, "for weak sisters—physically, mentally or emotionally." Entrance exams usually weed out those with physical and mental problems, she explained, but "emotional cripples" are more difficult to detect. Some homosexuals "slip by," among them "human vultures who blight the lives of youngsters." And thus "love, the force that leads a man to sacrifice his life for his brother on the battlefield, is warped and cheapened by these poor apologies for womanhood." As "brothers, husbands, sons and neighbors are giving their lives in Korea," Hallaren asked, how can servicewomen give less than their finest effort? Law doesn't guarantee survival, Hallaren reminded them, referring to the 1948 integration act that had joined the WAC to the regular army. Hallaren was explicit: ignoring any of these three transgressions was the same as tacitly condoning it, and that must stop. "The Corps cannot carry you," she instructed her subordinate officers. "[Y]ou must carry it."[26]

Concern about femininity, heterosexuality, and the irreproachable reputation of the WAC did not fade as the Women's Army Corps became more established. A 1968 chaplain's pamphlet, acknowledging that "women have become an integral part of our military services," nonetheless included a lengthy discussion on the proper grooming and comportment of the "military lady." An accompanying film, *The Lady in Military Service,* found emotional blackmail more effective than straightforward advice. This training film portrayed Wendy, a young sergeant in the Women's Army Corps, who begins to forget that she's a lady; she "no longer bothers to wear her hair becomingly, and forgets to use lipstick" (in the words of the training film synopsis). Wendy's older brother Bob, a Sergeant First Class, comes to meet his sister for lunch but is "outraged to see Wendy chew out a young WAC Pvt. in 'tough-guy fashion.'" Bob "stalks out of the office," leaving Wendy "hurt and bewildered." "He came to see his sister," the film synopsis explained helpfully, "but the hard-bitten soldier Wendy seems to have become 'isn't anybody's sister.'" WAC basic training, in 1969, included an instruction block titled "Personal Standards and Social Concepts," which *Army Digest* magazine explained was "a course to emphasize the feminine side of their soldiering." And the 1972 edition of the chaplain's guide still advised army religious officers to counsel WACs against "taking on masculine traits."[27]

Most of this rhetoric amounted to little more than cultural prophylaxis, attempts to define and reinforce the sorts of behavior, appearance, and standards that made the Women's Army Corps a reasonable choice for a respectable young lady, whether in her opinion or in the opinion of her parents. But leadership concerns about the reputation of the WAC had practical implications that went far beyond proper dress length, hairstyle, and application of makeup. In May 1970 the head of the Army Recruiting Command (USAREC) pointed out that it increasingly faced questions about alleged discrimination against women applicants. The vast differences in admissions standards for men and women, he noted, were difficult to defend in the midst of a "movement for more liberal moral standards" and a "rising emphasis toward equality of the sexes." Was it not possible, he inquired of the chief of staff for personnel (DCSPER), for the army to offer moral waivers to women who had "illegitimate" children or a record of venereal disease, given that neither of these factors barred men from admission—or even required a waiver?[28]

USAREC had no difficulty with the generally higher mental (overall) and physical (compared to other women) admission standards for women. Men had to meet mental and physical criteria as well, and the higher levels of education and test scores of women, as a group, were simply a result of the "supply and demand relationship," in the wording suggested for army public statements. Besides, as "quality" began to fall during the 1970s, women's higher rates of high school graduation and stronger AFQT scores, which were not separated out of army averages, leavened the alarming overall statistics at least a bit: in early 1974, for example, 35 percent of enlisted women had one or more years of college, compared to an infinitesimal number of enlisted men, and in 1975 98.6 percent of female accessions were drawn from mental categories I and II. But in 1970, it was mainly the nonparallel "moral" categories that attracted attention: that married women were not allowed to join the army, whereas married men could; that pregnancy and parenthood were automatic grounds for dismissal; that having a child outside wedlock or a history of venereal disease disqualified women but not men on "moral" grounds. The commander of USAREC had been right; by August the army was fielding complaints from members of Congress.[29]

The director of the Women's Army Corps (Hoisington, at this point) was appalled at the suggestion that the Women's Army Corps "lower" its standards. Rejecting the proposal that married women without previous army service be allowed to join the WAC, she insisted that "the Army is not a suitable side job for a woman who is already committed to maintaining a home, a husband, or a child." She was even firmer on the "moral" waivers: "American society" demands "higher moral character in women" than in men. According to Hoisington, when it came to women, a history of venereal disease or of unmarried pregnancy is a clear "indication of lack of discipline and maturity." The Women's Army Corps has an obligation, she wrote, "to parents who have entrusted their daughters in our keeping, and to itself," to "advance the standards of morality." And WAC enlistment standards must reflect "the necessity to maintain an impeccable public image." The proposed changes in admissions standards for women, however, did not stem from the army's embrace of "more liberal moral standards" or its desire to rethink the role of women in the army. There was an urgency for change, but only because it had become clear that such different regulations for men and women left the army on untenable legal ground. General Hoisington lost her fight for "standards" on almost every count.[30]

This WAC director was generally understood, even by WAC loyalists, to be conservative in her leadership and in her vision of women's proper social roles. For example, when pressed to explain why she believed a woman could not return to duty after having a child, Hoisington simply asked her audience to imagine the absurd scenario: "Corporal Susie Brown might then come home some night and say to Sergeant Charley Brown: 'Well, dear, I have orders for Japan. You'll have to take care of Junior and do your own cooking for a while.'"[31] For Hoisington, that story put an end to the discussion—perhaps a sign that she was not completely in touch with the culture of young American women in 1970.

Hoisington's successor, General Mildred C. Bailey, was somewhat less conservative in outlook. Bailey had grown up in Kinston, North Carolina and undertaken graduate work in languages at the University of North Carolina, Chapel Hill in the months immediately preceding America's entry into World War II. She spent the war as a member of the French Training Program at Craig Field, Alabama. She'd completed thirteen years in intelligence, been chief of WAC recruiting, commanded a detachment at Fort Myer, Virginia, toured with the U.S. Army Exhibit Unit, and served as a congressional liaison officer to the U.S. Senate. Her marriage to a marine sergeant major who left the service at the end of World War II had ended in tragedy when her husband died in an automobile accident in 1967. Bailey had, throughout her career, impressed others as bright, articulate, charming, and hyper-presentable, a lady in the best WAC tradition. As the author of an article in the *Recruiting and Career Counseling Journal* wrote in 1972, after describing her "warmth" and "merriment": "She appeared radiant, with her neat white hair, lovely smile and long-sleeved black evening gown."[32]

General Bailey, like many accomplished women of her generation, appears inconsistent if not contradictory when it comes to questions of gender. Though she spoke the language of equal opportunity, many of the policy proposals and public materials created during her tenure as director of the Women's Army Corps—from 1971 to 1975—could as easily have been created in the 1950s. Shortly after Bailey was appointed director of the WAC, General Westmoreland, then chief of staff of the army, gave her a difficult task: to recreate the image of army women. Her job, in Westmoreland's eyes, was to figure out how to draw enough women volunteers to keep the all-volunteer army afloat. Bailey received no specific instructions, and Westmoreland's wishes were not clear. In general, Westmoreland seemed to have little opposition to women, so long as they stayed in what he saw as their place. On the other hand, he wasn't especially sensitive to women's status as professionals. In 1964, when Westmoreland authorized assignment of a WAC officer to the headquarters of the Military Assistance Command, Vietnam (MACV), the MACV personnel officer had specified that she must be "beautiful." And in 1970, when Westmoreland awarded the first star to an army woman—fifty-one-year-old Elizabeth Hoisington, director of the Women's Army Corps—he had pronounced "a new protocol for congratulating lady generals" and kissed her on the lips.[33]

Bailey, left to her own devices, submitted ten "Recommendations to Improve the Image of the WAC." There was no introduction or broader vision statement on the future of women in the army. The document began with Item 1, a recommendation "[t]hat a new uniform be designed for Army women that will enhance the feminine image of women in the Army." Recommendation two also focused on "attractiveness," including optional wear of the white uniform shirt "as a means of presenting a more feminine image in uniform." Bailey's third recommendation was to reduce the maximum weight allowance for women, thus preventing enlistment of women who do not present "an attractive appearance in uniform"; recommendation four was to deny WACS who exceeded the new weight limit highly desirable overseas assignments. Other recommendations included a strongly worded request that instruction on the "Role of Women in the Army" be offered to male soldiers at all levels, from basic training through senior service schools and colleges, and a proposal to allow women to command men in administrative fields (though not in any others).[34]

Bailey also recommended that the army contract with a civilian agency such as the Barbizon School, Powers School, or Patricia Stevens to offer a good grooming course at the WAC Center. "Individual professional instruction in the use of cosmetics, hair styling, figure control and diet, selection of civilian clothes, poise in speech and body movement, would improve the personal attractiveness of most of the young women who enter the Army," explained General Bailey.[35] Only one of Bailey's recommendations proposed expanding women's roles in any fashion, and then only at the upper ranks of command. None suggested offering women new challenges—or even the same old ones. None attempted to build on the new social possibilities or the new economic realities of women's lives in the early 1970s. It is an ungracious observation about a woman who worked hard on behalf of the women under her care, but these recommendations came very close to portraying the Women's Army Corps as a charm school or matrimonial bureau. None of Bailey's recommendations suggest notions of citizen's duty, service to country, rational economic opportunity, physical and mental challenge, or the adventure of a lifetime.

Recruiting for women in the late 1960s through the mid-1970s reflects such assumptions, filtered through the lens of advertising agencies. These were the years in which National Airline ads offered customers mini-skirted stewardesses wearing buttons reading "I'm Cheryl. Fly Me!" Recruiting advertisements aimed at men took advantage of new cultural freedoms, and the promised attractions of "the Army's 16-month tour of Europe" most definitely included beautiful blonde *fraulein*s such as the one who sat with the soldier at the café table in the 1971 magazine ad. One of the army's most popular television commercials showed a young man using the news he'd joined the army to extricate himself from the loving embraces of an amazing number of girlfriends. (The magazine version called them "loose ends": "Shirley, Ellen, Pam, Nancy, Sally, Mary Anne, to name a few.")[36] But whether shown as pull or push to enlist, the women in these ads were not army women.

By contrast, recruiting advertising for women in the late 1960s and early 1970s offered women men—in the army. An ad in a spring 1970 issue of *Senior Scholastic* debunked "Great Myths about the Women's Army Corps." The first myth, that "It's against regulations to be feminine," was quickly put to rest. Myth two, that "Marriage is out for the duration," merited an illustration: a sergeant slipping a ring on the finger of a private first class. (And no, the man was not the private.) "The Corps wouldn't dream of cramping a girl's style in such an important thing as marriage," read the text. "After all, we're women, too!" Just a few months before, N.W. Ayer had created "The Army needs girls as well as generals." "Generals make the Army go. But so do girls," began the advertising text, which continued to describe army opportunities for women. The girl and the general in the accompanying illustration were a study in body language and power relations. He was well-built and craggily handsome, but she commanded the shot. Her eyes engaged the viewer, and her look was nothing if not knowing. Together they held a folder; underneath it, their fingers were intertwined.[37] In army advertising, girls always married (or whatever) up.

Recruiting ads offering women an abundance of male prospects, Hoisington's concern with "high moral standards" and the reputation of the WAC, and Bailey's emphasis on femininity and attractiveness were closely linked in the logic of the time. All were premised on the notions that most young women hoped to marry, that only women of good reputation could marry satisfactorily, and that the right sort of young women would enlist only if joining the WAC would not harm their reputations or, thus, their futures. Although gender roles and sexual mores were in upheaval during the early 1970s, it was not at all clear at the time what the outcome of this revolution would be. Even as society changed, parents continued to worry about their daughters' reputations. As late as 1976, "SGT Judy" told the *Recruiting & Career Counseling Journal* that parents were her biggest recruiting challenge. "Some parents," she explained, "have the impression their daughters will 'morally decline' if they join the Army."[38]

Despite General Bailey's seeming obsession with feminine attractiveness (she told the *Army Times* that her goal was to create a uniform women could wear in place of fatigues, "something that makes them look like women"), she was also adamant in her support of equal opportunity. It was on her initiative that many more MOSs were opened to women, from 185 to 437 of the existing 485, in 1972. She urged women to seek nontraditional assignments and worried about how to move young women from the "Cinderella image of life—school, marriage, family—in which they live happily ever after" toward a real commitment to "work and a career." When asked, she was willing to cite instances of "chauvinism": "As a commander of a unit, when I stood up for the women, I was termed aggressive and obstinate. When a male officer did the same thing, he was called a leader, willing to stand up for his men." She insisted that while a male officer "commands respect by virtue of his rank," a woman always has to prove herself. In her "End of Tour Report" in 1975, she emphasized the "entrenched psychological bias" that impeded women's advancement in the army. "Our culture and business society," she wrote, has "not taught men to work with women whose *only* relationship to them is that of co-worker, professional colleague." Women, she continued, "are saddled with overcoming negative assumptions," competing in a world in which "it is hard for men to discuss reasonably anything involving a woman's self-interest."[39]

Bailey was definitely aware of the obstacles facing working women, most especially those women who chose to make their lives or careers in the intensely male world of the U.S. military. But her blunt cautions about male chauvinism and psychological biases should not be mistaken for an endorsement of the movement for women's rights. She steadily insisted that there were fundamental differences between men and women. "The WAC Director," she wrote, referring to herself in the third person, "believes very strongly that men and women can be equal in dignity, opportunity, and status without being identical." Bailey warned Secretary of the Army Callaway, in her End of Tour Report, that he should expect continued "pressures from 'women's rights' organizations." And she was absolutely adamant that women's liberation was not responsible for women's growing opportunities in the army or, as she put it elsewhere, for the increasing opportunities available "for the young lady intent on becoming a soldier." Asked, at a 1972 event, if the women's movement had influenced her thinking, Brigadier General Bailey simply shook her head. "We haven't needed Women's Lib in the Corps," she said. "We have equality. Women's Lib really hasn't touched us."[40]

Bailey's insistence, while counterintuitive, made sense in two ways. First of all, "women's lib" was a complicated phrase in the late 1960s and early 1970s. In the popular sphere, it was closely tied to the rejection of standards of respectability, to claims of sexual freedom and autonomy. When, in 1970, a man asked a woman, "Are you liberated?" he rarely meant "Do you believe in equal pay for equal work?" He more often meant "Do you have sex?" and quite frequently he meant, "Will you have sex with me?" The phrase "women's lib" carried with it all the sexual baggage that WAC leaders had been trying to escape since the bad old days of World War II.

Although that is certainly not what most questioners meant when they asked General Bailey about opportunities in the Women's Army Corps, her sensitivity to the issue was not misplaced. For example, when *Mademoiselle* ran a highly positive feature on the Women's Army Corps in 1976, the article began by dismissing the stereotype that WACs were "invading a man's world to nab a man, lesser versions of [TV show *M.A.S.H.*'s] Hotlips Hoolihan." And when the *Today Show* scheduled a special on the Women's Army Corps for March 1, 1974, NBC television submitted a list of questions to the Director's Office. Of eighteen questions, ten concerned sex. Question three requested the number of WACs "released in the past year for homosexuality"; question four sought the number who had received abortions; question five concerned the army budget for "female birth control devices, to include pills." The American public was evidently eager to know whether WACs were required to wear a bra while on duty, whether a "female" can enlist while pregnant, and if "P.G. during basic training" disqualified a recruit. The final question was: "Are all married men who serve as supervisory or Cadre personnel with WACs required to have written consent from wives?"[41]

It was not only a historically conditioned sensitivity to issues of sex and respectability that led General Bailey to dismiss the role of "women's lib." She, along with most other senior career army women, had no intention of crediting outsiders—especially a bunch of outsiders that in the early 1970s appeared unthinkingly antimilitary—with the results of the hard work and professional performance of army women over the past three decades. No matter that WAC leadership had become profoundly conservative; no matter that the ideal gender roles of the 1950s still structured WAC policy in the early 1970s. The director of the Women's Army Corps credited army women with responsibility for change. She said that the women's movement had little to do with the increasing opportunities for women in the army.

She was wrong. The women's movement, most particularly the Equal Rights Amendment and the series of legal challenges mounted during the 1970s, had a profound impact on the armed forces. As in so much of the history of civil rights in the United States, "sex" piggybacked on concerns about race. Faced with growing racial unrest and violence in the army, and under pressure from the White House and the Department of Defense, in June 1971 General Westmoreland began developing an affirmative action plan for the army. One result was the creation of an Army Office of Equal Opportunity (OEO). The U.S. Office of Equal Opportunity monitored discrimination on the basis of sex as well as race, though, in 1964, when Congress had surprised much of the nation by including "sex" as a protected category in a bill designed to guarantee the civil and employment rights of black men, many of those in power did not take the inclusion of sex seriously. The head of the OEO, when asked by a reporter, "What about sex?" joked, "I'm all for it!"[42] By 1971, enough had changed that issues of sexual discrimination automatically fell under the purview of the Army OEO, and without jokes. But both the army's affirmative action committee and its OEO were primarily concerned with race, which was, in their logic, a category that applied to men. Nonetheless, the army's OEO provided a mechanism for promoting gender equity once concerns about gender came to the fore.

The move from the draft to an all-volunteer force also propelled changes in women's roles. Army manpower analysts were well aware that young men might not flock to join the new all-volunteer army and equally conscious that the cohort of 17- to 21-year-old men would shrink by 15 percent during the 1980s. From the beginning they had proposed expanding the use of women, although oddly, and not insignificantly, members of the Gates Commission never once considered that idea. In 1971, as Secretary of the Army Froehlke confronted projections of a serious recruiting shortfall with the end of the draft, he supported a plan to double the size of the Women's Army Corps—to 23,800 enlisted women—by June 30, 1978. Under continued pressure from the Pentagon, in 1973 the army raised that goal to 50,400 by the end of 1979. With good publicity about opportunities for women in the army, the WAC volunteer rate began to climb for the first time in decades. Secretary Callaway, Froehlke's successor, proposed that the army "exploit success" and rely even more heavily on women, but hard-headed information about the logistical complexities of expansion and the lead time required to develop facilities and create training slots moderated his initial enthusiasm.[43]

Nonetheless, the army was proposing to increase the size of the WAC by more than 400 percent in less than eight years. The numbers were not, as a percentage of the army, very large: a 38,000 increase in an army of approximately 800,000. And the WACs would simply be making up a larger, though still single-digit, share of the enlisted ranks, not enlarging the army's overall size.[44] But men and women were not interchangable in the army. All women, other than physicians, were assigned through the Women's Army Corps, no matter where they were stationed or what they did. Women were trained separately from men, and differently from them, as well. They were guaranteed a different level of privacy, different sorts of facilities. There were severe restrictions on the assignment of women—restrictions that went well beyond barring them from combat. Thus, for the army to meet its allocated strength by increasing the number of enlisted women meant that the army had to do some serious rethinking of women's roles in the army.

General Bailey had overseen the opening of all but directly combat-related MOSs to women in the summer of 1972. Women could now be trained as dog handlers and tank mechanics, ammunition specialists and plumbers. But the newly opened MOSs did not translate directly into broader use of womanpower. Just because a woman could train as a dog handler or tank mechanic did not mean that she was eligible for all such positions in the army. As the civilian labor market had done until the practice was outlawed by the Civil Rights Act of 1964, the army designated positions—not only general job categories, but individual slots—by gender: M, F, or I (for "interchangable"). There was no point in increasing WAC enlisted strength to 50,400 if there were only 19,000 slots army-wide that were coded "F" or "I," as was the case in the summer of 1972.

In 1973, the army began to reevaluate its gender designations. Although all noncombat positions might, at least theoretically, be designated "I," that was nowhere near the case. The army sought an appropriate balance of men and women in each unit, with the acceptable percentage of women dropping dramatically as the unit's primary mission took it closer to the battle front. Designation of positions by sex took into account issues of privacy, of isolation, even the availability of bathing facilities. A fair number of slots were designated "M" to ensure equitable promotion possibilities for men, because women made up a separate promotion pool. And commanders had the last word when it came to designating slots. Most were aware—whatever their prejudices or sympathies—that the integration of women into nontraditional slots would not always go smoothly, whether women had anything to do with the difficulties or not. Many commanders preferred to avoid the potential for trouble. Nonetheless, a significant number of new slots opened to women in the mid-1970s. And General Bailey, acting on principle, designated a staff position in her office "I" and filled it with a man.[45]

The necessities of a marketplace model forced the army to expand and rethink the role of women. But the most significant pressure for change came from external forces. Through most of the 1970s, Congress strongly supported equal rights for women. The judicial branch steadily struck down gender-based distinctions. And the Pentagon, under congressional pressure, increasingly involved itself in the details of service policies that distinguished military personnel by gender.

In March 1972 the Senate approved the Equal Rights Amendment with a vote of 84 to 8, sending it on to the states for ratification. The amendment was elegantly simple: "Equal rights under the law shall not be denied or abridged by the United States or any State on account of sex." The simplicity of the amendment suggested that judicial interpretation would be critical; that, in fact, was one of the grounds offered for opposition. Questions about military implications abounded. Many argued that the courts had traditionally allowed great flexibility in military determinations about national defense. Others pointed to existing equal opportunity case law to demonstrate a history of judicial restraint. But Congress did not mean to exempt the military from the effects of the ERA. When Senator Sam Ervin proposed an amendment that would have exempted laws barring women from combat, it was defeated 71 to 18.[46]

In 1972, it seemed extraordinarily likely that the ERA would be ratified. Both congressional Democrats and Republicans had supported it in strength, and though the groundswell of support would soon founder on well-organized opposition coordinated by conservative activist Phyllis Schlafly, twenty-two of the necessary thirty-eight state legislatures ratified the amendment in 1973. The army, seeing what appeared to be the handwriting on the wall, established an "ERA Committee" in August 1972. Despite proposing some changes to bring the army's policies in line with contemporary society, the committee focused on policies members believed the army should struggle to retain. Gender equity, the ERA committee acknowledged, would likely require admitting women to the U.S. Military Academy at West Point. But military necessity, the committee report argued, should offer sufficient legal justification for maintaining a separate women's army corps, using different admissions standards, training women separately and differently from men, discharging those who became pregnant, and barring the use of women in combat.[47]

As the ERA moved steadily toward ratification and pressure from the Pentagon increased, the deputy chief of staff for personnel had his staff take another look at the issues, offering them the simple guidance: "Do what is best for the Army and best for women." This second study, in prize-winning bureaucratese, noted: "The starting point of this concept is to assume that women are completely equal with men and can do everything a man can. Recognizing also the practical limitations of this assumption, there are valid constraints." This report counterintuitively took a negative approach, moving from those things "women 'never' should do," such as combat and "assignments which preclude privacy in the field," to a list of things the army should "continue to do," such as "[m]onitor progress of the Equal Rights Amendment." Once again, the army plan was generally conservative, seeking means to maintain distinctions between male and female soldiers. On the civilian side, however, things were moving in the opposite direction. Both Secretary of Defense Laird and Secretary of the Army Froehlke made clear that it was time, in the words of one key memo, "to fully integrate the utilization of women into the Army" or, in other words, to eliminate the separate Women's Army Corps.[48]

Nothing happened quickly. There was a fair amount of turnover in civilian leadership during those days, and within the army General Bailey was fighting hard to preserve the corps. She, along with many other senior—and thus older—women leaders, believed that full integration was not the best path to equality. Women, thrown in with men to sink or swim, would face prejudice and suspicion. They would be expected to compete on "male" terms. They would lose the separate path to promotion they were currently guaranteed, and—perhaps most fundamentally, in Bailey's eyes—they would lose the impassioned champion for their well-being in the position of the director of the Women's Army Corps. Women leaders may well have drawn lessons from the racial integration of public schools, where African American teachers and principals typically lost position and influence when integrated into the predominantly white system. But WAC leadership's vision of "separate but equal" was not compelling in post–Civil Rights movement America or to the very broad coalition of liberal feminists in the 1970s.

Bettie Morden tells the story of the struggle over the future of the Women's Army Corps—or what Chief of Staff Abrams referred to as "distaff personnel assets"—in careful and complete detail in her official history of the WAC. There were multiple positions and rationales, and a series of sophisticated political strategies within the military. But in the end, it was Congress that made the difference. In hearings during June 1975, ranking members of the relevant subcommittee argued that the army was using the Women's Army Corps "as a cover to provide the opportunity for continued discrimination." The following week, Secretary Callaway agreed to the elimination of the WAC.[49]

The army began the gradual process of disestablishing the corps, but the legislation, attached to a larger and more complex bill, was stalled. The process dragged on until July 1978, when Secretary of the Army Clifford Alexander weighed in, finding an ally in Senator William Proxmire of Wisconsin, who had made his reputation as an opponent of defense department spending and waste in America's massive defense industry. Proxmire, introducing the legislation, asked fellow senators to "Imagine a separate personnel system for Blacks or Catholics or Chicanos. The country would not stand for such a thing . . . The Women's Army Corps is the last vestige of a segregated Military Establishment." The legislation was passed by Congress and signed by President Carter. And on October 20, 1978, the Women's Army Corps was officially discontinued.[50] There was little response. Given the changes that had already taken place, most Americans thought it had been dissolved years before.

As the WAC fought rearguard actions for survival, the civilian forces continued to press for change. In 1973, the Supreme Court had ruled that the military practice of automatically awarding men dependent benefits for both spouses and children but requiring women to prove that they were the sole financial support for their spouses was not constitutional. The armed forces were in full support, and had been pushing legislation to this end for years. In Congress, the voices of equal opportunity had been growing. Reports that Representative Patricia Schroeder, a junior member of the House Armed Services Committee, advocated the use of women in combat (her exact statement was: "It's outrageous that they limit the number of women in the Army because they say they can't handle combat roles") made many uneasy.[51] But army leaders were still shocked when Congress voted to open the national military academies to women.

In congressional hearings, the military offered one key objection. Military academies, one leader after another told the House Armed Services Committee, trained officers for combat. And admitting women to the nation's military academies either meant that America would begin sending women into combat, or it was a "waste of a scarce and costly resource" on those who would not fulfill the mission of Academy graduates. When West Point graduate Secretary Callaway testified in opposition, he nonetheless surrounded his statement with testimony supporting the army's record on equal rights for women. "I would contend," he told the assembled representatives, "that no other institution has actually done more—not talked about, but *done* more—to advance the cause of women than has the Army." Given the mood of the committee, it's possible that he didn't help his case when he listed the contributions women had made to the army as "skills and attitudes and—yes—charm."[52]

There was some debate in the House. Georgia's Larry McDonald, from the far right wing of the Republican party, asked his colleagues if they could "seriously imagine an officer giving a lecture or leading a tank column but requiring a pause to breast-feed her infant?" Rather than turning to policy and professional standards for a practical answer to McDonald's question, the outspoken advocate for women's rights, Bella Abzug of New York, replied: "women were lactating on the frontier of this Nation; and women were lactating on the frontiers of Israel when they fought to establish that homeland. They were lactating during wars throughout the history of this great nation and the history of the world. Somehow or another that did not stop progress."[53]

Despite the excessive interest in women's breasts and their functions, statistical social science data allowed members of Congress to override military objections. Research showed that slightly more than 12 percent of those graduated from West Point did not enter the combat arms. Thus, there was precedent. Neither the purpose of the academy nor the prohibition against women in combat need be changed in order to accommodate women at West Point. Military leaders argued that all West Point graduates were meant to join the combat arms, that the 12 percent figure being used to justify the end of an era represented those who had become physically incapacitated during the course of their education. But members of Congress understood the central place the U.S. Military Academy had in army careers, and they meant to remove as many obstacles to women's progress as possible. The House vote was 303 to 96. In the Senate, with support from Sam Nunn, conservative Democrat from Georgia, the measure passed easily in a voice vote.[54]

As civilian and military leaders struggled over gender policy, the army had to recruit, train, and "utilize" a steadily growing number of enlisted women. Beginning in 1974, recruiters were instructed to enlist women for nontraditional military occupational specialties and—to enforce the shift—the army dramatically cut the number of spaces available to women each month in the traditional fields of administration, medical care, and communications. In part because of young women's growing interest in new opportunities, but also because of such recruiting policies, the percentage of women in nontraditional fields jumped from 1.8 percent in 1972 to 22.4 percent in 1978.[55]

As the army made the commitment to assign women to a broader range of positions, it had to rethink training, as well. Commanders, urged to expand the number of interchangeable positions, often insisted that WACs were not able to meet basic requirements. For example, members of combat support units were required to patrol unit perimeters. But as WACs were not given tactical and weapons training, they could not do so; either a man would have to do double duty for every WAC assigned or—more likely—the slots would remain coded "M." Thus in 1974, defensive weapons were added to women's basic training. At first WACs were only required to "familiarize" themselves with the M16; those who requested were allowed to fire one. But within a year, WAC basic training required familiarization *and* qualification. Even though a writer for the Fort Jackson *Leader,* chronicling the process, did manage to locate a female trainee who obligingly told her, "I don't really believe in guns," weapons qualification removed one more objection to the use of women. As of September 1975, the Department of the Army stated officially that WACs were allowed to participate in all unit "activities," so long as "they are not perceived as combat soldiers." "Perceived" seems to have been the key word. Thus, training sites were urged to "avoid using pictures that could be misconstrued."[56]

In 1978, moving toward full integration, the army began to combine men and women in the same basic training companies. Reported responses from members of the first group, who had volunteered for the army but not for combined training, revealed some difference in perspective. Private Sandi Reed of Whitman, Massachusetts, said, "I was pretty excited when they first told us. There's more competition, and it's a bigger challenge"; Private Charles Simpkins, from New York City, replied, "Since women are into 'women's lib' and want the same opportunities, I think it's a good place to start." This training cycle experimented with identical physical training for men and women, with no modified push-up or sit-up option for female trainees. At the end of the first week, a feature article in the post newspaper reported, men were ahead of women in physical training. But according to at least one male drill sergeant, "Females catch on a lot quicker."[57]

Material intended for recruiters pushed change hard. After a 1976 report to Congress offered statistical data demonstrating that army recruiters had not told 54 percent of the women surveyed about nontraditional options, official publications worked to normalize the role of the women and to lessen the sense of distance between "WACs" and "soldiers." The recruiter's *Journal,* after noting that a WAC official had suggested replacing WAC with the terms "woman soldier" and "woman officer," suggested that—in the interest of equal opportunity—the terms "soldier" or "officer" might serve women better. General Eugene Forrester, head of the recruiting command, told his recruiters that enlisting women for nontraditional skills was a "prime element of our mission" and urged them to "Be aggressive." The *Journal* ran articles such as "'I Hate to Type'" and "'I am not typical: I'm a person,'" along with photographs of women operating bulldozers and repairing trucks.[58]

The army had to rethink its advertising strategy for men as it moved from the draft to all-volunteer. Recruiting advertising for women was caught up in the process. In 1972, even as the army opened all noncombat MOSs to women, the "creative boys" at N.W. Ayer were caught between models of femininity and opportunity. The lieutenant colonel—a former artilleryman—who managed army advertising described a campaign "directed at the young woman bored with her social life (or lack of it) and her direction, yearning for the excitement she cannot find, perhaps, in Minneapolis or Kansas or Sandusky." The heart of the new army campaign was a song, its melody "soft and sweet and gentle," its lyrics meant to "provoke a gauzy wistfulness":

When nighttime falls
And you're thinkin' about the life you're livin'
Ask yourself this:
Is it all you want and all that you wished for?
. . . Join the Women's Army Corps.

As Lt. Col. Childress explained, the song might move young women past the "hard-nosed, truckdriving-mama image the WACs have had. This outfit sounds feminine . . . professional . . . glamorous . . . *nice!*" And, in fact, the ad did seem to work.[59] Some other advertising efforts at that moment were less successful; when the advertising agency for the Army National Guard tried to recruit its first women members by offering, "Spend a weekend with the boys"—a slogan the recruiting command liked a lot—top guard officials ordered the entire batch of brochures shredded.[60]

As women's possible roles in the army changed, army recruiting advertising tried to keep pace. Someone eventually realized that advertising femininity and glamour might not be the most effective way to recruit women who wanted to repair trucks and operate bulldozers. So an advertisement created for *Life* magazine in 1973 asked, "What's new for women in today's Army?" and answered: "[A]lmost every job open to men is now open to women. At the same pay, $288 a month to start." "We've got over 300 good, steady jobs," offered another ad. "Jobs for young men. And young women." A 1977 ad for *Military Intelligence* simply referred to "the men and women of the Army's intelligence team." An ad the following year adopted the language of the women's movement. "If you like Ms., you'll love Pvt.," the headline promised.[61]

But with all the gender-neutral ads and the repeated claims that "Today's Army may be your most equal opportunity," recruiting advertising more or less painted itself into a corner. Although there were a great many things women could do in the army, there were a great many things they could not. Someone felt obliged to confront the issue (albeit "humorously") in an advertisement created for *Sourcebook,* an army publication aimed at high school students, in 1977. "Hey Sergeant!" the ad began.

"I'm a sensational looking chick. Can I ride up front in the tank?" The answer: "Ahem." The text continued: "Right now women are not allowed in combat specialties, so you can't be a 'tank crewperson,' or an 'infantryperson' . . . However, you can fix the tank if you want, or help plot where it's going to go." For all the talk about "hundreds of challenging specialties open to women in *every* field"—a claim repeated even in this ad—there was one huge omission.[62] Women were barred from combat.

In the mid-1970s, there was a strong sense of urgency surrounding the issue of women in combat. Many Americans, within and without the military, assumed that a decision had to be made, and to be made soon. And at that moment, the word floating around the Pentagon was "inevitable." All the pieces seemed to be falling into place. Congress had powerfully endorsed equal opportunities for women, from its strong vote for the Equal Rights Amendment in 1972 on through its decision to admit women to the service academies in 1975. Women's rights organizations felt confident; in 1976 NOW's Committee for Women in the Military, whose motto was "On land, on sea, and in the air—a woman's place is everywhere," rejected the question of combat as "irrelevant." "[I]f there are capable women who want these jobs," the committee stated, "the question that needs asking is . . . Does the military have the right to treat their women, regardless of ability, as children who must have their decisions made by others?" In 1977, the Women's Equity Action League judged prospects for women's opportunity in the military—including the end of the combat barrier—as "more promising now than ever before."[63]

Secretary of the Army Clifford Alexander, who saw enhanced social equity as the cornerstone of his administration, took the lead, pushing both the army and the Pentagon to end distinctions between men and women. "There are few things that men can do that women can't," he said, with an oblique reference to combat duty. "We cannot afford to waste human talent." Support was not only ideological. As the army steadily increased the percentage of women serving, assigning them ever more widely, drawing lines was less and less feasible. Army Chief of Staff Bernard Rogers, while having allowed that the notion of "women with rifles and fixed bayonets holding a forward position gives me heartburn," stated a firm official position in 1978. "Women are an integral part of the Army," he said. They are not "part-time soldiers—here in peace, gone in war." Should war come, women will deploy with their units and, like male soldiers, "share all risks . . . inherent in their specialty."[64]

The greatest sense of pressure, however, came from the congressional decision to admit women to the academies. The first class of women, which entered in 1976, found reasonable success; a higher percentage of women than men survived their first year. But as these first classes moved toward graduation in the spring of 1980, the question of what to do with the first women graduates became urgent. In fact, the issue was less pressing in the army, for it had much greater latitude than its fellow services. The Women's Armed Services Integration Act of 1948 specifically banned women from combat ships and cockpits. But in the wake of World War II, of the siege of Stalingrad and the bombardment of London, of the slow and violent liberation of France, of the purposeful firebombings of Dresden and Tokyo, of the atomic annihilation of Hiroshima and Nagasaki, the army had argued that battle fronts might not be clear and distant in the next war. "I do not believe," General Willard S. Paul testified, "that anyone in the city of Pittsburgh or any other industrial center is going to be in a rear area in the next war." Col. Hallaren, the director of the Women's Army Corps, had told the Senate Armed Services Committee that "it is impossible for the War Department to outline combat areas in the future since the experts advise that modern warfare makes the entire United States vulnerable as a combat area in the future." Congress, convinced by these arguments, had imposed no legislative restrictions on the army's use of women, leaving such decisions to the discretion of the secretary of the army.[65]

Thus, in 1980, the army would have some flexibility—limited by policy but not by law—in finding something worthwhile to do with the remarkable young women who had pioneered at West Point. But the equally remarkable young women who'd made it through the Naval Academy could not be assigned to combat ships. Many thought the problem demanded a servicewide solution—*before* these young women graduated in spring 1980. And as the Carter administration developed plans to expand the number of women in the military from 150,000 in early 1980 to 250,000 (both numbers including the reserves) by 1985, the Pentagon was pressing hard for more flexibility in their use.[66]

Some significant shifts were taking place in American society and politics, however, and the outcome of the debate about women in combat was not going to be what women's rights advocates had expected. Just as the virtual certainty that the ERA would pass pushed the army to offer women equal opportunity, the expanding roles of women in the military were heavily responsible—along with the supposed threat of co-ed toilets—for the defeat of the ERA. Even though a Gallup Poll found that two out of three Americans between the ages of 18 and 24 believed women should serve in combat, though only if they volunteered to do so, the threat that the ERA would put the nation's daughters in combat boots was the most effective argument against the ERA and the one that would bury it. When President Carter proposed registering women for the draft, Phyllis Schlafly proclaimed: "President Carter has stabbed American womanhood in the back in a cowardly surrender to women's lib."[67] A backlash was growing.

The growing conservative backlash undermined attempts to expand women's military roles, but so did concerns about the health of the all-volunteer force. As commentators and military analysts catalogued its problems in the late 1970s—problems of quality, of readiness, of size and training and capability—many began to include women as an item on the list. Many army officers had reservations about the rapid expansion of women in the ranks—some clearly chauvinistic, some more practically centered around the untested capabilities of women in combat or the potential impact of high pregnancy rates on mobility. These were not reservations made public, especially during the Carter administration, but military concerns were not simply fading away as women proved themselves. Despite many military leaders finding women to be excellent soldiers overall, there was a deep reservoir of concern, and of opposition, to women's growing role in the military.

The most powerful public critiques were offered by James Webb, the former marine infantry commander who would be elected to the U.S. Senate from Virginia in 2006. Webb steered clear of the conservative call upon "the deepest wisdom of the human race" that had animated writer George Gilder's "Case Against Women in Combat" in the *New York Times Magazine* in 1979. Instead, he saw the growing use of women in the military, the admission of women to the service academies, the notion that women might serve in combat, all as part of the larger failure of the volunteer force: the turn away from the "essential masculinity and rigorous nature" of military service, the replacement of discipline with notions of individual rights, the substitution of "job" for duty and commitment. In requiring admission of women to the service academies, Webb argued, Congress had fundamentally undermined their mission. Women would not make good combat soldiers, he insisted, and even more, women would never be able to lead men into combat. Webb rejected the idea that women were facing what black men had initially faced during racial integration of the military. That, Webb wrote, was "unfounded bigotry." Opposition to women, in contrast, was not due to cultural bias but to biological difference. "[D]espite what some would like to think," he wrote, "men and women are fundamentally different." With the integration of women and the resulting accommodations to their presence, training had been watered down. Combat readiness had been undermined by sexual attraction within a unit, by high rates of pregnancy, by double standards based on sex. And in the end, "after all of this confusion," the army had compromised the training of its combat officers and had taken in large numbers of soldiers who were weaker than their male peers, who had less endurance, and who were much more difficult to deploy.[68]

Changes in women's roles had not come easily during the 1970s. Though women had made enormous and rapid gains in public life, women's claims to equality were often met with opposition and ridicule. Nonetheless, advocates for equality in American life had been on the ascent, with victory after victory, since the Supreme Court's *Brown v. Board of Education* decision in 1954. Despite internal opposition, Congress had steadily enacted legislation to protect civil rights and guarantee equal opportunity. By the late 1960s, aware that too many of their number had taken the wrong stance on issues of racial justice, members of Congress were more willing to support legal remedies to discrimination. Mainstream advocates of women's rights had come to expect congressional support for their initiatives. The record was there, the trajectory clear. But by the late 1970s, something fundamental had altered the politics of the nation.

The advocates of women's equality who appeared before the House Armed Services subcommittee to discuss the utilization of women in the military in November 1979 were blindsided by those changes.[69] They had watched, with concern, the grassroots political movement to defeat the ERA; they had worried about the rise of a politically active religious right, with its notions about "traditional values" and the divinely ordained roles of women. But they had believed they had an ally in Congress. That was no longer true. By the late 1970s party discipline was breaking down. Senators and representatives were feeling pressure—or finding support—from a growing conservative movement that opposed government-mandated equality. And while there was no legitimate voice demanding the nation reverse the gains made by African Americans, a powerful movement now argued, straightforwardly and overtly, that the government should not guarantee women's equality to men in public life. Instead, its representatives argued, Americans should hold to the timeless truths, to the divine wisdom, to the traditional values that defined the differences between men and women. For many in this movement, the role of women in the armed forces was the line in the sand.

Opposition to women's changing roles in the military was not new. But by the end of the 1970s, the voices of opposition were based in increasingly well-organized and politically savvy organizations, and members of Congress gave them new levels of visibility and respect. The polarization was evident in the November 1979 hearings. Advocates and opponents of women's military equality seemed to be speaking different languages. The advocates used the language of law and logic. They offered social science data; they called for policy decisions based on rational investigation. The opponents claimed different sources of authority. They called upon timeless truths, on personal experience, and on God's will.

The staff counsel for the Women's Rights Project of the American Civil Liberties Union (ACLU) stressed the need for "thoughtful scrutiny," "reasoned analysis," and "rational examination." The chair of the National Coalition for Women in Defense cited army studies demonstrating that the presence of women did not impair the function of combat support and combat service support units. The Deputy Assistant Secretary of Defense for Equal Employment Opportunity explained a complex principle of U.S. employment law she believed would apply to the issue of women in combat: if the percentage of a group (here, women) qualified for a position (here, the infantry) under (gender) neutral standards was too low to be cost-effective, the military would not be required to screen women for that function.[70]

These advocates joined some of the traditional debates about the meaning of military service. Despite the move to a volunteer force, they insisted that the rights and responsibilities of citizenship were inseparable, that women's full citizenship required military obligation. They confronted the oft-stated conflict between national security and legislated equality, arguing that equality of *opportunity,* with judgments based on objective criteria, would do no harm to the necessary priority of security and strength. They straightforwardly argued that if women could not do the job, they must not. But they asked that women be given the opportunity to either succeed or fail. Their concern, they made clear, was not only with fostering women's equality but with maintaining the effectiveness of the U.S. military. Better to gather and analyze data during peacetime, insisted the EEO officer, than to face such decisions under pressure of war.[71]

In the testimony of those who opposed expanding women's roles, emotion, personal experience, and religious understandings replaced appeals to social science data and evidence based on "rational examination." A low point was the testimony of the Eagle Forum's national vice president, Mrs. Tottie Ellis. Speaking soon after a naturalized U.S. citizen who drew on her experience in Hitler's concentration camps to show "what war can do to women," Mrs. Ellis argued that the notion of putting women in combat "out-Hitler's Hitler." Women were not suited for combat, she explained, because combat is "violent and dehumanizing . . . In fact, men I have known who were in combat do not even enjoy war movies."[72]

With much greater credibility, two retired military officers offered their own experience to counter the advocates' social science evidence. With quiet intensity, retired Brigadier General Andrew Gatsis contrasted the isolated actions of training—firing a rifle on the range, parachuting out of an airplane and returning to the barracks—with actual combat: the "loneliness and desolation, weary marches, at times relentless heat, bitter cold, torrential rains, filth, pestilence, disease, the slime of dropping dugouts and the stench of human carnage." In Gatsis's view, the issue was not women's rights or opportunity, but the survival of soldiers. "Weak warriors," he argued, "become a burden on others, diminishing fighting power and increasing the likelihood of casualties." "It is a crime," Gatsis told the committee, that as the Soviet Union builds its "practically all-male army" to three times the size of the U.S. Army, "some American leaders regard combat chiefly as an obstacle to women's rights."[73]

The overwhelming bulk of testimony, however, was grounded in a sense of loss, framed as a means to stave off the destruction of the God-given American way of life. General Hoisington, former director of the Women's Army Corps, insisted that the question of women in combat was "not a matter of equal rights . . . not a matter of equal opportunity." But she did not see it as a matter of national security or military effectiveness, either. "It is a matter, ladies and gentlemen," Hoisington claimed, "of whether we are going to preserve the things our Nation stands for . . . Our constitution, our flag, our family life." Jeremiah Denton, a retired rear admiral who had spent eight years as a POW in Vietnam and would soon join the U.S. Senate, called proposals to use women "in mortal combat" a "frightening system of a relatively new but rapidly worsening spiritual illness," one that he "prayed that the sharp shock of recent national failures" would stem. But Denton—who was also the founder of the Coalition for Decency and a consultant for televangelist Pat Robertson's Christian Broadcasting Network—linked the question of women in the military to "godless Sodom and Gomorrah poison," instructed the committee that "all rights, including women's rights, take on grotesque perceptions" unless the nation admits that God is "the basis for government," and rejected the notion of women in combat with his claim that "the traditional principles of this Nation are the key to our goodness and to our success as a Nation."[74]

Phyllis Schlafly, predictably, condemned the "false dogmas" of the women's liberation movement, including those that suggested, in her words, that the nation must "accord the same dignity to lesbians and prostitutes as to wives, to illegitimate births as to legitimate, . . . [and] that we support immoral and antifamily practices with public funds," even in the armed services. "The very idea of women serving in military combat is so unnatural," Schlafly said, "so ugly, that it almost sounds like a death wish for our species." Instead of expanding women's roles in the military, she argued, the nation must "reestablish as a national principal that there are different roles for men and women." General Westmoreland, appearing at his own request and as a private citizen, addressed questions of military capability. But he also insisted, in his prepared statement, that "No man with gumption wants a woman to fight his nation's battles," and condemned female soldiers who bore babies "out of wedlock." "I believe," he said, somehow overlooking a few minor exceptions, such as slavery, "this is the first time that our nation has by its official policy sanctioned an immoral practice."[75]

For psychological insight, the committee turned to Dr. Harold M. Voth, a psychiatrist at the Menninger Foundation in Topeka, Kansas. Voth offered a state-of-the-art 1950s analysis of the "antifemininity or masculinity complex" that led women to "search for an identity and role which permits them to live out a pseudo-male identity." This "crazy quest to get women out to do all these things which men obviously do better," according to Voth, had yielded "social pathology" and social decline, manifest in 1970s America as "lowered productivity, . . . greater self-centeredness, trends toward mediocrity, [and a] high divorce rate." The quest for women's equality, Voth concluded, was destroying the family. And it was the family, after all, that "America was built on, a good solid American family."[76]

Final testimony was given by Charles Cade, operations director of the organization at the heart of the religious right—the Moral Majority. Though only a year and a half old, the group had drawn millions of members and was beginning to demonstrate its political muscle. Cade made the most extreme claim of all the witnesses. While all others had accepted some voluntary role for women in the military, Cade saw women's very presence as immoral, their violation of God-given roles as a sign of national decline. "Leadership and authority," he insisted, "are male attributes ordained by God." And soldiers "cannot be expected to be valorous and self-sacrificing when breathing in a self-indulgent and egocentric atmosphere" of a military integrated by women and undermined by the presence of birth control, abortion, and promiscuity. As "the moral corruption of false equality gnaw[s] at traditional family roles," he claimed, "the bedrock of our Nation hangs in the balance." Mr. Cade ended his testimony by thanking the committee for "letting God have the last say here."[77]

Cade's claim to speak for God took some members of Congress by surprise, but his basic message—that there was a large, growing, and politically active constituency devoted to a profoundly conservative vision of American life, and which did not believe in the equality of men and women—was clear. The political mood of the nation was shifting. There were strong hints that the subcommittee would recommend new legal restrictions on the army's use of women. That didn't happen. But only a few months later the same legislative body that had so recently endorsed the ERA with bipartisan support and opened the service academies to women buried the presidential request to register women for the draft in committee. It never even got to the floor of Congress.[78]

With President Carter still in office, plans to increase the number of women in the military continued. The administration's overall goal was to move from 8 to 12 percent (about 250,000 women in total) of the armed forces by 1985; more immediate army goals were to jump from 65,000 to 100,000 women in the early 1980s. The recruiter's journal, by this point re-named *all VOLUNTEER,* was doing its part. "It's happening everywhere in the Army, worldwide," began an unusually well-written article in February 1981, "and it happens all the time: The UH-1 'Huey' flares and hovers inches above the ground, and from the surrounding tree line, an infantry fire team . . . runs out to board the ship. The last of the heavily laden 'grunts' reaches up" and is "yanked aboard" by the crew chief "as the Huey pulls pitch out of the maneuver." The crew chief, of course, is a woman, as are the MP in Stuttgart and the commander of the Target Acquisition Battery who join her in "This *wo*man's Army." Of limits imposed on women in the army, this recruiter writes: "Those days are done, a thing of the past."[79]

Three months later, assuming it had the blessing of the new conservative president who had vanquished Carter so decidedly at the polls, the army instituted a "womanpause" and stopped recruiting women.

6 ⋆ THE ALL-RECRUITED ARMY

THE ARMY'S "WOMANPAUSE" certainly signaled strong resistance to expanding women's roles and numbers, but it was also evidence of continuing concern about the health of the all-volunteer force. No matter how enthusiastically the secretaries of the army cheered its progress, no matter how resolutely the commanders in the field stated their confidence in the men and women of the U.S. Army, a significant portion of army leadership had never really signed on to the notion of a Modern Volunteer Army. Change had come rapidly with the move to the market and almost everyone was uncomfortable with one piece or another of that transformation. Some, of course, just wanted to go back to the way things used to be. But for every commissioned officer or NCO who longed for the increasingly mythical good old days there were more who worried, concretely and specifically, about the viability of the army they had. Many in the army were not convinced that the all-volunteer force was working; some large sub-group was not convinced that it would ever work. And through much of the 1970s some portion of army leadership truly believed they were just marking time, waiting for the facts to win out, waiting for it to become patently obvious to all concerned that the nation had to return to the draft.

By the end of the 1970s, those facts were grim. The all-volunteer force turned out to be much more expensive than the Gates Commission had predicted, and Congress had been less than enthusiastic about allocating funds for recruiting, bonuses, and pay increases as inflation had skyrocketed. First-term soldiers complained about promises not kept, about mismatched MOSs, make-work, and tedium; army officers and NCOs complained about lax training and the seemingly oxymoronic "reluctant volunteer." Quality, as measured by test scores and high school graduation rates, was plummeting—even though no one yet knew the extent of the problem. America's enemies abroad read journalistic accounts of soldiers who couldn't read, tankers who couldn't aim, nuclear weapon maintenance crews who had no real idea what they were doing. Thirty-six percent of new enlistees didn't make it through their three-year term of service. The integration of women, many in authority believed, was undermining the training process and the resulting strength of the force. Re-enlistment rates were poor, and the army was desperately short of sergeants. Recruiter scandals made the news, prompting yet more congressional investigation. In 1979, the army missed its recruiting goal by 17,000 men and women, or almost 11 percent of recruiters' total mission. It was in the spring of 1980 that Edward C. "Shy" Meyer, the chief of staff of the army, said publicly that the United States had a "hollow Army." As if to prove the point, a postage-paid "for more information" postcard from army recruiting bore the photograph of a dubiously smiling soldier. "Nothing's perfect," read the caption. "But this is pretty good."[1]

These all-too-obvious problems, in an era of rising global tensions, prompted a serious debate about returning to the draft. It was not the first—or the last—of such debates. But in the late 1970s, the AVF *was* vulnerable. It may never have been so vulnerable as its congressional opponents thought, but the debates about its future were real. When a 1978 study of the army conducted by a congressional fellow in the office of Tennessee Republican representative Robin Beard began with the claim that "The United States Army is fighting one of the major battles of its history; it is fighting for a future," the nation's congressional representatives did not laugh at the author's temerity or dismiss him as politically naive.[2] Instead, they relied heavily on his claims as they argued over the future of the all-volunteer force.

The rhetoric of the Beard Study was often overblown, and the report as a whole could well have served as a brief for reinstituting the draft. Evidence of all the obvious problems was there in abundance. But the report also suggested a solution. It is easier, it asserted, to fight "an enemy that is seen and that is 'in force and in being'" than to face and conquer "other fronts": personnel management, declining budgets, and technological change. Stepping with both feet into the ongoing military debate about the relative importance of leadership versus management, the Beard Study claimed that the only way to control "the slippery facets of managing a 'peacetime' force" was to seek management solutions to army problems.[3]

The army found its manager in General Maxwell R. Thurman, a slight, pencil-necked man in thick glasses who used the word "volumetric" in sentences and signed his memos with smiley faces. He was also aggressive and hard-nosed, perfectly capable of humiliating a full colonel in front of his men, an officer with little patience for the slow, the stupid, the lazy, or those who disagreed with him, a man who earned the devotion of some as well as the nickname "Mad Max." When Thurman succumbed to leukemia in 1995, an army press release called him "a principal architect of the all-volunteer army" and credited him for "the modern professional Army we now possess."[4] Thurman, more than anyone else, addressed the management problems that were undermining the young all-volunteer force. His fundamental insight was that the army was not all-volunteer; it was all-recruited. And under Thurman's detail-oriented, hands-on, seven-days-a-week-including-holidays guidance, the all-volunteer army figured out how—as an institution—to recruit.

By the middle of the 1980s, the all-volunteer army had moved from its 1979 nadir to relative stability and success. Quality was up; boots were filled; pay was competitive (with a raise totaling almost 25 percent); the army's status had risen; training was improved; readiness was high. Thurman, obviously, did not accomplish these things on his own. Nor did the army. Even the best plans are subject to broad social forces and cultural shifts, to the upturns and downturns of the economy, to the vagaries of political change. The army benefited from economic recession during the early 1980s, as youth unemployment hit 17.4 percent (35.2 percent for black youth aged 16 to 19). The Reagan administration's overwhelming concern with Soviet power and its massive expansion of the defense budget played a role in recruiting, as did the growing distance from the Vietnam War and the emergence of a new public culture of patriotism inspired by the Reagan presidency.[5]

During the 1980s, army recruiting moved past the initial models of a supply-and-demand labor force. It went well beyond its initial, somewhat awkward forays into the consumer marketplace, and it shifted polarizing arguments over race and gender to the margins of its concerns after the vicissitudes of the prior two decades.[6] In this decade army recruiting staked its future—and the future of the all-volunteer army—on state-of-the-art econometric models and the details of market shares and media weight. It learned the lessons of corporate management and information economics. Working within this system, recruiters increasingly sent forward young men and women who became capable and motivated soldiers. As a result, the rest of the army began to believe in the all-volunteer force.

The all-volunteer army was saved, in some large part, by the recruiting system's mastery of modern corporate management. This is not a simple story of triumph, for there were tradeoffs. Standardization and systematization left less room for the more personal art of recruiting. Emphasis on social science research and econometric models crowded out the knowledge born of individual instinct and experience, and data based on aggregate success rates certainly foreclosed the against-the-odds success of many individuals. The transformations, furthermore, were not due solely to the discovery of new management techniques. Though the recruiting system needed to be managed, as had been obvious throughout the history of the army, management is no substitute for leadership. Individuals matter. In this instance, recruiting was in the hands of a commander who was willing to use leadership in the service of management. Max Thurman thought like a manager and trusted data analysis more than experience, but he also had the force of personality and the knowledge of how to work the army to make things happen.

Max Thurman never intended to join the army.[7] His older brother, Roy, had graduated from West Point, and Max's high school record made that a likely option for him, as well. But though the two men were legendarily close as adults—even wearing matching silver belt buckles that "Thurman the Younger" (or "Thurman the Lesser," both of which Max Thurman sometimes called himself until the day he outranked his three-star brother) had designed and ordered from a silversmith—that wasn't true in their youth. Thurman, highly aware of his own abilities in math and science, had decided to study engineering at North Carolina State University rather than to follow in his brother's footsteps. Nevertheless, North Carolina State issued Max Thurman an Army ROTC uniform during freshman orientation, for NC State was a land grant college and all male students at U.S. land grant colleges were then required to complete two years of ROTC training. Afterward, like all of his male classmates, Thurman was essentially required to join the reserves—otherwise, he would be automatically eligible for the draft. "I wasn't born yesterday," said Max Thurman, looking back. "I figured that I would just as soon not get drafted to go to Korea."[8]

Thurman did well in college; as he put it, he "knew which way the rabbit jumped on campus." At the end of his freshman year he was first in his class academically and "the number one kid in ROTC." During his sophomore year he carried a load of twenty-seven credits when the standard was eighteen. He majored in chemical engineering but also studied Russian, Shakespeare, and public speaking, played intramural sports, and managed his fraternity—a role he described as handling "irate complaints from all the dissatisfied proletariat." By senior year he was brigade commander of ROTC.[9]

The path to four star general, however, was far from clear. Thurman had little real interest in the army and even less interest in its traditions. At the end of his first year at NC State, he turned down the offer of a nomination to West Point and steadfastly refused to have anything to do with the traditional military organizations for ROTC cadets, such as Scabbard and Blade. "Isn't it interesting that the brigade commander didn't belong to any of that bullshit?" he asked later. When he graduated in 1953, even though he was warned that he would almost certainly be called to active duty in the reserves, he took a job in industry. His tenure as a "snotty-nosed, lack-luster, lout" of a rookie engineer at Carbine Carbon's petrochemical complex in West Virginia lasted only six weeks before he was called up by the reserves and assigned to serve as supply officer to the Army Depot in Anniston, Alabama.[10]

Second Lieutenant Thurman, resolved not to go to that "damn branch," showed a precocious understanding of how to work the army system. He'd been designated a Distinguished Military Graduate for his performance at NC State; that meant he had the option of selecting a commission in the Regular Army. He used it. And here, he meant to follow in his brother's footsteps—to the army's Airborne Division. The army assigned him instead to Ordnance. But Thurman had another card to play.

He did the basic ordnance course, but in the meantime the adjutant general got a call from the vice chief of staff and Thurman got orders for Field Artillery, from which he could volunteer for Airborne. Roy Thurman was the aide to the vice chief of staff; once Max had been called up for the reserves, Roy had made certain that his brother fell into the company of the vice chief.[11]

Thurman devoted the rest of his life to the army. They may as well have coined the term "life-long bachelor" for him; one former colleague described him as the poster boy for "If the Army wanted you to have a life it would have issued you one." Once he was in positions of command he rarely went home, even when he could, and he was likely to call someone at three in the morning if he'd had an idea he thought important. It may be that he came to love the army, as he spent thirty-seven years and seven months in its ranks. Or it may be that it was just not in the character of a man who took twenty-seven college credits in a semester because he "was capable of doing it" to behave otherwise.[12]

Thurman's competence was obvious, and his early career went smoothly. He served with the 11th Airborne Division in the 1958 Lebanon crisis and then did two tours in Vietnam, commanding the 2nd Battalion, 35th Field Artillery during the Tet Offensive. His appointment to the Army War College came in 1969; he later commanded the 82nd Airborne Division Artillery. But by 1977, he was director of Program Analysis and Evaluation (PA&E) in the office of the chief of staff of the army: the army's chief analyst and programmer. One of the chief problems Thurman had to confront in PA&E was recruiting, which was, in Thurman's assessment, "going to hell in a handbasket." Recruiters were not making mission. Congress had cut the recruiting budget, which meant that the number of recruiters had shrunk along with the recruiting command's advertising budget. And with the secretary of the army (Clifford Alexander) and the army staff constantly at war, there was no unity in direction.[13]

Thurman, as director of PA&E, made recruiting his business. He assigned an analyst to monitor issues of quality and attrition and took advantage of an opportunity to study advertising with New York–based consultants Canter, Achenbaum, Heekin, hired by the Department of Defense to evaluate military advertising. They took him through mountains of data—always something he found satisfying. Their recommendations, however, were another story. The official report to the secretary of defense concluded: "There is ample evidence that the Army is now offering a product which is being rejected by the target market. And it is axiomatic in marketing that you can't sell an inferior product with advertising." If that recommendation was accepted—and the "bad product" language was repeated by at least one congressman in appropriation hearings soon after—that meant no increase in advertising budgets until the army was deemed sufficiently improved for advertising to work.[14]

In these meetings, Thurman learned a great deal about advertising analysis, but not all Thurman's teachers made such dire evaluations. In September 1979 Tom Evans, the recruiting command's civilian deputy director of advertising and public affairs, brought a team of media analysts from N.W. Ayer to the Pentagon to make a case for reprogramming $63 million of already-allocated funds to advertising. If the agency was able to advertise most heavily early in the year, these analysts argued, the additional support would give recruiters a head start on the year's goal. PA&E support was critical in any request for reprogramming funds, so the Ayer team began its briefings with Thurman. These were not the usual agency briefings, in which the ads did star turns and the discussion concerned general strategy. This presentation was about the details—ad placement, the science of media scheduling, and the quantitative analysis of media weight. Thurman was fascinated. And convinced. At the next meeting that day, scheduled with the deputy chief of staff for personnel, Thurman did the briefing himself, quite comfortably, in the language of advertising and media analysis.[15]

In November 1979, Shy Meyer, the chief of staff of the army, summoned Thurman to his Pentagon office. Thurman had heard some talk about his being sent to recruiting to try to manage the biggest can of worms in the army, but he still had hopes he would get command of the 82nd Airborne instead. It was not to be. Thurman, Meyer announced, was going to Fort Sheridan to take over the Recruiting Command. The change of command was "fractious." Although the recruiting crisis may not have been the fault of the current USAREC commander, it was his responsibility, and it was clear to all that he was departing under a cloud. There was no orderly handover; there was no formal change of command. At six o'clock in the evening—well after dark in late November on the western shore of Lake Michigan—Major General Mundy accepted his Distinguished Service Medal and left Fort Sheridan. Early the next morning, Major General Thurman took charge. He found the atmosphere hostile at first, but he wasn't spending much time in his office.[16]

General Thurman, as he made clear in various public speeches, saw the army as a "gigantic business." He approached problems from his operations research background; it went without saying, for Thurman, that research and systems analysis outweighed gut-level response and the lessons of experience. As he approached the problem of recruiting, he kept the claims of the DoD advertising consultants in mind: one can't sell a bad product. But he wasn't at all convinced that the army was a bad product. And he was pretty sure that it wasn't really possible to change a two-hundred-year-old institution. "The Army is the Army," he said later. "The monolithic mother Army is the monolithic mother Army . . . It is what it is, and some major general can't easily change it."[17] This wasn't modesty, for Thurman was fairly confident that he *could* change the recruiting command. And despite his faith in management, Thurman did hold true to some traditional army principles, though more likely because of personality than because of the weight of prescription or tradition. He put his faith and his energy into rationalization and systematization, into the tools of management, but he did not experiment with management techniques. Thurman's USAREC was not ahead of the management curve in creating a democratic workplace. The first priority of the new commanding general of USAREC—aside from learning, in enormous, hands-on detail, about every step of the recruiting process—was making clear who was in command.

Thurman's goal for his first thirty days was to meet with every one of the commanders and sergeants major of each of the fifty-seven recruiting battalions, as well as the five brigade commanders and their sergeants major. He spent five days each week on the road for these meetings and the other two days at Fort Sheridan, working with army legal counsel on the recruiting malpractice cases (he called it "recruiter chicanery"). Thurman met with representatives of each brigade separately, beginning in the west. These were not simply meet-and-greets. General Thurman interrogated his subordinates. By the second day of his meeting in Kansas City, which was his second stop, he'd made one diagnosis. From what he'd heard, the basic problem with the recruiting command was that the officers weren't running it. The sergeants were. In Kansas City Thurman dismissed all the sergeants major from the meeting and informed the remaining officers that that wasn't the way it worked in the army.[18]

Recruiting was an odd field. Generally, army officers were "raised" in a branch—rising in rank and responsibility from lieutenant within artillery, for example, or infantry, or ordnance, or the quartermaster corps. Recruiting was a lateral transfer. Though captains were assigned to recruiting, they rarely had repeat assignments in the field. Virtually no one rose through the ranks to battalion commander. Instead lieutenant colonels, with no previous experience in recruiting, were brought in to command battalions. Not surprisingly, they looked to more knowledgeable senior NCOs, with years of experience in recruiting, for advice.[19]

Thurman had quickly identified what he saw as a problem in command—and clearly demonstrated his allegiance to rank and hierarchy in his diagnosis. But his proposed solution likely endeared him more to NCOs than to the officers in charge. Shortly before Christmas, Thurman was in San Diego to distribute awards at the annual recruiter banquet for the Santa Ana battalion. The awards that year were slim and, he felt, not particularly well deserved. Thurman had identified this battalion as one of his failures—not because of the recruiters, but because of their officers, none of whom, he'd decided, understood how to recruit. Standing before the assembled recruiters in their dress blues, all there to celebrate the accomplishments of a very difficult year, it occurred to Thurman (as a former field artillery officer who had, albeit indirectly, transferred laterally into recruiting) that the officers in the room couldn't pass a gunners test.

"Is there any sergeant in here," Thurman asked his audience, "who has come into the recruiting service from the artillery?" A few recruiters raised their hands, and Thurman pointed to one of them. Tell us what a gunners test is, he told the sergeant, who explained that a gunners test determines whether one knows how to man a howitzer. So, the commanding general of USAREC asked the recruiter from the failing battalion, now "tell me what the gunners test should be in recruiting." The recruiter gave the answer Thurman wanted: "to put a guy in boots." General Thurman made it an order: all officers in the recruiting command had sixty days "to put a guy in boots."[20] He wanted the officers to know, firsthand, what it was like to make dozens of phone calls that yielded no appointments, or to work for weeks with some young man who, at the very last minute, decided he'd rather stay home and marry his girlfriend, or go to college, or keep living rent-free in his parents' basement. Only then, he believed, could the officers properly manage their recruiters.

Thurman, himself, had little feel for the recruiter's life. He understood that recruiters were essential; he was certain that recruiting had to be an "eyeball-to-eyeball" process and made that argument strongly before

Congress. He respected what recruiters did and he meant to provide them with the resources to do it even better, but if someone had asked him whether recruiting was an art or a science, he wouldn't have pondered the answer. He certainly didn't waste time musing about "the nature of youth today." Thurman's goal was to figure out how to "provision" the army with people. "It sounds crass," he said later, but "provisioning in the people game is like provisioning in the bullets and beans game . . . It is a stock control function." In the winter of 1979–80, General Thurman was beginning to systematize that process.[21]

The most obvious sign that things had changed was the location and timing of the annual recruiting command "sales conference," an event that usually offered the recruiting commanders a bit of pleasure along with the work. But as Tom Evans, USAREC's acting director of advertising and public affairs during Thurman's first months and a man Thurman quickly came to respect, recalled that meeting at Fort Sill: "Lawton, Oklahoma, may in some seasons be a garden spot, but on that [February] weekend it was decidedly bleak, a bleakness augmented by the fact that arrangements had not been made to heat . . . the building where the meeting was held. Recruiting commanders and USAREC staffers sat shivering in jackets and scarves through seemingly interminable workshops dedicated to arcane, if important, aspects of recruiting administration." The chief of staff of the army flew in to give the major motivational speech on Sunday afternoon. Toward the end of his talk, still trying to warm up the room, Shy Meyer asked a former golfing partner he'd spotted in the first row, "What's your handicap these days, Zaldo?" "General Thurman Sir," the former golfer replied.[22]

Word of a new era had circulated rapidly through the recruiting command. Thurman, however, had also decided he needed to take charge of the advertising. He'd been impressed with Ayer's media analysts earlier that fall, but not so much with their advertising campaign. Thurman's take on "Today's Army Wants to Join You" was in keeping with most of the rest of the career army officers. That campaign, at least, had been "interruptive." Those that followed—"Join the People Who've Joined the Army," with several different subthemes—tended to blur. J. Walter Thompson, the advertising agency for the marines, tactfully described the army's advertising as "a wide-ranging approach (befitting the size of the service), but with no single, underlying emotional appeal." "This is the Army," the slogan instituted in late 1978, had clearly not brought droves of volunteers to the recruiting offices. It was a defensive campaign, instituted largely in response to charges by the Beard Study that the army was misrepresenting what it offered. Representative John Murtha, former marine and the first Vietnam veteran elected to Congress, had taken a passionate dislike to the advertising photo of soldiers in Europe visiting a castle, and as Congress controlled budgets it very much mattered what the more opinionated members of Congress thought.[23]

The new campaign spent little time promoting opportunities for leisure in the all-volunteer army. The "This is the Army" campaign tried, instead, to show army life as it was, from basic training on. The ads were chock-full of information, with column inch upon column inch of tiny text. Informative, yes, but not something to grab the attention of young prospects. There were a few light touches, but not the right ones. A television commercial showing an infantryman sinking out of sight as he tries to ford a stream in full gear had tested well with focus groups of current soldiers and pleased people in the Pentagon, but army recruiters reported that it worked even better for recruiters from the navy and the air force.[24]

Soon after taking command of USAREC, General Thurman arranged a "Come to Jesus" (his term) session with N.W. Ayer. He brought the agency personnel out to Chicago. In this case, at least, there was heat in the building. And lots of coffee. Thurman, by his own account, had decided that he needed to "break" the agency. So he ordered the USAREC staff not to drink any coffee—not the night before the meeting, not to wake themselves up in the morning, and not as they sat in the room going over the details of media weight and the comparative advantages of radio, television, and print. The agency people, of course, drank the coffee. Thurman ran a nonstop meeting. When the Ayer people increasingly urgently asked for a break, Thurman told each speaker he was welcome to leave, but the meeting would continue without him. After five hours, he reported, "they knuckled under." The N.W. Ayer people left that meeting, Thurman believed, with a clear understanding of who, in fact, was in charge of army advertising. And it wasn't N.W. Ayer.[25]

There was one more command issue that Thurman had to deal with—and this one was not by choice. Soon after Christmas the secretary of the army, Clifford Alexander, made the trip to Fort Sheridan. Alexander knew Thurman from his days in Program Analysis and Evaluation; he and the chief of staff of the army, General Meyer, had sometimes had Thurman, as chief programmer, deliver briefings to the House Armed Services Committee on their behalf. Alexander had not been pleased when Meyer appointed Thurman to USAREC. Alexander believed the army focus on quantitative measures of quality was veiled racism; Thurman was convinced by the data that there was a close relationship—in aggregate—between these measures of quality and successful completion of terms of enlistment. Alexander didn't want to write off the 50 percent or so of young men and women who would succeed despite their lack of high school diplomas; Thurman believed that if roughly half of non–high school graduates did not complete their enlistments, it was much more efficient to recruit from the population with a greater likelihood of success. More fundamentally, although Thurman understood that the army had to make numbers—its "volumetric" mission—he was much more concerned with the content of those numbers. Quality was going to be an absolutely key factor in his command, and he defined quality quantitatively, not experientially: as measured by the percentage of I—IIIA "mental categories" and of high school diploma graduates. It is no surprise that Clifford Alexander had reservations about Max Thurman.

Alexander's options, however, were somewhat limited. Although civilian control of the American military is enormously important, from the president's power as commander-in-chief to Congress's hands-on (and changeable) supervision, the direct power available to the civilian leader of the army is, structurally, somewhat limited and excessively blunt. The secretary of the army cannot issue orders to commanding generals. But he can "fire" them. Max Thurman was fairly confident that was the reason the secretary of the army was making the trip to Fort Sheridan in the dead of winter.

Thurman had no intention of being fired. Instead of waiting to see what would happen, he took the offensive. The USAREC staff at Fort Sheridan assembled six officers and six recruiters from varying parts of the country. The men had a range of experience; in each group was a man with three, six, nine, twelve, fifteen, and eighteen months in recruiting. Thurman made clear to his staff—and they to the men—that he didn't want to know who they were. There was no "pre-brief"; the only instructions they received were that they were to meet with Secretary Alexander and to speak freely with him. When Alexander arrived, Thurman gave him the agenda for his trip: the secretary would meet with the recruiters for an hour. When that was done, he would meet with the officers for an hour. When that was done, Thurman would return, tell the secretary what each group had said and then explain USAREC's new direction. That accomplished, they would have lunch together and then Secretary Alexander could "go about his business" in Chicago. That, according to Thurman, is exactly what happened. When Thurman joined Alexander after the two meetings, he told Alexander: "what you should have found out . . . is that all the NCOs could sell you the Brooklyn Bridge and none of the officers could tell you a goddamn thing about recruiting." In Thurman's account, Alexander replied: "Yes, that is right. How did you know that?" To which Thurman answered: "Because I am in charge here and I understand what is going on in my command." And then they ate lunch, and "Clifford Alexander went away and we were happy ever after."[26]

Thurman's desire to manipulate may well not have stopped with Ayer execs, USAREC battalion commanders, and the secretary of the army. His stories of taking command seem a bit exaggerated and well-rehearsed, even for a man who describes himself as not well known for tact and diplomacy.[27] But Thurman did bring together elements of management and leadership, along with his knowledge of how to make things happen in the army, to implement a new focus on data, analysis, and systematization. On these foundations, he began to reform the recruiting system.

The army dealt with three major recruiting issues during Thurman's reign. Though he only commanded USAREC from November 1979 through July 1981, he kept close control over recruiting issues during the following six years as deputy chief of staff for personnel and then vice chief of staff of the army.[28] During that period, the army systematized recruiting. It created and built an enormously successful advertising campaign that changed the image of the army. And it secured congressional support and funding for programs that would allow it to attract young people who did not see the army as employer of last resort.

The recruiting system Thurman and his staff meant to systematize was, in fundamental ways, a holdover from the years of conscription—though its roots lay in the nineteenth century. Developed over decades, it had been molded by experience, shaped more by the accretion of decisions and actions than by a systematic and centralized process. Initially, and for much of U.S. history, army units had directly recruited their own volunteers. The first general recruiting organization was established in 1822, but it added to the efforts of individual regiments rather than replacing them. The true move to a central recruiting service took place in 1872, when the function was assigned to the office of the adjutant general, which was the central coordinating bureau of the army. During a major army reorganization in 1962, recruiting functions, along with responsibility for examination, induction, and processing, were moved from the control of the adjutant general; by 1966 they would be supervised by the deputy chief of staff for personnel. The U.S. Army Recruiting Command was created in 1964.[29]

Elements of modern recruiting had emerged gradually, in response to the needs of the U.S. military and the changing organization of American society. Regional control became increasingly important as, from 1904 on, potential volunteers were examined, processed, and inducted at central recruiting depots instead of at local recruiting stations. Measurements of acceptability became standardized, as experts devised more instruments for evaluating potential capability. In fact, the army, which had pioneered the use of qualification exams and other classification tests, ran the Armed Forces Entrance and Examination Stations that served all branches of the military from 1950 until 1979, when the stations were brought under control of the Secretary of Defense and redesignated Military Entrance Processing Stations. Army advertising, too, developed relatively early. The Recruiting Publicity Center, formed during World War I by people from advertising and entertainment industries, created recruiting posters, brochures, and films under the supervision of the adjutant general's office.[30]

It was obvious to all concerned, as the army contemplated the move to an all-volunteer force, that recruiting would become critically important. But there was no clear central plan for recruiting's new role. Change was rapid and somewhat unpredictable during the 1970s. The army launched a major recruiting advertising campaign, but the slogans rolled through—three major campaigns with dozens of subthemes in the space of eight years. The number of recruiters jumped dramatically, more than doubling—from 2,200 to 4,762—at the beginning of the decade. New recruiting stations opened; the number of recruiting battalions, or "recruiting main stations," as they were called then, surged from forty to sixty-four. The army worked hard to replace draft-era recruiters, stereotyped as NCO order-takers on the verge of retirement, with some of the army's most talented young sergeants. The recruiting school began to develop a professional course in sales techniques, replacing training that one recruiter later irreverently described as a course on "how to shake hands."[31] Perhaps most important, USAREC implemented a new computer-based system, REQUEST, that allowed army guidance counselors, the very experienced recruiters who worked with applicants at the Military Entrance Processing Stations, to determine the terms of their enlistment, to know precisely when and where seats were available at different training schools. That information streamlined the process and made it possible for trainees to move from basic training to advanced individual training at the same post with no time wasted waiting for a training slot to open up. Now the army could boast: "We don't make promises. We make guarantees."[32]

But despite the new importance of USAREC and its rapid expansion in size and scope, much of the control over recruiting remained at the regional level. The practice of recruiting, from "prospecting" techniques (the ways in which recruiters generate leads, whether cold-calling or through relationships with high school guidance counselors) to record-keeping practices to station appearance and administration, varied greatly throughout the nation. Each of the five geographically based recruiting brigades, themselves made up of battalions that encompassed anywhere from a single metropolitan area to several states, depending on population density, had, over the years, instituted the techniques it found most successful in its region. There was a fair amount of latitude so long as recruiting goals were met.[33]

This—along with the widely publicized recruiting shortfall and the equally widely publicized cases of recruiter malpractice—was the situation when Thurman took charge of the recruiting command in November 1979. The problem with numbers disappeared in fiscal year 1980, when the recruiting command surpassed its objective. But while numbers went up, the percentage of high school graduates dropped significantly, from 64 to 54 percent.[34] That was definitely not the direction the army had in mind. As he worked to reform recruiting, Thurman had two goals: to improve the quality of recruits, and to rationalize and systematize the entire recruiting process.

Standardization was the first step. At the meeting of battalion and brigade commanders at Fort Sill that February weekend in 1980, Thurman asked participants to identify the best practices thus developed by battalions or brigades; his goal was to codify them and implement them nationally. Within months two new sets of regulations—the Recruiter Basic Management System and the Recruiting Station Management System—were distributed. New regulations for recruiting areas and districts followed soon after. And by 1988, under Thurman's more distant leadership, USAREC developed the "Recruiting Doctrine and Strategy Manual" modeled after the FM 100-5 ("how to fight and win") Operations Manual.[35]

Thurman was also intent on standardizing recruiting itself—not just prescribing the proper format of paperwork or the best prospecting techniques, but even controlling the precise ways and order in which recruiters made their pitch to prospects. In 1982, recruiters received the first version of JOIN (the acronym-friendly Joint Optical Information Network program). JOIN built on Navy research and development, offering computer analysis of applicants' suitability for different career fields and allowing the recruiter to show three- to six-minute videos—the "optical information"—about training for and practice of different MOSs for which the individual qualified, all in a carefully nonpromotional fashion. JOIN fit well with Thurman's desire for standardization. For its time, it was an impressively high-tech tool for selling the army and a real aid to inexperienced recruiters.[36]

But JOIN was also a response to the widespread charges of recruiter malpractice. Not only had the recruiting scandal undermined public belief in the army's believability and taken large chunks of Thurman's time as he moved to command USAREC, public suspicion of recruiters had been given new life by the 1980 film *Private Benjamin,* in which the spoiled and sheltered Judy Benjamin, played by Goldie Hawn, falls victim to a slick army recruiter who promises her nothing short of a rose garden. Benjamin's lament ("See, I did join the army, but I joined a *different* army. I joined the one with the condos and the private rooms") was simply an over-the-top version of complaints from first-term soldiers that they'd been misled by army advertising and army recruiting. JOIN was a more useful version of the "This is the Army" advertising campaign, an effort to make sure that recruits knew exactly what they were joining. It was also meant to prevent recruiters from making what the army investigation of malpractice characterized as "false promises."[37]

JOIN, of course, severely limited recruiter autonomy. It dictated the order in which the recruiter could ask questions and present information. It restricted a recruiter's ability to emphasize different selling points depending on his or her read of the person or of the situation. It discounted what recruiters knew: that appeals to patriotism and the military tradition worked in the south but not the northeast, for example, or that helicopter maintenance might be pitched differently to young women than to young men. Like most of Thurman's reforms, JOIN favored social science data over knowledge based on experience and instinct, and it sought the aggregate good at the expense of individual possibility. The best recruiters didn't like JOIN when it was introduced in 1982. But new recruiters were trained on it, and upgrades came steadily. By 1988, the *Recruiter Journal* pointed to JOIN as one of the things that distinguished the "'class' profession" of recruiting in the 1980s from the "naive, primitive and even unconscionable" recruiting that preceded it.[38]

Even as Thurman worked to standardize recruiting, he was launching the sort of research and systems analysis that would dramatically change aspects of USAREC's one-size-fits-all labor market model to encompass a sophisticated understanding of niche markets. It had become clear to Thurman, based on his conversations with battalion commanders and on the mountains of accession data he'd ordered, that—even when simply thinking about numbers (the "volumetric" mission)—assignments to recruiting stations and battalions were made with very little knowledge of what was and should be possible. It's not that there was no logic to it; General Thurman was not the first person with above-average intelligence in the recruiting command. But Thurman meant to shift recruiting focus from filling boots to filling very specific "quality" categories, and he was certain that a blanket across-the-board approach would not work. Major changes were about to take place. But first someone had to do a great deal of econometric research and analysis.

Early on, Thurman had requested ten new people to do operations research and systems analysis at Fort Sheridan. During his years at USAREC and as deputy chief of staff for personnel, he had broadened the base of research on which decisions might be based and conclusions cross-checked. Thurman had been impressed with N.W. Ayer's market research and wanted more. And there was RAND, of course, "the daddy rabbit" in Thurman's terms, which had been doing independent and nonpartisan research for the U.S. military since its founding in 1948. Thurman, who wanted a "counter-weight" to RAND, established his own research shop in the U.S. Military Academy's department of social science. He also fostered an economic analysis "cell" at the Army Research Institute, better known for their psychological research; it grew in importance during his years as deputy chief of staff for personnel and vice chief of staff. All of these groups, along with the analysts now assigned to USAREC, investigated overlapping sets of questions about how to "provision" the army with people.[39]

The analysts at USAREC headquarters quickly began working on rationalizing mission assignment. Traditionally, the process worked through the basic chain of command. If the 6th Recruiting Brigade (then known as the Western Regional Recruiting Command and headquartered at the base of the Golden Gate Bridge in San Francisco) was to supply a certain number of recruits in the first quarter of fiscal year 1977, it divided that number among its subordinate battalions, and so on down the line, brigade to battalion, battalion to area, area to station, station to recruiter. The shares were not always equal; it was clear that brand new recruiters shouldn't be expected to match their most experienced counterparts, and that some areas were much more fruitful territory than others. But there was little data, beyond experience, on which to base allocations.[40]

The new plan was to allocate mission based on in-depth analysis of specific recruiting areas. Recruiting Zone Analysis Teams had begun quantitative evaluation of "relative market potential" in the vastly different regions and states and neighborhoods of the United States. They factored in prior recruiting results over time, but also everything from the level of traffic past an individual recruiting station to the percentage of high school seniors in that zone who were bound for college. The numbers generated by the analysis teams' manpower equations did not translate directly into individual recruiter missions. Those still had to be negotiated through the chain of command. But the second step toward rationalization focused directly on the individual recruiter. Recruiters would no longer be recruiting for volume, with points toward a gold recruiter's badge or a recruiter's ring. Instead, they were assigned "contract" missions. Every recruiter received a quarterly (later, monthly) "mission box," a card bearing the number of recruits from a variety of category combinations (for example, male high school diploma graduate, I-IIIA, combat arms) to be enlisted that period. It was mandatory to carry the card; if caught without it, "Woe is me," said General Thurman. Thurman's insight here was basic: "You tell [a recruiter] to go out and get a I–IIIA, they go get one. If you don't tell them to go get a I–IIIA, then you get just anything."[41]

Over the course of the 1980s, such basic—and seemingly obvious—insights fundamentally altered the work of military manpower analysts.

During the decade of the 1970s, they had focused on "supply factors," such as the declining number of eighteen-year-olds as the last of the baby boomers came of age, or the impact of unemployment on military enlistment. The new econometric theory stressed, in addition, the critical importance of "private agents' optimizing choices." In other words, "recruiters do not passively process enlistments." Instead, they focus their time and efforts in response to goals they are assigned or incentives they are offered. Somewhat belatedly, the analysts factored recruiters into their labor market models of supply and demand. As General Thurman liked to say, it was an "all-recruited" army. One equation even introduced a variable for General Thurman himself in recognition of how fundamentally his efforts changed recruiting outcomes.[42]

Thurman's final focus as commanding general of USAREC—and the one that had the greatest public impact—was on advertising. He knew that the army was still combating its image, not only still the least-favored service, the one that had no clear identity, but also the butt of negative press about recruiting shortfalls, "low-quality" recruits, and rates of incompetence. In May of 1980 the *Washington Post* reported that the House Armed Services Committee was contemplating a "full-blown congressional inquiry into the state of the Army." A Harris poll that year found that 64 percent of those surveyed believed that "the young people the military has recruited on a voluntary basis have mainly been those who couldn't get jobs elsewhere and have not made very good soldiers."[43] All the systematization in the world would not change those facts.

The slogan that would change the public face of the army had its roots in Thurman's obsession with research, but even more in the forces of chance and contingency and the specific history of one individual. In early April 1980, Thurman, who had recently ratcheted up the pressure on Ayer with a second version of his "come to Jesus" meeting, summoned major figures from the army's advertising agency to discuss a topic close to his heart: "Research in the Marketplace."[44] Like all meetings with Thurman, this one was full of detailed data and hard questions. And there was a difficult decision to be made. On the one hand, new research portrayed the "demographic, sociographic, and psychographic breakdown" of the army "market" in much greater detail than before. The army was now much better able to identify submarkets and to determine what approaches had most resonance with each. But on the other hand, "econometric" analysis pointed to the importance of "a strategy that maximizes coherence." And so, evidently, did the lessons of history. "The great agitators, demagogues and propagandists of history," argued Tom Evans in a memo on advertising strategy he prepared for Thurman in advance of the meeting, "have succeeded by insistent repetition of simple ideas." It would be "an uphill struggle" at the very least, Evans acknowledged, as the army made its case in a "cluttered commercial medium." But "insistent repetition" was Evans's key point, and that was the approach that Thurman embraced. Not only did he tell Ayer to develop proposals—four, he specified—for a single clear and coherent message to sell the army, he wanted a single message for all army recruiting: for officers, for the enlisted ranks, for ROTC, for doctors and nurses, and for the Army Reserve.[45]

Then, of course, Thurman wanted more research. Ayer's developmental lab tried out six different portraits of army service on carefully chosen representative groups in twelve different locations. The army was a place to find personal challenge. It was an institution full of smart people. Army service was "a good and necessary experience." It offered the chance to serve one's country. It was a good step in developing a career. It was the place to learn state-of-the-art technology. What Ayer researchers learned, from all the individual questionnaires and group discussions, is that young Americans thought army service was worthwhile. Just not for themselves. Only one approach increased individual propensity to enlist: the claim that the army has "more aircraft than United Airlines and more computers than IBM."[46] This finding fit well with army concerns. The institution was intent upon raising "quality," not only because high school diploma graduates who tested in the upper half of the qualifying test were more likely to complete their enlistments successfully, but also because the army needed an ever greater number of bright soldiers to operate its new technologically sophisticated equipment.

Back in New York at N.W. Ayer, the word circulated: Thurman wanted a new theme for the army, something that emphasized technology. Creative director Lou DiJoseph set up what advertising agencies called a "gang bang": an assignment given to several teams at once in competition with one another, with ideas culled from that process again assigned to several groups as competition continued. One of the men on the army account, Earl Carter, may have been a bit hungrier than the rest. He saw himself as low man on the totem pole at Ayer. Carter had grown up in the Bronx, he and his mother surviving on what was then called Home Relief, his father abusive, alcoholic, and often absent. He'd never quite developed the Manhattan smoothness common in the advertising business, even in a firm with deep roots in Philadelphia. Carter tended to say what he thought; he was territorial and bad at politics. But he was talented, and the draft notice that had interrupted his youth had given him more experience with the army than the other agency creatives who were looking for that winning phrase.[47]

Carter had one good idea: "Army. We'll Show You How." Another line he'd created, working with an art director the year before, had also been thrown into the mix: "The Advantage of Your Age." But he wasn't quite satisfied. Sitting in his office—"creepy, dark, no-windows," as he described it—trying to come up with a line to top "We'll Show You How," Carter found himself staring at the one spot of color, a poster for the School of Visual Arts he'd hung for inspiration. Carter had taken some advertising courses at the School of Visual Arts, and he had taken the words of its founder, Silas Rhodes, to heart: "To Be Good Is Not Enough When You Dream of Being Great," the poster reminded him. Reaching for an emotional connection, Carter thought about the sergeant major he'd so admired when he was serving in Germany. Then he thought of his childhood, his memories of sitting at the kitchen table listening to his mother talking about his father. "He could have been anything he wanted to be," she'd told her son. But for the drinking, "what he could have been."[48]

The words came to him "like a lightning bolt," Carter recalls. "I knew I had something special." It was not exactly on theme, but that was okay. He could make it work. At the very least, "all you can be" rhymed with "technology." That's what he gave them at the creative meeting:

Be all you can be
with Army technology.

Carter's slogan made the cut when Lou DiJoseph, the creative director on the army account, narrowed the list from sixteen to four. But despite Carter's confidence, it wasn't obvious to everyone else in the room that day that "Be All You Can Be" would become one of the great advertising slogans of the twentieth century. "Join Tomorrow Today" was the favorite, though one Ayer executive was pretty strongly committed to "We'll Show You How." Worse yet, from Carter's perspective, "Be All You Can Be" passed out of Carter's control the moment DiJoseph endorsed it. It would be more than twenty years before Carter got official credit for his words.[49]

Ayer presented four campaigns to Thurman and his staff in mid-June. Each of them—"Join Tomorrow Today"; "Army. We'll Show You How"; "The Advantage of Your Age"; and "Be All You Can Be"—had a set of layouts for print advertisements and storyboards for television commercials. There was a lot of discussion, and the decision was made by the process of elimination, wading through possible limitations of each slogan until only "Be All You Can Be" remained. It was Friday afternoon and the presentation to the Pentagon was scheduled for Monday morning. Once again, Ayer was going to have a long, hard weekend. On Monday, Ayer would present all four treatments to the Pentagon's Advertising Policy Council, because Thurman wanted to demonstrate that he'd explored all possibilities. But the presentation would be carefully scripted to produce the proper outcome. And only "Be All You Can Be" would have music. Ayer had Jake Holmes—who'd written Dr. Pepper's "Be a Pepper" jingle, not to mention music and lyrics for Frank Sinatra's *Watertown* album and the original version of Led Zeppelin's "Dazed and Confused"—standing by.[50] On Saturday Holmes wrote and recorded the first version of the song that would soon flood American airwaves. And on Sunday Ayer put pictures to the words. Thurman showed up at the Pentagon for a preview at 8 A.M. on Monday morning.

> I know this world is changing
> Changing every day
> And you've got to know
> your way around
> If you're going all the way

the lyrics began, as photographs of soldiers, male and female, people of different races and backgrounds, people who showed the diversity of America, moved across the screen. By the time the last of the music died away, the final appeal to "Be All That You Can Be/Because we need you/in the Army" trailing into silence, General Thurman was crying.[51]

When "Be All You Can Be" was rolled out for recruiters at their December 1980 sales meeting, they cheered. The ads premiered during college bowl games—first seen December 27, 1980, and then steadily thereafter. Research showed that the army needed to hit the market segment, youth between the ages of 16 and 22, at least eighteen times in the first thirty days. So it relied not only on high-profile TV commercials, but also on radio advertising, with the song done in different versions, from country and western to disco. They also orchestrated an arrangement for marching bands and distributed it free to more than 13,000 high schools throughout the nation.[52]

"Be All You Can Be" was a success. Recruiters liked it. Prospects liked it. Serving soldiers liked it. The advertising business loved it. Measuring its success was somewhat difficult—"akin to successfully nailing a jellyfish to a wall," concluded an article in the *Army Times*—but some data did support the campaign's effectiveness. One study traced major improvement in public perception of the army within eight months of the introduction of "Be All You Can Be." And according to the Youth Attitude Tracking Survey, on which the military relied heavily for its analysis of American youth, the army was steadily overtaking the navy and gaining on the air force in positive impressions among American teens.[53]

A year after the campaign's launch, Ayer executive vice president Ted Regan reassured recruiters that Ayer and the army were "staying with a good thing." "BE ALL YOU CAN BE appears to be all everyone thought it would be. And more," he wrote in the recruiter's journal, at that point titled *All Volunteer.* People are "feeling better than ever about the Army." Regan attributed some of those "positive feelings" to "a more conservative mood in the country and a new administration." But according to what "research tells us," the "Be All You Can Be" campaign had made a difference. Ayer was definitely proud of the campaign. It advertised its services to potential clients with the line: "When we tell young people to "Be all you can be" in the U.S. Army, that's human contact. That's Ayer." When Max Thurman's beloved dog died, he buried her on army ground under a stone inscribed, "She was all she could be." The line became a locker room standard. It turned up everywhere from religious exhortations to song lyrics. Even the Soviet Union copied it. "Byt vsyo shto mozhno byt," offered a campaign to sell young women on the "virtues of Soviet military life."[54]

"Be All You Can Be" established the army brand. It lasted for two full decades, through the administrations of Reagan, Bush, and Clinton, through Operation Urgent Fury (U.S. invasion of Grenada in 1983), Operation Just Cause (U.S. invasion of Panama, 1989), Operation Desert Storm (the first Gulf War, 1991), and NATO's Operation Allied Force (Kosovo, 1999). Most of these military operations, though controversial within the United States, were brief and, judged by military objectives, successful. During the 1980s and 1990s, fewer than two hundred members of the U.S. military died in combat. During the 1980s and 1990s it was not only the image of military life but its reality that became less closely associated with combat and the risk of death. That key fact also helped to shape the army brand.

"Be All You Can Be," created and developed during two decades of relative peace, continued to shift the focus from service toward opportunity, from obligation to benefit. Though the slogan was constant, the campaign itself evolved over the years, always in response to research on the army's "market." The initial appeal—"because we need you in the Army"—soon disappeared, replaced by the more affirmative "you can do it in the Army." When researchers discovered that young people were more likely to enlist if they saw army service as a practical step toward future success, the tagline became, "find your future in the Army." Although many of the benefits the "Be All You Can Be" army offered were intangible—the chance to become better, stronger, more disciplined, more mature; the chance to "reinvent" oneself—advertising promises became increasingly concrete.

By the mid-1980s, the word "college" was almost always visible in "Be All You Can Be" army ads. One fifteen-second television commercial, "Oath," showed a roomful of young adults being sworn into the army, right hands raised. "Now the Army offers up to $50,000 for college," said the voiceover. "If you could use that kind of money, raise your hand." In print advertising, striking photographs of tanks moving across rough landscapes were captioned, "The road to college isn't always paved," or "These soldiers are on their way to college." Specialist Mark Butcher, Airborne Scouts, told readers, "I found a road to college that's making me feel exhilarated, exhausted and proud."[55]

The recruiting command had long understood the relationship between college funds and quality; they attributed much of the decline in quality during the late 1970s to the expiration of the G.I. Bill in 1976. They had fought hard for renewed funds: a limited experiment with VEAP (Veterans Education Assistance Program) in the early 1980s; then the 1982 Army College Fund, and finally Congressional approval of the 1985 Montgomery G.I. Bill. But it wasn't only the specific educational benefits that mattered. College benefits were a way to rebrand the army. According to the research of the day, mothers were the most important "influencers" in their children's lives. They had the most impact on the decision to—or not to—enlist. And mothers, according to this research, wanted their children to go to college, because they saw college as success and other paths as failure. So army advertising played up college. Joining the army was not a failure or a detour, not even a different choice. It was a path to college, and even better, a sign of independence as young people earned their own way to a degree. The majority of army veterans did not go on to graduate from college. But by creating the mental association between army and college, "Be All You Can Be" continued to rebrand the army.[56]

In 1987, the army demonstrated its commitment to "Be All You Can Be," if not to N.W. Ayer. There had long been troubles with Ayer's army account, not over content but in the complicated interface between a civilian advertising firm and rigid federal regulations about documentation and accounting practices. In the end Ayer's downfall was—in true 1980s fashion—due to the greed of an individual, a "minor executive" who was caught taking kickbacks from subcontractors on the army account. The man was eventually convicted and fined $50; no evidence ever surfaced that Ayer had prior knowledge of his financial malfeasance. But the army opened the account for bids while Ayer was suspended, and Young & Rubicam claimed the army account in 1987.[57] They thought they'd be able to go with the campaign they'd pitched: "Army. Get an Edge on Life." But no one wanted to scuttle "Be All You Can Be." "Get an Edge on Life" became the new tagline and the new last line of the song, as advertisements moved ever further toward the "functional benefits" of army life. By the end of the decade, the "Army Advantages" tagline focused on "post-service civilian success."[58]

"Be All You Can Be," in the space created by an era of relative peace and limited deployments, developed and reinforced a consistent message. As the research director at N.W. Ayer explained to the *Army Times* in 1985, it was "aimed at the type of person that Horatio Alger might have written about—the serious, goal-oriented person who wants to get ahead in life and thinks of achievement in occupational terms. Today, that means skills that translate into civilian occupations—skills that pay well. They realize that getting ahead depends on finding the right niche in the world of work. Our aim is to get them to thinking about the Army as a stepping stone, rather than a detour." *Time* magazine put it a bit differently. Noting that promises of success heavily outweighed notions of "service and patriotism" in army recruiting ads, the author suggested that the army was trying "to produce a corps of Yuppies in uniform." An army spokesperson tried to counter the charge with the claim that advertising portrays the army "as a springboard to personal satisfaction in a complex world." But when it came to defining personal satisfaction, he fell back on notions of material success: "The thrust is that the Army increases your chances of doing well in your future life."[59]

Time magazine's image of "a corps of Yuppies in uniform" may have captured the spirit of the ad campaign in the mid-1980s, but it wasn't fair to the young men and women who enlisted in the army. They rarely came from the ranks of the privileged and entitled; if they were drawn by promises of money for college or by their desire to develop skills necessary for "success," they nonetheless earned those funds or those skills, and in so doing they served their country. Nonetheless "Be All You Can Be" did help to shift understandings of the meaning of military service from obligation to opportunity. It also helped to transform the army. In fiscal year 1980, only 54 percent of new recruits had graduated from high school, and well over half were Category IV. By 1987, 91 percent had graduated from high school; only 4 percent fell in Category IV. In 1992, only 2 percent of army recruits lacked a high school diploma.[60]

"We bent metal," said General Alan Ono, a protégé of Thurman who took over command of USAREC in the mid-1980s. "We took the Army and . . . with the force of our muscles and minds we shaped it and redirected it. When people thought it was not possible, we showed that it could be done."[61]

7 ✶ THE ARMY AS SOCIAL GOOD

AT THE END OF THE 1980S it was abundantly clear that America's army had been shaped, in fundamental ways, by the ongoing Cold War between the United States and the Soviet Union. In the years following World War II a large standing peacetime military had been justified—against national tradition and inclination—by the threat of the Soviet Union and of communist expansion. The Cold War had made hot wars (Korea, Vietnam) appear necessary, with obvious consequences for America's military. The vision of a world divided between two superpowers determined where American troops were stationed; it shaped military training and doctrine; it justified military budgets. And then suddenly, in 1989, the world changed.

"It was one of those rare times when the tectonic plates of history shift beneath men's feet," wrote *Time* magazine just days after the fall of the Berlin Wall, "and nothing after is quite the same." Of course there was enormous practical uncertainty about relations between the United States and the nation Ronald Reagan had not so long before dubbed "the evil empire," not to mention longstanding suspicion of Soviet motives despite Gorbachev's policies of *glasnost* and *perestroika.* Nonetheless, the American press was drawn to a language of victory, eager to chronicle the moments that served as symbolic evidence that the West had won the Cold War. Of that night in early November when "crowds of young Germans danced on top of the hated Berlin wall," the *New York Times* exulted: "They danced for joy, they danced for history." And as U.S. president George H. W. Bush and Soviet premier Mikhail Gorbachev met on stormy seas off the coast of Malta in early December 1989, struggling against the forces of history and of nature to forge a new path for their nations and the world, the American press described U.S. first lady Barbara Bush, back in Washington at the Kennedy Center Honors gala, enjoying the Red Army Song and Dance Ensemble's rendition of "'God Bless America' in their distinctive Russian accents."[1]

As American soldiers and other members of the military watched the stunning collapse of a bipolar world order, many realized just how fundamental—and close to home—the effects would be. The end of the Cold War put the army in a position of uncertainty. It was just days after the Malta summit that *U.S. News and World Report* made the point in blunt terms. "It was hard to watch the spectacle of the Red Army Chorus belting out 'God Bless America' . . . on the stage of Washington's Kennedy Center last week," the relatively conservative news magazine noted, "without realizing that the assumptions guiding America's military strategy for four decades are rapidly becoming as obsolete as muskets and men-of-war." In large, bold letters the article's headline asked: "Does America Need an Army?"[2]

U.S. News, not surprisingly given its general editorial stance, argued strongly against any precipitous reduction of military spending or military force, quoting Democratic congressional representative Barney Frank's declaration that "We're going to cut the hell out of [the Pentagon budget]" as evidence that Congress, controlled by Democrats, lacked the prudence necessary in such uncertain times. Nonetheless, the questions *U.S. News* raised could not be so simply put to rest. If the current U.S. military was, more than anything else, a product of the Cold War, what, now, was the purpose of the army?

During the 1990s, as the army cut its ranks by almost a third and worked to manage the resulting congressionally mandated "transformation," it struggled with that question. The army was not contending with a contrast between peacetime and wartime footing. In fact, the U.S. military was deployed at much higher rates, engaged in many more major military operations, between the end of the Cold War and the 2001 terrorist attacks on the World Trade Center than during the years between 1973 and 1989. What changed was that there was no more implacable enemy, no more absolute vision of strength as deterrence, no more fundamental struggle against a major power for the future of the world. In the 1984 presidential election, with no hot war on the horizon, Ronald Reagan had staked his successful campaign in large part on the Soviet enemy. "There is a bear in the woods," one of Reagan's most powerful campaign ads began. "Some people say the bear is tame. Others say it's vicious. And dangerous. Since no one can really be sure who's right, isn't it smart to be as strong as the bear?" In 1986, U.S. military spending reached 6.2 percent of the nation's gross domestic product. By 1999 it had fallen to less than half that figure.[3]

With the demise of the Soviet Union, the American public lost its sense of clear and present danger. There were those who pointed to the increased complexity and unpredictability of the post–Cold War era, and in retrospect it is clear that the world was nowhere near "the end of history" and that there were significant conflicts already in play. But as Congress mandated a major downsizing of force, the army had to rethink its purpose and organization. As an institution, it had to justify itself to the American public and their congressional representatives.

During the 1990s, army doctrine increasingly emphasized "operations other than war" that ranged from international peacekeeping missions to domestic disaster relief. Debates about the roles and mission of the army were most significant internally, for they were meant to determine how, in the words of the army's 1994 Field Manual 100-1, its "capstone document," "we think about the world and how we train, equip, and organize our forces to serve the Nation."[4] But they were also part of the army's attempt to "sell" Congress and the American people on its continued importance. Definitions of army mission shaped recruiting goals and methods: how many new recruits the Army sought each year, with what sorts of skills and abilities, for which military occupational specialties and career fields. And public understandings of the role of the army determined levels of public support, which in turn made recruiting more or less difficult, and which translated through Congress into defense dollars and cents.

As the army attempted to answer the fundamental question—what is the purpose of the army—in terms of doctrine, it also attempted to demonstrate its relevance in the new world order. Although it never set aside the understanding that the army's fundamental purpose is to fight wars, during the 1990s the army also sold itself to the public as a provider of social good.[5] It portrayed itself as a site of equality and opportunity for all America's citizens. And it emphasized the "value added" by the army to American society, as young men and women were returned from military service to the civilian sector with education and training and with heightened senses of responsibility and discipline.

Social good, however, was a controversial mission for the army. Through much of the twentieth century such social good, including the racial desegregation of the military and growing opportunities for women, was perceived instead as social experiment. And social experiment, in turn, was portrayed as a threat to unit cohesion, to military readiness, and to national defense. Even as the army offered, both actually and symbolically, an unprecedented level of equal opportunity and inclusion across the boundaries of race and gender during the 1990s, debates about social experiments versus national defense never quite disappeared. By the end of the last decade of the twentieth century—well before the planes crashed into the Twin Towers and the Pentagon and precipitated another shift in "the tectonic plates of history"—the army had begun recasting its emphasis from social good to a newly articulated "Warrior Ethos."

The army, bottom line, has little control over its fate or its future. Responsibility for command and control of the nation's armed forces is vested, respectively, in the president and in Congress. The army, as an institution, officially affirms the principle of constitutionally mandated civilian control at the beginning of each version of Field Manual 100-1, its fundamental statement of "who and what we are as an institution."[6] But civilian control means that the army often finds itself coping with mandates that represent neither its design nor its desires, such as the shift to an all-volunteer force, or the ban on paid commercial advertising, or the directive to admit women to West Point. It was difficult for the army to imagine they would benefit from the promised "peace dividend" at the end of the Cold War. And as the declining Soviet threat combined with a growing budget deficit, the Republican administration of George H. W. Bush joined Congress in a move to "substantially" (the army's term) reduce defense spending. Early in the summer of 1990 Dick Cheney, then secretary of defense, proposed cutting active army strength by close to one-third within the next five years.[7]

The army's view of the drawdown is clear in its official annual "historical summary" for 1990 and 1991: "As the U.S. Army began the last decade of the twentieth century, it faced uncertain times and substantial downsizing, even though on two occasions during FY 90 and 91 it engaged in major military operations." The military successes of Operation Just Cause (the 1989 U.S. invasion of Panama to oust Manuel Noriega) and Operation Desert Storm (the U.S.-led military intervention following Iraq's 1990 invasion of Kuwait) had paradoxical results. Rather than demonstrating to the American public that serious international threats demanded continued military strength, the "100 Days War" in the Gulf that looked so much like a video game on American television convinced much of the American public that the nation's military was strong, technologically sophisticated, and probably undefeatable. The army didn't necessarily see it that way. "Despite these new challenges," the army's historical summary noted, with clear concern, "the public mood continued to call for a smaller military establishment. . . . [and] the drastic downsizing of the military force structure, regardless of long-term policies. Rapidly changing foreign developments and new fiscal realities within the United States, however, have not altered the fact that the world remains a dangerous place."[8]

For perspective, it's important to remember that the U.S. military budget accounted for more than 45 percent of the entire world's military spending in 1990, and that over the following decade that percentage never dropped below 41, in part because of continued spending on major weapons systems.[9] Nonetheless, the army did have to figure out how to cut almost 250,000 people from its ranks, and how to do so without losing necessary expertise or absolutely destroying morale. A presidential commission appointed by George H. W. Bush debated recommending that the military use the downsizing to eliminate women from its ranks. Senator Edward Kennedy publicly expressed concern that the commission's recommendations would be "Neanderthal," and rumors about the commission's deliberations fueled an exchange in a congressional hearing in the summer of 1992. Representative Pat Schroeder, Congress's strongest advocate for women's opportunity in the armed forces, questioned the army chief of staff about his reaction to that possible recommendation. He flatly rejected the proposal: "The Army cannot function without women." In fact, he noted, women were reenlisting at a higher rate than men, and would likely become a larger percentage of the force as the downsizing continued.[10]

Many Americans, including some members of Congress, saw an obvious solution. If the military needed fewer people, it should simply recruit fewer. But the obvious answer—stop recruiting—was no answer. Soldiering, as the saying used to go, is a young man's game. The army is dependent on a steady supply of fresh recruits not only to fill the infantry and to do the heavy lifting, "to maintain its vitality," but also to keep the proper balance and pace of promotion through the ranks. As one Department of Defense representative explained to Congress, if the military cut accessions further, it would have "an overly senior, stagnant force . . . [with] severe shortages of senior personnel in the long term."[11] The army has to be shaped like a pyramid. It can't become top-heavy, can't manage the military equivalent of being tenured up.

The army's recruiting objective was, in fact, lowered at the beginning of 1990: from 119,901 in fiscal year 1989 down to 78,241 in fiscal year 1991. Lower objectives allowed the army to concentrate even more on quality, and by 1991 less than one percent of new accessions scored in Category IV and almost 98 percent were high school graduates. But the institution still had to contend with the hundreds of thousands of mid-career men and women, many of whom had hoped to spend their twenty-years-to-retirement in the army, as well as with the more than 40 percent of first-term soldiers who wanted to reenlist in 1991.[12]

Overall, the Department of the Army tried to minimize the threat of involuntary separation, offering those with between six and twenty years of service economic incentives to leave the army and expanding a program that allowed soldiers in "overstrength" MOSs to depart before their terms of enlistment ended. It also took advantage of the drawdown to improve the quality of the existing force. Soldiers whose performance was judged deficient were put on six-month probation. They had a choice: "voluntary separation" during that period, or accepting their commander's choice of either continued probation or "separation on grounds of unsatisfactory performance or misconduct" at the end of the six months. Between the usual retirements, the incentives, and the not-so-friendly pushes, almost 100,000 enlisted men and women left the army in fiscal year 1992 alone.[13]

The plan to cut the army's strength by a third seemed earthshaking from the inside. Colin Powell, chair of the Joint Chiefs of Staff, offered a militarywide comparison: "General Motors is eliminating 74,000 employees over three years. We're doing that many alone from January to September of this year [1992]."[14] The rapid drawdown was, in some ways, more complicated than the demobilizations following World War II and Vietnam, though of course not nearly of the same scale as the end of WWII. These were not draftees whose lives had been disrupted against their will, nor men who had gone to do what they thought necessary and now wanted nothing more than to return to their homes and families and whatever sort of normal life they could find. Many of these were men and women who had volunteered for the army and had planned military careers. Many of them had never held another job.

Some of those being pushed out of the army had developed marketable skills during their service, but others found their skills were not easily transferable. As one veteran of Desert Storm told a reporter, "Driving a tank in combat isn't exactly the greatest preparation for civilian life." To help with the transition, the Pentagon set up seminars on how to write resumes and handle job interviews. But it was an uphill struggle. In 1992 the nation was in the midst of the recession that prompted Clinton campaign advisor James Carville to post his powerful reminder in the Little Rock campaign headquarters: "It's the economy, stupid." When *Soldiers* magazine looked for some positive way to begin its article on "Reshaping the Army" in 1991, the best it could offer was: "Change is life's only constant, and the Army is not immune." The historical comparison it drew was not designed to be reassuring. By the middle of the 1990s, the article pointed out, the army would be "reduced to a level not seen since the 1930s." Two years later the magazine offered cold comfort with its tentative judgment that "the worst may be over."[15]

These were turbulent times for USAREC. The recruiting command's home, Fort Sheridan, had appeared on the list generated by the first round of Base Realignment and Closure (BRAC) proceedings in 1988. Plans were made to move to Fort Benjamin Harrison, which housed the army recruiter school. But Fort Benjamin Harrison turned up on the second BRAC list in 1991. USAREC then began making plans for a move to Fort Knox, Kentucky.[16] It wasn't simply the logistics of the move or the uncertainty about the future that was disruptive. USAREC relied on a significant number of civilian employees, some of them (such as Tom Evans, who was in charge of advertising) with significant responsibility and years of hard-won knowledge. Unlike the men and women in uniform, the civilians could not simply be ordered to relocate from the shores of Lake Michigan to northern Kentucky.

Recruiting also came under particular scrutiny as Congress weighed base closings against local economies, weapons systems against personnel, facilities against family support programs. And advertising, once again, seemed an easy target. Senator David Pryor, by his own admission playing to the folks back home in Arkansas, stood on the floor of Congress and condemned the "big-city, Madison Avenue" agencies who "continue to get fat . . . at the taxpayer's expense," along with the nation's military services, who seem to think that "spending money is part of their job description." It makes no sense, Pryor asserted, to pay people "to get out of the service" and at the same time spend "all these millions of dollars to get more people to come in." Logic like that likely drove the army's deputy chief of staff for personnel crazy. But there was a more reasonable case to be made. Army recruiting objectives had shrunk dramatically, from 211,600 in fiscal year 1974 to less than 79,000 in fiscal year 1991.[17] The recruiting climate was strong. Numbers were good; quality was high. Advertising had succeeded in establishing a brand identity, in defining the "Be All You Can Be" army. The Gulf War demonstrated the volunteer army's success. Why let what were essentially start-up expenses for the AVF become the new baseline for business-as-usual?

Major General Jack Wheeler, commander of USAREC, offered an early version of the army's defense to Congress in May 1991, soon after the end of the first Gulf War. It doesn't matter, he argued, that the Patriot missile system had—according to *U.S. News and World Report*—"restored faith in American technology." Despite the dramatic televised images and army claims of deadly precision, the lesson of the Gulf War was not that technological change has made the individual soldier irrelevant, that "smart" weapons have made smart soldiers unnecessary. Soldiers operate the Patriot missiles. And, in general, the more complex the technology the more capable its operators must be. But bright and capable soldiers—the "high quality" ones, the ones who have other options—are more expensive to recruit. Like all the other partisans who tried to ward off the budgetary axe, Wheeler claimed the centrality of his mission: cutting the recruiting budget would be very bad for the army.[18]

Thirteen of the army's fifty-five recruiting battalions—along with the brigade headquartered at Fort Sheridan—were closed in 1992. Advertising budgets were cut by almost two-thirds in the first years of the decade—43 percent from 1990 to 1991 alone. Funds available for enlistment bonuses dropped by close to 80 percent. And recruiting became more and more difficult. As army advertising disappeared from its usual venues and headlines about cutbacks and downsizing and drawdowns filled the press, people began to assume that the army had no openings. The army recruiting office in Falls Church, Virginia, hung a huge banner, the white letters on green background proclaiming: "U.S. Army, We're Still Hiring."[19]

"We're Still Hiring" is scarcely an inspirational message, but it was the necessary one. Through the 1990s, as the economy recovered and then boomed, the army worked hard to draw new recruits. Until 1999, when all the services failed to meet recruiting goals, it largely succeeded. But throughout this decade the army faced a major advertising challenge. Much as it did in the 1970s, army advertising reached beyond its immediate target of potential recruits to make the case that the army contributed to American society in times of peace as well as in times of war.

Army recruiting ads continued to offer the concrete benefits of service: money for college, job skills, and training in state-of-the-art technology. And there was always the intangible opportunity to "be all that you can be." But during the 1990s, army advertising fundamentally shifted the terms of the debate. Critics had worried, back in the 1970s, that if the army recruited young Americans with promises of opportunity rather than with calls to service it would attract the wrong sorts of people, play to pernicious forces of selfishness and individualism among American youth rather than to their latent idealism, and undermine the public good. In the 1990s, army advertising recast that initial tension. The conflict was not between visions of individual opportunity and the public good. Instead, the opportunity the army offered was *itself* a social good. In blunt terms, the army marketed itself as the embodiment of the American dream of full inclusion and equal opportunity. And it presented itself as a force for good in civilian society. It was a provider of education, of training, of discipline. It was a creator of good citizens, of good employees, and of good leaders. It took America's youth and from them it created strong, principled, and committed men and women, men and women who made America a better place.

To make its case, the army turned to quantitative evidence. According to army research, military service gave those who completed enlistments and returned to the civilian job market an "Army Alumni advantage," a set of traits and skills valued by employers. In its memo to the Advertising Policy Council, the army proposed to use this finding not only to attract volunteers, but also to position itself with other "important public and private initiatives to resolve the highly publicized 'skill gap' problem" that worried American economic and labor analysts in the late 1980s. Army advertising could craft a "coherent presentation of a positive Army message to the general public" in an era of economic uncertainty by making one fundamental point: "Because it adds value to human capital entering the work force, Army service contributes to the future health of the economy." The strategy was to present the army "as a vital American institution playing a role that transcends its national security mission."[20] Thus when Major General Wheeler, USAREC commander, appeared before the House Armed Services Committee to argue against cuts in the army's advertising budget, his case went beyond the possible impact on recruiting. "We have an opportunity to demonstrate to Americans that their Army is a resource not only for defense, Mr. Chairman," Wheeler argued, "but for education, a resource for business, and a resource for society, while simultaneously providing for a strong national defense."[21]

Throughout the post–Cold War, pre-9/11 era, the army made this claim frequently and in a variety of ways, even moving beyond claims of social good to visions of social redemption. A series of "Be All You Can Be" recruiting commercials featured individual young men, most of them African American, all of whom could be seen, depending on one's politics and position, either as at-risk or potentially disruptive or dangerous. But the ads showed men who emerged from army training and service strong, disciplined, and responsible, one proud that he had not disappointed his mother, who had always believed in him, another that he had lived up to the expectations of his elementary school teacher, who never would let him settle for a "C."

"I think many of the kids today are lost," the USAREC commander told a congressional subcommittee in 1997, offering a similar message of army redemption. "They are looking for core values. They are looking for something they can anchor their lives to, something that is larger than themselves." Today's youth, he continued, are smarter than those that came before them. But they are also "less committed, they are less focused, and they are softer physically." Recruiters who testified earlier that day had chosen their words less carefully. "They are fat, dumb and happy living at home," one said, with "parents [who] let them get away with anything they want to." Schools are so poor, according to another, that the class valedictorian from one of his Dallas high schools scored a 19 out of 100 possible points on the ASVAB—"and she actually tried on it." The recruiting commercials' positive portrayal of parents and teachers was crafted to appeal to the adults—parents, teachers—who influenced the decisions of youth, even though representatives from the army, navy, air force, and marines placed little faith in their advisory capacities. All said there was a fundamental problem with the values of contemporary youth, and all located that problem in family life. "We are finding kids going home, and there are no parents," said the air force recruiting commander, and the head of navy recruiting chimed in: "We are talking to a significant number of young people who come from very troubled families." Many new navy recruits had been abused when they were children, he told them, and "are in fact troubled" themselves.[22]

The USAREC commander was speaking genuinely and without cynicism when he offered an answer to the dilemma, but his answer fit very well with the current "value-added" message about the purpose of the army. The "youngster" who entered basic training was not the same youngster who left. "Having had Army values instilled in them," he said, "a sense of purpose, a sense of duty, they were happier. They seemed to have a greater sense of purpose in life." And while some of them fell off the wagon, failing to fully grasp the "message that there is something larger than what feels good at the time," others were redeemed. How, then, he asked the roomful of senators, could the army "get to as many" of America's challenged youth as possible and "assist" them in their struggles to become "more productive citizen[s]"?[23]

The army continued to link redemption and productivity as it crafted its peacetime public image. In 1999, with a booming economy, Chief of Staff Eric Shinseki credited "the presence of a . . . robust Army" for much of America's prosperity. "What we send back to our community is a great citizen," Shinseki said, a young man or woman who has learned army values that make him or her "an asset to employers and to the community." In April 2001 the army offered a new "brand statement" that moved quickly from national defense to a catalog of those army values: loyalty, duty, respect, selfless service, honor, integrity, and personal courage. The army, explained Major General Dennis Cavin, commander of USAREC, "invests in each individual . . . [and] equips them to make a significant difference, on foreign soil or within their communities, as soldiers and as citizens." The army takes young people "from all walks of life," he continued, and "return[s] to America better citizens."[24]

As the army made its value-added case, it also portrayed its policies of equal opportunity and inclusion as contributions to the social good. Such claims, often made implicitly in army advertising images, were very much in keeping with the widespread American celebration of diversity during the 1990s. At the same time, portrayals of diversity in army advertising were nothing new. Army recruiting ads had carefully managed race and ethnicity since the 1970s, when the move to an all-volunteer force made it necessary to envision an army in which all belonged. Non-Hispanic whites were actually underrepresented in the initial 1972 "Today's Army Wants to Join You" ad. Two of the nine young men pictured were black, though African Americans made up about 12 percent of the nation's population, and one was Hispanic, even though Hispanics then made up less than 5 percent of the nation's total numbers. The army paid attention to portrayals of ethnicity, as well. One early recruiting commercial was discarded after army officials objected to the way it portrayed an Italian-American family.[25]

During the 1970s, as a rule of thumb, if four or more young men appeared in a print advertisement, one of them would be black (and one of them would be wearing glasses). There was some awkwardness in the handling of race. A 1972 "Today's Army Wants to Join You" ad in *Sports Illustrated* offered "Mike, Rocky, Leroy, Vince, and Bunts," who were "taking the Army's 16-month tour of Europe. Together." Four white kids; one black. The black kid (Bunts, if the names are in order) was the one holding the basketball. And although photographs of single-sex groups usually included one young black man, it wasn't until 1980 that a black man and a white woman appeared as part of the same group, in this case, in "a special offer for buddies" to enlist, train, and serve together. Spanish-language print ads began appearing in the late 1970s—"Unete a la gente que está en el Army"—but again with some miscues; in one, a lengthy testimony in Spanish was attributed to Corporal David Shaul of Ft. Riley, Kansas. The ad was originally in English; as with early ads that substituted black models for white models, Ayer had simply "translated" the appeal. But by the early 1980s, N.W. Ayer was subcontracting with Sosa & Associates for Latino-focused ads.[26]

The biggest change was not in the portrayal of race but of gender. By the 1980s ads about femininity and marriage prospects were long gone. But the language of equal opportunity, the ads that proclaimed "Some of our best men are women" and promised "If there's one place where opportunity is genuinely equal, it's in the Army," also became less common. Women, increasingly, simply appeared as one of the team, interchangeable with the men. In 1981 an ad in the women's magazine *Dawn* asked, "Why Should the Army Be Easy, Life Isn't?" Over a stark-contrast photograph of four paratroopers—their sex impossible to determine—the ad copy ran: "In the Modern Army, the Cavalry flies, the Infantry rides, and the Artillery can hit a fly in the eye 15 miles away."[27] Some ads were still addressed specifically to women, but more and more often advertising text avoided gender altogether. Women appeared in the ad illustrations, but—like men—as soldiers.

It had not been until the late 1970s, as the House Armed Services Committee passed from Congressman Hébert's chairmanship in 1977, that the army could expand to regular television advertising. Television recruiting ads generally, to the extent that race or ethnicity was visible, pictured the diversity of the army that was and included women in discussions of possible army benefits. But while army ads had been racially inclusive during the 1970s and 1980s—especially in comparison to the portrayals of America in the surrounding advertising—something fundamental changed during the 1990s. No longer did the signature advertisements simply picture an inclusive army. Instead, some offered inclusiveness as a key message, a central point.

The 1990s attempt to portray the army as a place of inclusion and opportunity that unifies a diverse society is clearest in contrast to what came before. The army's most highly produced this-is-who-we-are ad from the 1980s was "Freedom Isn't Free," a 1988 country-inflected tribute to the imagined small town that—seemingly—lay at the very heart of America. "I'm from a town," began the lyrics that substituted for voice-over, "where things are as good as they come. And it's pictured in my mind just as clear as the midday sun." The picture was of rural white small-town life, of pick-up trucks and dirt roads and diners, working men in cowboy hats and hardhats and baseball caps, a pregnant wife, a pretty girlfriend, and lots of carefree children. As the song played in the background the images shifted to pouring rain, soldiers advancing up a stream, men huddled, shivering, under the scant shelter of a tree. "Now I'm out here in the darkness, and the rain is coming down," the lyrics continued, and the rain continued, too, as soldiers leapt from helicopters hovering low over the ocean. "It never was like this in my hometown." There is no "be all you can be" in this commercial. It's meant to transcend the army's recruiting slogan, to make a larger claim about the purpose of the army. As the commercial's producers instructed Army Specialist Giandomenico and Sergeant Kijewski, the soldiers who were sitting under that tree in the Indian Dunes north of Los Angeles being doused with "rain" from giant overhead pipes, they were "to give the impression of soldiers suffering to maintain freedom." "My hometown," the song finished, "It's not like this, but that's all right with me. See, I'm out here for my hometown, 'cause freedom isn't free."[28]

This vision of a Norman Rockwell America, in which every adult is white and the soldiers are all men and none of the women work makes Ronald Reagan's 1984 "Morning in America" campaign commercial look positively progressive. Its picture of American society is not meant to represent reality, of course, but to symbolize what must have seemed a marketable vision of all that was best about America, to represent what was defined as pure and sacred and true, what justified the sacrifices of American young men. There are obviously problems with a commercial that, in 1988, portrayed an all-white, all-male army and used an all-white old-fashioned small town to represent American freedom. But the contrast between the actual American society and this "ideal" America is matched by the contrast between this commercial and its 1990s counterpart.

"Soldier's Pledge," the army's highly produced defining statement from the 1990s, is a powerful vision of American strength through diversity, of the integral connections between soldiers and the society they protect, and of the values they hold firm. As voices recite the Soldier's Creed—"I am an American soldier. I am a member of the United States Army—a protector of the greatest nation on earth," the camera moves over historical images of men at war. There is no voiceover, no song lyrics, no narrative, just the woven voices of Americans paying tribute to their soldiers. They are people from the full spectrum of American life, a diversity that could be nothing but American, not only of race or ethnicity and age and gender, but of region and culture and creed. "You are my brother," it begins, and the voices join, sometimes overlapping, as do the images, speakers and soldiers. "You are my brother. You are strong. You are not afraid. You are my sister. You are my sister. You are not afraid. You are my son. You are my grandson. You are my granddaughter. You are a leader. You are my daughter. You are brave. You are brave. And full of courage." "You are a peacekeeper," say two police officers. "You are the one I look up to." "You make me proud," offer several voices as the camera lingers on an African American soldier in Special Forces beret and then cuts to a young African American boy. "You are the heart and soul of my country," says a Native American woman, her arm around her daughter, land unfolding into the distance behind her. "When others cower, you stand tall." "You are my hero." "You are the defender of democracy." "You keep freedom alive."[29]

The 1980s portrayal of America's army, "Freedom Isn't Free," created a powerful and unbreachable distinction between "my hometown," where people pursued good lives and simple joys, and the world of the soldier who sacrificed to make that possible. The only uniform that appeared in the hometown itself was that of the high school football team. The two worlds were completely separate, and that was the point. "Soldier's Pledge" wove the worlds together. While images of what would later become "the homefront" were clearly different from those of soldiers in training, in tanks and in planes, even in historical scenes of combat, American civilians were not oblivious to the men and women "who keep democracy alive." The connections are immediate, and proud. And while no word of race or gender was ever spoken, this portrayal of the army emphasized inclusiveness in every second of its duration. Members of different races served with pride and with distinction. And it was decidedly "the men and women of the U.S. Army" that this commercial celebrated, for while women were not shown in roles forbidden to them, the montage kept returning—seven times—to a slight and pretty female specialist who stood a full foot shorter than the male soldiers on either side of her and who jumped from a plane as the words echoed: "You are brave . . . and full of courage."

The army so successfully conveyed the message that it offered equal opportunity and created strength through diversity, that it was a "resource for society" in ways that reached beyond national defense, that this understanding passed for conventional wisdom. Army officials may have wondered whether its marketing of social good had too far eclipsed its image of military strength when a 1995 *New York Times* article casually noted: "Whatever its ability to wage war, the all-volunteer military has made enormous strides since its creation in 1973 as a vehicle for racial integration and upward mobility of men and women who otherwise might not have had the opportunities that the armed services have provided."[30]

"Soldier's Pledge" was a brilliant work of advertising and a powerful symbolic claim, but it raises fundamental questions. How well did the army's concrete record match its portrayal in "Soldiers' Pledge"? Was the army truly a source of social good for the nation, building unity through diversity and strength through inclusion? By the mid-1990s, the army had moved far beyond the racial crisis of the 1970s. It had worked very hard to overcome the violent and angry divisions of those years, conducting major studies of race relations, creating mandatory race-relations courses, adopting race-conscious promotions policies, investigating charges of discrimination and maltreatment, and holding leaders responsible for achieving racial calm and fostering the sort of teamwork that transcends divisions of race or creed. These efforts made a difference. And so did broader cultural changes, as the nation moved further from the intense and angry confrontations of the 1970s. By the mid-1980s, Amy recruits—white and black—also were much more likely to be people of competence and ambition, much less likely than those who, as recruiters sometimes said, had been pulled from the dregs of society to seek violent solutions to racial difference.

In 1996 military sociologists Charles Moskos and John Sibley Butler argued that the army had not only conquered its race problems, but that it offered the entire nation a model for race relations. These scholars described a black and white world, however, a model that was increasingly out of date in a nation with a Latino population of almost 10 percent. It was less so in the army; in 1996, Hispanics accounted for only 5.3 percent of soldiers, whereas blacks made up 27 percent and whites 62 percent.[31] But even setting aside the bipolar model of race, the optimistic picture offered by these social scientists was controversial, for Americans—especially black Americans—were well aware that peacetime military opportunities could quickly change to wartime military casualties, and that the high rates of black enlistment in the army were closely tied to the limited civilian job opportunities for young black men and women. Butler and Moskos did, however, make a strong argument for black opportunity in the peacetime army. Although the army "is not immune to the demons that haunt race relations in America," they wrote, it was unequaled in its level of racial integration and was possibly "the only place in American life, where whites are routinely bossed around by blacks." Even more, they argued, no other majority-white institution had so fundamentally incorporated the African American "heritage" into its institutional culture.[32]

As the army raised its recruiting standards, black enlistment remained high. And by many measures blacks, on average, were more likely than whites to succeed in the army. Blacks were much more likely than whites to successfully complete their first term of enlistment; for black women, the likelihood was double. One of every four white men was discharged for indiscipline, lack of aptitude, or physical/psychological problems during his first term; five of six black men completed their terms of enlistment successfully. Black men and women were also much more likely than white soldiers to reenlist.[33]

The army was well aware that the black men and women it recruited faced continuing disadvantage in the civilian labor market. Many had attended failing public schools. Others came from backgrounds of social disadvantage, or lived in areas with few good jobs, or encountered barriers that had to do with race. So army recruiters sold army opportunities. Black enlistees, research showed, were looking for education and training. Money for college was a critical incentive for 51 percent of black volunteers as compared to 32 percent of whites. And in the mid-1990s, 80 percent of black army veterans used the G.I. Bill for further education. Those educational benefits, many concluded, were the army's biggest contribution to equal opportunity in America.[34]

The gap between average scores of white and black recruits on the military entrance test remained, though it had grown smaller since the 1970s. But with hardly any soldiers from Category IV, white or black, the testing gap was no longer a major public issue. Fifty-nine percent of black recruits scored in Categories IIIA or above during the 1990s. That compared to 14 percent of black youth nationwide. Exam scores were still used to determine specialties or career fields, and lower average scores meant that blacks were proportionally underrepresented in some high-tech areas. Though slightly more than a quarter of active duty soldiers were black in the mid-1990s, for example, they accounted for only 11 percent of those assigned to electronic warfare specialties. But black men were also slightly underrepresented (in proportion to their numbers in the army) in the combat arms, for most black men sought training and experience that would transfer to civilian life.[35]

During the 1970s, the army learned that strong and visible black leadership improved racial comity within the ranks. So, in its own self interest, the army worked hard to increase the number of black commissioned officers, creating internal programs to prepare those with poor academic backgrounds, recruiting heavily for West Point, and building ROTC programs at historically black colleges. In 1975, only 3 percent of commissioned officers were black; that figure was 11.4 percent in 1995. The senior NCO ranks had no lack of black representation; by 1990 almost a third of first sergeants and sergeants major were black (up from 14 percent in 1970). Army policies were explicitly race-conscious, and the army judged them a success. When the Supreme Court considered the legitimacy of University of Michigan policies meant to promote racial diversity in its student body in 2003, retired army generals weighed in heavily in support of affirmative action.[36]

From the beginning of the all-volunteer force, black Americans had joined the army in large numbers. Some had been disappointed; others had found opportunity. But the concern had always been, as blacks filled the ranks in disproportionate numbers: What if there is a war? Would black casualties be disproportionate, as well? The first Gulf War seemed to settle that question, at least for a time. Thirty percent of army troops sent to the Persian Gulf were black. Twenty-eight black soldiers died. They represented 15 percent of those killed in action. Their deaths were mourned, but they were not protested—except as all deaths in that war were protested. Black soldiers had not been cannon fodder. And during Desert Storm, there was not a single racial incident significant enough to draw the attention of the military police.[37] Enormous changes had taken place over the past two decades, and by the 1990s the army's claims of equal opportunity had real substance.

Military regulations had insisted on the equal rights and opportunities of soldiers regardless of race ever since Truman issued his executive order desegregating the army in 1948. It was never so simple, and racism marred institutional culture as well as individual lives. But the army's official policy on race was no impediment to equal treatment. Women, however, were in a different category. Women were covered by different rules, subject to different regulations, restricted—by policy if not by law—from being treated as indistinguishable from their male counterparts.

The army had instituted a "womanpause" in spring 1981, assuming that with Jimmy Carter out of the White House and Clifford Alexander no longer secretary of the army, things could go back to "normal." Many high-ranking army officials believed the "experiment" with women had moved too far and too quickly. So with Carter's defeat, the army moved quickly, too. It put an end to gender-integrated training. It announced that it would hold women's numbers to 65,000. The Carter administration had planned for 87,000 women, or 12.5 percent of the enlisted force, but even that number was vastly lower than the 159,000 that the Evaluation of Women in the Army study had defined as the theoretical maximum in 1978. Field commanders, the Department of the Army informed Reagan's transition staff, were concerned about "combat readiness" in the wake of women's "attrition, pregnancy, sole parenthood, and strength and stamina." Thus the army proposed to undertake yet another major study of the utilization of women and women's effect on combat readiness.[38]

As army leaders watched the fundamental political shift from President Carter to President Reagan, they understood that the military's world was about to change. Reagan intended to dramatically increase the size of the army. Secretary of Defense Weinberger was floating queries about what it would take for the military to absorb half the nation's GNP in the event of war (Vietnam had accounted for 8.5 percent of the nation's GNP; Korea 15 percent). Defense spending was going to skyrocket; long-deferred needs and desires, from military pay and facilities to major weapons systems, were materializing. In this climate, the Department of the Army may have believed it had a blank check. But it made a fundamental miscalculation. In 1981, with the disastrous decade of the 1970s still shaping army policy, army leadership had no confidence that it could increase its strength by almost 100,000 volunteers—or that, if possible, those volunteers would be of sufficient quality to keep the nation safe. And this time, the Department of the Army meant to hold the line on women; the army would not solve its enlistment problem by increasing the number and percentage of women soldiers. Looking to Reagan's defense-oriented administration, the Department of the Army proposed—in a "secret" report that was described almost immediately in the *Washington Post*—to return to the draft.[39]

The Pentagon shook to its roots. Secretary of Defense Weinberger was "livid." The Reagan administration made abundantly clear that it did not intend to return to the draft. As Reagan officials watched the army push back on the issue of women, they drew the line. Women, even Ronald Reagan's Pentagon believed, were key to the survival of the AVF. Caspar Weinberger clarified Pentagon policy. "Qualified women are essential to obtaining the numbers of quality people required to maintain the readiness of our forces," he announced. "This Administration desires to increase the role of women in the military . . . This Department must aggressively break down those remaining barriers that prevent us from making the fullest use of the capabilities of women in providing for our national defense."[40]

During the 1980s, despite this affirmation, army women made few gains. The study undertaken by the army was a major anticlimax, its release repeatedly postponed. Members of DACOWITS protested its findings; "nothing but a snow job," said one social scientist. Overall, argued those who supported women's increased role, it seemed that the army repeatedly sought evidence that women undermined readiness and discounted studies that suggested otherwise. Those who opposed expanding women's roles generally focused on the question of combat. Quantitative statistics, such as the fact that women's upper body strength averages 42 percent less than men's, was repeated from source to source, but in opponents' arguments the lessons of "experience" often outweighed social science evidence. There was no way, opponents argued, for training exercises or carefully crafted studies to simulate the reality of combat. And in combat, what was at stake was not the principle of women's equality but the lives of soldiers.[41] The Women in the Army Policy Review focused on issues of physical strength and proximity to combat, and led the army to close twenty-three more MOSs to women. It was clear to all that this was not a time of opportunity for women in the military. One writer for *U.S. News and World Report* concluded in a 1982 article subtitled "End of a Honeymoon," "Whatever happens, there can be little doubt that the tide has turned for the female soldier." And the reassurance offered by Reagan's assistant secretary of defense for manpower, Lawrence Korb, that "women who are already in the Army can stay in if they want to" likely did little for women's morale.[42] Nonetheless, because the Reagan administration was committed to maintaining an all-volunteer force even as it expanded the size of the military, women maintained a significant presence in the army.

In early 1988, due in large part to the efforts of DACOWITS, the Department of Defense reevaluated its regulations governing the issue of women in combat. Secretary of Defense Frank Carlucci announced that the military would apply a standard "risk rule" to determine which positions would be open to women. Women were still barred from direct ground combat and from support positions that left them equally or more subject to direct combat, hostile fire, or capture than the combat unit they supported, but this policy did open more military jobs to them. Nonetheless, in a sign of the challenges ahead, this announcement was joined with a directive calling for the military to enforce regulations against sexual harassment more rigorously. As the *New York Times* explained the linked actions, the "steps announced today . . . represent a continuing effort by the armed forces to find a balance among military readiness, equal opportunity and social values as women are integrated into an institution that has traditionally reflected male values and is still dominated by men." Until 1988, the Army's Code of Conduct had begun with the words, "I am an American fighting man"—a difficult statement for women soldiers to make with any sense of legitimacy.[43]

Desert Storm would be a major turning point for military women, most of all because women performed well. Twenty-six thousand female soldiers were deployed to the Gulf; five were killed in action. As Assistant Secretary of Defense Christopher Jehn told Congress, "women who served in the Gulf performed their duties magnificently." But the Gulf War demonstrated something else. The "risk rule" was next to useless. In such environs, all uniformed personnel were at risk. Congress began, again, to debate the combat exclusion issue. The Bush administration appointed a commission to study "the Assignment of Women in the Armed Services." The commission was both controversial and acrimonious, but after its sixteen members heard testimony from more than 300 witnesses and reviewed more than 11,000 statements, it all came to little. The report, which offered findings that pulled in different directions and an "Alternate View Section" signed by five of the most conservative commission members, appeared after the 1992 election. Outgoing president Bush and secretary of defense Cheney paid it little attention; incoming president Clinton paid it even less. Clinton and his secretary of defense, Les Aspin, intended to expand military opportunities and roles for women. In 1994, the Department of Defense eliminated the risk rule, substituting a basic prohibition against assigning women to units (below brigade level) whose primary mission is direct ground combat.[44]

During the Clinton administration, the army looked a fair amount like its advertising representation. Gender-integrated training reappeared in 1994. Women's representation grew, even as army numbers shrank.

Black women made up an ever-larger share of the Army; in the mid-1990s 48 percent of female soldiers were black. Fourteen percent of the army was female; fourteen percent of commissioned officers were female. Still, relatively few women had reached the top ranks of the military. There is no such thing as lateral hire in the army; all officers must rise through the ranks. And since women made up a tiny percentage of soldiers until after the move to an all-volunteer force, and since the first women were not graduated from West Point until 1980, time in service was still an issue during the 1990s. Restrictions on women's roles mattered, as well; two-thirds of general officers came from tactical operations fields in which women were very poorly represented. The first brigadier general—the commander of the Women's Army Corps—was appointed in 1971. The first female major general came seven years later. It was nineteen more years before a woman reached three-star rank. And the first woman joined the tiny number (210 in the history of the U.S. Army) of four-star generals in 2008.[45]

By the 1990s, the army not only presented itself as a site of equal opportunity and inclusion, but came close to matching its claims. It is quite possible to argue that, despite remaining problems, the army offered more opportunity to racial minorities and to women than almost any segment of civilian society. That doesn't mean, however, that notions of social good dominated military thinking. Even as the peacetime army sought public support by emphasizing the value it added to American society, its primary mission was always national defense.

America's military had a long history of framing externally mandated moves toward inclusion or equal opportunity as stark conflicts between "social experiment" and national defense. The nation fought for democracy in World War II with a racially segregated military; military and government officials set fundamental questions of legitimacy and morality aside, insisting that nothing mattered more than ending the war. It was an effective argument. If white racism was so powerful that the Red Cross segregated "white" and "Negro" blood and racial violence was common or barely contained throughout the war, many believed, the project of forced integration might well undermine war aims.[46] Notions of social good versus national defense had also been at the root of the ongoing struggle between civilian Secretary of the Army Clifford Alexander and army leadership during the late 1970s. Such models were not restricted to the military. "I don't think we should crucify the national defense capability on the cross of an equal opportunity slogan," conservative Georgia representative Larry McDonald testified during Congressional hearings on the utilization of women in 1979.[47]

As America struggled through its deep and divisive "culture wars" during the 1990s, questions about the army's role in American society and the proper relationship between goals of inclusion and military preparedness spiraled into intense partisan debate. Americans from widely different backgrounds and with vastly different levels of knowledge argued over whether army policies of inclusion and equal opportunity were vital to the success of the all-volunteer force or were social experiments that almost necessarily undermined military readiness. A key disagreement was over how far policies of equal opportunity and inclusion should reach, and what methods should be employed to implement them. The army's race-conscious policies were brought into heated debates over affirmative action and racial preference.[48] Arguments over the utilization of women were never resolved. The most explosive and vitriolic version of this longstanding controversy, however, centered on the issue of "gays in the military."

In October 1991 presidential candidate Bill Clinton had pledged during a little-noted speech that he would, if elected, end the ban against gays in the military. This ban, like the regulations governing women's roles in the army, was a matter of policy rather than of law. From World War I on the military had prohibited consensual sodomy and attempted to screen out those who manifested the "stigmata of degeneration" or evidence of "sexual psychopathy"; by World War II the focus had shifted from prohibiting sodomy to excluding homosexuals. In 1949 the new Department of Defense officially barred homosexuals of either sex from serving in the military. The Department of Defense issued a new policy statement in 1981, declaring for the first time that "homosexuality is incompatible with military service." Government statistics showed that 16,919 men and women had been discharged from the armed forces for homosexuality between 1980 and 1991, and a number of legal challenges had been mounted in response to the DoD directive.[49] Clinton's proposal was in line with his broader platform of inclusion and equal opportunity for all Americans, but he had no idea how much opposition it would face.

The promise to end the ban on gays in the military got little attention during the campaign, but it did nothing to endear Clinton to military leaders. He had, in any case, little military support. Clinton was the first president since FDR who had no military experience. During the 1960s he had opposed the Vietnam War and, like many young men of his generation, had used the means within his reach to avoid military service. His actions were legal, but they did not fit military notions of honor and patriotism. Policy proposals also undermined military support: in his campaign, Clinton made clear that he intended to build domestic social programs, not defense spending. And in his first act as president, historian Michael Sherry notes, Clinton replaced the usual metaphors of war with those of seasonal rebirth, promising in his inaugural address to "force the spring" of "American renewal."[50]

There would have been military resistance to ending the ban on homosexuals no matter how the majority of military leaders felt about this president. But the fact that Clinton wasn't one of theirs, that he didn't speak their language, that he had "shirked" the obligations of military service—all that well-spun history shaped relations between the military and its new commander in chief. And the issue of gays in the military provided Republicans in Congress with their first tactical opening in the larger culture wars. They pushed it to the top of the agenda in the first days of the Clinton presidency, diverting the Clinton administration from its intended focus on economic issues and creating a crisis that undermined Clinton's authority with Congress, the Joint Chiefs, and even some of his supporters. That the opposition to Clinton's plan was led by Sam Nunn, Democratic senator from Georgia and Congress's most powerful authority on military affairs, and General Colin Powell, who Clinton had appointed chair of the Joint Chiefs of Staff, made the situation that much more impossible.

Clinton had seen trouble coming and had sent a member of his transition team to negotiate with the Chiefs of Staff before his inauguration, hoping to develop a plan that would end the ban "with minimum disruption to combat effectiveness." The Chiefs of Staff agreed to a first step: their respective services would stop screening prospects for homosexuality. They would not, however, sign on to an Executive Order ending the official ban on gays in the military. During the first week of February, Senator Nunn condemned Clinton's proposal in what *Time* magazine described as a "withering" twenty-five-minute speech on the floor of Congress. Nunn posed forty-two questions about integrating gay men and women into the military, many of them going beyond the immediate concern of military readiness and national defense. "What restrictions," he asked, "would be placed on displays of affection while in uniform, such as dancing at a formal event?" Soon an inflammatory video that included highly sexual images from gay pride parades began circulating on Capitol Hill. Opposition was consolidating. Having long ago lost control of the process, Clinton tried to manage the fallout. In a compromise negotiated with Nunn, he agreed to delay action for six months, giving Nunn "his time in the sun" in a series of congressional hearings while working with the Joint Chiefs to find an acceptable compromise. Nunn, in return, agreed to help block a Republican attempt to write the ban, which was at that point under executive authority, into law.[51]

Spring hearings before the House Armed Services Committee returned, repeatedly, to seemingly nonideological claims about the importance of national defense. That greater good was often framed against the narrow self-interest of "homosexual activism." Committee chair Ron Dellums, who had played a role in Vietnam-era struggles over race, attempted to reframe the debate as one between those who hold "a commitment to one of America's most fundamental ideas; elimination of discrimination" and those who are driven by "tradition, societal taboos or strongly held religious beliefs," but the ranking minority member, South Carolina Republican Floyd Spence, quickly pushed back. "Lifting the ban on homosexuals serving in the military," Spence said, "should not be a question of civil rights, equal rights, or gay rights." Instead, he insisted, it is a question of "military readiness," of "cohesion, discipline, and morale."[52]

One witness, in language that found a rough poetry, tried to lay the old model of social experiment versus national defense to rest. "I am going to be blunt, maybe even a little crude with some of what I say about the infantry and combat," Colonel Lucian Truscott III (U.S.A., Retired) told committee members. "The question of gays in the military demands an answer to their serving in a real war, at dirt level . . . down where men kill and get killed, down where 85 percent of all of the casualties in all of the wars have occurred."

> Down there we need to know: Will he fight? Will he be there when the going gets tough? Is he willing to take a hill in the pouring rain, walk in among the enemy dead, see their bloated bodies . . . the trash, the filth, the piles of excrement . . . the stench of that mixed with that horrible sweetish smell of rotting flesh? Is he willing to push a dead soldier out of a fox hole

> so he can get into it? Is this guy willingly [sic] to aim his weapon right at somebody and kill them? Can he take it if his best friend, the guy he went through basic training with and shared a hole with for the past 3 months, gets shot through the middle of his forehead and he has to sit there with his body all night? If the answer to all of these questions is yes, then we don't care if he is white or black or brown or red or yellow. We don't care if he is Christian, Jew, Muslim, or atheist. We don't give a damn if he is gay. We wouldn't even care if he were a she.[53]

But testimony against the change took center stage, and in the end the committee concluded that lifting the ban against homosexuals would "create an unacceptable risk to the high standards in morale, good order and discipline, and unit cohesion that are the essence of military capability."[54]

What became clear, during the winter and spring of 1993, was that the nation was divided. While a Time/CNN survey in mid-January found that 57 percent of Americans believed gays and lesbians should not be banned from the military, one conducted only a week later found 43 percent in support with 48 percent opposed. The difference may have been the wording of the question; only in the second was the move identified as "Bill Clinton's plan." But it was clearly Clinton's plan, and it was getting a lot of attention. By the end of the month, 51 percent of Americans believed that "admitting gays to the military would undermine discipline and morale." That was the same percentage that agreed with the statement "Homosexuality is wrong, and this policy would be condoning it." For context, shortly before Truman issued his executive order integrating the armed forces, 44 percent of white Americans polled believed that "Although Negroes should not be mistreated by whites the white race should always keep its superior position" and an additional 20 percent took a stranger stance: "Because Negroes are so different from white people as a race . . . they should not be allowed to mix with whites in any way."[55]

Opinion about lifting the ban was not so divided within the military. A poll conducted by the *Los Angeles Times* found that more than three-quarters of active duty enlisted personnel—across all services, and with no significant difference by race or ethnicity—opposed the change. And an unpublished internal poll conducted by an unnamed service found that 80 percent of enlisted personnel thought recruiting would suffer if the ban were lifted and 85 percent believed disciplinary problems would increase.

The Republican co-chair of the congressional hearings asked, rhetorically: "How can sentiment of this intensity against the lifting of the ban not negatively impact cohesion, discipline, and morale?"[56]

Leadership, more than anything else, determines the success of military policies and regulations. A study by the Center for Strategic and International Studies argues, "The most powerful and direct influence on organizational culture [in the military] comes from within the officer corps . . . Officers turn values into action, bring coherence out of confusion, set the example, and articulate the viewpoint of the military institution."[57] In the case of gays in the military that leadership was not forthcoming. General Powell, speaking at Annapolis, told sailors he would understand if they resigned from service if the president lifted the ban. The Commandant of the Marine Corps reportedly handed out antigay videos at one meeting with Secretary of Defense Les Aspin; another chief opposed the admission of "fags." Clinton's secretary of defense met repeatedly, intensely, and heatedly with the Joint Chiefs; there was no give. "Don't Ask, Don't Tell"—a policy that ended questions about sexual orientation at the time of enlistment, but required discharge of anyone who made his or her sexual preference known—was as far as they would go. And then, in the middle of the summer, Senator Nunn jumped ship. In a move that surprised even his colleagues in Congress, he announced that he would propose legislation solidifying the ban on gays in the military. "Don't Ask, Don't Tell" would become the law of the land.[58] Army claims of inclusion and equal opportunity had much substance during the 1990s, but they also had very definite limits.

★

During the 1990s, the army increasingly focused on operations other than war and sold itself to the public as a provider of social good. And it also worked harder and harder to recruit and retain soldiers. Sooner or later, some began to make a connection between the two. In a world where Colin Powell found it possible to joke, "I'm running out of villains. I'm down to Castro and Kim Il Sung," some of those who tracked military recruiting began to ask whether the sort of young men who had joined the army to defend the free world, the sort who sought hardship and challenge and adventure, the ones who wanted to blow things up—in short, the ones who wanted to fight—were less motivated by the prospect of peacekeeping missions and humanitarian relief. "Without an Enemy," asked an article on army recruiting in *Time* magazine, "What Makes a Soldier's Heart Sing?" The army continued to focus—not always by choice—on inclusion and questions of equal opportunity. In 1998, following assaults on female trainees by drill sergeants at Aberdeen Proving Ground in 1996 and evidence that male soldiers had committed at least thirty-four sex crimes, including rape of female soldiers, during the Gulf War, the army responded by adding fifty-four hours on army values and human relations to basic training. But a debate had begun, urged on by the polemics of civilian critics. The Army War College class of 2001 found "The Code of the Warrior and the Kinder, Gentler Army" on its list of suggested research topics. The new Field Manual 22-100 (Army Leadership) attempted a definition of "the Warrior Ethos" for the first time.[59] In an army of social good, a movement had begun to reinvigorate the army's warrior culture and the army's warrior image.

8 THE WARRIOR ETHOS

ON MARCH 19, 2003, at 10:16 P.M. Eastern Standard Time, President George W. Bush sat behind his desk in the Oval Office, looking into the television cameras that linked him to the nation. American and coalition forces, he informed the American people, had begun "military operations to disarm Iraq, to free its people and to defend the world from grave danger." The United States, Bush told a divided public, "will not live at the mercy of an outlaw regime that threatens the peace with weapons of mass murder. We will meet that threat now, with our Army, Air Force, Navy, Coast Guard and Marines, so that we do not have to meet it later with armies of fire fighters and police and doctors on the streets of our cities." Assuring the nation that "this will not be a campaign of half measures, and we will accept no outcome but victory," the president offered prayers for the "defenders of our nation," that those who serve "will return safely and soon."[1]

Forty-three days later, on May 1, 2003, George W. Bush donned flight gear, took the navigator's seat in a U.S. Navy S-3B Viking antisubmarine aircraft, and—in a carefully staged scene of triumph—made a tailhook landing on an aircraft carrier returning from the Gulf. Standing before a banner proclaiming "Mission Accomplished," Bush declared victory in Iraq. The Battle of Iraq, he told the cheering sailors and the world, "is one victory in a war on terror that began on September the 11th, 2001." When

Bush announced the end of major combat operations that day, 139 American servicemen had lost their lives. Iraqi losses, military and civilian, were much higher.[2]

As the *New York Times* hailed the "end of the combat phase of one of the swiftest wars in American military history," it also offered more measured language. American military forces in Iraq were beginning stability operations, explained an army officer, but it was important to understand that stability operations tend to be characterized by "momentary flareups of violence." In words much more accurate than "mission accomplished," the chief of staff for the army's V Corps cautioned: "It will look at times like we are still at war." Three and a half years later, with no weapons of mass destruction ever found, the nation marked the day when it had fought in Iraq longer than it fought in World War II. Between March 19, 2003 and November 27, 2006, the war had claimed the lives of almost 2,900 American servicemen and women. Twenty-two thousand more had been wounded. And more than two-thirds of those casualties came from the army.[3]

For most of the life of the all-volunteer force, few Americans—at least among those in positions of power—believed the United States would ever fight an extended war without a draft. In the initial debates of the Gates Commission, in the Carter administration's decision to reinstate selective service registration when the Soviet Union flexed its muscles in Afghanistan, in countless congressional hearings and serious discussions in the inner offices of the Pentagon, most of America's civilian and military leaders had assumed that the AVF was in essence a peacetime military, one that would serve as the core of the nation's forces in the event of war. In 1981, when the Reagan administration was on the verge of ending draft registration (reversing the Carter administration's actions), the Joint Chiefs of Staff made that clear. "The AVF policy provides peacetime manpower," wrote the chairman of the Joint Chiefs to the Secretary of Defense. "Selective Service registration supports mobilization for war."[4]

What they meant by war, of course, is the issue. The United States has not declared war since 1941. Given that more than 162,000 American troops (and hundreds of thousands of Koreans and Vietnamese, along with soldiers and citizens of nations including Grenada, Panama, Iraq, Somalia, Haiti, and the Balkan states) died in U.S. military operations of various sorts during the last half of the twentieth century, definitions of "war" are obviously complicated. But when it came to the balance between the AVF and the draft, these politicians and military officers and planners tended to think in terms of the big one. They imagined the clash of massive armies: American tanks arrayed along the Soviet border; millions of troops trying to stem a "Red Chinese attack in Asia."[5]

The distinction between a peacetime and a wartime military gradually receded, at least in public discussions during the last two decades of the twentieth century. Assumptions that the all-volunteer force was the peacetime-only version of the nation's military faded, and just as Americans who had argued so strenuously over the existence of a standing peacetime army came to see the draft as a normal fact of life in the decades following World War II, Americans eventually stopped using the phrase "all-volunteer" to talk about the nation's military. Secretary of Defense Caspar Weinberger was well ahead of the curve in 1983 when he half-joked that the all-volunteer force was so successful he thought he'd drop the term and order everyone to start calling America's military "the armed forces."[6] In 1984, however, the army changed the title of its recruiters' journal from *All Volunteer* to the simple, eponymous *Recruiter Journal.* Full acceptance came in the 1990s. The Cold War was over; the Soviet threat dissolved. In the first Gulf War, where technology played the role of hero and victory was declared in 100 hours, the AVF was judged a grand success—in war, not only in peace. The experiment was over. People still talked about returning to a draft in the years that followed, but the distinction they made was not between peacetime volunteer force and wartime conscription.

When the American military launched its campaign of "shock and awe" in March 2003, some critics raised the specter of Vietnam and warned of the possible quagmire to come. As it became clear that the "images of celebrating Iraqis" did not necessarily reveal what U.S. president Bush called the "ageless appeal of human freedom," and that the major problem faced by the occupying force would not be "what to do with all the floral gifts" (in the words of the British *Guardian*), Americans began to talk about what it meant to fight this war with an army of volunteers.[7] It was simply a new chapter in a longstanding debate, as there was no political will for a draft and quite arguably no need for one. The military, in fact, was strongly opposed to conscription. But proposals to return to a draft were made newly powerful by each individual death, by each life compromised or destroyed as the United States sent its "warriors" to fight in a voluntary war.

In the first decade of the twenty-first century the modern army faced, for the first time, the challenge of recruiting during an extended war with no threat of conscription to motivate volunteers. And the war in Iraq posed a particular set of challenges. In Iraq, it was not only those in the combat arms that were at risk. There was no clear battle front. The insurgents did not wear uniforms; their weapons-of-choice were improvised explosive devices, or IEDs, which exploded without warning and with no regard for combat designation. In this war, there were many fewer "safe" MOSs for which to volunteer—and those, of course, were not the ones that carried enlistment bonuses of twenty or thirty thousand dollars. Once in the army, soldiers faced repeated tours in Iraq, while stop-loss provisions could prevent them from leaving the military when they completed their terms of enlistment.[8] And those who had joined the U.S. Army Reserve, with its recruiting promise of "one weekend a month," were not exempt. Controversy over the war itself also made recruiting more difficult. It wasn't like the war in Vietnam, when public anger over the war too often spilled over onto those who fought it. This war's critics were careful to make clear that they honored the service of those who fought even as they questioned the political leaders who had initiated it. But because the war was enormously unpopular with African Americans, for example, enlistment rates for black youth dropped precipitously.

This war, many argued, had no clear definition of victory or plan for withdrawal. It was all too much like the nation-building projects presidential candidate George Bush had garnered support from military personnel by opposing back in 2000. And while some large percentage of American 18-year-olds continued to believe, against all evidence, in the immortality of youth, their parents looked at the photographs of painfully young soldiers killed in action and read the stories about massive head trauma and PTSD rates and the prevalence of sexual assault with different eyes. Struggling recruiters learned that, for this cohort of youth, parents' opinions really did matter.

In response to a difficult situation, the army changed both the way it recruited and the ways it portrayed itself to the American public in the first decade of the twenty-first century. Oddly enough, however, it wasn't the war in Iraq alone that prompted those changes. A major shift had begun before the invasion of Iraq—before the body count continued to rise in 2003, before American troops landed in Afghanistan in 2002, before al Qaeda attacked the World Trade Center and the Pentagon in 2001. The war in Iraq did affect army recruiting and change the ways that Americans understood the meanings of military service. These war-induced changes, however, belong to a longer story of transformation that reaches back to the post–Cold War world of the 1990s and the ongoing struggle over the purpose and future of the U.S. Army.

Those who worked, during the 1990s, to sell the army to the American people as a provider of social good, as a site of equality and opportunity for all America's citizens, had a perfect example in the top military and civilian leaders of the army. The army's chief of staff was Eric Shinseki, the first Asian American to wear four stars. Ric Shinseki had been born to Japanese-American parents in 1942, just short of a year after the Japanese bombed Pearl Harbor. Although his birthplace—the small town of Lihue, Kaua'i, in the Territory of Hawai'i—saved him from the incarceration in "relocation camps" that Japanese Americans endured on the mainland, he nonetheless began his life classified as an "enemy alien." Louis Caldera, secretary of the army, was born in 1956 to Mexican immigrants in El Paso, Texas, and had lived briefly in public housing when his family moved to California when he was four.[9]

Both men paid public tribute to their backgrounds; when General Shinseki was sworn in as the 34th Chief of Staff of the U.S. Army he wore a lei of maile leaves from Kaua'i, and he often spoke of his uncles who had fought with the "Go for broke" 442nd regimental combat team and the 100th Battalion during World War II. Caldera paid tribute to his immigrant parents, who had taught him "that this is a land of great opportunity and I had a responsibility to give something back." He frequently spoke of the patriotic beliefs of young Latinos and urged the army to worry less about high school diplomas than about who would make good soldiers, since at the time Latinos had only a 50 percent graduation rate.[10] Yet in the last years of the Clinton administration, these leaders talked little about the army as a producer of social good. They saw an army in crisis yet again and facing a future of even greater challenges. In the final months of the twentieth century General Shinseki and Secretary Caldera were both, in different ways, working hard to transform the army to face those challenges.

General Shinseki began his four-year term as chief of staff of the army with a sense of urgency. "The time is right," he explained to an interviewer who questioned his commitment to rapid transformation. "Our country is at peace, and we lead the world economically. There is potential here. There is a pause in world affairs where we can advantage ourselves to make some changes with minimal risk."[11] While Shinseki publicly emphasized the opportunities offered in a time of extended peace, he was well aware that the 1990s had been a tough decade for the army. It had faced a rapid reduction in force, ending the decade with 35 percent fewer troops than it had begun. Recruiters struggled to fill an ever smaller number of boots. Funding had dropped from a height of more than 6 percent of GDP in the 1980s to less than 3 percent. With a smaller force and a broader set of missions, contingency deployments had increased from a Cold War average of one every four years to one every fourteen months. Most were brief, but others—such as those related to the conflict in the Balkans—had become longstanding commitments that drained army capability to execute the two-major-theaters-of-war scenario that had formed the basis of military planning since 1993. At the turn of the century, 140,000 army personnel were committed outside the nation. And many believed these deployments—whether the difficult task of "peacekeeping" and stability operations, combating drug trafficking, and providing humanitarian assistance on foreign soil; or domestic tasks that included fighting wildfires and cleaning up after massive hurricanes—undermined not only army readiness but army recruiting. As the Republican chair of the House subcommittee on military personnel put it in highly partisan language, under President Clinton the nation's armed forces "have begun to resemble an international fire brigade with poorly defined, helter-skelter responsibilities."[12]

Despite public perceptions of army success in the first Gulf War and in the Balkans, military planners saw major problems with army warfighting capability. The army was simply not mobile enough. When Iraqi forces overran Kuwait City in 1990 and continued rapidly toward the Saudi border and thus toward the airfields and ports where America's heavy mechanized forces would arrive, the army's best recourse was to airlift a brigade of the 82nd Airborne Division into the desert and charge it with blocking the Iraqi advance. It was no one's idea of an ideal battle plan: a light infantry brigade facing the heavy mechanized forces of the Iraqi Army. But for reasons no one in the United States ever figured out, Iraq had stopped its advance and the U.S. Army had six months to move equipment (a U.S. armored division's machines weighed, in total, more than 300,000 tons) into position. In the 1999 war in Kosovo, it had taken the army so long to get its Apache helicopters to their mobilization point in Albania that the term in general circulation was "embarrassing."[13]

Shinseki's goal was to create an army that was agile, flexible, and versatile. He proposed to create medium-light brigades of mechanized infantry that could be deployed anywhere on earth within ninety-six hours and that were capable of the wide range of missions the army confronted in the new post–Cold War world. He had great faith in technology, and planned for a future combat system that included nanotechnology and incorporated information systems first developed by the entertainment industry in Hollywood. But unlike Bush's secretary of defense, Donald Rumsfeld, who sought to substitute long-range precision strikes for boots on the ground—"immaculate warfare," in the army's skeptical terms—Shinseki refused to compromise on the size of the force. In his ideal army, the soldier was key. All soldiers, insisted Shinseki, had to be more versatile. They had to be able to judge situations, to engage in nonlinear warfare, to shift from peacekeeping to warfighting in the space of a moment. "[H]ow have you prepared your youngsters," Shinseki asked rhetorically, "both intellectually, from a point of being trained and prepared, and with equipment, to be able to very quickly prevail in that more intense higher mission requirement?"[14]

Although the specifics of Shinseki's plans for transformation provoked debate, they had the full support of Clinton's secretary of the army. Louis Caldera, like Eric Shinseki, was a West Point graduate. But unlike Shinseki, who was graduated in 1965 as the United States expanded its presence in Vietnam, Caldera completed his West Point years in 1978 and entered the army at its all-volunteer nadir of quality, competence, and morale. Caldera left the army after his required five years of service, which included time as admissions director at West Point. He liked to say that he hoped to be thought of as "the Soldier's Secretary," but he often relied more on what he had learned in business school at Harvard and in his years in California politics than on the lessons of army leadership from his undergraduate days. Caldera, who saw the late 1990s as a "time of great challenge" for the army, believed that he must sell the army to the American public and, most of all, to Congress. He told a reporter in 1998 that he intended to "tell that story . . . to sell that story" of the "tremendous job we're asking soldiers to do every day." Driving that point home,

Caldera believed, was the best way to ensure that the army had the resources it needed. From his first days as secretary of the army, Caldera was thinking about marketing.[15]

As Shinseki and Caldera tried to "jump-start transformation" of the army, a third strand of reform was gaining power. In 1996, Thomas E. Ricks, then a reporter for the *Wall Street Journal,* argued in the *Atlantic Monthly* that the army was suffering a post–Cold War "identity crisis." More and more frequently, in the following years, public discussions of this "identity crisis" centered around the notions of the soldier as "warrior." Some argued that military operations other than war (OOTW) "detract from the 'warrior' capabilities of the armed forces." Widely read works positioned "warrior" in opposition to "women" and their increasing presence in the military. Elliott Abrams and Andrew Bacevich, two of the most influential scholars writing about the military, argued that "the identity of the 'soldier as warrior' has become obsolete" in the modern army, but insisted that even in a new era of post–Cold War, high-tech warfare, the need remained for "a traditional combat ethos—the mix of physical and mental toughness, discipline, raw courage, and willingness to sacrifice that was the hallmark of effective militaries in the wars of the 20th century."[16]

These three strands—Shinseki's plan for transformation, Caldera's faith in marketing, and the emerging focus on a warrior ethos—all came together at the cusp of the new century. In 1999, the army missed its recruiting goal. Badly. It needed only 74,500 new soldiers, and it fell 7,000 short. The army was not alone; the navy's shortfall in 1998 was "disastrous." Even the air force was struggling. ("It really is against the laws of God and Nature for the Air Force to have recruitment difficulties," noted a prominent military expert.) Analysts offered a range of reasons for the recruiting crisis. First and most basic, there were simply fewer young people. In 1999 there were 21 million Americans between the ages of 18 and 22—a drop of almost 20 percent since 1980. A great number of them were unqualified: the army required that 90 percent of volunteers have earned high school diplomas (not GEDs), and it virtually ruled out the bottom two "mental" quintiles. As manufacturing jobs disappeared and a college degree seemed a necessary requirement for middle-class lives, more and more high school graduates headed straight to college—a 20 percent increase during the 1990s. The Clinton administration believed in education, and the army's offer of funding for college increasingly competed with other sources of loans, grants, and employer benefits. The economy was booming, jobs were plentiful, and the papers were full of stories of twenty-somethings making fortunes on start-up companies run out of their parents' basements. As the days of the draft grew more distant, fewer parents, teachers, coaches, or counselors—those that recruiters call "influencers"—looked back with pride on their own military service. In 1999, fewer than 6 percent of Americans under the age of 65 had any military experience at all.[17]

Once again, critics claimed that the all-volunteer force was in jeopardy. Senator John McCain began musing—publicly—about reinstating the draft. The *Army Times* flatly endorsed one. The word "draft" began popping up in newspapers and in current event magazines.[18] Relatively few members of the American public remembered how often the volunteer force had been declared dead during the preceding two decades, and the reports of shortfalls created a sense of urgency to which the army had to respond. USAREC was taking concrete action—increasing the number of recruiters, creating new enlistment options, contracting research—but both the secretary and the chief of staff of the army believed it necessary to fight this war on symbolic terrain.

In October 2000, Army Chief Shinseki announced that, beginning on June 14, 2001—the army's first birthday in the new millennium—black berets would be standard issue for all the army's soldiers. For the 94 percent of Americans under the age of 65 who had never served in the military, this directive on headgear did not seem critically important. But it set off a firestorm in the army. In an institution where much recognition of achievement is symbolic, Shinseki's decision to take the black beret, the hard-earned symbol of excellence worn by the elite infantry cadre of Army Rangers, and give it to brand new privates who had struggled through basic training and to those who manned desks and shuffled paper or fried hamburgers and peeled potatoes seemed the ultimate insult. Shinseki had a reason: he meant the black berets to symbolize the army's commitment to transformation. He meant to encourage all members of the army to think of themselves first and foremost as soldiers, unified by their excellence and by army values. Although Shinseki was not narrowly focused on recruiting, retention, or morale, the black berets were part of his larger attempt to recast the meaning of soldiering. "With a stroke of the general's pen," one editorial proclaimed, "America will have a grander image of modern soldiering."[19]

Shinseki's action fit quite well with the growing insistence that the army needed to recapture a warrior ethos. But it didn't sit well with the army's "Real Warriors" (as some Rangers signed themselves). Shinseki's order, one Ranger told a reporter for the conservative *Weekly Standard,* speaking on condition of anonymity, devalued warrior culture. Command desire to pretend that "lesser" soldiers were the equal of the elite—"warrior-norming," in the words of the *Weekly Standard* reporter—did not correct the perceived failures that led critics to call for a return to the warrior ethos. It was instead a further sign of its loss.[20]

While those on active duty offered no attributed comments to the press—though one Ranger did state, anonymously, "If the chief of staff told me to wear a clown hat, that's what I'm gonna wear"—anger was not contained. "We filled the *Army Times* with letters," a retired command sergeant major wrote in retrospect, "we plugged up Internet discussion forums and our conversations were of little else . . . but the issue of who gets to wear what colored hat." One former Army Ranger, reported CNN, had walked 750 miles to Washington, DC to join a protest march over the proposed beret change. Even the newly inaugurated president got involved: George Bush ordered his new secretary of defense, Donald Rumsfeld, to investigate the situation.[21]

The heated words about headgear drew just the wrong kind of attention to the army. "At the dawning of a new century," reported the *New York Times,* "the United States Army is undertaking what its chief of staff, Gen. Eric K. Shinseki, calls a 'transformation.'" The article, titled "Fashion Forward Armed Forces," continued: "This is a big deal, so big, in fact, that last week the general announced that all of his soldiers would get new caps." And when it seemed things could not get worse, Congress discovered, in the midst of international tension over the midair collision of a U.S. surveillance plane and a Chinese fighter jet over the China Sea, that the army had ordered hundreds of thousands of the berets from a factory in China. Congressional hearings began in April. On May 2nd, the army announced that it would recall and dispose of all the Chinese-made berets. In the end, Army Rangers switched to tan berets. Army paratroopers kept theirs in maroon. And all the rest of the army's soldiers donned made-in-America black berets as "a symbol of unity"—not in celebration of the army's birthday on June 14, 2001, but after the newly ordered berets arrived in the very different world of post-9/11 America.[22]

On Thursday, January 11th, 2001, in a commercial aired during an episode of *Friends,* the U.S. Army made the biggest move to recast its image since the "Today's Army Wants to Join You" campaign three decades before. A lone soldier runs, at dawn, through the barren landscape of the Mojave Desert. In the beginning he is only a speck in the distance, moving toward us through rising dust and waves of heat. As he comes closer his dogtags catch glints of the rising sun; we hear his steady breathing, his heartbeat. A squad of soldiers jogs past in the opposite direction; a helicopter passes overhead. And he runs on. "Even though there are 1,045,690 soldiers just like me," he says, in voiceover, "I am my own force. With technology, with training, with support, who I am has become better than who I was."

> And I'll be the first to tell you,
> that the might of the U.S. Army doesn't lie in numbers.
> It lies in me.
> I am an Army of one.[23]

It was a striking ad, visually powerful, its message left unfixed, like the most sophisticated campaigns of an era that played to the postmodern impulses of contemporary youth. This was no soft-focus tribute to "my hometown," aimed at the conservative heart of small-town America. This was no celebration of diversity (though the soldier in this ad, Corporal Richard Lovett, was of Panamanian and Native American descent), seeking recruits among women and racial minorities, appealing to liberal notions of social good.[24] This was a redefinition of the army soldier in an era of transformation.

"We are seeking smart, technologically savvy people," USAREC's director of advertising said of the new campaign. "The Army is in a transformation stage now, needing to become more agile and rapidly deployable." Said Secretary Caldera: "The world has changed dramatically over this past decade. And no one understands this reality better than the American soldier who finds him- or herself maintaining stability in a dangerous, complex world, day in and day out." When American soldiers confront "the inherent challenges" in operations in "Bosnia, Kosovo, East Timor, Haiti," explained the vice chief of staff of the army in a press conference introducing the new campaign, we "expect them to do what is right." And "[w]e expect them to get it right with minimal direct supervision. That requires a special individual, someone with mental and physical toughness, someone with a strong moral fiber, someone with a heart, and someone with maturity, and someone that does what is right when no one is looking. This kind of a soldier is what is exemplified in this campaign."[25]

In its new campaign, the army attempted to portray the importance of the soldier in an army less likely to face mass warfare than potentially explosive situations in which the training, judgment, and individual competence of each soldier would be critical. The images of Corporal Lovett running through the desert, along with the entire "An Army of One" rebranding, was meant to decisively shift the army's portrayal of itself. This army wasn't about benefits, not about money for college and the chance to learn computer skills. This was an army of warriors in training. This was an army in which the individual competence and judgment of every soldier mattered.

The criticism came hard and fast. "An Army of One," mused *Army Magazine.* "Bereft of a verb, it looks a little naked by itself, confusing in meaning and purpose." Marveling at the ad that showed Corporal Richard Lovett, "slogging all by his lonesome through the desert with flashing dog tags (an excellent way to attract sniper fire) as his troops head in the opposite direction," a critic noted, "It's not clear if he's going AWOL or about to make a kamikaze charge." "Has anyone considered," asked a distinguished military sociologist, "that 'An Army of One' isn't likely to scare potential enemies?"[26]

Among those who had already joined the army, the new slogan was about as popular as "Today's Army Wants to Join You" had been, back in the 1970s. The new recruiting campaign, wrote one former soldier, "has been greeted by soldiers with the same enthusiasm and vigorous support associated with the black beret, anthrax vaccinations, and Christmas Day Charge of Quarters." Once again, it was the emphasis on individuality that rankled. The locker room standard—"There is no 'I' in Team"—got a lot of play, and many of those who'd been there speculated about how the appeal to individuality fit with the way the army *really* worked. General George Patton, wrote Specialist Lindsay Pike of Fort Richardson, Alaska, had had this to say: "The Army is a team. It eats, sleeps, fights, dies as a team. This individuality stuff is a bunch of crap." "[I]t sounds like something out of a comic book," said Elaine Donnelly, director of the Center for Military Readiness, who had led campaigns in the 1990s against gays in the military and women in combat with claims that either change would destroy unit cohesion. It is "directly at odds with a classic concept that is essential . . . and that concept is unit cohesion." Several critics wondered what would happen when the "smart, independent-minded young people" the army was recruiting found out that the real army "doesn't live up to the image in the ad they saw on 'Friends.'" And one soldier, in the midst of a flood of letters to the *Army Times* decrying the campaign, suggested a replacement slogan: "Be a Man, Join the Marines!"[27]

Perhaps it is no surprise that the most insightful criticism came from the world of advertising—for after all, this was an ad campaign, not a documentary about army life. "Here is propaganda as pure as poetry," wrote a columnist in *Advertising Age's Creativity* magazine,

> celebrating the power of one man as an instrument of destructive power, as an intelligent cog in the great machine of liberty, and as master of his own epic journey. I bristle at the dishonesty and expediency of this message at face value. But I marvel at its structural brilliance and its daring, subversive unveiling of a higher universal truth: We are a selfish people.[28]

Back in 1998, when Louis Caldera first began talking about rebranding the army, he criticized the longstanding and well-loved "Be All You Can Be" campaign for focusing on "you personally, as opposed to serving your country." He hoped to replace it with appeals based on duty and honor and love of nation. But had he learned nothing else in Harvard's MBA program, he knew better than to base a massive marketing campaign on his own vision of the "product."

Secretary Caldera didn't need mountains of research to tell him that "Be All You Can Be" had become wallpaper, background noise, incapable of luring America's youth through the doors of a recruiting office. And from the beginning he understood quite clearly that the army's contract with Young & Rubicam did not work to the army's advantage. No one really "owned" army advertising, he realized. The Army Advertising Council, the army's voice in the process, consisted of seven or eight people who already had full-time assignments. They met once a quarter and offered very limited guidance. And Young & Rubicam did not do dedicated research for the army. It wasn't in the budget.[29]

Advertising decisions were based on the Youth Attitude Tracking Study, prepared annually since 1975, in a process that a scholarly evaluation ordered by the Pentagon would soon conclude was methodologically outdated and insufficient. With four-year government contracts signed, sealed, delivered, there was nothing to motivate the army's advertising agency; there was nothing at risk. There wasn't even much competition for the account. Faced with mountains of specifications and an up-front bidding cost that approached a million dollars, most firms didn't think it worth their while. As Caldera took over stewardship of the army, he resolved that it was time to run army recruiting like part of a Fortune 500 company. It was time to rethink everything: to make the army's ad business competitive, to put an incentive clause into the advertising contract so that the agency earned more if the army met its recruiting goals, to do the serious research on American youth, and to invest in army marketing, media affairs, and public relations efforts to interpret the military to the civilian population.[30]

Serious research efforts began in 1999: first a study by the consulting firm McKinsey & Company, then one by RAND, and one by Yankelovich Partners, Inc. American youth, researchers learned quite definitively, were not motivated by appeals to duty or service or patriotism. Summing up the "important learnings about prospects" for the army's Recruiting Research Consortium, one presenter offered the phrase "Me. Now." Young people, she elaborated, want "a world where I'm in control—doing things I want to do, not things I'm told to do." As a senior executive at Leo Burnett, the advertising agency that would put this research to use, explained: "The two overriding themes for young adults are 'What's in it for me?' and a need for immediate gratification, or 'nowness.' Any notion that it's the right thing to do for somebody else or your country wasn't going to resonate for them."[31]

Initial research in hand, the army put out the word that it was looking for a change. "Be All You Can Be," after all, was older than the kids the army was trying to recruit. And the problem wasn't only that the slogan had become, in the frequently used phrase, wallpaper (even "faded wallpaper"). It was that—research showed—young people heard it as nagging. "Kids . . . say it's the voice of their parents telling them what to do," explained another advertising executive at Burnett. So as the army sought what Secretary Caldera called a "new marketing strategy," it turned to an agency with lots of experience in the youth market. Leo Burnett counted McDonald's, Walt Disney, and Coca-Cola among its clients.[32]

To those who'd been around long enough, the way researchers and advertisers and critics talked about American youth and the new army campaign sounded eerily like the early 1970s all over again. It was all about individuality. American youth didn't want to become "nameless, faceless people in green uniforms," said the researchers and the advertisers. Critics pointed out, as they had three decades before, that perhaps the army was not the best fit for those who ranked "individuality" at the top of their list of career goals.[33]

But just as there were powerful similarities between the two moments, there were important differences. In the early 1970s, "individuality" was about the imperative to "do your own thing." It was about the existential problem of alienation, of impersonal bureaucracy, of the system as machine. Individuality meant the right to use black power handshakes and claim pride in racial identity. It meant a modicum of privacy and the right to personalize the space in which one slept, to express individual opinions in "rap sessions," to have choices about what to eat for dinner. It meant not having to cut your hair. Lots had changed in thirty years. As young Americans faced the new millennium, research found, most had a powerful desire to belong to something larger than themselves. But they also needed to believe that they, as individuals, mattered. They didn't want to be invisible. And they, in the best possible reading of "a need for immediate gratification," wanted to make "an immediate and noticeable impact on the world." "What we are telling them," said Caldera during the campaign launch, just days before George Bush's inauguration and the end of Caldera's tenure as secretary of the army, "is that the strength of the Army is in individuals. Yes, you're a member of the team and you've got support from your fellow teammates, but you as an individual make a difference."[34]

Just as "Today's Army Wants to Join You" tried to speak the language of 1970s youth, "An Army of One" tried to make the army "cool." Yet the language in which the army explained its new campaign was the language of the educational institutions in which these young people had grown up. The army, according to the "Army of One" launch guide, "empowers" its members. Everyone, in this army, matters. The army's new marketing, a retired major general explained elsewhere, was, like the move to put all soldiers in the Rangers' black berets, meant "to make enlisted members feel valued and not less important than those serving in the elite beret-wearing units." Just as the early 1970s campaign tried to court the do-your-own-thing individualists, this campaign had roots in the educational theory—and educational systems—that emphasized individual empowerment over evaluation, participation over competition, the notion that there were different styles of learning and different measures of success. It is easy to see the "Army of One" individualism as playing to the same cultural impulse that had national park rangers explaining, as they led tours of the new World War II memorial on the mall in Washington, D.C., that the men delivering the mail on the homefront had played just as important a role in the war effort as the men in uniform who had fought their way up Mt. Suribachi or died on the beaches of Normandy.[35]

The army, however, gambled that young people would understand that "As a whole, you're helping the Army because you're the best as an individual." And a few people even ventured to point out that the well-loved "Be All You Can Be" was, in fact, about "You," that the army had been selling individual benefits and individual transformation for years, and that perhaps this new campaign was actually less devoted to selfishness and self-actualization than its predecessor. Secretary Caldera, however, made the ultimate point. The beautifully shot footage of Corporal Lovett running through the desert was not the army's mission statement. Nor was "An Army of One." They were, instead, a byproduct of the turn to the market, sophisticated images based on state-of-the-art research and high-priced creative energy and the work of extraordinarily talented filmmakers and composers and artists. Caldera had always understood the importance of selling the army. If it took promises of individual importance and immediate gratification to draw volunteers, that was okay. It wasn't even untrue—if individual importance meant doing one's part and immediate gratification meant responsibility. And in the end, the army would make volunteers into soldiers. "They are going to get the ethic of selfless service, duty, honor and country in basic training and in every unit they are assigned to," the secretary of the army insisted. "But you've got to get them in the door to try selfless service."[36]

Critics and commentators and people on the street debated the army's new slogan and the sixty seconds of its theme commercial, but the changes taking place were much larger and more significant. Caldera presided over a shift from advertising to marketing, from slogan to brand, from old media to new. In early 2000, the army set up an "Army Brand Group," based in the Pentagon and composed of civilian marketing professionals. Concluding that "the Army is not a brand; it's a collection of different products, websites, messages and creative looks," the group worked with Leo Burnett to create "a strong, unified brand identity" represented by a new logo: a white star, outlined in gold, imposed on a black background. The Army Brand Group was responsible for the line, "enlisting in the Army is a big decision made by young consumers." It was also the source of a wealth of instructions to recruiters, meant to standardize the army's brand and improve the "sub-optimized" "consumer contact and sales process." In a document specifying the color of paint for recruiting offices (Bone White, Benjamin Moore) and the allowable number of "G.I. Joe-type toys, toy tanks or helicopters, etc." (three), the "2004 Phase II Army Merchandising Kit" offered "merchandising elements" (posters) that "share a similar color palette to create synergy throughout the accessions corridor experience." The introductory memo explained: "By correctly representing the Army brand throughout the accessions corridor—our brand is enhanced and reinforced."[37]

Marketing professionals understood that the army needed to move from old media to new. Although Leo Burnett's decision to shift television ads from sports events to shows such as *Friends* and *Buffy the Vampire Slayer* acknowledged changes in the youth market, the real move was to the Internet. Everything that showed up in print or broadcast media was crafted to drive people to the army's new Web site. And at goarmy.com, they found a smart, user-friendly, beautifully designed interface, crafted both to "intrigue" and to reassure. Research had found that young people had no idea what one does in the army. ("March?" ventured one interviewee.) Too many images of the army came from Hollywood, and Hollywood had not been kind to the army. Kids had the idea, said Caldera, looking back, that joining the army meant four years of crawling through the mud with sergeants yelling at you all the time in the company of people who had joined the military because they like to hurt little animals. When asked what movie they most associated with the army, a large majority of young people said *Full Metal Jacket*. They remembered the scenes from basic training, the drill instructor screaming obscenities: "You are not even human-fucking-beings!" They didn't remember that *Full Metal Jacket* was about the marines.[38]

Goarmy.com gave the army a chance to change that image. For reassurance, it picked up on the current fad for reality TV and followed six new recruits through basic training. The reality-TV move was a gamble; for there to be any drama, there had to be some doubt. And these were real volunteers, no matter how carefully chosen. There was also a section meant to reassure parents, and information on "212 ways to be a soldier." The promised "intrigue" came fast and loud: "The badass quotient is high," said one senior designer. With more than 90 percent of the army's target audience online at least once a week in 2001, goarmy.com jumped from an average of 7,300 hits a day before the "Army of One" campaign aired to 14,000, and then to 28,000 hits a day when the basic training reality series went online. According to the army, about 750 people chatted with "cyber-recruiters" every day, and about 10 percent of them ended up enlisting.[39]

Moving far beyond the TV box, the army launched a computer game at the 2002 E3 (Electronic Entertainment Expo) that completely blew away the gaming-software competition. "America's Army" was "a deep marketing effort—a branding tool" in a world in which, according to an industry executive, "marketers can't ignore the fact that they need to have a video-game strategy." Public events also figured in the army's marketing campaign. Turning from the one-size-fits-all advertising campaign to events aimed at specific markets, the army took on a National Hot Rod Association team in 2000. The Army NASCAR team appeared in 2002, with Jerry Nadeau and then Joe Nemechek as sponsored drivers. Next came a rodeo team with seven cowboys and a cowgirl. The army teamed up with *The Source* magazine for a "Take It To The Streets" campaign, sending a tricked-out bright yellow Hummer with a hip-hop soundtrack not only to the streets, but to college campuses and Black Entertainment Television (BET)'s Spring Bling. "Our research tells us," said the head of the army's Strategic Outreach Directorate, "that hip-hop and urban culture is a powerful influence in the lives of young Americans. We try to develop a bond with that audience. I want them to say, 'Hey, the Army was here—the Army is cool!'" The recruiters in the Hummers—of which there were several, all custom-made—had a better line.[40]

Despite it all, recruiters were never quite sold on "An Army of One." Recruiters had cheered the first presentation of "Be All You Can Be"; they were largely silent when confronted with the new campaign, slow to clear out the now-forbidden posters from recruiting offices, reluctant to embrace the slogan and the new corporate logo and the drive-them-to-the-Web tactics. It's not clear what would have happened over time. Perhaps recruiters would have come around as the new slogan became more familiar. "Be All You Can Be" was immediately popular, in part, because army advertising had been floundering for years. It wasn't hard to improve on "This is the Army."

The attacks of September 11th, 2001, however, changed the landscape in which the army had to recruit. In their immediate aftermath "An

Army of One" disappeared from the airwaves, along with all other commercial advertising. As programming began to return to normal the army aired "Generations," historical footage of an army that had fought America's wars. Its tagline: "Every generation has its heroes. This one is no different." The army met its recruiting goals six weeks ahead of schedule that fiscal year—and it made much of that fact, as no one had been sure what effect the "war on terror" and the move into Afghanistan would have on recruiting. But despite notable individuals, such as Pat Tillman, who walked away from a million-dollar-a-year contract with the Arizona Cardinals to become an Army Ranger, most of the lines in the aftermath of 9/11 were formed by people waiting to give blood, not to sign up for the military. In a candid moment, the head of army recruiting pointed to the fundamental reality: there was a "surge of people buying American flags after 9/11. But there was no surge of people rushing in saying that they wanted to join the Army." Soon enough the "Army of One" campaign returned and army recruiting continued, very much as it had before.[41]

The attacks of 9/11 and the Bush administration's Global War on Terror set the stage for America's preemptive invasion of Iraq. America would be, for the first time in its modern history, fighting an extended war with a volunteer force. As the war began, Americans saw not only televised footage of troops moving into Baghdad, but the army's own carefully crafted images, as well. The commercial "Victors" called on history: tight close-ups of the faces of soldiers filmed in the sepia tones of old photographs; a voice declaring: "There is no second place. There is no runner-up." "Creed," with its mottoes of service and sacrifice and its silent soldiers looking steadily into the camera, reminded Americans what the nation asked its army to do. "We will always win," read the last motto, as the symphonic score swelled to a climax. And then its tagline: "These words are our promise. Together, we are an Army of One."[42]

These commercials—extraordinary examples of the advertiser's art—had been in production since the fall, part of what Leo Burnett called "communications plans to anticipate contingencies." As hundreds of thousands had gathered around the nation and the world to protest the anticipated invasion of Iraq, the army had some stake in shifting attention away from the political conflict to the soldiers themselves, and to the army's long history of service and sacrifice.[43] As they faced the prospect of war—and one of different scale than the military operations in Somalia or Bosnia—those charged with managing the army brand and filling the army ranks looked back to the last time the United States had sent troops to the Gulf. In January 1991, the army had pulled all its recruiting messages. "The reality of war, the reality of what could be the most televised conflict in history, is bound to drown out the effectiveness of our message," said a senior vice president at Young & Rubicam.[44] But by the time hostilities in the Gulf ended, the army was airing "Count on Me," a montage of images over a new jingle by "Be All You Can Be"'s Jake Holmes:

> I am a soldier, I am skilled and smart,
> I've got the training, and I've got the heart.
> I'm the defender of our liberty.
> I am the soldier. Count on me.
> Rising to the challenge, whatever it may be.
> I am the soldier. Count on me.

"Army cheapens thrill of victory with its excessive, gloating ad," responded *Advertising Age*. "We don't need TV spots to tell us the Army performed brilliantly; the news has pictures galore of the charred Iraqi dead."[45]

In fact, in 1991 army recruiting had tried to distance itself from the war. As the *New York Times* ventured that, with "all the glamour and accolades" brought by this victory, the war must seem like an advertising copywriter's "dream," USAREC's director of advertising demurred. "You've got to be careful how combat, or the potential for combat, is displayed in your commercials," he said. "We don't want to be misleading, but too much combat footage interferes with the longterm attributes of Army service that we want to portray: money for college, skills training and relevance to a civilian career."[46]

His statement reveals a tension at the heart of the all-volunteer army. The end of conscription did not change the army's purpose: the fundamental mission of the U.S. Army is to fight and win the nation's wars. Combat, of course, is the means to this end. But the all-volunteer army had, quite purposefully and more powerfully over time, tried to recast the meaning of military service. It downplayed notions of duty and service and obligation; it sold itself to potential recruits and to the broader American public as a source of opportunity. Neither combat footage nor the reality of war fit well with the army's recruiting message about the "longterm attributes of Army service." A great many men and women did find some form of opportunity in the army during the decades of relative peace, but peace was never guaranteed. Was it legitimate, critics asked, to sell the army as money for college or as job training or as a source of health coverage for one's children when those erstwhile students or skilled employees or parents would also be soldiers, subject to orders that would override other obligations and other roles, and that could even end their lives? In 1978, when the false promises of some army recruiters made news and drew the attention of Congress, recruiters were ordered to give all applicants a written reminder. "The Army is a military organization," the statement read, "which may be called upon to participate in combat operations (to fight) while you are a member of it."[47]

In 1992, taking another approach, General Thurman angrily rebutted charges that army advertising misled the young by so decisively avoiding mention of war: "It's a stupid adult notion that kids don't know what an Army, Navy, Air Force and Marine Corps are about." In more measured tones, an account supervisor from Young & Rubicam pointed out that combat, killing, and dying are not exactly topics "for 30 seconds during 'The Cosby Show.'" Those issues, spokespeople agreed, were best handled by recruiters. Recruiters, however, like ad campaigns, are meant to sell the army. "This pamphlet is the sales doctrine of the United States Army Recruiting Command," begins the 1989 version of the USAREC recruiter training guide. (The 2006 version, in a more complicated recruiting environment, substituted "counselor" for "salesman" and compared recruiting to the infantry.) Recruiters are trained to handle questions about war and danger and the likelihood of deployment if they arise.[48] But they are not going to raise potential impediments the prospect hasn't yet considered.

Army advertising's loud silence about killing and dying is, paradoxically, less a problem when soldiers are actually fighting and dying. In that case, it is hard for potential volunteers to avoid knowledge of that possibility. But as extended warfare receded further and further into the nation's past in the years following the Vietnam War, what young people knew about the army increasingly came—as the army knew very well—from advertising and marketing campaigns and popular culture. The army's televised offers of self-transformation and fulfillment, of practical skills and concrete benefits, were not, like the highly regulated pharmaceutical advertisements, accompanied by a rapid monotone reading of the product's potential risks. One can understand the bitterness of members of the Army Reserve, which had relied for years on the recruiting slogan, "One Weekend a Month," who in 2003 embellished their Army Reserve truck in Iraq with a sign: "One Weekend a Month, My Ass!"[49] It is perfectly reasonable to note that the risks of military service are obvious and widely understood. This, however, is a nation in which massive financial judgments were rendered against tobacco companies not because cigarettes cause cancer, but because—even though it is universally known that smoking causes cancer—advertising campaigns celebrated the pleasures of smoking and were silent about its costs. If the army is a "product" and prospects are "consumers," what, after all, is the difference?

In 1978, a military court had confronted that question. The army had charged Captain Leon T. Davis, a 30-year-old radiologist, with refusing to obey orders, desertion, and missing his deployment to Korea. If court-martialed, Davis faced a sentence of up to eight and a half years at hard labor. Capt. Davis claimed that in a volunteer force, military service was based on a two-way contract. In this "voluntary-contract military," Davis said, if the army breached its contract he was "legally and morally excused" from fulfilling his contractual obligations to it. His willingness to enter army service, he and his attorneys claimed, was based on promises made by army advertising and army recruiters. Those promises had not been fulfilled—most particularly, the promise that army doctors would have modern, state-of-the-art medical equipment. The radiological equipment at Walter Reed, four of his former colleagues testified, was so antiquated that it posed a danger to their patients.[50]

The army prosecutor characterized Davis (who the *Washington Post* described as the first "to literally make a federal case out of the obligation of the military to fulfill recruitment promises") as "naive." Army recruiting ads, he asserted, were just "puffery," "a commercial thing" done by ad agencies in New York, "simply braggings on the part of the government and not actual contractual rights." The military judge finally asked, incredulously: "Is that the government's position?" Capt. Davis was court-martialed, though a $2,000 fine replaced the years of hard labor. The judge's verdict was not based on prosecutors' disparagement of advertising, but on contract law. The Supreme Court had found, in 1890, that military enlistment was, in fact, contractual. But as that contractual act changes an individual into a soldier, it changes the status of the individual. And once status is changed from civilian to soldier, no breach of contract can destroy the new status or relieve one from the obligations it carries.[51]

No matter what implicit promises had drawn young men and women to change their legal status from "individual" to "soldier" in the months and years prior to March 2003, the new war in Iraq fundamentally changed what the army expected of a great many of its soldiers, both active and reserve. General Shinseki, chief of staff of the army, had committed what Secretary of Defense Rumsfeld saw as a major act of insubordination when he told a congressional committee in late February 2003 that it would require several hundred thousand troops to establish peace in postwar Iraq. The Secretary of Defense, calling Shinseki "far off the mark," staked the lives of American soldiers and marines on a commitment to technology over personnel. He believed in a came-saw-conquered scenario that offered no significant plan for what would happen once major combat operations ceased. Meanwhile, a civilian Pentagon official told a reporter that Shinseki's projections were just "bullshit from a Clintonite enamoured of using the army for peacekeeping and not winning wars."[52] Shinseki, with war on the horizon and, as time would prove, a correct understanding of the task ahead, had continued along the path he'd begun in 2000, rethinking the role of the army soldier.

During the winter of 2003, Shinseki had directed the army's Training and Doctrine Command (TRADOC) to come up with a definition of "the Warrior Ethos." Their efforts were clearly shaped by the conditions of combat in Iraq, as well as by the recent death of eleven soldiers and the capture of 20-year-old maintenance clerk Jessica Lynch and her five comrades in an attack on their eighteen-vehicle convoy. The 507th Maintenance Company "found itself" (according to the official account of the U.S. Army) "in a desperate situation due to a navigational error caused by the combined effects of the operational pace, acute fatigue, isolation and the harsh environmental conditions." All soldiers, the task force concluded, no matter their MOS or their gender, had to be prepared for combat.[53]

By May, 2003, the TRADOC task force had forged a vision of "the Objective Force Soldier We Need . . . A Soldier of character, imbued with a warrior spirit, persuasive in peace . . . INVINCIBLE IN WAR!" Army leaders acknowledged that they were looking to the marines, who insisted that every marine was first and foremost a rifleman, as they considered how to recruit and train soldiers for a "dispersed, non-linear battlefield" in which "all soldiers—regardless of battlefield location—must be fully prepared to engage in close combat." That month, Shinseki approved a new version of the Soldier's Creed.[54] The former creed, adopted in the years after the

Vietnam War, began: "I am a member of the United States Army—a protector of the greatest nation on earth." It contained no language of combat; soldiers vowed not to "do anything . . . which will disgrace my uniform, my unit, or my country." The new creed replaced "I am a member of the United States Army" with "I am a Warrior and a member of a team," and centered on a four-line statement of the "warrior ethos":

> I will always place the mission first.
> I will never accept defeat.
> I will never quit.
> I will never leave a fallen comrade.

An army in which all soldiers were issued dogtags bearing these lines, one in which all soldiers vowed, "I stand ready to deploy, engage, and destroy, the enemies of the United States of America in close combat," was not an army that defined its purpose as the provision of social good.[55] And it was not one that could recruit with simple promises of money for college.

As the wars in Iraq and Afghanistan continued and casualties rose, the American public saw photographs of the dead, displayed "here, in silence," in the words of the PBS *Newshour*'s Jim Lehrer. They read stories about IED attacks and the inadequate armor on U.S. military vehicles, about the shameful events at Abu Ghraib, about Walter Reed's neglect of wounded soldiers in its care and the use of "stop-loss" orders that kept soldiers in uniform after their voluntary terms of service ended. The army nonetheless met its recruiting goal every year from fiscal year 2000 through fiscal year 2004, though as the army's 2004 "Military Image" study concluded, "Recruiting for an all-volunteer Army in times of war is increasingly difficult."[56]

By fall 2004, a year and a half into the war, enlistment numbers were beginning to drop. The army, in fact, had met its recruiting goals in fiscal year 2004 by raiding its DEP pool. The delayed entry program, which allowed "future soldiers" up to one year before reporting for duty, provided recruiters with a cushion: in 2004, 45 percent of the army's total recruiting goal was already in the DEP pipeline. In many cases, those future soldiers were called to duty sooner than they had expected. From the army's perspective, that made sense. Research showed that the longer those who signed waited to leave for boot camp, the greater the chance for "buyer's remorse," especially as the war continued. Almost a quarter of those who had signed up to join the army in the fiscal year ending in September 2004 never made it to basic training. That figure was 90 percent higher than in fiscal year 2002. But robbing Peter to pay Paul (or, as one recruiter put it, "eating their seed corn") by relying so heavily on the delayed entry program left the army with a major shortfall in fiscal year 2005. In March 2005, the army reported, only 7,800 soldiers had completed infantry training at Fort Benning. According to army projections, that number should have been 25,541. And by 2006, the delayed entry program provided less than 10 percent of the army's total recruiting goal.[57]

True to patterns developed over time, when the army faced recruiting troubles it turned to research. A major study contracted in 2004 found that much had changed since the last major studies, done in 1999 and 2000—before the attacks of 9/11 and the wars in Afghanistan and Iraq. In 2000, young people hesitated to join the army because they saw it as giving up control over their own decisions. They worried about "inconvenience." In 2004, young Americans worried about dying. Black youth told researchers they didn't want to fight for a cause they didn't believe in. Those sentiments helped explain plummeting enlistment figures among African Americans—down 41 percent since 2000. Mothers, researchers found, were possibly the biggest obstacle to enlistment. They needed reassurance. Young people still found money for college the best reason to join the army, even though such promises had largely disappeared from recruiting ads. And "An Army of One" badly needed reevaluation "in light of the current communication objectives."[58]

The army worked hard to address those problems and to fill its ranks. It put a thousand new recruiters in the field in less than ten months and allowed them to wear battle fatigues instead of the green slacks and shirts that (some had complained) made them look like security guards. It offered enlistment bonuses in rapidly increasing amounts: from a maximum of $6,000 in 2003, $15,000 in 2004, $20,000 in 2005, and $40,000 in 2008. The Army College Fund offered "those who select high-priority specialties" up to $70,000. A student loan repayment program targeted college graduates.[59] The army raised the maximum enlistment age from 35 to 40 in January 2006, and then to 42 in June of that year. It began a trial "prep school" to help those who lacked basic education requirements earn a GED; it sent new recruits to "fat camp" to prepare them for basic training. Recruiters went to Indian reservations, offering Native American youth the chance to fulfill their tribal "warrior tradition" by joining the army; they crossed into Mexico seeking young men with U.S. residency papers. The Bush administration offered citizenship—in a highly accelerated process—to those from other nations who agreed to fight in the uniform of the United States.[60]

With NPS (nonprior service) recruits harder to find, the army focused much more on retaining the soldiers it had. The budget for reenlistment bonuses increased sixfold between 2003 and 2007; two out of every three soldiers who reenlisted got tax-free bonuses ranging from $10,000 to $30,000. A very few commanded from $50 to $150 thousand. The army also tried to cut attrition. Many who joined never made it through their first term; many of those didn't even complete basic training. Unsatisfactory performance or problems with conduct, alcohol or drug violations, "failure to meet body fat standards," or pregnancy were all grounds for "separation," at the discretion of battalion commanders. Pointing out—perhaps unnecessarily—that "we are an Army at war," a 2005 memo from the Department of the Army made it much more difficult for battalion commanders to get rid of an unsatisfactory soldier. Reducing attrition by just one percent, it noted, meant 3,000 fewer soldiers to recruit or retain.[61]

Recruiters, meanwhile, shifted their focus to parents. "If you want to get a soldier, you have to go through mom," said one of those who crafted the approach. As a recruiting station commander in Florida put it, "If you don't have a good relationship with the parents, you're not going to go anywhere. The kid might want to do it, but it's all about mom and dad." Even people in their late twenties, he said, tell him, "I need to speak to my mom." And parental support for enlistment, research found, was low and still sinking. A new advertising strategy began bypassing prospects for their parents. In yet another well-crafted set of ads, the army offered realistic conversations between skeptical parents and their sons or daughters. To his daughter's thoughtful explanation of why she wants to join the army, a father responds, "When did you start talking like me?" "All that came from you," says a young man to his mother, listing the values that led to his decision. This series's tagline was directed at parents, not youth: "Help them find their strength."[62]

After the army missed its recruiting target in 2005 by a higher number than at any time since 1979, it dropped both ad agency Leo Burnett and the slogan "An Army of One." Army representatives had been complaining, privately, about Leo Burnett's "significant lack of respect" for army input since mid-2002. The recruiting shortfall offered an opportunity to sever relations, even though recruiting troubles likely had much more to do with the casualty rate in Iraq than with confusion over the meaning of "An Army of One." The new campaign launched by McCann Worldgroup in November 2006 was, however, clearly intended for an army at war.[63] In the signature "Brand Ethos" video, a triumphal symphonic score swelled over images of an army that clearly understood its purpose. There was no jingle. No words were spoken. The message was conveyed by images of soldiers, by the massive power of a moving tank, by the words that appeared on the screen, gold letters against a black background: "There's strong. And then there's Army Strong." The new campaign flatly rejected the "Me. Now" rationale, defining "Army Strong," in part, as "The strength to get over yourself." This high-budget, beautifully edited piece of filmmaking offered one central claim:

> There is nothing on this green earth
> That is stronger than the U.S. Army
> Because there is nothing on this green earth
> That is stronger than a U.S. Army soldier.[64]

This was an army that meant to scare potential enemies.

The army's presentation of the new campaign, which, though labeled "confidential" and "for internal use," was posted on an army Web site, drew direct connections to the war in Iraq. Those who join the army today, its author noted, "understand that they are joining a warrior culture and are willingly accepting the distinct possibility of serving in a combat zone." "We need," he wrote, "a campaign that measures up to that standard," one that offers "soldiers today . . . a tribute that swells their chest with pride," and one that acknowledges the "strength of young Soldier's parents, who are filled with pride—and fear—and longing to see their Soldier safely home again."[65]

Despite all the army's best marketing efforts, the fact remained: this was an army at war. Recruiters felt the pressure intensely. It had taken, on average, 120 significant contacts to yield one recruit in the years before the war. That, looking backward, seemed like the good old days. "We call this the pressure plate, like on a land mine," said one, pointing to the recruiter patch he wore. "If you push it too hard, we'll explode." By early 2005 thirty-seven recruiters had gone AWOL. Recruiters were more likely to commit "improprieties" than ever before: substantiated violations jumped from 186 in 2000 to 459 in 2004. On May 20th, 2005, the army held a "values stand-down," in which all 7,500 recruiters and every other member of the recruiting command were reminded of the rules that governed their actions. "It's ethics-under-pressure training," said the army's chief of public affairs. "We want to emphasize that bending the rules is not the way to make mission."[66]

Following its recruiting shortfall in 2005, the army made its numbers in the years that followed. But it did so by lowering quality. It is relatively difficult to get into the army. Roughly seven out of ten young adults in America today do not meet its standards. Of 31.2 million Americans aged 17 to 24, only 4.7 million are considered "qualified military available." And only 1.6 million of them are in the army's "target market." More than 30 percent of young adults don't have a high school diploma or GED—and high school graduation rates in the United States are falling. About 17 percent of Americans in their late teens are significantly overweight or obese, and thus disqualified. Although the army insisted that its qualification tests do not measure intelligence, Categories IV and V are roughly equivalent to an IQ of 90 or below. Those regulations rule out most of the bottom third of the youth population. Young people taking medication—Ritalin, antidepressants—are prohibited, though they make up a rapidly increasing segment of today's youth; potential recruits must certify that they have been off such medication for a full year to qualify for enlistment. Those with criminal records require waivers and decisions are on a case-by-case basis, with anyone convicted of sexually violent crimes, drug trafficking, or more than one felony absolutely barred from enlistment. With automatic fingerprint checks, an arrest or conviction is not something potential recruits can simply forget to mention. Recruiters are prohibited from asking about sexual orientation, but those who are openly gay face a serious hurdle. Complicating everything is the fact that almost two-thirds of the army's target group, those who have graduated high school, enroll in college within a year after graduation.[67]

In the years following 2005, the army met its recruiting goals but missed the DoD benchmarks that were meant to guarantee quality. With a 90 percent goal for recruits with earned high school diplomas, the army attracted just over 70 percent in 2007. Two-thirds of all recruits were supposed to fall into Categories I–IIIA, scoring above the fiftieth percentile mark on the military entrance exam. Army recruiters missed that mark by almost 6 percent. The allowed percentage of those who scored in Category IV, previously limited to 2 percent and actually accounting for only

0.6 percent in 2004, was doubled. More alarmingly, the number of "moral waivers" jumped 65 percent between 2003 and 2006, when almost 12 percent of those entering the army had some form of criminal background (convictions for using marijuana did not require a waiver).[68] These were not promising trends. On the other hand, it is a clear sign of success when the fact that 4.1 percent of new recruits were drawn from category IV raised cries of alarm. In 1980, more than half of all new recruits had been classified Category IV.

In the aftermath of the 1991 Gulf War, when U.S.-led UN forces defeated Saddam Hussein's Iraq in just 100 hours, commentators and critics had declared that the all-volunteer force had been tested and had triumphed. Well-educated, well-trained, well-motivated soldiers did perform well in 1991. But that brief war, with its quick victory and low U.S. casualty rate, was not a true test. The real test of the all-volunteer force was the preemptive war that the United States launched against Iraq in 2003. The nation sent its troops into a difficult operational environment without adequate protections ("you have to go to war with the Army you have," said Secretary of Defense Rumsfeld, when asked why soldiers were having to scrounge through landfills for scraps of metal to "up-armor" their vehicles), and then, because the U.S. lacked sufficient troops to meet all its military commitments, extended soldiers' tours mid-course, invoked stop-loss protections, and sent men and women in uniform back to Iraq for second and then third tours of duty.[69]

Many who originally supported the move to an AVF believed that reliance on volunteers would make it more difficult for the United States to send troops to war. The war in Iraq proved them wrong. During the Vietnam War the draft had commanded the attention of the nation. It had ensured that the broader public felt—in some limited way—the force of war, saw its physical and psychological toll, understood something of the blood sacrifice being demanded of its nation's youth. Because the draft potentially affected the children of senators and CEOs as well as those of small shopkeepers and factory workers, it had compelled public engagement, and so provided a focus for mobilizing either antiwar protest or support for the war. The all-volunteer military, in contrast, allows most Americans the safety of distance not only from war but from the possibility of military service, even from their fellow citizens who have volunteered to serve. The AVF was no solution to American military adventurism, which is how a growing number of Americans saw the war in Iraq. Recognizing that failure, some critics argued forcefully for the return of the draft: if the American people were not willing to fight for a cause, to share the burden of service and sacrifice, then the nation should not be going to war.

The civilian planners of the war in Iraq did not envision the extended conflict it became, and the problems with planning and conducting the ongoing war in Iraq were largely independent of the all-volunteer status of the military. The shortage of troops, for example, was not due solely to the military's dependence on volunteers. The desired end-strength of the U.S. military is determined by Congress, not by the vagaries of the marketplace, though different branches of the military sometimes fail to meet those numbers. But the army's all-volunteer status did matter. In 2007, as military leaders insisted that the all-volunteer force was stretched to its breaking point, Congress authorized an increase in the size of both the army and the marines. A larger force, supporters argued, would allow combat-weary troops longer periods between deployments; it would also give the United States more latitude in a world where potential crises were not restricted to the Middle East. Increasing the size of the military, however, is not easy. The nation could not simply raise the number of draft calls. Those new soldiers would have to be persuaded to volunteer. And as the war ground on, the army was already struggling to recruit and retain a sufficient number of men and women to fill the ranks.

In this climate, Americans once again debated the viability of the all-volunteer force. For most of those in the defense establishment, the fundamental measures of success and failure were practical. How did the volunteer army rate on readiness and deployability? How well had soldiers carried out their missions? Had the army drawn volunteers who were competent to "maintain stability in a complex and difficult environment . . . with minimal direct supervision"?

The extended war in Iraq highlighted the consequences of demographic changes in the all-volunteer force. While Americans had worried, in the early years of the AVF, about the overrepresentation of African Americans or the growing number of women in the military, few had anticipated that the shift to volunteer status would produce a family-oriented army. In the first decades of the all-volunteer force, the army moved from the draft era's young and mostly single conscripted and short-term enlistees to a professional force. Volunteer soldiers were older; their enlistment terms were longer. More and more of the volunteer soldiers were married, and more and more of them had children. And while reenlistment rates of under 10 percent had sufficed when conscription guaranteed to fill the ranks, the volunteer army needed reenlistment rates of over 50 percent. Research found that soldiers' decisions about reenlistment were heavily influenced by family concerns. And morale, it became obvious, was closely linked to the stability and satisfaction of soldiers' families. In 1983 the chief of staff of the army, John Wickham, initiated an Army Family Action Plan to build systems of support. Policies that offered comprehensive family health care, child care, and benefits based on the number of a soldiers' dependents made re-enlistment attractive to those with young families. By 2000, 62 percent of soldiers were married and an additional 4 percent were single parents. The percentage of married soldiers dropped to just over half by 2008, but at that point 10.7 percent of soldiers were single parents and more than 22,000 dual-uniform marriages—many with children—further complicated the mix. Army families reported more than 700,000 minor children. No matter how often the army proclaimed that the warrior ethos defined its soldiers, families also lay at its heart. During the wars in Iraq and Afghanistan, parents were repeatedly separated from their families, and many single parents and those married to members of the armed forces had to activate the family care plans they had filed, leaving their children with family members or friends who had agreed to serve as "long term care providers" in case of deployment.[70] The new demographics of the all-volunteer army had serious impacts on readiness, deployability, and morale.

The quality of the volunteer force also became an issue during the Iraq War, and in ways that went beyond quantifiable measures of high school graduation rates and test scores. Wartime experience in both Iraq and Afghanistan led to significant changes in army doctrine: a new counterinsurgency manual that emphasized the importance of "culturally astute leaders" and a flexible force in 2006, along with an unprecedented new doctrine defining "stability operations" as the key to military success in 2008.[71] What was asked of soldiers in Iraq and Afghanistan became increasingly complicated. At the same time, soldiers' actions at Abu Ghraib and reports of female soldiers raped by male comrades raised questions about the quality of those who were drawn to enlist. Final judgments about the performance of enlisted men and women would come in post-war assessments, but during the war America's soldiers were praised by their leaders and, despite profound divisions over the legitimacy of their mission, treated with respect by the American people in whose name they fought. Some soldiers violated army values, a few crossed all lines of humanity, but overall the army proved itself, once again, competent and able.

A second practical measure was whether, during an ongoing and increasingly unpopular war, enough young men and women would volunteer to serve. Those individual decisions are what makes a volunteer force possible—no matter how much they were fostered by financial incentives or by the stirring images of pride and power in high-budget recruiting ads, no matter whether they were induced by the testosterone-laced appeal of the first-person shooter *America's Army* game or by the flattering attention of an army recruiter who wanted only to "help you find your strength." Judgments of success, here, are less clear. Through most of the course of the war in Iraq it took 7,500 recruiters and a budget of hundreds of millions of dollars each year to convince 80,000 young people to join the army. In 2009, however, as the Obama administration promised phased withdrawal from Iraq and casualty rates remained low for a second year, a deep recession sent youth unemployment above 20 percent and military enlistment jumped—despite the prospect of military escalation in Afghanistan.

The lessons to be drawn about fighting an extended war with a volunteer force are uncertain, for it is not clear whether young Americans were reluctant to volunteer because of the circumstances of this particular war, which Americans increasingly viewed as illegitimate, or whether the impediment to voluntary service was war itself. In either case, the challenge posed by the Iraq War only intensified an ongoing problem. The all-volunteer army had succeeded during the previous decades, according to the practical measure of meeting recruiting goals, in large part because the size of the army had been dramatically reduced in the years following the Vietnam War. It was much easier to recruit 80,000 volunteers a year than 240,000.

One further measure of success moves beyond practical criteria. In late 2002, watching the mounting pressure for war, Korean combat veteran and U.S. congressman Charles Rangel called for reinstatement of the draft. "A disproportionate number of the poor and members of minority groups," he wrote in an editorial in the *New York Times,* "make up the enlisted ranks of the military, while the most privileged Americans are underrepresented or absent." If America goes to war, he insisted, "all Americans should share the burden."[72] Rangel's criticisms were echoed in starker terms over the following years: the war is being fought on the backs of the poor and the black.

That claim was, in fact, more false than true. America's army—even its enlisted ranks—is fairly solidly middle class. In 2007, across the military as a whole, 25 percent of enlisted recruits came from census tracts with family incomes in the nation's top 20 percent, while only 11 percent of recruits came from the bottom quintile. (Army statistics would be skewed a bit lower.) Those numbers are potentially misleading in a society in which many of those with household incomes of $200,000 a year or higher consider themselves middle class. In 2007 the average household income was $50,428, and $65,000 put one into the top 20 percent. Nonetheless, the poor were underrepresented compared to the more well off.[73] Young people from America's poorest families, by and large, don't meet current army standards. They are more likely to have dropped out of high school. Poor schools leave them ill-prepared for written qualification tests. They are more likely than their peers to have criminal convictions or significant health problems. In times of peace, for those who see the army as a site of intervention and producer of social good, such standards seem to discriminate against the poor. In times of war, they could be seen as protection from exploitation. So while most upper- and upper middle-class youth make other choices, and the poor find themselves with one fewer option, the army draws primarily from those in between.

Similarly, people of color have not borne the brunt of the war. In the years since the attacks of 9/11, African American enlistment rates dropped from 23 percent of new enlistments in 2000 to 12 percent in 2005.[74] Blacks are still overrepresented in the army compared to their numbers in the general population, but they are proportionately represented in each yearly cohort of new recruits. That is because African Americans, especially African American women, are more likely than whites to reenlist. And since the 1980s, young black Americans had been, very decidedly, enlisting in fields other than the combat arms. Black youth wanted money for college and leadership skills and job training. Most had little interest in carrying a gun.

During the war in Iraq, both whites and blacks were very slightly overrepresented in the military. The recruit-to-population ratio was 1.05 for whites in 2007, when 62 percent of the male population between 18 and 24 were classified as white. It was 1.08 for blacks. Hispanics were significantly underrepresented, with a troop-to-population ratio of .65. The most overrepresented group in the military was, in fact, a geographic one. Southerners made up 40 percent of new military recruits in 2007. And of the 2,825 soldiers who had died in the course of Operation Iraqi Freedom as of April 5, 2008, a disproportionate majority, 2,106, were white. Three hundred and twelve were black. And 266 were Hispanic.[75]

From the beginning of the AVF, Americans had been worrying about the question of representativeness. Did the benefits of service in time of peace outweigh the possibility of exploitation in time of war? Would an all-volunteer force be a force of the poor, the black, and the disadvantaged? In some ways, the war in Iraq has answered those questions. Though a great many Americans, at a distance from the military, still see the army as the final refuge for those with no other options, it is not.

The debate about race, class, and equity, however, though legitimate and well-grounded in history, obscures a more significant question. Is it just or fair for a small number of Americans to bear the heavy burden of military defense while the rest of the nation is asked no sacrifice? As the vast majority of Americans remain untouched by war, not even subject to the shared risk of the draft or the obligation of service, the lives of others—those who volunteer— are disrupted or destroyed.

This moral question is significant, but it runs up against another truth. A volunteer force offers the best means of national defense—at least as military planners now envision the future battlefield. It takes a fair amount of intellectual competence to be a soldier in today's army, and it takes a great deal of training. Although a no-deferments draft would definitely capture more of America's most competent youth, it would also capture a great many more of the less competent. Drafting young men and women, as a matter of course, for more than a year's term would be hard to justify. But a one-year stint in the army doesn't offer time for adequate training on increasingly sophisticated weapons; it doesn't allow a new soldier time to develop the necessary experience and instincts to function in complex and rapidly changing operational environments. And, as the army learned all too well in the last years of conscription, those who are drafted against their will tend to be much less highly motivated than those who have volunteered. Bottom line: less able, less well trained, less experienced, less motivated soldiers are more likely to fail in their missions. And they are more likely to get themselves—and their comrades—killed. Despite the army's enormous reservations about the move to an all-volunteer force back in the early 1970s, it even more strongly opposes the return to the draft today.

In most ways, the discussion is moot. Short of massive, total war, the United States is not going to reinstate the draft. There is little public desire; there is no political will. The majority of citizens in this democratic nation have chosen to define military service as a choice rather than an obligation. In practical terms, a volunteer force provides best for the defense of the nation. An institution that once seemed mired in crisis has achieved remarkable successes, both as purveyor of military force and provider of social good. The history of the all-volunteer army is, in very many ways, a tale of progress and achievement. Nonetheless, in a democratic nation, there is something lost when individual liberty is valued over all and the rights and benefits of citizenship become less closely linked to its duties and obligations.

ABBREVIATIONS

NOTES

ACKNOWLEDGMENTS

INDEX

ABBREVIATIONS

AT	*Army Times*
AVA—CMH	All-Volunteer Army—Misc., Center of Military History, Fort McNair, Washington, DC
AVA—MHI	All-Volunteer Army Collection, Military History Institute, Carlisle, PA
AWC	U.S. Army War College
AWCSRP	Army War College Student Research Paper
Ayer Collection	N. W. Ayer Advertising Records, Archives Center, National Museum of American History, Smithsonian Institution
CMH	Center of Military History, Fort McNair, Washington, DC
CSA	Chief of Staff of the Army
CSM	*Christian Science Monitor*
DA	Department of the Army
DAHSUM	Department of the Army Historical Summary
DCSPER	Deputy Chief of Staff for Personnel
DDEL	Dwight David Eisenhower Library, Abilene, KS

M&RA	Manpower & Reserve Affairs
MHI	U.S. Army Military History Institute, Carlisle, PA
NARA	National Archives and Records Administration, College Park, MD
NMAH	National Museum of American History
NYT	*New York Times*
OASA	Office of the Assistant Secretary of the Army
R&CCJ	*U.S. Army Recruiting and Career Counseling Journal*
R&RJ	*Recruiting and Reenlisting Journal*
RJ	*Recruiter Journal*
SA	Secretary of the Army
SAMVA	Special Assistant, Modern Volunteer Army
SOOHP	Senior Officers Oral History Project, MHI
USAREC	U.S. Army Recruiting Command
USN&WR	*US News and World Report*
WAC	Women's Army Corps, 1945–1978, RG 319, NARA
WSJ	*Wall Street Journal*

NOTES

1. Individual Freedom and the Obligations of Citizenship

1. David Farber and Beth Bailey, *The Columbia Guide to America in the 1960s* (New York: Columbia University Press, 2001), 374, 376–377. For a superb institutional history of the creation of the all-volunteer army, see Robert K. Griffith, *The U.S. Army's Transition to the All-Volunteer Force, 1968–1974* (Washington, DC: U.S. Army Center of Military History, 1997). Bernard Rostker, *I Want You! The Evolution of the All-Volunteer Force* (Santa Monica, CA: RAND Corporation, 2006), offers a detailed policy history with an accompanying CD including archival documents. David R. Segal, *Recruiting for Uncle Sam: Citizenship and Military Manpower Policy* (Lawrence: University Press of Kansas, 1989) offers a history of manpower policy from colonial times through the 1980s. For other fundamental works, see Eliot A. Cohen, *Citizens and Soldiers: The Dilemmas of Military Service* (Ithaca, NY: Cornell University Press, 1985), as well as sociological or policy analysis by Charles Moskos, David R. Segal, Mady Weschler Segal, and Martin Binkin. This book focuses on the active army; for a study of the reserves, see Stephen M. Duncan, *Citizen Warriors* (Novato, CA: Presidio, 1997).
2. Richard Nixon, "The All-Volunteer Armed Force," address on CBS radio network, October 17, 1968, AVA—CMH.
3. Thomas W. Evans, "The All-Volunteer Army after Twenty Years: Recruiting in the Modern Era," *Army History* 27 (Summer 1993): 40; Janice H. Laurence and Peter F. Ramsberger, *Low-Aptitude Men in the Military: Who Profits, Who Pays?* (Westport, CT: Praeger, 1991), 63.
4. Term from Christian G. Appy, *Working-Class War: American Combat Soldiers*

and Vietnam (Chapel Hill: University of North Carolina Press, 1993); Nixon, "All-Volunteer."

5. Richard Gillam, "The Peacetime Draft: Voluntarism to Coercion," *Yale Review* 57 (January 1968): 499.
6. Ibid.
7. Segal, *Recruiting,* 18–24.
8. Segal, *Recruiting,* 23.
9. Gary W. Gallagher, *The Confederate War* (Cambridge, MA: Harvard University Press, 1997), 28–29; Segal, *Recruiting,* 25–26; Iver Bernstein, *The New York City Draft Riots: Their Significance for American Society and Politics in the Age of the Civil War* (New York: Oxford University Press, 1990), 5; George Q. Flynn, *The Draft, 1940–1973* (Lawrence: University Press of Kansas, 1993), 167–168.
10. Lt. General Lewis B. Hershey, "Outline of Historical Background of Selective Service (From Biblical Days to June 30, 1965)," rev. ed. (N.p., n.d.); Segal, *Recruiting,* 31.
11. Throughout this section I have relied heavily on George Q. Flynn, *The Draft, 1940–1973.* On the origins of the selective service system, see John Whiteclay Chambers II, *To Raise an Army: The Draft Comes to Modern America* (New York: Free Press, 1987).
12. Flynn, *Draft,* 20 (original source *NYT,* November 10, 1940).
13. See Christopher Capozzola, *Uncle Sam Wants You: World War I and the Making of the Modern American Citizen* (New York: Oxford University Press, 2008); Bernard C. Nalty, *Strength for the Fight: A History of Black Americans in the Military* (New York: Free Press, 1986).
14. See the special issue on psychiatry and the armed forces, based on series of seminars held by the Menninger Clinic in June 1941, *Bulletin of the Menninger Clinic* 5 (September 1941); Allan Berube, *Coming Out Under Fire: The History of Gay Men and Women in World War Two* (New York: Free Press, 1990); Beth Bailey, *Sex in the Heartland* (Cambridge, MA: Harvard University Press, 1999), 56–61.
15. Flynn, *Draft,* 68–73.
16. Ibid., 61, 95–96.
17. Ibid., 97.
18. Ibid., 96.
19. "I need you again," advertisement #44-1948, N. W. Ayer Collection, NMAH.
20. Nalty, *Strength for the Fight,* 214–216, 224–225; Flynn, *Draft,* 88–113.
21. Flynn, *Draft,* 88–113.
22. Ibid., 136, 164. Reporting on the 1951 draft bill, a joint congressional committee insisted that "The duty of bearing arms in defense of the Nation is a universal duty."
23. "Service and Citizenship," part 3 of *Are You Ready for Service?* (Coronet Instructional Films, 1951), Prelinger Archives, www.archive.org, accessed December 12, 2008.
24. Flynn, *Draft,* 140, 148.
25. Ibid., 140, quoting Selective Service press release, April 9, 1958.
26. Flynn, *Draft,* 165; Segal, *Recruiting,* 33.

27. The number of 19–25 year-old men jumped from 8 million in 1958 to 12 million in 1964. Flynn, *Draft,* 169.
28. Flynn, *Draft,* 164; "The Draft," *Newsweek,* April 4, 1960, 40.
29. Flynn, *Draft,* 169; Segal, *Recruiting,* 33.
30. Segal, *Recruiting,* 34.
31. James S. Olson and Randy Roberts, *Where the Domino Fell: America and Vietnam, 1945–1995,* 2nd ed. (New York: St. Martin's Press, 1996), 127; Robert Dallek, *Flawed Giant: Lyndon Johnson and His Times, 1961–1973* (New York: Oxford University Press, 1998), 271–277.
32. Dallek, *Flawed,* 276–277.
33. Ibid., 277.
34. Doris Kearns Goodwin, *Lyndon Johnson and the American Dream* (New York: Harper & Row, 1976), 282–283; see also Dallek, *Flawed Giant.*
35. Flynn, *Draft,* 166–168.
36. Susanna McBee, ". . . The Hullabaloo Is Old Hat to Hershey," *Life,* August 20, 1965, 29.
37. Olson and Roberts, *Domino,* 119.
38. Matthew Newman, "A Vital Service to Their Country: U-M Faculty's Historic Teach-in of 30 Years Ago," *Michigan Today,* October 1995.
39. Douglas Robinson, "Induction Center Picketed by 400," *NYT,* July 30, 1965; Penelope Adams Moon, "'Peace on Earth—Peace in Vietnam': The Catholic Peace Fellowship and Antiwar Witness, 1964–1976," *Journal of Social History* (Summer 2003). According to James D. Tracy, *Direct Action: Radical Pacifism from the Union Eight to the Chicago Seven* (Chicago: University of Chicago Press, 1996), 63–64, draft cards were first burned at a rally led by the literary critic Dwight Macdonald in protest against President Truman's 1947 call for universal military training.
40. "Mendelian Domain," *Time,* June 21, 1968; Steven Waldman, "Governing Under the Influence," *Washington Monthly,* January 1968; "Biographical Information," L. Mendel Rivers Collection, Special Collections, College of Charleston Library, http://www.cofc.edu/~speccoll/lmr.html.
41. *Prohibition of Destruction or Mutilation of Draft Cards,* HR 10306, 89th Cong., 1st sess. August 9, 1965; "Stiff Penalties Voted In House for Burning Draft Registration," *NYT,* August 11, 1965, 14; "Strom Thurmond Biography," The Strom Thurmond Institute of Government and Public Affairs, Clemson University, http://www.strom.clemson.edu/strom/bio.html; *Prohibition of Destruction or Mutilation of Draft Cards,* S 2381, 89th Cong., 1st sess., August 12, 1965.
42. "Protests on Principle and Some Practical Options," *Life,* August 20, 1965, 30; "Students at UC March on Draft Board," *Los Angeles Times,* May 6, 1965, 3; "Berkeley Students Protest 'Invasion,'" *NYT,* May 6, 1965, 13. This Associated Press article does not seem to have appeared in Washington, DC papers.
43. Richard Eder, "Hasty Marriages No Bar to Draft," *NYT,* September 1, 1965.
44. Moon, "Peace," 1043; "Vietnam Protesters Plan Drive to Avoid the Draft," *NYT,* October 18, 1965, 9.
45. "Student Protest in Iowa," *NYT,* November 4, 1965, 9 (this brief notice appeared after David Miller had been extensively covered as the first to defy the

law); George Starbuck, "Of Late," *The Works: Poems Selected from Five Decades,* ed. Kathryn Starbuck and Elizabeth Meese (Tuscaloosa: University of Alabama Press, 2003), 27.

46. "Out of the Kitchen Into the Soup," *Time,* November 5, 1965; "Draft Protester Is Seized by F.B.I. for Burning Card," *NYT,* October 19, 1965, 1.

47. Robert B. Semple, Jr. "Johnson Decries Draft Protests; Presses Inquiry," *NYT,* October 19, 1965, 1; On the International Days of Protest, see Melvin Small, *Antiwarriors: The Vietnam War and the Battle for America's Hearts and Minds* (Wilmington, DE: SR Books), 32–33; on the draft resistance movement, Michael S. Foley, *Confronting the War Machine: Draft Resistance during the Vietnam War* (Chapel Hill: University of North Carolina Press, 2003).

48. David Lawrence, "Basic Causes of Campus Disorders," *USN&WR,* May 25, 1970.

49. Nixon, "All-Volunteer."

50. Ibid.

51. Edward F. Sherman, "The Great Draft Debate," *New Republic,* May 18, 1968, 36.

52. Quote from Peter Barnes, "All Volunteer Army? No—But Not the Present System Either," *New Republic,* May 9, 1970, 19.

53. Marie Smith, "Draft Proposal Drafter," *Washington Post,* April 24, 1970.

54. Martin Anderson, "An Analysis of the Factors Involved in Moving to An All-Volunteer Armed Force," typed paper, July 4, 1967, AVA–MHI; Smith, "Draft Proposal"; Sol Tax, ed., *The Draft* (Chicago: University of Chicago Press, 1967).

55. Anderson was a special assistant to the president and served as part of the transition team headed by Arthur Burns. On the transition process, also see Rostker, *I Want You!*

56. Rostker, *I Want You!* 63–65. Quotations about economists are from Alfred B. Fitt, "Arguments Against a Special Commission," Memorandum to Melvin R. Laird, Washington, DC, January 29, 1969, Rostker CD, G0260.pdf.

57. Nixon to Laird, January 29, 1969, AVA–CMH; Griffith, *Army's Transition,* 20–21.

58. Rostker, *I Want You!* 66; Martin Anderson, *The Making of the All-Volunteer Armed Force* (Palo Alto, CA: The Hoover Institution Press, 1991), 5.

59. List of Members in President's Commission on an All-Volunteer Armed Force: General Correspondence (2) folder, box 135, Lauris Norstad Papers, 1930–1987, DDEL; Melvin R. Laird, "Memorandum for the President," February 7, 1969, Rostker CD G0265.pdf. On Laird's list of proposed members, Nobel was the sole entry under the category "Women," and "Women" was the only category on the list that did not describe a professional field or expertise, i.e., "Military," "Educators," "Industry," "Management Expert."

60. "President's Commission on an All-Volunteer Armed Force" Series, folder I, box 1, Alfred M. Gruenther Papers, DDEL.

61. Greenewalt profile from DuPont historical Web site, http://heritage.dupont.com.

62. Gates Commission, Minutes of May 13, 1969 meeting, 9, folder 1, box 1; Minutes of September 6, 1969 meeting, 23, folder 5, box 1; both in Gruenther Papers, DDEL.

63. Gates Commission, Minutes of June 28–29, 1969 meeting, 11–12; Minutes of July 12–13, 1969 meeting, 9; David J. Callard, memo to Commission Members, "Soliciting Public Opinion and Hearings," September 16, 1969, with sample letter and list of organizations attached, in Correspondence, Aug.–Dec. 1969 folder, box 2, Gruenther Papers, DDEL.
64. Gates Commission, Minutes of September 29, 1969 meeting, 3, folder 6, box 1, Gruenther Papers, DDEL.
65. American Legion, "Statement of James R. Wilson," attached to Gates Commission, Minutes of September 29, 1969 meeting, folder 6, box 1; National Student Association, "Statement of Jim Sutton," ibid.; Young Americans for Freedom, "Why 'Conservative' Students Support an All-Volunteer Military," ibid.; Gates Commission, "Notes on Meeting, September 29, 1969," ibid.; Gates Commission, Minutes of October 4, 1969 meeting, folder 7, box 1, all in Gruenther Papers, DDEL.
66. President's Commission on an All-Volunteer Armed Force, *The Report of the President's Commission on an All-Volunteer Armed Force* (Washington, DC, 1970), x. Meckling was dean of the business school at the University of Rochester; Oi received his Ph.D. in economics from the University of Chicago in 1961 and in 1967 was a full professor in the Graduate School of Management at Rochester, www.defenselink.mil/prhome/dacmc_oi.html, accessed December 12, 2008.
67. Gates Commission, Minutes of July 12–13, 1969 meeting, 3, 6, folder 4, box 1, Gruenther Papers, DDEL.
68. Ibid., 3–5.
69. Ibid.
70. Stephen E. Herbits to Thomas Gates, August 1, 1969, in Correspondence, Aug.–Dec. 1969 folder, box 2, Gruenther Papers, DDEL.
71. Gates Commission, Minutes of October 4, 1969 meeting, 49, 33, folder 7, box 1, Gruenther Papers, DDEL.
72. Gates Commission, Minutes of September 6, 1969 meeting, 24–25, folder 5, box 1, Gruenther Papers, DDEL.
73. "Catching GIs Without a Draft," *Business Week*, January 10, 1970, 32.
74. *Report of the President's Commission*, 6, 14.
75. Richard Nixon, "To the Congress of the United States," April 23, 1970, 5, in President's Commission on an All-Volunteer Armed Force—General Correspondence Folder, box 135, Norstad Papers, DDEL.

2. Repairing the Army

1. Samuel Zaffiri, *Westmoreland: A Biography of General William C. Westmoreland* (New York: William Morrow, 1994), 35, 314–316; "Slugger's Turn," *Time*, June 14, 1968.
2. Zaffiri, *Westmoreland*, 40; "A White House Vignette," *Time*, July 19, 1968; "The Guardians at the Gate: Man of the Year," *Time*, Jan. 7, 1966; "Slugger's Turn"; "Cards on the Table," *Time*, May 5, 1967.
3. Zaffiri, *Westmoreland*, 324, 330–332; W. C. Westmoreland, "Talking About the Army," *Vital Speeches of the Day* 35 (May 15, 1969): 451.
4. Directorate of Personnel Studies and Research, Office of the Deputy Chief of

Staff for Personnel, U.S. Army, *PROVIDE: Project Volunteer in Defense of the Nation,* vol. 1 (executive summary), June 1969, 11; Griffith, *Army's Transition,* 53.

5. For analysis of this crisis (what the author terms a "nervous breakdown"), see Ronald H. Spector, "The Vietnam War and the Army's Self-Image," in *Second Indochina War Symposium,* John Schlight, ed. (Washington, DC: U.S. Government Printing Office, 1986), 169–185.
6. "Who Gets Drafted?" *New Republic,* August 2, 1969, 9. Hershey refused to officially inform draft boards that a U.S. Court of Appeals had ruled that it was illegal to use the draft as a punishment.
7. Griffith, *Army's Transition,* 17–19.
8. Ibid., 21–24; Directorate of Personnel Studies and Research, *PROVIDE,* vol. 1; Lieutenant Colonel Butler to DCSPER, September 29, 1969, AVA—CMH.
9. See Griffith, *Army's Transition,* chaps. 2 and 3, for detailed description and analysis.
10. George I. Forsythe, oral history, 1974, SOOHP, 488, 496; Griffith, *Army's Transition,* 48; William C. Westmoreland, "Towards a Volunteer Army," *Vital Speeches of the Day* 37 (December 1, 1970): 98–100. (*Vital Speeches* incorrectly indicates Westmoreland's speech took place on October 30, 1970.)
11. Zaffiri, *Westmoreland,* 323–329; "Changing of the Guard," *Time,* April 19, 1968; Kevin P. Buckley, "General Abrams Deserves a Better War," *NYT Magazine,* October 5, 1969.
12. Ron Ridenhour, letter, March 29, 1969, under "Peers Report" on William Eckhardt, "The My Lai Courts-Martial 1970," www.law.umkc.edu/faculty/projects/ftrials/mylai/mylai.htm, accessed December 13, 2008.
13. For a comprehensive analysis, see William M. Hammond, *Public Affairs: The Military and the Media, 1968–1973,* United States Army in Vietnam Series (Washington, DC: Center of Military History, 1996), on Alpha Company Affair, pp. 193–200.
14. Neil Sheehan, "Letters from Hamburger Hill," *Harper's Magazine,* November 1969, 41, 52.
15. W. C. Westmoreland and Stanley R. Resor, "Memorandum for Lieutenant General William R. Peers," November 26, 1969, http://www.law.umkc.edu/faculty/projects/ftrials/mylai/directive.html, accessed November 28, 2008.
16. Chief of Staff, U.S. Army, to Commandant, AWC, "Subject: Analysis of Moral and Professional Climate in the Army," April 18, 1970, included in AWC, *Study on Military Professionalism,* Carlisle Barracks, PA, June 30, 1970, 53.
17. ". . . and the Home Front," *NYT,* May 5, 1970; "Death on the Campus," *NYT,* May 6, 1970.
18. Directorate of Personnel Studies and Research, *PROVIDE,* vol. 1, 8.
19. AWC, *Military Professionalism,* i, 1.
20. Ibid., iii, v, 26.
21. Ibid., 23, 24, 29, 26; David H. Hackworth, "Commentary: A Soldier's Disgust," *Harper's Magazine,* July 1972, 75.
22. AWC, *Military Professionalism,* B-45.
23. Griffith, *Army's Transition,* 49–52. Westmoreland quotation from interview by Griffith, February 28, 1983, 61, 7n.

24. William K. Brehm and Walter T. Kerwin, interview by Robert K. Griffith, April 13, 1983, transcript in AVA—MHI; Pete Dawkins, telephone interview by author, February 5, 2008; Forsythe, oral history, 516; Thomas W. Scoville, *Reorganizing for Pacification Support* (Washington, DC: Center of Military History, U.S. Army, 1982), see esp. chap. 4; Griffith, *Army's Transition,* 64.
25. Forsythe, oral history, 459–461.
26. *Army 75 Personnel Concept Study,* prepared by Battelle Institute under contract to Personnel Studies and Research, Office of the Deputy Chief of Staff for Personnel, 5.7–5.9, in "Women and the AVF" folder, AVA—MHI.
27. Forsythe, oral history, 454–464.
28. Westmoreland, "Towards a Volunteer Army," 98–100. In his address, Westmoreland used the phrase "volunteer Army" but never "all-volunteer." On the Pentagon announcement: "Toward an Ideal Army," *Time,* October 26, 1970.
29. William C. Westmoreland, keynote address, Army Commanders' Conference, The Pentagon, November 30, 1970, edited transcript, 1, 2, 4, 12. On officer ethics, AWC, *Military Professionalism.*
30. Westmoreland, keynote, 4, 7, 11–12.
31. Ibid., 6–8, 13. On changes implemented, see Griffith, *Army's Transition,* chaps. 6 and 7.
32. Henry G. Gole, interviews by Beth Bailey, December 16, 2004 and September 28, 2005. On social science, see Ramon Nadel, "Suggestions for General Westmoreland," February 1971, AVA—CMH.
33. Office of the Assistant Secretary, DA, to Assistant Secretary of Defense (M & RA), "Subject: Experiments Associated With The Modern Volunteer Army Programs," December 29, 1971, AVA—CMH; Griffith, *Army's Transition,* 82–87.
34. Griffith, *Army's Transition,* 64–65.
35. Bill Mauldin, "Willie and Joe Visit the New U.S. Army," *Life,* February 5, 1971, cover, 2A, 20–27; G. D. Barrante, "What Hasn't Changed," *R&CCJ,* March 1971, 10–12. Robert K. Griffith, personal correspondence with author, November 2008; Robert M. Montague, Jr., interview by Robert K. Griffith, March 11, 1983, 17–18, AVA—MHI; Griffith, *Army's Transition,* 65; "Humanizing the U.S. Military," *Time,* December 21, 1970, 16–22. The article in *Time* focused on Zumwalt and the navy, portraying the army as playing catch-up.
36. L. James Binder, "MVA: The Now Very In at Fort Benning," *Army,* April 1971, 24; George C. Wilson and Haynes Johnson, "Retraining the Leaders of Today's G.I.," part seven of series, "The Army in Anguish," *Washington Post,* September 18, 1971, 1; Richard J. Levine, "General Westmoreland Puts Forth New Plan for Rebuilding Army," *WSJ,* September 15, 1971, on the "Master Program for the Modern Volunteer Army" booklet; Leavitt A. Knight, Jr., "What the Army Is Doing to Make Out without the Draft," *The American Legion Magazine,* April 1971, 4; Westmoreland, keynote.
37. Binder, "MVA," 26; Wilson and Johnson, "Retraining the Leaders"; "Editor's Note: Forward March," *R&CCJ,* December 1971, 25.
38. Special Subcommittee on Recruiting and Retention of Military Personnel, House Committee on Armed Services, *Recruiting and Retention of Military Personnel,* September 29, 1971, 59. This is a stenographic transcript of hear-

ings with editing inserted by hand, in AVA—MHI; quotation from unedited version, which is what was said during testimony.

39. Binder, "MVA," 23, 25, 29; Griffith, *Army's Transition,* 85–86. For army enlisted pay grades and rank chart, with insignia, see http://www.defenselink.mil/specials/insignias/enlisted.html.
40. Binder, "MVA," 27; "The Modern Volunteer Army: A Program for Professionals" (Washington, DC: OSAMVA, 1971), in "Misc. Interviews & Notes & Phones" folder, AVA—MHI; House Committee, *Recruiting and Retention,* 59–60, unedited version.
41. "Humanizing the U.S. Military," 18.
42. LTC Broady, "Talking Paper, Subject: Status of the VOLAR Experiment," January 21, 1971, attached to minutes of SA/SAMVA meeting, January 21, 1971, AVA—CMH; Binder, "MVA," 24, 26, 28–29.
43. Office of the Assistant Secretary, DA, "Subject: Experiments."
44. Dana Anderson Schmidt, "The New Army—2," *CSM,* March 24, 1973; Michael Klare, "Can the Army Survive VOLAR?" *Commonweal,* January 18, 1974, 384–389.
45. B. Drummond Ayres, Jr., "Army Is Shaken by Crisis in Morale and Discipline," *NYT,* September 5, 1971.
46. Richard Reeves, *President Nixon: Alone in the White House* (New York: Simon and Schuster, 2001), 265; James J. Kilpatrick, "Looking Behind the Triggers in Ohio," *The National Guardsman,* Florida Edition, June 1970.
47. Mauldin, "Willie and Joe"; Griffith, *Army's Transition,* 110.
48. Griffith, *Army's Transition,* 112.
49. Pete Dawkins drafted the "professionalism" pamphlet over a single weekend; it was intended primarily for the institutional army. Dawkins, interview.
50. House Committee, *Recruiting and Retention,* 56.
51. Ibid., 51, 62–68.
52. Ibid., 70, 74–77. Lombardi led the Washington Redskins to a victorious season in 1969, then died of cancer in DC little more than a year before this testimony. Despite his fame, the transcript consistently read "Vince Lombardy." I corrected it in this text.
53. Ibid., 73–77; Forsythe, oral history, 470.
54. B. Drummond Ayres Jr., "Army Softens Rigors of Recruits' Training," *NYT,* August 29, 1971.
55. Ayres, "Army Softens"; "Sergeant Major," "Anyone Listening?" *AT,* May 5, 1971; SFC Theodore Evans, "Commentary: The Non-Professionals," *AT,* June 9, 1971.
56. Captain MVA, "A Letter to Sarge," and response, M.Sgt. James C. Guyton, "The NCO's Function," both in *AT,* May 5, 1971.
57. Lt. Col. Emmett F. Knight, letter to the editor, "Haircut Policy," *AT,* July 21, 1971.
58. "Sergeant Major," "Anyone Listening?"; "Big Bite" (Combat Arms Feature), *R&CCJ,* December 1971, 15.
59. House Committee, *Recruiting and Retention,* 54; on leadership, see U.S. Army Command Information Unit, "Special Events Speech for the Modern Volunteer Army No. 1," ref. # HRC327.02, AVA—CMH.

60. Binder, "MVA"; Wilson and Johnson, "Retraining the Leaders"; "Editor's Note: Forward March"; DA, *The Modern Volunteer Army Program: The Benning Experiment, 1970–1972* (Washington, DC: 1974); DA, *Building a Volunteer Army: The Fort Ord Contribution* (Washington, DC: 1975).
61. "Forward March," *R&CCJ*, December 1971, 25.

3. The Army in the Marketplace

1. Benjamin F. Schemmer and George F. Weiss, "Will Fate of President Nixon's All-Volunteer Force Hinge on 'Competition' for Nation's 50th Largest Ad Contract?" *Armed Forces Journal* 108 (March 15, 1971): 40–41 (original copyright *Army and Navy Journal*, 1971); Philip H. Dougherty, "Ayer Keeping Army Account," *NYT*, January 11, 1971. McCann-Erickson, Marschalk, Creamer-Colarossi, and N.W. Ayer bid for the Army account.
2. Schemmer and Weiss, "Will Fate"; Donald H. McGovern to George I. Forsythe, December 18, 1970, AVA—CMH.
3. Schemmer and Weiss, "Will Fate."
4. See Lizabeth Cohen, *A Consumers' Republic: The Politics of Mass Consumption in Postwar America* (New York: Knopf, 2003); Meg Jacobs, *Pocketbook Politics: Economic Citizenship in Twentieth-Century America* (Princeton, NJ: Princeton University Press, 2005); David Farber, *Sloan Rules* (Chicago: University of Chicago Press, 2002).
5. Directorate of Personnel Studies and Research, *PROVIDE*, vol. 1, 8, 3.
6. "Army Enlists Ayer for Blitz," *Broadcast Advertising*, date illegible (before March 9, 1971); clipping in AVA—MHI.
7. "Grand Old Adman," *Time*, July 4, 1960; Peggy J. Kreshel, "John B. Watson at J. Walter Thompson: The Legitimization of 'Science' in Advertising," *Journal of Advertising* 19 (1990): 49–59; Brehm for Kelley, Assistant Secretary of Defense (M&RA), June 12, 1969, quoted in Griffith, *Army's Transition*, 32.
8. Colonel Beuke, Director of Advertising and Information, USAREC, Presentation to Joint Recruiting Conference, November 5–6, 1970, 6, AVA—MHI.
9. A. O. Connor, DCSPER, to Commanding General, USAREC, "Advertising and Publicity Plan Concept for FY 70," October 7, 1968, AVA—CMH.
10. Ted Rogers, interview by Robert Griffith, August 25 [1983?], handwritten notes in "USAREC and Recruiting" folder, AVA—MHI; LTC Broady, "Talking Paper, Subject: Advertising," in SA/SAMVA meeting Memorandum for Record, January 21, 1971; SA/SAMVA meeting Memorandum for Record, January 28, 1971, AVA—CMH. Meetings of key members of the army secretariat and the army staff were held each Thursday at the request of the secretary of the army, who attended regularly.
11. Ted Regan, interview by Robert Griffith, August 1983, handwritten notes in "USAREC and Recruiting" folder, unpaginated, AVA—MHI; N.W. Ayer, "United States Army Recruiting Advertising," n.d. (January or February 1972?), from personal files of Thomas W. Evans, former deputy director of Advertising and Sales Promotion, USAREC, copy in author's possession. The N.W. Ayer document combines its original 1971 presentation with one given the following year.

12. Directorate of Personnel Studies and Research, "Supporting Analysis," PROVIDE, vol. 2, 15–11; Opinion Research Corporation, *Reaction of 17 to 21 Year Old Males, Not in College, to Enlistment in the Army and its Combat Branches* (Princeton, NJ, 1971) emphasizes negative attitudes toward the military.
13. Forsythe, oral history, 27; LTC Stromberg, "Modernizing the Army," for *Four-Year Report of the Chief of Staff*, April 26, 1972, AVA—CMH.
14. Forsythe, oral history, 27.
15. Ibid.
16. Regan, interview.
17. N.W. Ayer, "Recruiting Advertising."
18. Forsythe, oral history, 30; Regan, interview.
19. William Kelley, interview by Robert Griffith, August 1983, "USAREC and Recruiting" folder; AVA—MHI.
20. N.W. Ayer, "Recruiting Advertising."
21. Ibid.; [William Westmoreland?], "A Note on the Army's Theme," speech, September 1971, AVA—MHI.
22. Schemmer and Weiss, "Will Fate," 40–41; BG Robert Montague, Jr., "Talking Paper on Paid Army Television and Radio Advertisements," August 1972, AVA—MHI.
23. "Bobby-Soxer's Gallup," *Time*, August 13, 1956; Office of the Assistant Secretary, "Subject: Experiments"; Market Facts, Inc., "Youth Attitude Tracking Study, Fall 1975," (Chicago, IL, February 1976), 1; on women, Defense Technical Information Center, oai.dtic.mil, accessed November 6, 2008.
24. The term "important psychological needs" comes from Opinion Research Corporation, *Reaction*, xxxiii.
25. Opinion Research Corporation, *Reaction*, xvii, xxxiii; Scott M. Cunningham, *The Volunteer Soldier: His Needs, Attitudes, and Expectations*, Report Number 72-2 (Cambridge, MA: Cinecom Corporation, 1972), vii, 8.
26. "Today's Army wants to join you" advertisement, *Senior Scholastic*, October 4, 1971.
27. "Today's Army wants to join you" advertisement, *Senior Scholastic*, November 29, 1971.
28. On race and advertising decisions, Tom Maxey (former president, vice chairman, and chief operating officer of N.W. Ayer), interview by author, Philadelphia, PA, November 9, 2005.
29. Series of advertisements, "When was the last time you got promoted?" (1973), folder 5, box 3, Ayer Collection; on "special interests of black Americans," Opinion Research Corporation, *Reaction*, xxiii–xxv, xxxiii.
30. 16-month tour ad, 1971, folder 3, box 2, Ayer Collection; Mike, Leroy, Rocky ad, *Senior Scholastic*, November 8, 1971.
31. U.S. Army Audiovisual Center, Office of the Chief Signal Officer, *The Army Reports*—"Today's Army . . . Is It Your Bag?" n.d. (1971 or 1972?), in Motion Picture, Sound, and Video Branch, NARA—College Park.
32. Subcommittee on Communications and Power, House Committee on Interstate and Foreign Commerce, *Expenditure of Public Funds for Broadcast Advertis-*

ing: Hearings on H. Con. Res. 215, 92nd Cong., 1st sess., April 21–22, 1971, 183; Beuke, Presentation, 7; Minutes, SAMVA meeting with OSD, Navy, Marines, and Air Force representatives, February 20, 1971, 2–4, AVA—MHI; James D. Hittle, Assistant Secretary of the Navy, Memorandum for the Assistant Secretary of Defense (Manpower and Reserve Affairs), Subject: Project Volunteer—Paid Advertising, February 24, 1971, AVA—MHI.

33. Art Buchwald, "Selling the Military," *Washington Post,* March 28, 1971; Stanley W. Cohen, "Marines Set Counterattack Following Army Ad Campaign," *Advertising Age,* May 17, 1971; John G. Kestor to Assistant Secretary of Defense (Manpower and Reserve Affairs), Proposed Marine Corps Advertisement, May 10, 1971, AVA—MHI.

34. Office of the Assistant Secretary, DA to Deputy Assistant Secretary of Defense (Manpower Research and Utilization), Subject: Army Advertising Program, March 23, 1971, "USAREC and Recruiting" folder, AVA—MHI; Maurine Christopher, "Army's Enlistment Campaign is Blockbuster Test of Radio-TV," *Advertising Age,* March 1, 1971, 2, 6; Stanford Research Institute, *Effectiveness of Modern Volunteer Army Advertising Program* (Menlo Park, CA, 1971), 98.

35. Rome Arnold & Company, "U.S. Army Recruiting Advertising Test," conducted for U.S. Army Recruiting and N.W. Ayer & Son, Inc., September 1971, 3, AVA—MHI.

36. Ibid., 12, 17.

37. Memorandum for Secretary of Defense from Assistant Secretary of Defense, June 30, 1971, AVA—MHI.

38. N.W. Ayer, "Recruiting Advertising"; "Talking Paper: Status of Advertising," July 1, 1971, CSA/SAMVA Meeting Agenda, AVA—CMH.

39. Hadlai Hull, Memorandum for the Record, Subject: Advertising, July 8, 1971, AVA—MHI.

40. Columbia Broadcasting System, *From Subpoena to Recommittal,* broadcast transcript of *The Selling of the Pentagon,* February 23, 1971, 1.

41. CBS, *Selling of the Pentagon* transcript, 15 (Hébert), 1 (Mudd); Jack Gould, "TV: CBS Explores Pentagon Propaganda Costs," *NYT,* February 24, 1971, 83.

42. CBS, *Selling of the Pentagon: Postscript* transcript, 2, 1; House Committee, *Expenditure,* 173 (Hébert quoted from *Advertising Age,* April 5, 1971); Maurine Christopher, "Army Gets Okay for Second Wave of Radio-TV Advertising," *Advertising Age,* July 19, 1971, 12.

43. House Committee, *Expenditure,* 2.

44. Ibid., 148–149.

45. "The Military's Four-Year Crusade to Break into Broadcast," *Media Decisions* (October 1976): 67.

46. Ibid.

47. Kelley, interview.

48. Thomas W. Evans, "Recruiting Advertising" (overview historical essay by deputy director of Advertising and Sales Promotion, USAREC, to prepare LTG Elton for "Hill" testimony about Army advertising), July 27, 1983, p. 19, AVA—

MHI; Thomas W. Evans, interview by author, Highwood, IL, December 22, 2005.

4. Race, "Quality," and the Hollow Army

1. "Draft-Free Army," *NYT,* April 21, 1974; "Volunteer Army in Trouble: Back to the Draft, or What?" *USN&WR,* October 15, 1973, 63.
2. Robert L. Goldich, *Recruiting, Retention, and Quality in the All-Volunteer Force,* Report No. 81-106F (Washington, DC: Congressional Research Service, Library of Congress, 1981), p. xi.
3. On World War I registration and induction, see John Whiteclay Chambers, *The Oxford Companion to American Military History* (New York: Oxford University Press, 1999); Walter V. Bingham, "How the Army Sorts Its Manpower," *Harper's Magazine,* September 1942, 426, quoted in Daniel J. Kevles, "Testing the Army's Intelligence: Psychologists and the Military in World War I," *Journal of American History* 55 (December 1968): 567.
4. On WWI mental testing, see Paula Fass, *Outside In: Minorities and the Transformation of American Education* (New York: Oxford University Press, 1989), and Kevles, "Testing the Army's Intelligence."
5. Kevles, "Testing the Army's Intelligence," 572.
6. "Secret Mind Tests of the Army," *NYT Magazine,* February 16, 1919; Kevles, "Testing the Army's Intelligence," 572–578.
7. "Secret Mind Tests"; Ellen Herman, *The Romance of American Psychology* (Berkeley: University of California Press, 1995), 55.
8. Private Seth Dennis, "For Each Soldier the Right Job," *NYT,* February 21, 1943; Senate Armed Services Committee, *Department of Defense Authorization for Appropriations for FY 1983,* part 3, 97th Cong., 2nd sess., March 2, 1982, 1571.
9. Fass, *Outside In,* 139–154; on psychologists and the notion of "salvage," Bailey, *Sex in the Heartland,* 55–61.
10. *The Inductee's Mental Test* (New York: Arco Publishing Co., 1942), 7, 3; Fass, *Outside In,* 151, 149.
11. See Paul Foley and Linda S. Rucker, "An Overview of the Armed Services Vocational Aptitude Battery," in *Testing: Theoretical and Applied Perspectives,* ed. Ronna F. Dillon and James W. Pellegrino (New York: Praeger, 1989), 16–33; Rostker, *I Want You!* 481—482.
12. Homer Bigart, "M'Namara Plans to 'Salvage' 40,000 Rejected in Draft," *NYT,* August 24, 1966; on Project 100,000, see Janice H. Laurence and Peter F. Ramsberger, *Low-Aptitude Men in the Military: Who Profits, Who Pays?* (Westport, CT: Praeger, 1991); Lisa Hsiao, "Project 100,000: The Great Society's Answer to Military Manpower Needs in Vietnam," *Vietnam Generation* I (Summer 1989):14–37; I. M. Greenberg, "Project 100,000: The Training of Former Rejectees," *Phi Delta Kappan,* June 1969, 570–574; Appy, *Working-Class War,* 32–33.
13. Laurence and Ramsberger, *Low-Aptitude Men,* 15–19, 21; U.S. Department of Labor, Office of Policy Planning and Research, *The Negro Family: The Case for*

National Action (Washington, DC: GPO, 1965) (the "Moynihan Report"); Bigart, "M'Namara Plan."

14. Laurence and Ramsberger, *Low-Aptitude Men,* 36–43.
15. Michael T. Klare, "Can the Army Survive Volar?" *Commonweal,* January 18, 1974, 384 quotes Westmoreland's 1972 comment; "Big Changes in the Army: Interview with Gen. William C. Westmoreland, Chief of Staff," *USN&WR,* June 19, 1972, 59.
16. Fanteau testimony, House Committee on Armed Services, *Recruiting and Retention of Military Personnel,* March 6, 1972, Stenographic Transcript of Hearings, vol. 14, 1100–1150, Columbia Reporting Company, Washington, DC, in "Beard Report" box, AVA—MHI.
17. Griffith, *Army's Transition,* 165–167, 182. The size of the active duty military dropped from 3.5 million in January 1969 to 2.3 million in spring 1972; the army fell from 1.5 million to 974,000 active duty troops.
18. Griffith, *Army's Transition,* 165–167.
19. Ibid., 186–188; Rostker, *I Want You!* 268–275.
20. Griffith, *Army's Transition,* 186–188; Army Personnel Research Office, Fact Sheet, 1965, sent by A. J. Martin to Richard Danzig, September 4, 1980; George Doust, interview by Robert K. Griffith, March 30, 1983, AVA—MHI. The 1965 fact sheet notes that the correlation between the AFQT and individually administered intelligence tests is "high"—"about .8"—but that "no direct one-to-one correspondence between AFQT percentile scores and IQ scores can be stated."
21. Rostker, *I Want You!* 268–271; Howard H. Callaway, interview by Robert K. Griffith, Denver, CO, September 23, 1983, 28–35, AVA—MHI.
22. Callaway, interview, 6–7.
23. Ibid., 2, 4, 5.
24. Howard H. Callaway, keynote address, Association of the United States Army, Washington, DC, October 15, 1973, AVA—MHI; "Army Secretary Confident that Volunteer Army is Working" (army press release), October 15, 1973, AVA—MHI.
25. Callaway, interview, 14.
26. Ibid., 10.
27. MSG Nat Dell, "In Step with the Times," *Soldiers,* January 1975, 40, 41. General Bruce C. Clarke (Retired), Address to Graduates of the Army Recruiter and Career Counselor Course, Fort Benjamin Harrison, IN, October 22, 1971, AVA—CMH.
28. Callaway to Representative Frank Horton, November 1, 1973, AVA—MHI; Callaway, interview, 16–17; Eugene P. Forrester Papers, MHI; Dell, "In Step"; LTC Paul McCarthy, "So You Want To Wear the Recruiter Badge," *R&CCJ,* April 1976, 9.
29. Official form letter to "Dear Recruiter Candidate," *R&CCJ,* April 1976, 11; David Pankey, correspondence with author, 2004; *MacNeil-Lehrer Report,* "Uncle Sam Requests The Pleasure Of . . ." (transcript), no date (1974?), AVA—MHI.
30. David R. Boldt, "The Army Recruiter: 'I Wave at Everyone,'" *Washington Post,* June 25, 1972.

31. CPT Karen K. Psimadis, "A New Way to Make Points," *R&CCJ,* October 1973, 30; SP4 Stephen McMinn, "QIPS: Quality Counts!" *R&CCJ,* September 1974, 30–31.
32. Leonard Trasciak, "I sure like working with quality material!" cartoon, *R&CCJ,* December 1974, 39; Major General William B. Fulton, "Views and Reviews," *R&CCJ,* September 1974, 3.
33. Callaway, interview, 15, 25; Fulton, "Views and Reviews," 3; William K. Brehm, "All Volunteer Force: A Special Status Report," *Commanders Digest,* February 28, 1974, 4.
34. CPT Daniel O. Nettesheim, "The Recruiter's Unique Incentive System," *R&CCJ,* April 1976, 12; "Gold Star Recruiters," R&CCJ, December 1974, 13; Eugene P. Forrester, SOOHP, MHI, 640–643.
35. Jack Anderson, "Are We Staffing the Army With Military Misfits?" *Washington Post,* September 8, 1974; Boldt, "The Army Recruiter."
36. Daniel Huck, "Recruiter Malpractices," OASD (M&RA), November 9, 1973, in Rostker CD, G0082.pdf; William P. Clements and Lt. Gen. Robert Taber, news conference (transcript), July 18, 1973, AVA—MHI.
37. Herbits to Brehm, October 17, 1973, in Rostker CD, S0106.pdf; "Army's Elimination of Category IV's," Herbits to Brehm, October 16, 1973, AVA—MHI; Rostker, *I Want You!* 268–271; "The Volunteer Army," *Atlantic Monthly,* July 1974, 6–12.
38. George F. Will, "The Army's Problem," *Washington Post,* September 28, 1973, sent by Representative Frank Horton to Callaway with request for answers to allegations, AVA—MHI. See also Martin Binkin and Mark J. Eitelberg, *Blacks and the Military* (Washington, DC: Brookings Institution, 1982).
39. Clements and Taber, news conference.
40. See Appy, *Working-Class War,* 32–33, and Hsiao, "Project 100,000"; Eliot A. Cohen, "Why We Need a Draft," *Commentary,* April 1982, 35.
41. Joe Sharkey, "The Selling of the 'Modern Army,'" *Today/The Philadelphia Inquirer,* December 17, 1972; U.S. Department of Labor, http://www.bls.gov/cps/prev_yrs.htm, accessed November 14, 2008; advertisement, *Ebony,* December 1972; advertisements, folder 6, box 59, N.W. Ayer Collection—NMAH; "The Volunteer Army—One Year Later," Callaway to Nixon, February 14, 1974, V-4, AVA—MHI.
42. Gates Commission, Minutes of September 16, 1969 meeting, 41, Greunther Papers, DDEL; Charles B. Rangel, "Black Hessians in a White Man's Army," *NYT,* April 17, 1971, 29; Ronald V. Dellums, *Lying Down with Lions* (Boston: Beacon Press, 2000); www.thecongressionalblackcaucus.com, accessed November 19, 2008.
43. Dellums to Milton Francis, Deputy Assistant Secretary of Defense (Equal Opportunity), October 11, 1973; Assistant Secretary of Defense (M & RA), proposed reply to Dellums, January 31, 1974; Brehm to Deputy Secretary of Defense, "Marine Corps Minority Procurement Policy," memorandum, February 14, 1974, all in Rostker CD (G0548.pdf).
44. Ibid.
45. Ibid.

46. Department of the Navy, proposed reply to Dellums, February 4, 1974, Rostker CD, G0548.pdf.
47. Sol Stern, "When the Black G.I. Comes Back From Vietnam," *NYT Magazine,* March 24, 1968.
48. Ibid.
49. Ibid.
50. Ibid.; for army counter-argument, "The Volunteer Army in Review," *Atlantic Monthly,* December 1977, p. 12.
51. "The Other War: Whites Against Blacks in Vietnam," *New Republic,* January 1969, 15–16; Thomas A. Johnson, "Negroes in 'The Nam,'" *Ebony,* August 1968, 31–38.
52. "Racism in the Army," *Chicago Daily Defender,* January 28, 1970; on race relations policy and action in the U.S. Army, see "Department of the Army (DA) Policy and Activities," in *Race Relations Research in the U.S. Army in the 1970s,* ed. James A. Thomas (Arlington, VA: United States Army Research Institute for the Behavioral and Social Sciences, 1988), 32–47.
53. Hans J. Massaquoi, "A Battle the Army Can't Afford To Lose," *Ebony,* February 1974, 116, 117, 118, 120.
54. Ibid., 120, 118.
55. Congressman Augustus F. Hawkins, "U.S. Military Threatened By Racism," *Pittsburgh Courier,* December 2, 1972.
56. Benjamin E. Mays, "My View: New Secretary of the Army Fought Civil Rights," *Chicago Defender,* May 19, 1973; George M. Coleman, "Blacks Get 'Square Deal' in Army, Callaway Avows," *Atlanta Daily World,* July 7, 1974.
57. On "Callaway shift," see Rostker, *I Want You!* 275; Kenneth Y. Tomlinson, "How Good Is Our All-Volunteer Army?" *Readers Digest,* October 1975, 193.
58. John W. Lewis, Jr., "Say Military Is Using Tests to Curb Black Enlistments," *New York Amsterdam News,* April 23, 1975.
59. Howard H. Callaway, "Response to Congressman Dellums on Quality Standards and Discrimination," memorandum to Deputy Secretary of Defense, May 31, 1975; Callaway to Dellums, May 22, 1975, both in Rostker CD, G0665.pdf. The two-page letter was accompanied by six pages of responses to specific questions and ten pages of charts and supporting material.
60. Callaway to Dellums, May 22, 1975.
61. Ibid.
62. "Boss Man of the Army," *Ebony,* June 1977, 36, 38; Mary Brown, "Clifford Alexander: Boss!" *New York Amsterdam News,* May 13, 1978; "Secretary of the Army Clifford Alexander . . . Wants YOU," *Senior Scholastic,* November 3, 1977, 16–17.
63. "Boss Man of the Army," 35, 38.
64. John M. Swomley, Jr., "Too Many Blacks? The All-Volunteer Force," *The Christian Century,* October 1, 1980, 903; Benjamin L. Hooks, "Our New Day Begun: Bringing Back the Draft, Part II," *Atlanta Daily World,* June 7, 1979; Robert Phillips, "Historical Development of the Army College Fund," n.d., AVA—MHI.

65. "Army Is Disturbed by Recruit Quality," *NYT,* January 11, 1977; Goldich, *Recruiting, Retention, and Quality,* 26–27; Robert B. Pirie testimony, Subcommittee on Manpower and Personnel, Senate Armed Services Committee, "Department of Defense Authorization for Appropriations for FY81, part 3: Manpower and Personnel," March 10, 1980, 96th Cong., 2nd sess., 1290, Rostker CD, S0567.pdf.
66. "Doubts Mounting about All-Volunteer Force," *Science,* September 5, 1980, 1095–1099.
67. David Llorens, in "Why Negroes Re-Enlist," *Ebony,* August 1968, 90, quotes sociologist Donald F. Hueber's description of the AFQT as "a measure of the individual's participation in the culture, as well as a measure of innate ability," and notes, "In this case the culture reflected in the test is *white*"; "A Test for Recruiters," *R&CCJ,* January 1972, 24; "Doubts Mounting"; Goldich, *Recruiting, Retention, and Quality,* x, xiii.
68. MG DeWitt C. Smith, Jr., DCSPER, "Fact Sheet on Volunteer Army," memorandum for Information Officers Worldwide, April 23, 1974, AVA—CMH; Eliot A. Cohen, "Why We Need a Draft"; LTC William J. Taylor, "Random Observations of Soldier Attitudes at the Army Training Center, Fort Dix, New Jersey," memorandum for BG R. D. Tice, January 31, 1974; Subcommittee on Manpower and Personnel, Senate Committee on Armed Services, *Status of the All-Volunteer Armed Force,* 95th Cong., 2nd sess., June 20, 1978, 84–86; Michael Specter, "Is the Volunteer Army a Failure?" *The Nation,* June 19, 1982, 743–745; "Who'll Fight for America?" (cover story), *Time,* June 9, 1980, 24, 25.
69. David Cortright, "Our Volunteer Army: Can a Democracy Stand It?" *The Nation,* October 16, 1976, 360–361 (includes information from *Army Times*); "Doubts Mounting"; Senate Committee, *Status of the All-Volunteer Armed Force,* 8.
70. James Fallows, "The Civilianization of the Army," *Atlantic Monthly,* April 1981, 102; Lucian K. Truscott IV, "Notes on a Broken Promise: An Assessment of the Volunteer Army," *Harper's,* July 1974, 20–21; "Big Switch: Military Finding Favor with New Generation," *USN&WR,* May 3, 1976, 36.
71. Fallows, "Civilianization," 98, 102, 104–106.
72. Senate Committee, *Status of the All-Volunteer Armed Force,* 8; Truscott, "Notes," 20.
73. Sharkey, "The Selling of the 'Modern Army,'" 6; "Tell Them about the Warts," *R&CCJ,* October 1974, 28; Evans, "Recruiting Advertising," 18–19; J. L. Reed, "The Beard Study: An Analysis and Evaluation of the United States Army," April 1978, appendix to Senate Committee, *Status of the All-Volunteer Armed Force,* 157, in AVA—MHI; Drew Middleton, "Pentagon Chiefs, Supporting the Volunteer Army, Admit It Has Faults, but Oppose Return to Draft," *NYT,* July 5, 1977; on congressional inconsistency, Rostker, *I Want You!* 273.
74. R. Matthew Lee, "Flagging Vigilance: The Post-Vietnam 'Hollow Army,'" M.A. thesis, Texas A&M University, 2001, 16–18, www.geocities.com/rmatthewlee/index.html, accessed December 12, 2008; Middleton, "Pentagon Chiefs."
75. Senate Committee, "Department of Defense Authorization for Appropriations for FY81," 1286–1287; Rostker, *I Want You!* 396–399, 480.

76. Ibid.
77. Senate Committee, "Department of Defense Authorization for Appropriations for FY81," 1290–1293.
78. Ibid., 1309, 1299; House Committee on Appropriations, *Department of Defense Appropriations for 1981,* part 5, 96th Cong., 2nd sess., April 1, 1980, 63–65; Lee, "Flagging Vigilance," 12.
79. Senate Committee, *Department of Defense Authorization for Appropriations for FY 1983,* part 3, 1571–1572; "How Smart Are U.S. Soldiers?" *Newsweek,* March 8, 1982, 64.
80. "How Smart Are U.S. Soldiers?"; "Doubts Mounting"; Fallows, "The Civilianization of the Army," 102; Winston Williams, "U.S. Aide Says Allies Criticize Blacks in Army," *NYT,* June 6, 1982. Black versus white high school graduation rates for new military accessions were 65 percent to 55 percent at the end of the 1970s; 90.6 percent to 76.3 percent in fiscal year 1981.
81. "Doubts Mounting"; House Committee, *Department of Defense Appropriations for 1981,* part 5, 66.
82. "Army Secretary Alexander Under Attack by Nunn," *Atlanta Daily World,* June 29, 1980; George Davis, "Blacks in the Military: Opportunity or Refuge?" *Black Enterprise,* July 1980, 30.
83. "Angry Mothers and Draft Resisters," *Newsweek,* August 3, 1981, 33; Carl Rowan, "Moshe Dayan insults Black Gis [sic]," *New York Amsterdam News,* December 20, 1980; Williams, "U.S. Aide Says Allies Criticize Blacks in Army," 21. Reagan opposed draft registration during his presidential campaign, but shifted position after the election.

5. "If You Like Ms., You'll Love Pvt."

1. President Jimmy Carter, State of the Union Address, January 23, 1980, Washington, DC, http://www.jimmycarterlibrary.org/documents/speeches/, accessed November 27, 2008; video of address in Rostker CD, S0589.mov. President Ford had ended draft registration on March 15, 1975, putting the selective service system into "deep standby mode." See Rostker, *I Want You!* 422–428.
2. "The Carter Doctrine: Is the Draft Really Needed?" *Newsweek,* February 4, 1980, 29.
3. "Statement by the President," Office of the White House Press Secretary, February 8, 1980, Rostker CD G1186.pdf; Melinda Beck, "Women in the Armed Forces," *Newsweek,* February 18, 1980, 34; James Earl Carter, "Presidential Recommendations for Selective Service Reform: A Report to Congress Prepared Pursuant to P.L. 96-107," Washington, DC: The White House, February 11, 1980, Rostker CD S0561.pdf. See Linda Kerber, *No Constitutional Right to Be Ladies: Women and the Obligations of Citizenship* (New York: Hill and Wang, 1998), 278–302.
4. House Committee on Armed Services Military Personnel Subcommittee, *Registration of Women,* Hearings on H.R. 6569, 96th Cong., 2nd sess., March 5–6, 1980, 2–5.
5. House Committee, *Registration of Women,* 2–5, 103–105, 17, 86.
6. Calculated from tables 2-13 and 2-19, "Selected Manpower Statistics," Depart-

ment of Defense, http://siadapp.dmdc.osd.mil/personnel/M01/fy95/SMSTOP .HTM, accessed November 21, 2008. All percentages are for enlisted active duty personnel.

7. Racial statistics calculated from Bettie J. Morden, *The Women's Army Corps, 1945–1978* (Washington, DC: Center of Military History, U.S. Army, 1990), 415 (Table 5) and Table 2-19, "Selected Manpower Statistics"; Martin Binkin and Shirley J. Bach, *Women and the Military* (Washington, DC: The Brookings Institution, 1977), 50. The Coast Guard Academy began admitting women before the Congressional decision.
8. Binkin and Bach, *Women,* 5.
9. Ibid., 6; Mattie E. Treadwell, *The Women's Army Corps* (DA, Office of the Chief of Military History, 1954), 12.
10. Binkin and Bach, *Women,* 6–7; Carol Woster, "The Women's Army Corps: The Past Is Their Prologue," *Army,* May 1974, 23.
11. Quote from Leisa D. Meyer, *Creating G.I. Jane: Sexuality and Power in the Women's Army Corps During World War II* (New York: Columbia University Press, 1996), 19–20.
12. Meyer, *Creating G.I. Jane,* 66–68, 77–79; Carol Burke, "'If You're Nervous in the Service . . . ,'" in M. Paul Holsinger and Mary Anne Schofield, eds., *Visions of War* (Bowling Green, OH: Bowling Green State University Popular Press, 1992), 129.
13. Binkin and Bach, *Women,* 6–9; Meyer, *Creating G.I. Jane,* 86–89; Morden, *Women's Army Corps,* 18–24.
14. Hallaren to General Brooks, "The Mobilization of Women" memorandum, n.d. (1950), no label on file, box 86, Women's Army Corps, 1945–78, RG 319, NARA.
15. Ibid. Statistics on the strength of the WAC during the war vary from source to source.
16. House Committee on Armed Services Military Personnel Subcommittee, *Women in the Military,* 96th Cong., 1st and 2nd sess., November 13–16, 1979 and February 11, 1980, 159–160; Linda Bird Francke, *Ground Zero: The Gender Wars in the Military* (New York: Simon & Schuster, 1997), 22; Directorate of Personnel Studies and Research, *PROVIDE,* vol. 2, chap. 9, 12; Binkin and Bach, *Women,* 11–12.
17. *Army 75,* chap. 8, 41.
18. House Committee, *Women in the Military,* 161; Binkin and Bach, *Women,* 13; *Army 75,* chap. 5, 6, 7, chap. 8, 10, 11; Morden, *Women's Army Corps,* 227.
19. *Army 75,* chap. 8, 3, 5, 9, 1, 10, 13, 14.
20. Directorate of Personnel Studies and Research, *PROVIDE,* vol. 2, chap. 9, 8, 16.
21. Woster, "The Women's Army Corps," 22; BG Mildred Bailey, "Speech on 32nd Anniversary of Founding of WAC," WAC 98 folder, box 14, WAC.
22. Meyer, *Creating G.I. Jane,* 49, 59. See also Donna B. Knaff, "'This Girl in Slacks': Female Masculinity in the Popular Graphic Art of World War II" (Ph.D. diss., University of New Mexico, 2006) and Ann Elizabeth Pfau, *MISS YOUR LOVIN: G.I.s, Gender, and Domesticity during World War II* (Gutenberg-e, Columbia University Press, 2008, http://www.gutenberg-e.org/pfau/).

23. "The Fashionable Choice," DACOWITS recruiting brochure for women in the armed services, folder 82, box 12, WAC.
24. Brief biography of Mary Agnes Hallaren, preface to oral history conducted by Col. Bettie J. Morden, CMH, April 10, 1979, no file label; Memo from Col. Hallaren to All WAC Officers, April 4, 1951, no file label, both in box 86, WAC.
25. Hallaren memo, April 4, 1951.
26. Ibid.
27. DA, *Duty, Honor, Country,* pamphlet 16-13 (Washington, DC: U.S. Government Printing Office, 1968), 37–39 (includes synopsis of *The Lady in Military Service,* Training Film 16-3415); DA, *Human Self Development: Our Moral Heritage,* Pamphlet 165-10 (Washington, DC: U.S. Government Printing Office, 1972, I-B-3); SP5 Richard A. Dey, Jr., "Training for Army Service," *Army Digest,* n.d. [clipping, 1969?], 41, 42, in 401–407 Magazine/newspaper articles, box 38, WAC .
28. Morden, *Women's Army Corps,* 232–235.
29. Ibid.; OASA(M&RA), "Talking Paper: Subject: TV Interview," March 21, 1974, WAC 289, 401–407, box 38, WAC; Mildred C. Bailey, "The View from Here," January 1974, 4, WAC 98 folder, box 14, WAC; Mildred C. Bailey, draft of *Commanders Digest* article, n.d. (1975?), Magazine/newspaper articles, 401–407, box 38, WAC.
30. Morden, *Women's Army Corps,* 232–235.
31. Col. Elizabeth P. Hoisington, "Making a Good Idea Work," n.d. (first half of 1970?), MVA (Modern Volunteer Army), folder 720, box 86, WAC.
32. "Brigadier General Mildred C. Bailey," BG Bailey papers, WAC 98, box 14, WAC; Betty T. Reid, "Projecting the Vision," *R&CCJ,* May 1972, 15; "WAC Chief visits DSA," *Defense Supply Agency News,* March 12, 1974, 1.
33. Morden, *Women's Army Corps,* 242, 258–259; "People," *Time,* June 22, 1970. For Westmoreland on women, see "Why U.S. Must Return to the Draft: Interview with Gen. William C. Westmoreland, Former Army Chief of Staff," *USN&WR,* May 12, 1980, 36.
34. Mildred C. Bailey, "Recommendations to Improve the Image of the WAC," General Bailey's Background Papers, 1971–75, WAC 99 file, box 14, WAC.
35. Ibid. All recommendations were initiated or implemented within the year except for the grooming course, which was deemed too expensive. Morden, *Women's Army Corps,* 258–260.
36. "Where She Is and Where She's Going," *Time,* March 20, 1972; "The Army's 16-Month Tour of Europe," 1971, folder 3, box 2, Ayer Collection; "Some Guys Need Six Months to Say Goodbye," television commercial, from USAREC, in author's possession; "Some Guys Need 6 Months to Say Goodbye" (for *Sr. Scholastic,* October 1970) folder 4, box 3, Ayer Collection.
37. "Great Myths about the Women's Army Corps," advertisement, N.W. Ayer, for *Sr. Scholastic,* April 20, 1970; "The Army Needs Girls as Well as Generals," advertisement, for *Ingenue,* December 1969, both in Ayer Collection.
38. PFC Ken Holder, "WACs on Production," *R&CCJ,* May 1976, 6. WACs were assigned to "recruiting production" (for both males and females) in 1976.
39. Larry Carney, "Bailey Expects Hike in WAC Strength," *AT,* n.d. [clipping, 1974] WAC 98 folder, box 14, WAC; Morden, *Women's Army Corps,* 264; Bailey, "The View from Here," 2, 6; Mildred C. Bailey, interview with handwritten

corrections, no further information, n.d. (post-1972, pre-1975), WAC 98 folder, box 14, WAC; Bailey, "End of Tour Report," for SA, July 28, 1975, WAC 98 folder, box 14, WAC. The number of occupational specialties open to women in 1972 is given as 434 of 484 in "Volunteer Army Report—One Year Later," February 20, 1974, provided to President Nixon by Secretary Callaway, in "All Volunteer Army HumRO Study," CMH.

40. Bailey, 32nd anniversary speech, 1974; Bailey, "The View from Here," 6; Bailey, "End of Tour Report," 3; Reid, "Projecting the Vision," 15.

41. Catherine Calvert, "If You Think Your Country Owes You a Living . . . Here's How to Get It," *Mademoiselle,* March 1976, 182; clipping accompanied by a letter from the *Mademoiselle* sales manager is in Magazine/newspaper articles, 401–407, box 38, WAC; "Questions from Tom Pettit, NBC, for WAC Show on Friday, 1 Mar 74," in Magazine/newspaper articles file, box 38, WAC.

42. Morden, *Women's Army Corps,* 261; David Farber, *The Age of Great Dreams: America in the 1960s* (New York: Hill and Wang, 1994), 246.

43. "Army Officials Alarmed by Drop In Number of Women Recruits," *NYT,* April 1, 1979; Gates Commission, Minutes of July 12–13, 1969, meeting, 20 (the sole mention of army women that appears in the minutes and supporting documents held in the Eisenhower Library is a brief suggestion to dispense with women altogether); Morden, *Women's Army Corps,* 264, 280, 50, 400; Testimony of BG James Wroth in *Grace Chandler v. Howard H. Callaway* et al., 13, in BG Bailey, WAC 99, box 14, WAC.

44. Wroth testimony, esp. page 2.

45. Binkin and Bach, *Women,* 27–28; Morden, *Women's Army Corps,* 265–269, 285.

46. Binkin and Bach, *Women,* 41–42, 44–45; Leslie W. Gladstone, *The Proposed Equal Rights Amendment,* Report No. 82-51 Gov (Washington, DC: Congressional Research Service, Library of Congress), CRS-17. A document titled "Treatment of Military Women," with no date (1973?) or source, in General Bailey's Background Papers includes the Judge General Advocate of the Army's conclusion that the "so called Equal Rights Amendment (ERA) to the Constitution," would likely end the separate women's corps (WAC 99, box 14, WAC).

47. Morden, *Women's Army Corps,* 299–300.

48. Forrester to Rogers, "A Concept for Expanded Use of Women in the Army," February 22, 1973, in Gen. Bailey's Background Papers, 1971–75, WAC 99, box 14, WAC.; Comptroller General of the United States, Report to Congress, "Job Opportunities for Women in the Military: Progress and Problems, Department of Defense," FPCD-76-26, May 11, 1976, 11; Hadlai A. Hull to Secretary of the General Staff, Subject: Women in the Army, March 7, 1973, in "Plateau Concept" folder, box 35, WAC.

49. See Morden, *Women's Army Corps,* 310–318, 394–397.

50. Ibid.; Office of the Chief of Staff, "Utilization of Army Women," C Draft, October 11, 1973, in Gen. Bailey's Background Papers, WAC 99, box 14, WAC.

51. The case, brought by an air force lieutenant, was *Frontiero v. Richardson.* See Binkin and Bach, *Women,* 45; Morden, *Women's Army Corps,* 276–277; "Army Urged to Let Women into Combat," *Baltimore Sun,* March 28, 1974, in Magazine/newspaper articles files, WAC 289, box 38, WAC.

52. Binkin and Bach, *Women,* 42–44; Morden, *Women's Army Corps,* 318–323; House Committee on Armed Services, Subcommittee No. 2, *Admission of Women to the United States Military Academy,* 93rd Cong., 2nd sess., n.d. [spring 1975], 2, in Policy File ODWAC, 1959–1973, WAC 272, box 35, WAC.
53. McDonald and Abzug quotes from Binkin and Bach, *Women,* 85.
54. Binkin and Bach, *Women,* 85, 42–44; Morden, *Women's Army Corps,* 318–323.
55. Morden, *Women's Army Corps,* 280. Female members of the military police increased from thirteen in 1973 to 1,495 in 1976 ("Sex Barrier: It's Falling Fast in the Military," *USN&WR,* June 28, 1976, 54).
56. Morden, *Women's Army Corps,* 281–282. Women had been trained on carbines until 1963, when use was discontinued and Army trainers declared the M14 too heavy for women. Ann Rose, "Just Call Me SOLDIER—Week 2," *Ft. Jackson Leader,* reprinted in the *R&RJ,* May 1978; Gayle White, "The Changing Role of Army Women, *Atlanta Journal and Constitution Magazine,* May 5, 1974 and "WAC's and Weapons," *The Maintainer,* November 1975, 6, clippings, WAC 704, box 86, WAC.
57. Ann Rose, "Just Call me SOLDIER—Week 1," *Ft. Jackson Leader,* reprinted in *R&RJ,* May 1978.
58. Comptroller General, "Job Opportunities," 10; "Female Soldiers of 1978 and Beyond," *R&RJ,* May 1978, 2; Eugene P. Forrester, "Views and Reviews," *R&RJ,* May 1978, 3; "'I Hate To Type,'" *R&RJ,* May 1978, 15–16; "'I am not typical: I'm a person,'" *R&RJ,* March 1978, 34–35; "Today's Woman Builds New Army Traditions," *R&RJ,* May 1978, 13–14.
59. Sharkey, "The Selling of the 'Modern Army,'" quotations in text are *Inquirer* paraphrase.
60. "Guard Changes Brochure for Women," *Advertising Age,* June 25, 1973.
61. "What's New," 1973, folder 5, box 3; "300 Jobs," folder 4, box 3; "Military Intelligence," 1977, folder 3, box 4; helicopter repair, 1978, folder 4, box 4; "Ms./Pvt.," 1978, folder 4, box 4, all in Ayer Collection.
62. "Sensational looking chick," 1977, folder 7, box 82, Ayer Collection.
63. George Gilder, "The Case Against Women in Combat," *NYT,* January 28, 1979; Martin Binkin, "Women's Rights and National Security," *Washington Post,* July 7, 1976; Women's Equity Action League, "Arms and the Woman: Equal Opportunity in the Military," *WEAL Washington Report* 6 (April 1977):1.
64. WEAL, "Arms and the Woman," 1; "Women in the Armed Forces," *Newsweek,* February 18, 1980, 34; "Army Chief Suggests Drafting of Women," *NYT,* April 7, 1977; General Bernard W. Rogers, "'Women are an integral part of the Army,'" *R&RJ,* June 1978, 26; "Women G.I.'s: No Longer 'Here in Peace, Gone in War,'" *USN&WR,* June 5, 1978, 36. In 1977, *U.S. News and World Report* concluded: "If the all-volunteer armed services are to survive, one thing is certain: Women will have to play a much bigger role—even in combat units." "One Way to Avoid a New Draft: Recruit More Women," *USN&WR,* February 14, 1977, 58.
65. "Women Warriors," *Newsweek,* September 19, 1977, 12; On the combat exclusion legislation, see Francke, *Ground Zero,* 25–26; Binkin and Bach, *Women,* 26–27.

66. Belinda Beck, "Women in the Armed Forces," *Newsweek,* February 18, 1980, 3; Carter, "Presidential Recommendations"; *Selective Service Reform,* H200–2, February 12, 1980, 96th Cong., 2nd sess.; "Women in Combat????" *DA Spotlight* (Command Information Division, Office, Chief of Public Affairs, DA), August 2, 1976, concludes that the question of women in combat must be resolved within the next four years. See also House Military Personnel Subcommittee Hearings, *Women in the Military,* 96th Cong., 1st and 2nd sess., November 13–16, 1979 and February 11, 1980, 1, 30–32.
67. Beck, "Women in the Armed Forces," 34. When the Supreme Court ruled that women were exempt from registration, Schlafly said: "This puts the nails in the coffin of the ERA." "Uncle Sam Says Men Only," *Newsweek,* July 6, 1981, p. 64.
68. Gilder, "The Case Against Women"; James Webb, "The Draft: Why the Army Needs It," *The Atlantic,* April 1980, 34–38, 42–44; James Webb, "Women Can't Fight," *Washingtonian,* November 1979 (included in *Women in the Military* Hearings, 361–369).
69. House Committee, *Women in the Military.* These were hearings on the Department of Defense proposal to rescind Sections 6015 and 8549 of navy and air force personnel policies, which restricted by law how these services could use women members. Army use of women was governed by policy, not by law, and the DoD sought the same flexibility for the navy and air force. Nonetheless, this hearing focused on women in combat and largely on the army.
70. Ibid., 252–255, 203, 34, 26.
71. Ibid.
72. Ibid., 249–250.
73. Ibid., 277–278, 280.
74. Ibid., 232, 217, 214, 221.
75. Ibid., 236, 237, 243, 75.
76. Ibid., 224–230. For another appearance of Dr. Voth, see Bailey, *Sex in the Heartland*, chap. 5.
77. House Committee, *Women in the Military,* 290–293.
78. For another account of these hearings, see Maj. Gen. Jeanne Holm, USAF (Ret.), *Women in the Military: An Unfinished Revolution* (Novato, CA: Presidio Press, 1982), 337–345. The "hints" of legal restrictions are from Holm, 344.
79. Kathy Sawyer, "Pentagon Reassessing Impact of Women in the Armed Forces," *Washington Post,* May 13, 1981; Brad Knickerbocker, "Fewer Jobs for Private Benjamin," *CSM,* August 30, 1982, 3; Pete Earley, "Women Ask if Army Is Going Off-Limits," *Washington Post,* August 4, 1982; SSG Dave Pankey, "This Woman's Army," *All Volunteer,* February 1981, 4. In 1982 the Army raised the number of job categories closed to women from 38 to 61, and the Pentagon lowered the projected number of women in the army from 100,000 to 70,000.

6. The All-Recruited Army

1. Maxwell R. Thurman, oral history, 1992, SOOHP, MHI, 225; "For more information" postcard, 1978, folder 4, box 4, Ayer Collection; J. L. Reed, "An Anal-

ysis and Evaluation of the U.S. Army (the Beard Study)," appendix to Subcommittee on Manpower and Personnel of the Senate Committee on Armed Services, *Status of the All-Volunteer Armed Force,* 95th Cong. 2nd sess., June 20, 1978, 144; Richard Halloran, "Army Chief of Staff Dislikes Troop Reduction Plan," *NYT,* June 14, 1980. Richard Halloran, "Outlook in the Army Brightens with Some Problems Resolved," *NYT,* April 30, 1983, put the NCO shortage at 17,000 in 1979, dropping to 500 in early 1983. In 1972, an entering soldier earned 111 percent of the federal minimum wage; by 1980, entering pay was at 84 percent of the minimum wage. George C. Wilson, "General Favors Volunteer Army Over Draft," *Washington Post,* August 8, 1980.

2. Reed, "Beard Study," 129–131; 133.
3. For the management versus leadership debate, see "Leadership: A Return to Basics," *Military Review,* June 1980, and Richard A. Gabriel, "What the Army Learned from Business," *NYT,* April 15, 1979. Gabriel, who co-authored the book *Crisis in Command,* argues that Robert McNamara, "the ideal corporate man," moved the army "ever closer to the modern business corporation in concept, tone, language and style," to the extent that the "functions of command were perceived as identical to the functions of departmental management." Quotations from Reed, "Beard Study," 131, 133.
4. Bethanne Kelly Patrick, "Army Gen. Maxwell Thurman: Visionary General Developed Recruiting Campaign That Transformed Post-Vietnam Army," www.military.com, accessed August 20, 2008.
5. George C. Wilson, "Recruiters Told to Stress Jobless Rate," *Washington Post,* June 11, 1980; Walter S. Mossberg, "Huge Military Buildup Won't Require Return to the Draft, Reagan Task Force Says," *WSJ,* October 19, 1982. Military spending rose 29.3 percent in real dollars from 1981 through 1985, surpassing the peak spending during the wars in Korea and Vietnam. Bill Keller, "Cut the Military Budget? Oh, Sure," *NYT,* January 14, 1985.
6. Richard Halloran, "Army Personnel Chief Disputes Reports on Draft and Black Soldiers," *NYT,* July 4, 1982. The issue of black representation did not come to the forefront again until Operation Desert Storm. See testimony of Prof. Ronald Walters, Howard University, in House Committee on Armed Services, *The Impact of the Persian Gulf War and the Decline of the Soviet Union on How the United States Does its Defense Business,* 102nd Cong., 1st sess., March 4, 1991, 124–156.
7. Thurman material throughout chapter based in part on Tom Evans to Lewis Sorley, March 5, 2000, copy furnished to me by Evans; Bernard Rostker, RAND Corporation, telephone interview by author, July 17, 2008; Lewis Sorley, interview by author, July 16, 2008, Carlisle, PA; Alan Ono, interview by author, July 29, 2005, Honolulu, HI; Tom Evans, interview by author, December 22, 2005, Highwood, IL; Maxey, interview; Robert Griffith, correspondence with author, 2008.
8. Receipt, "Silverware" folder, box 8, Thurman papers, MHI; Sorley, interview; Thurman, oral history, 1–20.
9. Thurman, oral history, 20–27, 30.
10. Ibid., 28, 31–32, 43.
11. Ibid., 34, 31, 34–36, 42.

12. "Resume of Service Career," attached to Thurman, oral history; "Maxwell Thurman, 64, General Who Led '89 Panama Invasion," *NYT,* December 2, 1995.
13. Thurman, "Resume of Service Career"; Thurman, oral history, 185.
14. Richard L. Gordon, "Army-Ayer Ad Program Takes Some Fire," *Advertising Age,* March 17, 1980, 3; Tom Evans, "All We Could Be: How an Advertising Campaign Helped Remake the Army," *Army History Research,* www.armyhistory.org, accessed August 8, 2008; "bad product" language used by Representative Davis in House Committee on Appropriations, Supplemental Appropriation Bill, 1980, 96th Cong., 2nd sess., 77.
15. Evans, "All We Could Be"; Thurman, oral history, 193; Evans to Sorley.
16. Thurman, oral history, 194–195; Sorley, interview.
17. David Comer, "Top Army Recruiter Cites Manpower Problems," *Northeast Mississippi Daily Journal* (Tupelo, MI), March 10, 1981; Doug Payne, "'Willie and Joe' Image Hurts Army Recruiting, General Says," *Savannah Morning News,* January 23, 1981; Thurman, oral history, 193. Thurman also described USAREC as "an enormous employment agency."
18. Thurman, oral history, 136.
19. Ibid., 200–201.
20. Ibid.
21. Ibid., 251, 203.
22. Evans, "All We Could Be."
23. J. Walter Thompson Company, "United States Marine Corps Recruitment Advertising Plan, FY'80," in Recruitment Advertising Plan folder, box MC11, U.S. Marine Corps Account Records, 1867–2003, John W. Hartman Center for Sales, Marketing, and Advertising History, Duke University, Durham, NC; Evans, "All We Could Be."
24. Thurman, oral history, 203; Evans, "All We Could Be"; "This is the Army" advertisements, box 4, Ayer Collection.
25. Thurman, oral history, 204; James Kitfield, *Prodigal Soldiers: How the Generation of Officers Born of Vietnam Revolutionized the American Style of War* (New York: Simon & Schuster, 1995), 209, verified by Tom Evans, "Observations about 'Prodigal Soldiers,'" furnished by Evans.
26. Thurman, oral history, 205.
27. Ibid., 254.
28. Thurman, "Resume of Service Career"; Thurman, oral history, 267.
29. Historical overview from Thomas W. Evans, "The U.S. Army Recruiting Command," chap. 2 of incomplete unpublished draft of manuscript on recruiting (copy given to me by Evans), 1–2.
30. Evans, "The U.S. Army Recruiting Command," 1–2.
31. Ibid., 8–9, 13; "From 'Amateur Hour' to 'Class' Profession: No Draft Forced a Recruiting Metamorphosis," *RJ,* July 8, 1988, 4–5.
32. "The Army's Giving Guarantees" advertisement, folder 1, box 5, Ayer Collection; illustration accompanying "From 'Amateur Hour.'"
33. The number of recruiting brigades has changed over time—from the original six down to five in the 1970s and 1980s, then to four in 1992, then again to five in the mid-1990s—but from the time USAREC was activated, brigades

have served as the highest field command and are led by full colonels who report directly to the commanding general of USAREC. Recruiters work from recruiting stations, which are commanded by experienced recruiters who are, by definition, NCOs. Five to eleven recruiting stations constitute a recruiting area, or company (commanded by a master sergeant until 1974, after which the positions were filled by captains). Recruiting areas, of which there were approximately 240 in the early 1970s, are organized into battalions, led by lieutenant colonels. While the number of battalions increased to sixty-four in the early 1970s, the number would decline again to forty-two over the following two decades. Evans, "The U.S. Army Recruiting Command," 12–14; 6th Recruiting Brigade homepage, www.usarec.army.mil/6thBde/history.htm, accessed August 12, 2008.

34. Statistics from "Chronology" in "20th Anniversary of the All-Volunteer Army" documents, n.d. (1993?), furnished to author by Tom Evans.

35. Thomas W. Evans, "The State of the Art" (chap. 3), unpublished draft of manuscript on recruiting, 11; "USAREC Drafts Recruiter 'How To' Manual," *RJ*, July 8, 1988, 1.

36. Evans, "The State of the Art," 11–13; Thurman, oral history, 235; Peggy McCarthy, "Films Show Army Life to Recruits," *NYT,* April 8, 1984, p. 1, discusses a slightly later version of JOIN (and brings up *Private Benjamin*).

37. Evans, "The State of the Art," 11–13; *Private Benjamin,* directed by Howard Zieff, was released October 10, 1980. General Thurman included a reference to *Private Benjamin* in the draft of his taped comments to recruiters for April 13, 1981. The line originally read: "As of late there has been some criticism of operations from such outlandish portrayals as those depicted in the movie Private Benjamin. Now, in my opinion, that movie had many redeeming social qualities since the young lady in the movie became very self-reliant and made something of herself as a result of her Army experience." He changed it to "There has been some criticism of our operations recently." "TV Tape," draft, April 13, 1981, 8, Thurman papers, MHI.

38. Evans, "The State of the Art," 12; "From 'Amateur Hour' to 'Class' Profession," 4.

39. Thurman, oral history, 210–211; Rostker, *I Want You!* 390; Rostker, interview.

40. Evans, "The State of the Art," 13–14; Thurman, oral history, 229–230; Evans to Sorley.

41. Evans, "The State of the Art," 6–7; Thurman, oral history, 188, 198–199, 209–210, 229–230; Evans to Sorley; Sorley, interview.

42. Rostker, *I Want You!* 621–627, 391.

43. George C. Wilson, "House Panel Plans Inquiry Into All-Volunteer Army," *Washington Post,* May 27, 1980; Survey by ABC News/Louis Harris and Associates, August 1–August 3, 1980, retrieved August 7, 2008 from the iPOLL Databank, The Roper Center for Public Opinion Research, University of Connecticut, libproxy.temple.edu:2705/ipoll.html.

44. Earl Carter, telephone interview by author, July 17, 2008; E. N. J. Carter, "That's Got His Own: How a Street Kid on Welfare Ended up Creating Some of Madison Avenue's Most Enduring Slogans," unpublished memoir furnished to author by Earl Carter, unpaginated manuscript; Thurman, oral history, 210–

212; Evans, "All We Could Be"; Thomas W. Evans, "Memorandum for Commanding General," March 28, 1980, copy furnished by Evans.

45. Thomas W. Evans, "Thoughts on Advertising Strategy: Some Discussion Points for 2 April Meeting with N.W. Ayer," March 28, 1980, 1–2, furnished by Tom Evans; Thurman, oral history, 210–212; Evans, "All We Could Be."
46. Evans, "All We Could Be."
47. Carter, interview; Carter, "That's Got His Own," chaps. 1, 18.
48. Carter, "That's Got His Own," chap. 18.
49. Ibid., chaps. 18, 19. Earl Carter was awarded the army's Outstanding Civilian Service Medal on January 30, 2003. David Keough, archivist at the Military History Institute, Carlisle, Pennsylvania, has pointed out the similarity of Stonewall Jackson's words, which are inscribed on the arches at the Virginia Military Institute: "You May Be Whatever You Resolve To Be."
50. For Jake Holmes, see his My Space page, http://www.myspace.com/jakeholmes; Will Shade, "Dazed and Confused: The Incredibly Strange Saga of Jake Holmes," *Perfect Sound Forever,* September 2001, www.furious.com/PERFECT/jakeholmes.html, accessed August 8, 2008.
51. Evans, "All We Could Be"; Thurman, oral history, 213–214; Evans, "Ads Countered"; USNPS PP5047, advertisement, Ayer Collection.
52. "Media Buys Zero In On Our Target Audience," *All Volunteer,* January 1982, 5; Thurman, oral history, 214–215.
53. "Uncle Sam Still Wants You," *AT,* July 21, 1986, 73; Evans, "Ads Countered"; Michael Sean McGurk, "Rebranding the Army: An Advertising Effectiveness Case Study" (master's thesis, University of Louisville, 1997).
54. Theodore M. Regan, Jr., "Staying with a Good Thing," *All Volunteer,* January 1982, 6; Sorley, interview; promotional ad, folder 3, box 4, Ayer Collection; Correspondence, June 1981 folder, box 12, Thurman papers; John S. DeMott, "Pitchmen on the Potomac," *Time,* March 7, 1983.
55. Evans, "Ads Countered"; television commercials supplied to author by USAREC, 2005; "Paved" ad, 1986, for *Senior Scholastic,* folder 4, box 6; "On Their Way" ad, n.d., USNPS PP3139, folder 10, box 82; "Road to College," USNPS 520304, 1985, folder 6, box 2; Ayer Collection. A 1984 study found that the "leading category of inducement-mentions in brochures advertising the regular Army is educational benefits." Leonard Shyles and Mark Ross, "Recruitment Rhetoric in Brochures Advertising the All Volunteer Force," *Journal of Applied Communication Research* 12 (Spring 1984): 41.
56. William L. Armstrong, "Needed: A G.I. Bill," *NYT,* June 10, 1980; Brad Knickerbocker, "New G.I. Bill Sought To Help Ensure a Flow of Recruits Into the Military," *CSM,* August 16, 1983. On education benefits, see Rostker, *I Want You!* 510–514.
57. For the most complete and balanced account of this event, see Janet Meyers, "No Victors: Army vs. Ayer: What Really Happened," *Advertising Age,* May 16, 1988, p. 24. On Ayer and the army account, see "An Ad Agency's War with the Army," *Business Week,* April 13, 1987, 102, 104; Mimi L. Minnick, Vanessa Broussard Simmons, and Kate Richards, "Finder's Guide to N.W. Ayer Advertising Agency Collection," National Museum of American History, 2002, revised 2004. Ayer also turned its recruiting expertise in another direction: the

ACKNOWLEDGMENTS

I LIKE TRAVELING to places that are strange to me, lands where I don't understand the language or recognize the characters that create its written form, cultures in which the rituals and conventions of daily life are complex and significant—and fundamentally foreign to the outsider I become. Beginning this book felt much like (for better and for worse) the first time I got seriously lost in Tokyo, or my attempts to find a house to rent in Jakarta when all the major thoroughfares were under two feet of water and I didn't yet recognize the polite form of "no." Thus I am more than usually grateful to the people and institutions who advised, supported, and encouraged me as I learned my way and made sense of what I found.

In so very many ways I owe this book to David Pankey, who, as I began this research, showed me what matters and made me care. That made all the difference. Bob Griffith, author of the army's official history of the transition to the AVF, contacted *me* to offer his help. I relied on his published work and on the vast collection of research materials he had compiled in army archives, but I depended even more on his email correspondence and day-to-day advice. He was the embodiment of intellectual generosity, and I am enormously grateful. Tom Evans gave me papers from his personal collection and a copy of his manuscript in progress as well as his insights and memories, and took me on a tour of the old USAREC headquarters on the shores of Lake Michigan one cold December afternoon. Sandy Cochran braved too many dashes across busy D.C. streets with me; he was endlessly patient and a great companion in my early explorations. Mike Sherry, once again, asked the right questions. Henry Gole made me see the U.S. Army as a living institution—and told me some great stories. Bob Goldich shared his vast knowledge; Bernard Rostker graciously answered my questions; and Bob Sorley gave me his historian's context. Chris DeRosa and Jeremy Saucier sent me documents they discovered in their own research. Jennifer Mittelstadt's insights helped shape my argument, as did Greg Urwin's knowledge of military history. Seth Tinkham was an extraordinary research assistant. Donna Knaff offered her growing expertise on women and the military and sent me care packages whenever I got discouraged. Alan Ono, former commander of USAREC, was immensely informative and equally charming. And Tom Maxey (N.W. Ayer), Pete Dawkins (SAMVA), Gary Stauffer (Portland Army Recruiting Battalion), Earl Carter (N.W. Ayer), Ann Fudge (Y&R), and Craig McCarthy (Mullen) were generous with their time, sharing expertise and recollections.

I am deeply grateful to the foundations and institutions that gave me financial support for research and writing. A fellowship from the National Endowment for the Humanities bestowed the time to immerse myself in multiple archives. A fellowship from the Woodrow Wilson International Center for Scholars allowed me to participate in a community that often bridges the divide between scholarship and policy, and that experience convinced me that policy was a critically important part of this story. The John W. Hartman Center at Duke University funded my travel so that I could use its collections. The University of New Mexico supported the first steps of this research, and Temple University gave me excellent colleagues and unusual freedom to pursue my academic passions. I will always admire Temple's former dean Susan Herbst, who had a vision, and my friend and colleague Richard Immerman, who put together all the pieces of the puzzle.

Archivists and librarians are critically important to historians' work, and I was very lucky in this project. I am especially indebted to David Keough at the U.S. Army Military History Institute. David Murray, at Temple University, was a wonderful resource. I am also grateful to Frank Shirer and the archive staff at the U.S. Army Center of Military History;

Leo Daugherty, command historian, U.S. Army Accessions Command; Janet Spikes, Woodrow Wilson International Center for Scholars; the archivists and librarians at the Library of Congress, the National Archives, the John W. Hartman Center, Duke University Libraries, and the entire staff of the Army Heritage and Education Center for their assistance. My thanks to Phil Fizur, Temple University; Kay Peterson, National Museum of American History; and Lori Mezoff, Patricia Morrison, and Suzanne Nagel, U.S. Army, for help in obtaining illustrations.

I presented my research in progress to a wide range of audiences, and I learned much from their questions and comments, as well as from fellow speakers and panelists. I appreciate the opportunities to speak at the Harrisburg Recruiting Battalion's training meeting; the Army Heritage and Education Center's Perspective in Military History series; the Modern America Workshop and a Woodrow Wilson School policy seminar at Princeton University; the Mayrock Lecture at Ithaca College; the Miller Center for Historical Studies, University of Maryland; the Center for Force and Diplomacy (CENFAD) and the Center for the Humanities at Temple (CHAT) at Temple University; the Woodrow Wilson International Center for Scholars; the Hall Center for the Humanities, University of Kansas; the University of Delaware; the University of Pittsburgh; the Women and War symposium at Sarah Lawrence College; and at the meetings of the American Historical Association, the Organization of American Historians, the Society for Military History, the Social Science History Association, the Pacific Coast Branch of the American Historical Association, and the European Social Science History Association.

Several people read this book manuscript in whole or in part. I benefited greatly from the comments of Mike Sherry and an anonymous reader for Harvard University Press, as well as from Bob Griffith's meticulous reading of the full manuscript. Joyce Seltzer's editorial wisdom sharpened my arguments and improved my prose, and I value both her skill and her friendship. I'm also grateful to Jeannette Estruth, Kate Brick, and Lisa LaPoint at Harvard University Press.

I began this book in one place and finished it in another–and my thoughts were shaped by two different academic communities and by friends from across the nation and over two decades. Fred Logeval, Charlie McGovern, Chester Pach, Eric Porter, Diana Robin, and Ann Schofield all sustain me in different ways. I miss the day-to-day Albuquerque friendship of Melissa Bokovoy, Virginia Scharff, Jane Slaughter, Andrew

Sandoval-Strausz, Cathleen Cahill, Durwood Ball, Tina Kachele, and Rebecca Ullrich enormously, and am grateful to all of them for staying close. My thanks to those nonhistorians who are important parts of my life (I know it isn't always easy): to my brother, Richard Bailey, and my mother-in-law, Nancy Farber; to Marion Immerman, who is family by now, and Saïd Gahia, who is getting close; to Charlie and Barbara Robinson, good friends and a model of lives well lived; and to Elena Vitenberg and Juliet Whelan, for the compelling ways they see the world.

I am grateful every day for my colleagues at Temple. Thanks to Bryant Simon for conversation, coffee, and caring about writing; to Vlad Zubok for the music and for broadening my horizons; to David Watt for the walks; to Laura Levitt for our excursions; and to Kevin Arceneaux for the perspective of another discipline and many wonderful meals. Drew Isenberg, Petra Goedde, Will Hitchcock, and Liz Varon—the usual suspects—have made my life much richer. It is wonderful to have both a cohort and a community of academic couples. Someday we really will get the T-shirts. Richard Immerman continues to amaze me after all these years; I suspect he can do anything. And, though he has left Temple, Todd Shepard (who always sees my point before I finish the sentence) is a friend for life.

Max Bailey/Farber, despite his embrace of anthropology rather than history, profoundly affected the course of this book. I began researching it in earnest just as he hit prime draft age, and in the midst of a war he strongly opposed. That ever-present fact made me confront the dilemmas surrounding military service in ways that went far beyond the academic. And David Farber listened and read and debated, pushed me to ask bigger questions, and took care of all sorts of things (including me) when I was writing ten hours a day. This would be a much narrower work—and I a less adventurous historian—without him. He has inspired me since the day we met. As always, my deepest thanks go to David and Max, who fill my life.

While writing this book I lost two of the people I cared about most: my father-in-law, Don Farber, a brave man whose kindness meant so much to me, and Tim Moy, friend and colleague, whose very presence made the world a better place, if all too briefly. I am lucky to have known them both.

INDEX